Apocalypse Then

Apocalypse Then

American and Japanese Atomic Cinema, 1951–1967

Mike Bogue

Foreword by Allen A. Debus

McFarland & Company, Inc., Publishers
Jefferson, North Carolina

LIBRARY OF CONGRESS CATALOGUING-IN-PUBLICATION DATA

Names: Bogue, Mike, author.
Title: Apocalypse then : American and Japanese atomic cinema, 1951–1967 / Mike Bogue ; foreword by Allen A. Debus.
Description: Jefferson, North Carolina : McFarland & Company, Inc., Publishers, 2017 | Includes bibliographical references and index.
Identifiers: LCCN 2017030121 | ISBN 9781476668413 (softcover : acid free paper) ∞
Subjects: LCSH: Nuclear warfare in motion pictures. | Science fiction films—History and criticism. | Monster films—History and criticism. | Motion pictures—United States—History. | Motion pictures—Japan—History.
Classification: LCC PN1995.9.W3 B65 2017 | DDC 791.43/6581—dc23
LC record available at https://lccn.loc.gov/2017030121

BRITISH LIBRARY CATALOGUING DATA ARE AVAILABLE

ISBN (print) 978-1-4766-6841-3
ISBN (ebook) 978-1-4766-2900-1

© 2017 Mike Bogue. All rights reserved

No part of this book may be reproduced or transmitted in any form or by any means, electronic or mechanical, including photocopying or recording, or by any information storage and retrieval system, without permission in writing from the publisher.

Front cover illustration by Todd Tennant

Printed in the United States of America

*McFarland & Company, Inc., Publishers
Box 611, Jefferson, North Carolina 28640
www.mcfarlandpub.com*

For Mom,
whose love never wavered

Acknowledgments

Many thanks to the following, who helped me during my quest to complete this manuscript: Mark Matzke for reading multiple drafts and giving me sterling feedback; Todd Tennant for his terrific cover and moral support; Allen A. Debus for his foreword and cogent authorial advice; Peter H. Brothers for his generosity; and the following friends for their support: Matt Hauger, Luke Heffley, Jerry Forbes, Leslie Davis, Bob Statzer, Don Stribling, Mike Murders, Gwen Faulkenberry, Nancy Milich, Tom and Beth Weaver.

And last but never least, my brother Frank and sister-in-law Debbie for their resolute love and encouragement.

Table of Contents

Acknowledgments — vi
Foreword by Allen A. Debus — 1
Preface — 3
Introduction — 7

PART I: MUTANTS

1. **All-American Aberrations** — 11
   1951–1959: *Ma and Pa Kettle Back on the Farm* 11 • *Captive Women* 12 • The Year 1953 15 • *The Atomic Kid* 16 • *Bride of the Monster* 18 • *Creature with the Atom Brain* 20 • *Day the World Ended* 23 • *The Werewolf* 27 • *World Without End* 30 • *The Amazing Colossal Man* 33 • *The Cyclops* 37 • *From Hell It Came* 40 • *The Incredible Shrinking Man* 42 • *Attack of the 50 Foot Woman* 45 • *Frankenstein 1970* 48 • *Monster on the Campus* 50 • *Terror from the Year 5000* 52 • *War of the Colossal Beast* 55 • *The Alligator People* 58 • *The Hideous Sun Demon* 61 • The Best and the Rest 64

2. **Mutations American Style** — 65
   1960–1967: *Beyond the Time Barrier* 65 • *The Beast of Yucca Flats* 67 • *Most Dangerous Man Alive* 69 • The Year 1962 71 • *Monstrosity* 72 • *The Horror of Party Beach* 74 • *The Time Travelers* 78 • The Years 1965–1966 84 • *In the Year 2889* 84 • After the Year 1967 86

3. **Rising Sun Terrors** — 87
   1958–1965: *The H-Man* 87 • *Frankenstein Conquers the World* 97 • Of Gelatin and Giants 104

4. **Marty vs. the H-Man** — 106
   1958: National Identity 106 • Radiation Perspective 109 • Implicit Worldview 110 • Man-Sized Mutants 112 • King-Sized Mutants 113 • From Mutants to Monsters 114

PART II: MONSTERS

5. **Red, White and Blue Behemoths** — 115
   1953–1963: *The Beast from 20,000 Fathoms* 115 • *The Magnetic Monster* 119 • *Killers from Space* 122 • *Monster from the Ocean Floor* 125 • *Them!*

126 • *It Came from Beneath the Sea* 131 • *Tarantula* 134 • *The Phantom from 10,000 Leagues* 139 • *Attack of the Crab Monsters* 142 • *Beginning of the End* 147 • *The Monster That Challenged the World* 150 • *Monster from Green Hell* 153 • *Attack of the Giant Leeches* 156 • *The Slime People* 159 • Almost Atomic 162 • Of Beasts, Bugs and Behaving 165

6. **Walking H-Bombs** 166
   1954–1967: *Godzilla / Gojira, King of the Monsters!* 166 • The Americanization 172 • *Godzilla Raids Again / Gigantis, the Fire Monster* 175 • *Rodan* 178 • *Mothra* 181 • 1962–1963 184 • *Giant Space Monster Dogora / Dagora, the Space Monster* 184 • *Mothra vs. Godzilla / Godzilla vs. the Thing* 186 • *Gamera, the Giant Monster / Gammera the Invincible* 190 • *Godzilla, Ebirah, Mothra / Godzilla vs. the Sea Monster* 195 • *Son of Godzilla* 197 • Almost Atomic 200

7. **Honda vs. Harryhausen** 204

Part III: Mushroom Clouds

8. **Twilight's Last Gleaming** 217
   1951–1964: *Five* 217 • *Invasion U.S.A.* 220 • *Teenage Cave Man* 223 • *On the Beach* 225 • *The World, the Flesh and the Devil* 230 • *The Last Woman on Earth* 233 • *Rocket Attack U.S.A.* 235 • *The Creation of the Humanoids* 238 • *Panic in Year Zero!* 240 • *This Is Not a Test* 245 • *Dr. Strangelove—or: How I Learned to Stop Worrying and Love the Bomb* 247 • *Fail-Safe* 251

9. **Rising Sun Apocalypse** 257
   1956–1961: *The Mysterious Satellite / Warning from Space* 257 • *Earth Defense Force / The Mysterians* 261 • *The Final War* 264 • *The Last War* 267

10. **Aftermath vs. the End** 273

Epilogue 283
Chapter Notes 287
Bibliography 293
Index 295

Foreword
by Allen A. Debus

Mike Bogue's publications coaxed me into writing about giant monsters and science fictional dino-monsters of literature and film. How did this happen? Well, I've known of Mike for almost two decades. It was in 1996 when I came across an intriguing magazine named *Scary Monsters*, spied on a rack in a now extinct strip mall comic book shop. Two years later, in the magazine's *Monster Memories Yearbook 1998*, I discovered Mike's well thought-out article "Redoubtable Rodan," about Japan's ginormous soaring pterodactyl—one of Godzilla's cohorts from the mid–20th century monster craze. *Rodan*'s story began with a bang in the 1957 American version, with a huge spliced-in nuclear explosion.

I eventually subscribed to *Scary Monsters*, encountering Mike's good name repeatedly therein as well as in J.D. Lees' *G-Fan*, a magazine devoted to all things Godzilla. Although I've always considered myself more of a "dinosaur-paleo-guy," off and on during this period I wondered if there was anything I could add to the mayhem that fanzine readers might enjoy, as seemed to be the case with Mike's steady flow of monster material. In 2001, I found myself compelled to pen a series of my own dino-monster, science fictional articles, with my words proliferating thereafter in several McFarland books. In an odd sense, all this was partly thanks to Mike's invisible hand.

There are dozens of sci-fi-horror conventions scheduled around the country, and I've been fortunate to regularly attend two such events held annually in Chicago. One is G-Fest, organized by J.D. Lees. In 2014, I was approached by my Facebook friend Mike, who was arranging a G-Fest panel discussion with the intriguing title "Atom Age Connections." Would I like to be included as a panel member? Sure! It was a thoughtfully prepared panel presented on July 14, with considerable audience participation. What I recall mostly about that event began during the late evening of July 13 on into the wee hours of the following morning when I really should have been resting for a long day, rather than fighting fatigue to stay awake and gab with Mike and another panel member, Mark Matzke. We talked about the old sci-fi and horror movies we'd enjoyed as kids either at the cinema or on television that stayed with us all these years and the harrowing messages presented therein. Many were low-budget black-and-white films, often fraught with dismal plotting or subpar acting. Although some are laughable today for any number of reasons, subliminally, they deeply affected us. And that's the main point.

It was a vastly different time then. Even though we live our everyday, ordinary lives today, never minding the possibility of nuclear attack, back during the 1950s and through the mid–1960s, at least subconsciously, more than anything we dreaded the hydrogen bomb. A thermonuclear global annihilation could happen at any moment, it seemed, as launching of Soviet intercontinental missiles could spark a chain of mushroom clouds and radioactive fallout over civilization. Bomb shelters were built while families cowered in front of their TV sets as the grim Cuban Missile Crisis unfolded. Later, there was speculation whether JFK's assassination would trigger World War III. We cringed at the sound of air raid missile warning sirens being tested ("Is this finally 'the big one'?"). I wondered how long the supply of canned soup and Sterno stockpiled under our downstairs bathroom sink would keep us alive after the fireball swirled over our house. In grade school we were led into the hall during air raid drills and instructed to sit on the floor, bend our heads between our legs and kiss our glutei maximi goodbye just as we were about to erupt in radioactive flames. Mentally, I hedged my bets, fantasizing that I just might be able to outrun the fiery bomb blast, sprinting out the east door of the school, across the ball field toward the basement of our home and those Sterno cans. Precariously, it seemed, we lived on the fault line of disaster, as mirrored in the movies (and sci-fi television programs) that stoked our imaginations.

I recall agitating my frantic mother one afternoon when one of my younger brothers and I were playing with our army men on the basement floor, launching rubber band–powered plastic "nuclear" missiles at one another's aligned tanks and "troops." Supposing we were presaging World War III (which everyone just *knew* would be nuclear) in her very own home, she screamed at us to stop. It was merely her way of unleashing pent-up panic over what might someday come. And I had a recurrent nightmare of the skies to the north of our neighborhood suddenly darkening to black, spreading rapidly in my direction, but then instead of a tornado unfurling, in the distance I spied the enormity of an approaching colossus, Godzilla—heading directly toward *me*.

Spencer R. Weart documents in his *Nuclear Fear: A History of Images* (Harvard University Press, 1988) how psychologically scarred many of us (especially child Baby Boomers growing up then) became during this early phase of the Cold War. No—the threat of terrorist groups wasn't as prevalent then as we are too often shocked, distracted and revolted by many "breaking news" events of the present day. But even though the Cold War is now considered history, in our increasingly unstable world, the awful truth is that probability of nuclear attack remains imminent.

How odd to become so nostalgic about living with the threat of being nuked! Yet such things consumed our minds during the evening of that July 13, 2014, as we plotted how to emphasize a mere handful of old movies, reflecting images of doomsday, presented in Mike's "Atom Age Connections" panel. And that panel has wended its way into this book.

I've come to know Mike as a total enthusiast and a gentleman. His knowledge of this genre is prodigious—he lived the times he's writing about. So I know you will become absorbed in this book, somewhat fearfully, yet at the end uttering another Hollywood-ish "happy ending" sigh of relief because the movies detailed within are only a reflection of what *might have been* then. But what of the future...?

A life-long dinosaur enthusiast, Allen A. Debus is a retired environmental chemist who has authored five books, has regularly contributevd to Prehistoric Times, G-FAN, Mad Scientist, *and* Scary Monsters, *and has also contributed to the peer-reviewed journal* Science Fiction Studies. *He lives in Hanover Park, Illinois.*

Preface

Ever been awakened by a nuclear explosion? In 1985, I was asleep on the couch having a nightmare about nuclear war. I awoke with a start when a booming noise rattled the windows. *"Please, God, no...!"* Was I hearing the concussive sound wave from an ICBM that had just struck Fort Smith, Arkansas, 37 miles to the west? Within seconds, wakefulness jolted me into reality, and I realized the boom I'd heard was not a nuclear blast, but just a good old-fashioned thunderstorm, and a wave of relief washed over me.

The atomic anxiety that provoked this episode had been the background noise in my life, and in the lives of millions of Americans, for decades. I recall being a lad of ten in 1965 and assuming, matter-of-factly, that a major nuclear war would occur by 1970 (I probably got this cheerful idea of an atomic Armageddon being just around the corner from genre movies and mass media). Unlike Dr. Strangelove, my generation perhaps did not learn to love the Bomb, but we did learn to take it in stride, and science fiction movies played a major role in our outlook.

This was true not only for Americans, but for the Japanese as well. Both America and Japan produced a number of science fiction movies in the 1950s and 1960s directly or indirectly tied to the nuclear threat. Though each country's atomic age movies shared surface characteristics, their subtexts clashed. American science fiction films of the 1950s and early 1960s tended to suggest it was possible to put the nuclear genie back in the bottle. However, the Japanese science fiction films of that same era were inclined to suggest that once freed, that genie could never again be imprisoned. These movies tended to end pessimistically with the nuclear threat still present; the danger was only temporarily contained.

For the purposes of this book, the term "nuclear threat" refers to nuclear testing, nuclear accidents, nuclear fallout, nuclear radiation terrestrial and extraterrestrial, and/or nuclear war. In addition, we confine our examination of these films to the years 1951 through 1967. During this period, the number of American and Japanese sci-fi movies associated with the nuclear threat peaked. Radioactive mutants and monsters glutted movie screens, and atomic anxiety reigned supreme.

As the late Bill Warren stated in the preface to Volume 1 of his wonderful *Keep Watching the Skies!*, "Radiation was used to explain many wonderful things, from giant insects to walking trees to resurrecting the dead. This was not a form of nuclear paranoia, merely cheap and simple plotting."[1] I agree that radiation in 1950s movies sometimes (perhaps often) operated like magic and could make almost anything happen. But I also think radiation in these films can be more than a mere plot device.

Warren states, "[Radiation] was just a gimmick. In the 1930s the equivalent gimmick was electricity; in the 1920s, it was surgery and often gland operations. In the 1950s, it was radiation that got the monster going."[2] The latter is true, but cinematically, radiation was far more significant than glandular surgery or electricity. Warren rightly says that no one in the 1930s feared "electrical annihilation."[3] Likewise, no one in the 1920s feared the rout of civilization due to glandular surgery. But for purposes of our discussion, let's stick to electricity (a plot gimmick used in the 1940s as well as the 1930s).

Unlike radiation, society didn't consider electrical power a threat. Its societal context was almost overwhelmingly positive, certainly not the case for radiation. No key event in the history of electrical power strikes the public with foreboding, but radiation has such a historical event: the August 6, 1945, atom bombing of Hiroshima. Though the atom may have a positive side (the admittedly debatable use of nuclear power plants), people mostly think of it in the context of a nuclear accident, or fallout, or H-bomb testing, or nuclear war. Writers, journalists and scientists have spilled far more ink alerting humankind about the dangers of radiation than warning people not to stand too close to electrical power lines.

Many critics and fans contend that in the original 1954 *Gojira*, Godzilla is a stand-in for the atom bombings of Hiroshima and Nagasaki, essentially a walking H-bomb. *Gojira* director Ishiro Honda said that Godzilla was an attempt to make radiation visible.[4] However, we never saw the embodiment of an electrical power grid decimate a Japanese city.

While radiation directly or indirectly led to giant movie monsters both American and Japanese, the same cannot be said for electricity. Yes, the successful 1952 re-issue of *King Kong* no doubt paved the way for the brisk box office of 1953's *The Beast from 20,000 Fathoms* and all the giant monster films that followed. However, why was *King Kong* a major hit in 1952? Three years earlier, the giant ape film *Mighty Joe Young*, filled with stunning Ray Harryhausen/Willis O'Brien special effects, had failed at the box office. But in 1952, nuclear testing was at its height, as were Cold War fears of an atomic war. Could this public anxiety have unconsciously contributed to Kong's reissue success? I don't at all suggest this was the main reason or even a substantive one for the movie's brisk box office, but I believe it could have been a minor contributing factor. As the theory goes, giant monsters were stand-ins for the nuclear threat, in that nuclear explosions were likewise gigantic and destructive.

Warren does allow the possibility that fears of radiation might have unconsciously contributed to 1950s science fiction films when he says, "[A]lthough the 1950s did tend to be worried about atomic warfare, radiation in SF films wasn't a means of expressing this fear, probably not even unconsciously."[5] However, I think that unconscious symbolism can often be more powerful than intentional symbolism.

Of course, symbolism's context is often (if not always) in the eye of the beholder, and in some cases, the studio or filmmakers in question might say that they used radiation merely as a plot contrivance (*Attack of the Giant Leeches* might be a good example). However, just as one can make a Freudian slip that might reveal what is actually (but unconsciously) on one's mind, so too can a movie reveal its makers' underlying concerns. After all, movies of any era tend to say far more about the age in which they were made than was intended by the filmmakers. I think this is largely true for 1950s American and Japanese science fiction movies dealing with the nuclear threat.

Accordingly, as dinosaur scholar Allen A. Debus notes, it is probably no coincidence that almost all the giant monster movies, including the original *Gojira*, were made in the wake of the first H-bomb tests. As Debus states, the H-bomb "mostly inspired [giant monster movies], shifting the world's perspective on the likelihood for our long-term survival."6

I do agree with Warren that some 1950s filmmakers consciously used radiation as a plot gimmick. These films provide little visual or contextual evidence for the nuclear threat; a good example is 1957's *The Cyclops*. But other movies, such as 1952's little-seen *Captive Women*, employ the nuclear threat as more than a plot convenience. The best, such as 1954's *Them!*, tend to put the nuclear threat front and center.

During the 1960s and '70s, I grew up watching 1950s and early 1960s nuclear threat movies on a Sears black-and-white portable TV. For me, any movie that had a monster or a mushroom cloud was a "must-see." The local stations showed a slew of American International, Allied Artists and Universal-International movies from the '50s that exposed me to all things atomic. My brother Frank, three years my elder and a rabid science fiction fan, assured me that radiation did not mutate bugs or make people 50 feet tall. Still, at times the more serious nuclear threat movies confused or disturbed me. For example, at a very young age I saw 1959's *On the Beach*. At the end, a Salvation Army band sports a banner proclaiming, "There's still time, brother" as the band plays and people gather around them. When you next see that street, it is completely deserted, not a soul in sight. My interpretation: Radiation disintegrates you.

For this book, I have gone to the primary sources, the movies themselves. I have also employed a wealth of scholarly popular culture books and genre periodicals, as well as mainstream non-fiction books dealing with the nuclear threat. I have cautiously consulted the Internet. For each movie entry, I include the plot, one or more technical aspects, a personal evaluation and the film's connection with the nuclear threat.

The book is divided into three sections: Mutants (humanoid); Monsters (non-humanoid); and Mushroom Clouds (serious treatments of nuclear war). For each section, I look first at the relevant American films, next at the relevant Japanese films, and then compare and contrast the two.

This examination includes only American and Japanese science fiction films made between the years 1951 and 1967. Not included are British and European movies concerning the nuclear threat. Consequently, in this book you won't find commentary on noteworthy British films such as 1962's *The Day the Earth Caught Fire* or 1965's *The War Game*. Tellingly, British films on the subject of atomic science fiction tend to be more pessimistic than similar American movies. For example, 1959's British-made *The Giant Behemoth* (known in England as *Behemoth the Sea Monster*) ends on a cautionary note: Although the monster has been killed in the Thames, legions of dead fish have washed up on America's East Coast, implying more Behemoths are coming into the world.

When a movie's status for this book is uncertain, I have tended to err on the side of inclusion. Example: 1951's *Ma and Pa Kettle Back on the Farm*. In this one, radioactive coveralls give Pa the ability to power electrical machines just by touching them; this makes him, by definition, a humanoid mutant of the atomic age. Consequently, you will find a brief entry for this movie in Chapter 1.

Another occasional problem: deciding into which section to list a movie. For example, 1956's *World Without End* depicts a fairly serious post-atomic holocaust world, which would suggest including it in the book's third section, "Mushroom Clouds." However, the movie also includes multi-eyed, humanoid mutants, which would suggest its inclusion in the book's first section, "Mutants." I have decided to place it and all other post-holocaust movies containing humanoid mutations in the "Mutants" section.

Another problem: What to do with a movie like 1958's *Teenage Cave Man*? It includes only one mutant seen in a scientist's flashback of the immediate post-atomic holocaust world,[7] but includes no mutants in the immediate present that the movie depicts. Also, the film features what appear to be prehistoric animals, a fairly unlikely consequence of nuclear war. But because the film includes no humanoid mutants in the current world it portrays, I have placed *Teenage Cave Man* in the "Mushroom Clouds" section.

The book's first section, "Mutants," includes four chapters. Chapter 1 covers American-made humanoid mutant movies from 1951 to 1959. Chapter 2 deals with the same genre from 1960 to 1967. Chapter 3 covers the Japanese-made humanoid mutants from 1958 to 1965, and Chapter 4 compares and contrasts the American and Japanese humanoid mutant movies produced between 1951 and 1967.

"Monsters," the book's second section, comprises three chapters. Chapter 5 looks at made-in-America non-humanoid monster movies (primarily of the giant variety) from 1953 to 1963, and Chapter 6 examines Godzilla and the many Japanese monsters that graced movie screens between 1954 and 1967. Chapter 7 discusses the similarities and differences between American and Japanese (mostly giant) atomic monster films.

The book's third section, "Mushroom Clouds," examines the more serious nuclear threat science fiction movies. Chapter 8 looks at American-made nuclear war films from 1951 through 1967, including 1959's *On the Beach*, 1962's *Panic in Year Zero!* and 1964's *Fail-Safe*. Chapter 9 scrutinizes the only two serious Japanese movies on the subject, 1960's *The Final War* and 1961's *The Last War*. Chapter 10 compares the Japanese and American nuclear war movies discussed in the previous two chapters.

Though many other books have surveyed American and Japanese 1950s and 1960s science fiction films, no previous book has focused exclusively on 1950s and 1960s genre movies of these two countries dealing with the nuclear threat. The years 1951 to 1967 cover a range of tones and treatments, from the monster-on-the-loose thrills of *The Beast from 20,000 Fathoms* to the we're-all-going-to-die sobriety of *The Last War*, with plenty of stops in between. The nuclear genie has indeed escaped its bottle and taken up residence in the fever dreams of nuclear threat cinema. Let's pray that it is content to remain there. For next time I wake up from a dream about nuclear war, I want that percussive boom to still be thunder, not the apocalypse.

Introduction

In the world of nuclear threat cinema, we find strange bedfellows.

How strange?

How about Edward D. Wood, Jr., celebrated as one of the worst filmmakers of all time, and Stanley Kubrick, celebrated as one of the best? Yes, our examination of nuclear threat cinema will cover films as derided as Wood's 1955 *Bride of the Monster* and as acclaimed as Kubrick's 1964 *Dr. Strangelove*. After all, nuclear war jitters were not respecters of prestige, just fear.

And from the early 1950s through the mid–1960s, fear of atomic war preoccupied both America and Japan, a dread expressed in the science fiction movies of both countries. On the American side, the theatrical cycle began with 1951's low-budget *Five*, the story of the only five survivors of a nuclear war. Soon, American movie screens teemed with Big Bugs, Big Beasts and Big People. *Them!*, a big grosser for Warner Bros. in 1954, began the Big Bug cycle with its tale of giant mutated ants terrorizing New Mexico, then nesting in the storm drains of Los Angeles. A wave of colossal creepy-crawlies followed in *Them!*'s wake, including 1955's *Tarantula* (giant arachnid on the loose in Arizona), 1957's *Beginning of the End* (giant locusts on the march in Chicago) and 1958's *Monster from Green Hell* (giant wasps on the rampage in Africa).

Of course, the Bomb also produced plenty of Big Beasts. For 1953's *The Beast from 20,000 Fathoms* and 1955's *It Came from Beneath the Sea*, legendary stop-motion animator Ray Harryhausen supplied the technical effects.[1] In *Beast*, a nuclear test explosion frees a hibernating Rhedosaurus, an amphibious dinosaur that ravages New York City. For a wide-eyed six-year-old (my age when I first saw this movie), what could possibly be better? And what could top the monster crushing a car underfoot or smashing through a multi-story building? For my pre-adolescent money, the answer was *It Came from Beneath the Sea*, in which a colossal cephalopod attacks San Francisco, a major highlight the six-armed monster's obliteration of a section of the Golden Gate Bridge.

Of course, the Bomb also produced Big People in the land of *E Pluribus Unum*. Producer-director Bert I. Gordon gave us monstrous men in 1957's *The Cyclops* and *The Amazing Colossal Man* and 1958's *War of the Colossal Beast*. Not to be outdone, the formidable Allison Hayes represented the female gender in 1958's *Attack of the 50 Foot Woman*.

Let us not forget the human-sized mutants of 1950s American science fiction cinema, including atomic age wolf men (1956's *The Werewolf*), were-lizards (1959's *The Hideous Sun Demon*) and 'gator men (1959's *The Alligator People*). These unfortunates showed the admittedly fictional but still potent effects that radiation poisoning had on the individual.

Interestingly, the American theatrical cycle began with a relatively credible nuclear threat film—*Five*—and ended with another credible story, *Fail-Safe*. Neither *Five* nor *Fail-Safe* features the monsters that frequently populate 1950s genre cinema. But by the early '60s, the nuclear threat had reached emergency levels via October 1962's Cuban Missile Crisis, an event discussed at the end of Chapter 8.

Japan likewise experienced nuclear fear in the '50s and early '60s, but theirs was more acute than that of other nations, for they were the only country on Earth to have suffered atomic attack. Their cinematic nuclear threat cycle begins with 1954's *Gojira* (a.k.a. *Godzilla*) and thematically ends with 1961's *The Last War*, both Toho productions. (Technically, Japan's atomic cycle continued through 1964's *Space Monster Dogora*; 1965's *Gamera, the Giant Monster*; and the Godzilla franchise from 1962 to 1967. But in each of these films, the nuclear threat was not the main theme; in fact, usually a minor element.)

One needs little imagination to see Godzilla's attack on Tokyo as a stand-in for the nuclear bombings of Hiroshima and Nagasaki. Freed by nuclear testing, Godzilla is radioactive *and* invulnerable both to the Bomb and to conventional weapons. Much like the nuclear threat itself, he is indestructible ... almost. Every good monster fan knows that the Oxygen Destroyer literally disintegrated Godzilla as well as the apparatus' creator, Dr. Serizawa.

But Godzilla returned, launching a movie franchise that still thrives decades later. He also inspired other giant Japanese monsters, many of whose films we will examine, including jet-propelled *Rodan* (1956) and unstoppable *Mothra* (1961), two of Godzilla's best supporting *daikaiju* (giant monsters). As for human mutants, we will look at 1958's *The H-Man*, in which H-bomb radiation turns Japanese sailors into homicidal blobs, and 1965's *Frankenstein Conquers the World*, in which the radiation-immune titular character grows from man-sized to king-sized and battles a prehistoric monster.

Unlike the film industry in America, which in the '50s generally considered science fiction films inferior to mainstream movies, in Japan there was no loss in prestige from 1954's *Godzilla* to 1961's *The Last War*, despite the fact that the former features a fantastic monster and the latter attempts to realistically portray a nuclear war. After all, Toho, the studio of Godzilla, was also the studio of Akira Kurosawa, considered one of the best filmmakers of all time. Acclaimed actors such as Taksahi Shimura moved easily from monster movies to Kurosawa films such as *The Seven Samurai*. Likewise, Kurosawa films often shared the same producer (Tomoyuki Tanaka) and the same composers (Akira Ifukube and Masaru Sato) as Toho's Godzilla movies.[2]

The nuclear threat cycle in Japan began by featuring metaphors of giant monsters such as in *Godzilla* (1954) and *Rodan* (1956), and ended with realistic portrayals of a near-future atomic war as found in Toei's *The Final War* (1960) and Toho's *The Last War* (1961). Although Japanese filmgoers could apparently stomach allegorical recreations of the two atom bomb attacks on the country *à la* Godzilla,[3] it took time to build up to a vision of a near-future nuclear war in which not just two Japanese cities, but also the entire island nation is laid waste.

America's outlook on the nuclear threat differed from Japan's; after all, the U.S. was the nation that had dropped two atom bombs on the island nation in 1945. Almost inevitably, a tension bristled between the victor (America) and the vanquished (Japan), especially given America's postwar occupation and recreation of Japanese society and politics. The U.S. delivered the hammer blow, Japan received it, and both nations recoiled from the impact.

As a consequence, Japan and its leaders tended to wholeheartedly denounce nuclear weapons, an attitude found in the country's nuclear threat movies. But though it feared nuclear weapons as well, America, or at least its leadership, tended to implicitly endorse nuclear weapons as a necessary means to prevent Communist domination of the world, an attitude that seeped into many American science fiction films of the '50s.

By the early to mid–1960s, American and Japanese nuclear threat movies began thematically to harmonize. For example, *Fail-Safe* sets up a horrific lose-lose scenario, and *Dr. Strangelove*'s finale appears to usher in the literal end of the world. These fates are similar to the nuclear annihilation shown in *The Final War* and *The Last War*.

This book covers the serious as well as the frivolous, running the gamut from fanciful Grade-B monsters to grim grade–A Armageddons. Some entries may give you a smile, some a shrug, some a shudder. If you (like me) are a Baby Boomer, you may at times experience a welcome nostalgia *vis-à-vis* memories of monster matinees on Saturday afternoons—and at other times, a not-so-welcome nostalgia *vis-à-vis* memories of duck and cover drills in grade school. After all, nuclear threat cinema does make for strange bedfellows.

PART I: MUTANTS

1. All-American Aberrations

1951–1959

Classic film fans know that *Marty* was the name of an award-winning 1955 drama starring Ernest Borgnine, but they may not know that Marty was also the nickname for the three-eyed mutant in 1955's *Day the World Ended*.

Marty was one of many Hollywood mutants born of radiation. Atomic testing, fallout, accidents and/or nuclear war—all of which fall under this book's definition of the nuclear threat—figured prominently in several human mutant movies in the 1950s, including *Day the World Ended* as well as 1956's *World Without End* and 1957's *The Amazing Colossal Man* and *The Incredible Shrinking Man*. In this chapter, we will look at these films year by year from 1951 through 1959.

For our first stop on our U.S. humanoid mutations tour, we visit perhaps the least likely mutant to grace 1950s movie screens: Pa Kettle.

Ma and Pa Kettle Back on the Farm (Universal-International, 1951)

Credits: Directed by Edward Sedgwick; Screenplay by Jack Henley; Produced by Leonard Goldstein; Associate Producer: Bill Grady, Jr.; Art Direction: Bernard Herzbrun and Emrich Nicholson; Set Decorations: Russell A. Gausman and Oliver Emert; Photography: Charles Van Enger; Music Score: Milton Schwarzwald; Music Direction: Joseph Gershenson; Sound: Leslie I. Carey and Robert Pritchard; Editor: Russell Schoengarth; Special Effects: David S. Horsley; Makeup: Bud Westmore; Assistant Director: Bill Holland.

Cast: Marjorie Main (Ma Kettle); Percy Kilbride (Pa Kettle); Richard Long (Tom Kettle); Meg Randall (Kim Parker Kettle); Ray Collins (Jonathan Parker); Barbara Brown (Elizabeth Parker); Emory Parnell (Billy Reed); Peter Leeds (Manson); Teddy Hart (Crowbar); Oliver Blake (Geoduck); Edward Clark (Dr. Bagley); Edmund Cobb (Train Engineer); Harold Goodwin (Conductor); Jerry Hausner (Steve); Jack Ingram (Deputy); Rex Lease (Sheriff); Anne O'Neill (Nurse); Harry Von Zell (Mr. Chadwick); Dale Belding (Danny Kettle); Teddy Infuhr (Benjamin Kettle); Sherry Jackson (Susie Kettle).

Black-and-white; 81 minutes; released on May 10, 1951. Available as one of ten films on the DVD set *Ma & Pa Kettle Complete Comedy Collection*.

Though this folksy comedy's atomic angle is slight, it is still pertinent, for Pa Ketttle does develop a superhuman power thanks to his nephew's radioactive coveralls.

During the late 1940s and 1950s, Universal-International featured Ma and Pa Kettle, amiable hayseed characters who originated in 1947's *The Egg and I*, in a series of their own films (nine in all, not counting *The Egg and I*). In this third entry, feisty Ma (Marjorie Main) and low-key Pa (Percy Kilbride) are excited that they have become grandparents. Their grandson is the offspring of son Tom (Richard Long) and his wife Kim (Meg Randall). However, Kim's parents the Parkers have arrived, and while Jonathan Parker (Ray Collins) is easygoing enough, Elizabeth Parker (Barbara Brown) is a blueblood terror, horrified by the Kettles and their country ways (think *The Beverly Hillbillies*' Mrs. Drysdale vs. the Clampetts).

In reaction, Ma and Pa and their numerous children move back into their old house. There, while using dynamite to blast a new well, Pa gets stuck in the resultant mound of earth. His two Native American friends dig him out, and Pa discovers he can now power electrical objects just by touching them. Jonathan deduces that the well soil must have contained uranium, which has subsequently given Pa his new superhuman ability. Ma, Pa and Jonathan later discover that it is not uranium in the soil that has given Pa his new power, but rather the radioactive coveralls of his nephew, who witnessed an atomic bomb test in the Pacific.

Despite Pa becoming a human generator, the special effects are scant, basically just metallic objects tagging along after him when he walks past them. We also see him holding the plugs of several electrical appliances, including a vacuum cleaner, to give them juice. Whether he still has this power at the end of the movie is unclear.

The radiation in this movie is magical and seemingly harmless. Instead of developing radiation poisoning, Pa becomes, in Jonathan's words, "a human dynamo." No one seems too worried about the highly radioactive coveralls Pa has kept stashed under his bed. By rights, Ma's hair should be falling out and Pa should be at death's door, but in the cheerful universe of the Kettles, reality need not apply.

Although unashamedly formulaic, this film does have a certain charm, even though I didn't personally find it particularly funny. Marjorie Main plays the part of Ma with real gusto, and Percy Kilbride's Pa is so laid-back he seems almost catatonic. No doubt there are many Ma and Pa Kettle fans in the United States who treasure these films, and more power to them. As for the film's connection to the nuclear threat, it is slimmer than a supermodel.

Captive Women (RKO, 1952)

Credits: Directed by Stuart Gilmore; Written and Produced by Aubrey Wisberg and Jack Pollexfen; Associate Producer: Albert Zugsmith; Production Designer: Theobold Holsopple; Set Decorator: Clarence Steensen; Photography: Paul Ivano; Sound: Frank McWhorter; Editor: Fred R. Feitshans; Special Effects: Irving Block and Jack Rabin; Makeup: Steven Clensos; Mechanical Effects: Rocky Cline; Assistant Director: Ken Walters.

Cast: Robert Clarke (Rob); Ron Randell (Riddon); Margaret Field (Ruth); Stuart Randall (Gordon); Robert Bice (Bram); Gloria Saunders (Catherine); William Schallert (Carver); Eric Colmar (Sabron); Douglas Evans (Jason).

A Wisberg-Pollexfen Production; black-and-white; 64 minutes; released on October 10, 1952. Alternate title: *1,000 Years from Now*. Not available on home video.

Emphasizing adventure, action, and boorish male behavior, this poster for *Captive Women* (1952) downplays its post-apocalyptic milieu.

Depicting the long-term aftermath of a nuclear war, *Captive Women* could qualify for inclusion in "Mushroom Clouds," the third section of this book. However, the movie does include human mutants. Although they are not far-fetched (they sport only minor facial disfigurements), they are still mutants birthed by the nuclear threat, hence the film's inclusion in this section.

One of the earliest World War III aftermath movies, *Captive Women* takes place in a bombed-out New York City centuries after a major nuclear war. Three tribes of humans inhabit what's left of the Big Apple and the surrounding area: the Norms, non-mutants who more or less hold on to many American traditions from the twentieth century; the Upriver Men, scheming and amoral bad guys out for themselves; and the Mutates, humanoid mutations who kidnap Norm women to bear their children.

Led by callous Gordon (Stuart Randall), the Upriver Men accept an invitation to a Norm wedding. However, the wedding serves as a diversion for the Upriver Men, who attack the Norms on their home turf. Slaughtering many males, including the Norms' ruler, the Upriver Men also capture several Norm females. The slain ruler's son Rob (Robert Clarke) and his friend Bram (Robert Bice) escape; the Mutates give them shelter due to Rob's having earlier saved the life of a Mutate leader named Riddon (Ron Randell).

A bitter Mutate named Carver (William Schallert) challenges Riddon to combat, but Riddon beats him and subsequently banishes him from the Mutates. Revenge-minded Carver scurries to Gordon and shows him the secret underground passage (beneath a river) leading to the Mutates' homeland. Meanwhile, Rob and the Mutates free Norm women whom Gordon and the Upriver Men have held captive.

The Mutates, aware of Carver's treachery, rig their underground tunnel to collapse when the Upriver Men invade it, and sure enough, the timbers burst and the flooding river waters drown Gordon and his amoral associates. The film ends with an "inspirational" wedding between Riddon and a Norm woman, their betrothal not the result of a Mutate conquest of an unwilling Norm woman, but rather of love.

While its plot is predictable, *Captive Women* explores many interesting ideas. Instead of being pure good guys, the Norms have their flaws, not the least of which is their veneration of the Devil. As Rob says at one point, the Devil has "proved himself stronger than God. His works endure." Apparently, the "normal" survivors of World War III could not reconcile a God of love and mercy with the horrors of nuclear holocaust—but such atrocities *would* occur if the Evil One were in charge.

On the other hand, the Mutates, despite their oppressed status, have held onto Judeo-Christian religion for centuries. As a Mutate leader says, "We kept our faith." Yet it would seem that given their facial and physical deformities, the Mutates would be more likely to curse God than embrace him, and certainly more likely to do so than the Norms, who appear to have a better lot in post-nuke life. However, the Mutates identify with the founder of Christianity having been a man of many sorrows, apparently finding comfort in a divine being who likewise suffered unjustly at the hands of persecutors.

The Mutates are more or less the Native Americans of A.D. 3000. The opening narration tells us that the Mutates are "a people living in fear and terror," poorly regarded not just by Upriver Men but by Norms as well. For example, after seeing an Upriver Man kill a Mutate for sport, Rob wants to intervene, but his Norm friend Bram notes that the slain man was "only a Mutate." Gordon makes this bias more explicit when he says that the "only good Mutate is a dead one. We all know that."

And yet the Mutates are not without moral as well as physical blemish. They frequently kidnap fertile Norm women in the hopes of perpetuating their kind without passing on physical defects. They rationalize their barbarism, as we humans do so easily whenever it suits our purposes.

Having both the Mutates and the Norms exhibit good *and* bad traits gives each tribe nuance, and increases plausibility. On the other hand, the Upriver Men exhibit no redeeming traits. They are evil through and through, post-atomic Snidely Whiplashes in leather overalls. Indeed, the narrator tells us the Upriver Men are the disreputable types responsible for the nuclear war.

The movie doesn't play completely fair. For example, Riddon is a Mutate, yet his face is unblemished and his body whole, so it's something of a pulled punch to have him be the first Mutate to marry a Norm woman for love. As Dana Carvey's Church Lady might say, "How convenient."

Still, when it comes to the nuclear threat, the film clearly indicates that World War III was a catastrophe that has profoundly affected Western civilization. (We can speculate that the same is true elsewhere in the world as well. It might have been interesting to see what tribal groups had developed in Asia, Europe and South America.) As the narrator introduces the Mutates, he calls them "innocent victims of the black [twentieth] century," and says their unfortunate tribe was the result of "evil men's misuse of atomic power." This implies there is (or was) a valid use of atomic power in the twentieth century, a hint of optimism even in the bleak nuke-aftermath world of *Captive Women*. It also begs the question, who were the "evil men" who abused the power of the atom?

The opening narration seems somewhat inconsistent in its worldview. It champions the then-fledgling United Nations as the major hope of the world, and doesn't resort to the shrill tactics of 1953's *Invasion U.S.A.* (examined in Chapter 8). The latter film implied that a nuclear war between the superpowers (then the U.S. and the Soviet Union) was inevitable, so why not get it over with while America still had a clear nuclear advantage? Some influential Americans of the day, including Strategic Air Command's head honcho General Curtis LeMay,[1] apparently shared this view.

Captive Women champions international cooperation as the world's best hope of averting nuclear war. Yet at the same time, the "we" referred to sometimes seems to imply the world, and sometimes the United States only. For example, note this passage from the opening narration: "*We who control the weapons of peace* must be forever on guard to guarantee to the world that the forces of good will never be turned into forces for evil. *If we relax, lose our strength, our preparedness, what you are about to see is what might happen*" (emphases mine). The "we" in this case appears to be the U.S., not the Soviet Union. Note also the phrase "weapons of peace." Since this refers to nuclear weapons, the irony is rich: Can weapons, especially nuclear weapons, ever be used for peace? Perhaps, some would argue, to maintain peace. But this still appears to be doublespeak, since their actual use would be anything but peaceful—bear witness to Hiroshima and Nagasaki. The Bomb may have ended the Pacific War, but it didn't do so "peacefully."

Also, the narrator counsels that "we" (again, the 1952 American audience watching the film) should remain ever-vigilant, and this implies maintaining a nuclear parity with the Soviet Union. Indeed, the narrator warns us that if "we" do "lose our strength, our preparedness," then "what you are about to see is what might happen." Overall, the narration suggests (1) hoping for the best via the U.N. but (2) planning for the worse via a burgeoning nuclear arsenal. The film counsels that if we fail to do this, the movie's New York City of A.D. 3000 could become a reality.

The Year 1953

While 1953 was a fertile year for some of the most influential American science fiction movies, including *The War of the Worlds* and *Invaders from Mars*, that year saw no humanoid mutants begat by the nuclear threat. There *was The Beast from 20,000 Fathoms*, a film that influenced not only 1950s American monster movies but also led in part to the creation of everyone's favorite King of the Monsters, Godzilla. Chapter 5 covers *Beast*, along with the re-release of *King Kong*.[2] And speaking of famous stars who debuted in the 1930s, we now turn to Mickey Rooney in an ill-advised atomic age comedy from 1954.

The Atomic Kid (Republic, 1954)

Credits: Directed by Leslie H. Martinson; Screenplay by Benedict Freedman and John Fenton; Story by Blake Edwards; Produced by Mickey Rooney; Associate Producer: Maurice Duke; Art Director: Frank Hotaling; Set Decorators: John McCarthy, Jr., and George Milo; Photography: John L. Russell, Jr.; Music Score: Van Alexander; Sound: Dick Tyler, Sr., and Howard Wilson; Editor: Fred Allen; Special Effects: Howard and Theodore Lydecker; Makeup: Bob Mark; Assistant Director: John K. Grubbs; Second Assistant Director: Buddy Messinger; Script Supervisor: Gerry Wright; Technical Advisor: J.L. Cassingham.

Cast: Mickey Rooney (Barnaby "Blix" Waterberry); Robert Strauss (Stan Cooper); Elaine Davis (Audrey Nelson); Bill Goodwin (Dr. Rodell); Whit Bissell (Dr. Edgar Pangborn); Hal March (Ray); Peter Leeds (Bill); Fay Roope (General Lawlor); Stanley Adams (Wildcat Hooper); Robert Emmett (Mr. Reynolds).

A Mickey Rooney Production; black-and-white; 86 minutes; released on December 8, 1954. Available on VHS, DVD and Blu-ray.

Full disclosure: I am not a Mickey Rooney fan. I am not a Mickey Rooney non-fan either. A talented performer, he could be a fine actor, especially in serious roles. But when it comes to his over-the-top clowning, count me out. Indeed, calling Rooney's comedic acting broad is like calling the ocean wet—a severely malnourished understatement, to say the least.

But I also realize comedy may be the most subjective of movie genres. Yes, all genres are subjective, but comedy more so than most. For one thing, in a movie theater, you can tell if a comedy is working because if it is, people laugh. On the other hand, if the movie is supposed to be a comedy but no one laughs, the movie clearly is not working. Well, I didn't laugh once during *The Atomic Kid*, though admittedly, I was an audience of one in my den.

After spending days in the desert searching for uranium, friends Blix Waterberry (Mickey Rooney) and Stan Cooper (Robert Strauss) believe they have hit upon a mother lode. Actually, they have happened upon a nuclear testing site, and they spend the night in a deserted test house filled with dummies. Stan leaves the next day to file a claim in town, but soldiers stop him and pull him into a trench two miles from the blast area. The bomb goes off, and with Blix still back in the test house, it's apparently curtains for the hapless prospector.

But Blix miraculously survives, now radioactive and initially talking in a sped-up voice. The government quarantines him and runs tests to discover what made him immune to the nuclear test blast (they never find out). During this time, Stan lines up a seemingly lucrative deal to write a book about Blix. In actuality, a spy is using Stan to find out information about his bomb-resistant friend.

Blix and his pretty nurse Audrey Nelson (Elaine Davis) fall in love. As Audrey tells Blix, "I always pictured my dream man as being tall, dark and handsome. And then you come along—short, red-headed and radioactive." He even glows in the dark and literally lights up a room when he and Audrey kiss.

Eventually, Blix loses his radioactivity, and he inadvertently captures the spy who

1. All-American Aberrations: 1951–1959 (*The Atomic Kid*) • 17

Audrey Nelson (Elaine Davis) is startled as the radioactive Blix Waterberry (Mickey Rooney) glows in the dark in 1954's *The Atomic Kid*. **Rooney also produced the film.**

had been using Stan. Now a hero, Blix marries Audrey. Blix and Audrey drive to a secret location—but he accidentally drives onto a nuclear testing site. Discovering this, a panicked Blix races away from the test house in fast motion.

Rooney and Strauss play off each other *à la* Abbott & Costello, with Rooney the somewhat dim innocent and Strauss the get-rich-quick schemer. While on one level their clowning is professional, on another level, it's painful. The script (based on a story by Blake *Pink Panther* Edwards!) gives them little to work with.

For example, at the beginning after they've blundered onto the bomb site, they wonder why there appear to be no people in the test house. Rooney says, "You know what? Maybe this is one of those families that moved way out here in the desert to get away from the atom bomb." This is typical of the movie's wit, or lack of same. The physical comedy fares no better, and the radioactive gags likewise fall flat.

While today the idea of a comedy involving nuclear bombs and radiation wouldn't raise an eyebrow, in 1954 it must have appeared a tad peculiar if not tasteless. For Japanese audiences of 1954, *The Atomic Kid* may have seemed as inappropriate as hoofers dancing a soft shoe routine in the ruins of Hiroshima. And even though the movie tries hard to laugh at the nuclear threat, unintentional seriousness seeps through like a radiation leak from a lead-lined barrel. For example, the film opens with stock footage of a nuclear detonation in the Pacific, from which the title *The Atomic Kid* springs. During this brief opening, there is no music, and for a few seconds things become somber until the music score kicks in. In a later sequence, a news reporter, recording a news story prior to the blast, documents the various items that have been strategically placed near the spot where the bomb will detonate: military vehicles, a bomber plane, civilian autos, dummies. Says the newsman about the latter, "Let's hope that real people will never be so close to an atomic explosion." That quote harbors an apparently unintended but grievous implication, namely that the Japanese civilians in 1945 Hiroshima and Nagasaki must not have been "real people" since they had been "so close to an atomic explosion."

As the journalist continues to record his story, we see the test house set 200 yards from the detonation tower as well as the carefully positioned dummies inside the home. As the camera shows us the dummies, the reporter says, "After the bomb explodes, scientists will move in to check the damage to see exactly what an atom blast could do to Mr. and Mrs. Average American." The words clearly imply that many Mr. and Mrs. Average Americans may indeed be subject to such a nuclear blast during the 1950s, a brief but chilling statement in the midst of a lightweight comedy vehicle for Mickey Rooney. (If you watch the aforementioned scenes with the audio cut off, they seem almost eerie.)

The film reminds its 1954 audience that the search for bigger and better (read: more destructive) bombs continues apace. Says one of the scientists, "Strange, isn't it? The most powerful atomic bomb yet developed, and it's already outdated."

"Yes," his fellow scientist replies. "Right now in some secluded laboratory, they're already putting on paper a weapon that'll make this look like a firecracker."

As far as atom-spawned mutants go, Blix is played strictly for laughs. No one mentions that as he becomes more radioactive when he gets excited, i.e., when he gets close to Audrey, that he will contaminate others—including Audrey of course—who might then succumb to radiation sickness or even death. However, in the world of *The Atomic Kid*, radiation is a lark.

Bride of the Monster (Banner Pictures–Rolling M Productions, 1955)

Credits: Directed by Edward D. Wood, Jr.; Story and Screenplay: Edward D. Wood, Jr., and Alex Gordon; Produced by Edward D. Wood, Jr.; Associate Producer: Tony McCoy; Executive Producer: Donald E. McCoy; Photography: William C. Thompson and Ted Allan; Music Score: Frank Worth; Sound: Dale Knight; Sound Effects Editing: Marshall Pollock; Editor: Mike Adams; Special Effects: Pat Dinga; Makeup: Louis J. Haszillo and Maurice Seiderman; Property Master: George Bahr; Assistant Directors: William Nolte and Robert Farfan.

Cast: Bela Lugosi (Dr. Eric Vornoff); Tor Johnson (Lobo); Loretta King (Janet Lawton); Tony McCoy (Police Lt. Dick Craig); Harvey B. Dunn (Police Capt. Tom Robbins); George Becwar (Professor Vladimir Strowski); Paul Marco (Officer Kelton); Don Nagel (Detective Marty Martin); Ann Wilner (Tillie); Dolores Fuller (Margie); William Benedict (Newsboy); Ben Frommer (Drunk).

Black-and-white; 67 minutes; released on May 11, 1955. Available on VHS and DVD.

Edward D. Wood, Jr. The name strikes joy into the hearts of bad movie fans everywhere.

Though considered by many critics to be one of the worst filmmakers of the twentieth century, Wood is more famous than hordes of more capable genre movie directors

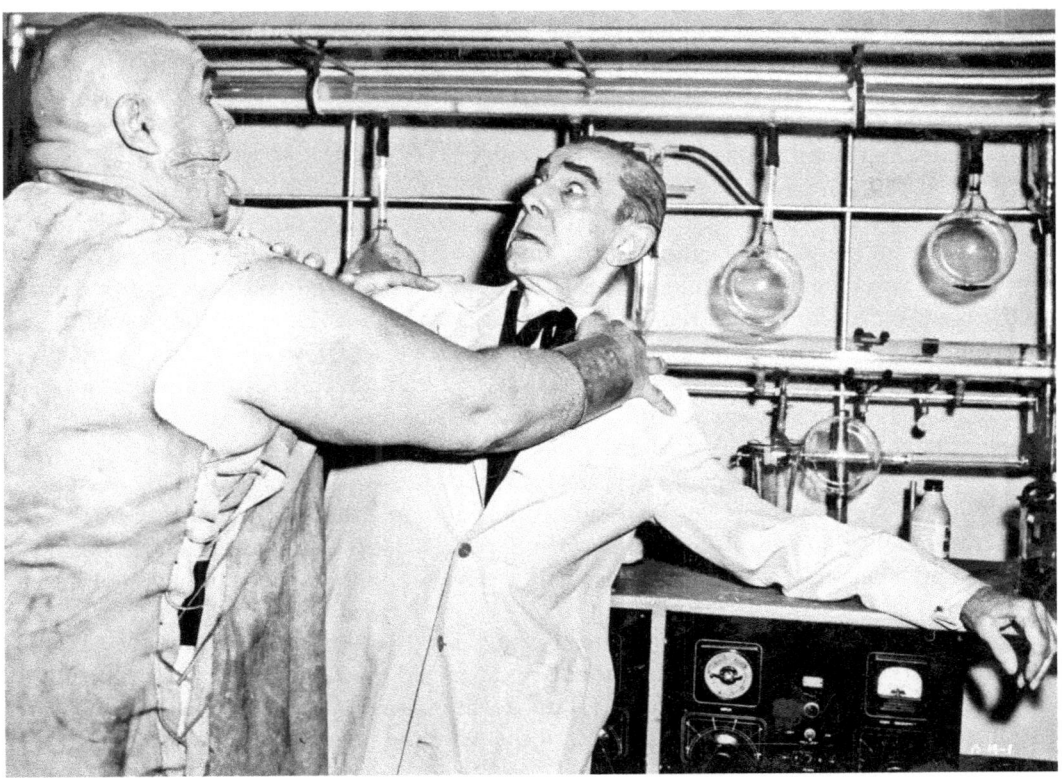

The mountainous Lobo (Tor Johnson) attacks a terrified Dr. Eric Vornoff (Bela Lugosi) in director Ed Wood's *Bride of the Monster* (1955).

whom time has forgotten. Tim Burton's 1994 movie *Ed Wood*, which painted the director's career with a broad and often inaccurate brush, has added to Wood's fame. *Bride of the Monster* doesn't let his fans down. And as bad movies go, it actually has a couple of bright spots.

Dr. Eric Vornoff (Bela Lugosi), a mad scientist, conducts experiments in a supposedly deserted house located somewhere in a Hollywoodized swamp. Periodically, Vornoff has his servant Lobo (Tor Johnson) drag hapless victims into his mad lab. Vornoff's hope is to create a race of "atomic supermen which will conquer the world," but his test subjects, with the exception of Lobo, invariably die when exposed to the scientist's atomic ray apparatus.

A scoop-happy reporter, Janet Lawton (Loretta King), wants to know where a number of missing men have gone; she believes a monster is responsible. Her policeman boyfriend Dick Craig (Tony McCoy) pooh-poohs this notion. Professor Strowski (George Becwar) is hunting for Vornoff, and believes the unhinged scientist may be behind the recent disappearances.

Janet becomes Vornoff's latest victim: Lobo brings her to Vornoff's house, where he courts her favor with food and conversation. Meanwhile, Strowski finds Vornoff and tries to persuade the scientist to return to his native country. Vornoff harbors a grudge against his homeland for having banished him and separated him permanently from his wife and son. Out of patience, Strowski pulls a gun on Vornoff, but Lobo gets the drop on Strowski. At Vornoff's command, Lobo tosses the terrified Strowski to Vornoff's "pet" octopus (a prop that Ed Wood may or may not have stolen from a movie studio). Strowski's demise has to be one of the longest death scenes in cinematic history.

Bizarrely, Vornoff has Janet don a wedding dress (!), and after she's strapped to the lab table, he gleefully tells her his atomic ray will transform her into "the Bride of the Atom!" Lobo, who has taken a shine to Janet, frees her and turns on Vornoff, subjecting the mad scientist to a dose of his own ray. This results in a super-sized, super-strong Vornoff who quickly dispatches Lobo and spirits Janet into the night.

The heroes, among them Dick, trail the atomic superman into the swamp, and once the new, improved Vornoff sets Janet down, Dick sends a boulder hurtling towards the mad scientist. Vornoff tumbles into a lake, where his own octopus seizes him. Next, lightning strikes the scientist and the cephalopod, and both inexplicably explode in a stock shot of a billowing nuclear mushroom cloud. Despite their close proximity to the blast, the protagonists remain unaffected.

Bride of the Monster sports the usual Ed Wood faults—poor continuity, unconvincing sets, flamboyant dialogue, etc.—but also offers a couple of genuine nuggets among its cache of fool's gold. One is Lugosi's performance. Yes, it is over the top, but it is also energetic and sincere. Regardless of the subpar material, Lugosi handled it like the pro that he was.

Another gold nugget is the theme of Beauty and the Beast played out between Lobo and Janet. Like Kong to Ann Darrow, Lobo is attracted to Janet, but also feels protective, so he frees her and goes after Vornoff. I don't want to over-praise this aspect of the film, but when Lobo tenderly regards Janet on the lab table before breaking her bonds, the pathos almost works.

But then again, this *is* an Ed Wood film, so hardly anything else works. His real masterpiece (if it can be called that) is 1958's *Plan 9 from Outer Space*. *Bride of the Monster* comes far closer to achieving mediocrity than *Plan 9*, which has little other than unintentional humor to recommend it, and hence falls far short of average.

As for the nuclear threat, Vornoff's goal of creating a super-race via atomic radiation has a definite totalitarian ring. Strowski clearly represents a Communist country, plugging into 1950s fears that the Soviet Union might defeat the West via superior nuclear weaponry. Of course, this talk of a "super-race" smacks of Nazi eugenics, and even a moviemaker as loopy as Ed Wood must have realized this. Thus, the Communists are being equated with the fascists of World War II as harbingers of ruthless domination.

Creature with the Atom Brain (Columbia, 1955)

Credits: Directed by Edward L. Cahn; Story and Screenplay by Curt Siodmak; Produced by Sam Katzman; Art Director: Paul Palmentola; Set Decorator: Sidney Clifford; Photography: Fred Jackman; Music Conductor: Mischa Bakaleinikoff; Sound: Josh Westmoreland; Editor: Aaron Stell; Special Effects: Jack Erickson; Assistant Director: Eddie Saeta.

Cast: Richard Denning (Dr. Chet Walker); Angela Stevens (Joyce Walker); S. John Launer (Captain Dave Harris); Michael Granger (Frank Buchanan); Gregory Gaye (Professor Wilhelm Steigg); Linda Bennett (Penny Walker); Tristram Coffin (District Attorney MacGraw); Harry Lauter, Larry Blake (Reporters); Charles Evans (Chief Camden); Pierre Watkin (Mayor Brener); Lane Chandler (General Saunders); Nelson Leigh (Dr.

Magnifying glass in hand, police doctor Chet Walker (Richard Denning) pauses to consider the intricate wiring inside a hi-tech zombie's skull in *Creature with the Atom Brain* **(Columbia, 1955).**

Kenneth C. Norton); Don C. Harvey (Lester Banning); Paul Hoffman (Tom Dunn); Edward Coch (Jason Franchot); Karl Davis (Willard Pearce); Michael Ross, Charles Horvath, Dick Crockett, Boyd "Red" Morgan (Creatures); Richard H. Cutting (Broadcaster).

A Clover Production; black-and-white; 69 minutes; Released in July 1955. Double-billed with *It Came from Beneath the Sea*. Available on DVD as a stand-alone or as part of the DVD set *Icons of Horror Collection: Sam Katzman* (with *The Giant Claw, Zombies of Mora Tau* and *The Werewolf*).

Castle of Frankenstein magazine (#8, 1966) succinctly summed up this movie "Gangster uses scientist to make humans into zombie-like robots. Movie makes audience into zombie-like robots." Clever, to be sure, and they did get the plot right. But their harsh opinion is just that—a harsh opinion. While obviously no prize-winner, *Creature with the Atom Brain* is a decently made B-grade programmer that will probably appeal to most Baby Boomers, though perhaps to no one beyond that generation. (Gen-Xers need not apply.)

Gangster Frank Buchanan (Michael Granger) employs the services of European Professor Steigg (Gregory Gaye) to exact revenge. Steigg has developed a technique in which he bombards dead men with radiation and implants an electronic brain; this imbues the reanimated corpses with super-strength and immunity to bullets, allowing Buchanan to order the radio-controlled Atom-Brained Creatures (ABCs for short) to find and kill those who sent him up the river.

The murders baffle the local police, particularly scientist Chet Walker (Richard Denning) and Captain Dave Harris (S. John Launer). Walker discovers that the ABCs leave behind radioactive traces and deduces that radiation is somehow empowering the assassins. The authorities call in the military, the latter using jet planes and specially equipped trucks to track down the source of the radiation. But Buchanan and Professor Steigg's residence and lab are lead-lined and thus immune to detection.

Nevertheless, through an ABC who phones the police station, Buchanan threatens to terrorize the city if the authorities don't call off the search. The authorities refuse to give in to Buchanan's demand—otherwise, where would his demands stop?—but they discover soon enough that the criminal mastermind wasn't bluffing. ABCs instigate a series of deadly accidents, including plane, bus and train crashes, causing the governor to declare a state of emergency and cancel all transportation.

Buchanan has Captain Harris killed and turned into an ABC; in turn, Harris murders two men that the police were hiding from the vengeful gangster. The authorities capture Harris, but let him go since Walker deduces that the atom-brained captain will lead them to his power source, which he does. After hitting Steigg in the head, presumably killing him, Buchanan orders all the ABCs in the lab to kill the soldiers and police officers outside.

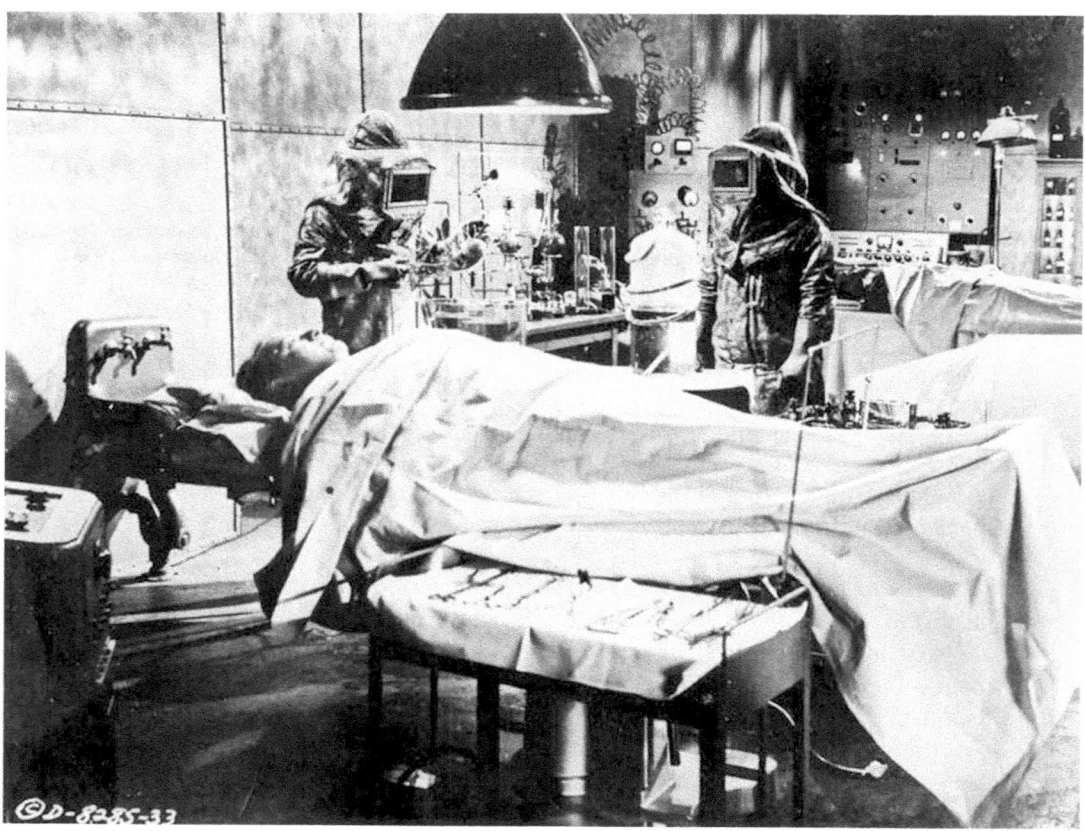

Prof. Wilhelm Steigg (Gregory Gaye, left) prepares to implant an electronic brain in Capt. Dave Harris (S. John Launer, on operating table) while vengeful gangster Frank Buchanan (Michael Granger, right) observes in *Creature with the Atom Brain* (Columbia, 1955). Both Steigg and Buchanan are wearing radiation suits, a sign of the atomic times.

A major battle ensues, with Harris strangling Buchanan to death before Walker short-circuits the lab, cutting off the power supply to the ABCs, who promptly drop to the ground like sacks of concrete.

It's probably unfair to probe the script too much—after all, its aspiration was just to be the second half of a 1950s "thrill bill"—but certain plot oddities make one wonder. For example, at the end, Buchanan orders the ABCs, including Harris, to kill the soldiers and police. But Harris comes through the window and kills Buchanan instead. Why? Because some vestige of Harris still lived on in the police captain's radio-controlled skull? Also, why does the atom-brained Harris dismember the doll belonging to Walker's daughter? Apparently to show us he had become a literal monster and to cancel any viewer sympathy with the ABC. In addition, until Harris, all the ABCs have spoken with Buchanan's voice. But wouldn't the men's voices sound the same as when they were alive rather than like Buchanan's?

Atomic rays charge the ABCs, but in this sense radiation truly seems like a gimmick; in a 1940s movie, electricity would have probably brought these same radio-controlled murderers to life. However, the movie uses certain sights and sounds emblematic of the then-newish nuclear threat: Geiger counters clicking, military trucks searching, fighter jets soaring. Also, Professor Steigg and Granger wear radiation suits when operating on ABCs, and such garb was certainly a sign of the atomic times. Steigg represents a foreign power that made nuclear breakthroughs ahead of the West, leaving America vulnerable, anathema to the spirit of the day.

An excellent primary source for the movie's effect on members of its intended 1955 audience is *Keep Watching the Skies!* author Bill Warren, who wrote, "*Creature with the Atom Brain* is, at best, undistinguished. Unless you're 12 years old, and it's grist for your mill. When I returned home after seeing this and its co-feature [*It Came from Beneath the Sea*], I entered in my diary that I had just seen the two best movies ever made."[3] Any self-respecting Monster Kid completely understands these sentiments.

Day the World Ended (American Releasing Corporation, 1955)

Credits: Produced and Directed by Roger Corman; Screenplay by Lou Rusoff; Executive Producer: Alex Gordon; Presented by Samuel Z. Arkoff and James H. Nicholson; Set Decorator: Harry Reif; Photography: Jock Feindel; Music Score: Ronald Stein; Sound: Jean Speak; Editor: Ronald Sinclair; Wardrobe: Gertrude Reade; Makeup: Steven Clensos; Script Supervisor: Barbara Bohrer; Monster Costume: Paul Blaisdell.

Cast: Richard Denning (Rick); Lori Nelson (Louise Maddison); Adele Jergens (Ruby); Touch [Mike] Connors (Tony Lamont); Paul Birch (Jim Maddison); Raymond Hatton (Pete); Paul Dubov (Radek); Jonathan Haze (Half-mutated Man); Paul Blaisdell (Mutant).

A Golden State Production; black-and-white; 79 minutes; released in December 1955. Double-billed with *The Phantom from 10,000 Leagues*. Remade in 1967 as *In the Year 2889*. Available on DVD double-billed with *The She-Creature* (1956) as part of the *Samuel Z. Arkoff Collection Cult Classics* series.

This film's distributor, American Releasing, quickly became American-International Pictures, or AIP for short. Headed by president James H. Nicholson, former Realart sales

This triple-eyed mutant (Paul Blaisdell inside the monster costume he designed) carries unconscious Louise (Lori Nelson) through a post–World War III valley in 1955's *Day the World Ended* **(American Releasing Corporation).**

manager, and his v-p Samuel Z. Arkoff, Hollywood lawyer, this company shrewdly tapped into teenage sensibilities with box office hits such as 1957's *I Was a Teenage Werewolf*. AIP released a slew of double creature features to movie theaters during the 1950s, many of them playing the lucrative drive-in circuit. *Day the World Ended* filled half a double bill with *The Phantom from 10,000 Leagues*. This twin science fiction horror show netted $400,000 in only two months, quite a bit of money in those days.[4] *Day the World Ended* is a modest but effective World War III aftermath drama that tries to have it both ways: score some serious points with its nuclear threat storyline while at the same time tossing in a monster to keep things commercial.

Produced and directed by Roger Corman, often dubbed "the King of the B's," *Day the World Ended* begins with portentous lettering that tells us "Our Story begins with…. THE END!" Immediately following is stock footage of a nuclear explosion. We see stock footage of a bombed city (probably from World War II Europe); the ominous voiceover narrator tells us that Total Destruction Day has left the world a radioactive shambles. Global thermonuclear war spread death and devastation over all the Earth. However, the narrator says, "But there is a force more powerful than man, and in His infinite wisdom, He has spared a few."

Those "few" dwell in a lead-lined valley: no-nonsense survivalist Paul Birch and his daughter Lori Nelson. Against Birch's better judgment, he and Nelson take in five survivors: geologist Richard Denning, petty crook Touch (a.k.a. Mike) Connors, stripper Adele Jergens, radiation-infected Paul Dubov and prospector Raymond Hatton. Survival is anything but assured as they wait to see whether they will eventually die of fallout or the lack of uncontaminated food and water. An equally unsettling prospect is that they might all turn into mutants.

Birch shares with Denning that an H-bomb test in the Pacific turned three animals into bizarre mutants with tough-as-metal skin. Denning determines that there are four mutant stages, and that they are all in Stage 1. Radiation-infested Dubov is Stage 2; he shuns food and water but goes out at night to feast on irradiated wildlife. Stage 3 is a mostly mutated man who descends into the valley through a thick radioactive mist; before he dies, he tells Birch and Denning an eerie story about fully transformed mutants battling it out for food in the fog above. These unseen beings are Stage 4. A Stage 4 mutant stalks them in their valley habitat. Nelson "hears" it "calling" to her telepathically.

Eventually, the stalking Stage 4 mutant kills Dubov. Prospector Hatton foolishly walks into the contaminated mist at the valley's edge to dig for gold, but the lethal radiation quickly finishes him. Trying to save the old man, Birch himself absorbs too much radiation and spends the rest of the film dying on the living room couch. Connors tries to force Nelson to become his girl, but she will have none of it and flees as Jergens confronts the two-faced hoodlum. After a brief argument with Jergens, Connors kills her and drops her body over a cliff.

The stalking Stage 4 mutant spirits Nelson away, but she escapes into a pond where the mutant refuses to go. Denning shoots at the monster to no avail, then also wades into the water. Rain gushes from overhead, killing the mutant, whose body belches smoke. It turns out that the rainwater is pure, and thus killed the mutant, who could only survive in an impure (i.e., radioactive) world. Birch shoots Connors to keep him from plugging Denning. After Denning and Nelson steal into the house to attend to Birch, the survivalist breathes his last.

Next, we see Denning and Nelson sporting backpacks and heading out of the valley arm in arm, given that the uncontaminated rain has (unconvincingly) cleansed radiation from the world outside the valley. The movie ends with the optimistic words "The Beginning."

Day the World Ended is a decent low-budget nuke aftermath drama. Corman brought several cash-strapped Grade-B science fiction movies to the screen in the 1950s, including *It Conquered the World* (1956), *Attack of the Crab Monsters*, *Not of This Earth* (both 1957) and *War of the Satellites* (1958). *Not of This Earth* is easily the best (and best written, with a script by Charles B. Griffith and Mark Hanna) of Corman's '50s genre films.

The *Day the World Ended* actors give professional performances. Denning, sometimes a villain (as in 1954's *Creature from the Black Lagoon*), brings a sincerity to his geologist role, just as Adele Jergens invests her heart-of-gold stripper with bittersweet authenticity. As Baby Boomers know, Mike Connors was the star of the hit TV detective series *Mannix* (1967–75).[5] The monster keeps the film from being taken *too* seriously and likewise satisfies the monster-loving kiddos.

The movie alerts its audience to the fact that atomic devastation could come at a moment's notice. This was a common fear in the '50s, reflected in Civil Defense flicks such as *Survival Under Atomic Attack*, distributed to more than 20,000,000 public school students in 1950,[6] and *You and the Atomic Bomb*, distributed to American citizens in 1952.[7] *Day the World Ended* also indicates that there will be survivors, some of them unscathed. We don't know exactly *how* they remained unscathed. Denning, Connors, Jergens, and Hatton appear to have no injuries of any kind. The radiation seems to have affected only Dubov, with burns covering one side of his face.

The film asserts that the unharmed survivors of a nuclear war would face personal tragedies. For example, Denning tells us that his younger brother, who was training to be "a man of God," died 30 feet away from him. Likewise, Nelson's boyfriend Tommy, whom we see in a framed photo of the two of them, did not make it to the house. Birch speculates that the young man has died, but he has actually become the Stage 4 mutant.

We know that about two months pass for the seven valley-huddled survivors, and it's interesting that all maintain regular grooming habits—bathing, washing and combing their hair, ironing their clothes, shaving, etc. Keeping to one's regular routines would help to keep things from becoming too horrific, and could help to keep tempers from flaring and souls from imploding. Jergens plays records to pass the time. And in an otherwise downbeat story, we see one brief moment of joy: Jergens dancing and saying to Denning, "What's my roentgen count—read me, daddy!" Denning and Nelson smile at this light-hearted quip. But scant moments later, Jergens stops cold and weeps.

Although the characters are stock types, Lou Rusoff's script makes occasional attempts to flesh them out. Connors, despite being a third-rate hood, says that he can't countenance smokers or boozers. But a movie like this probably needs stereotypes to give us a good look at how typical Americans from all walks of life would behave following a nuclear war. Also, the survivors being stalked by a monster—the Stage 4 mutant in this case—is a theme found in other 1950s science fiction films such as 1951's *The Thing from Another World*, 1958's *It! The Terror from Beyond Space* and 1959's *The Killer Shrews*.

What about the longer-term aftermath following World War III? *Day the World Ended* tells us that the good (read: young and attractive) will live, i.e., Denning and Nelson, but that the bad (Connors), the weak (Jergens), the foolish (Hatton) and the old (Birch) will not. Also, the continuing aftermath will wreak unexpected changes in human beings resulting in mutations. As Birch tells Denning, the atom's "true force has never been fully understood." He also says, "There's no such thing as logic any more." And yet there *is* a logic of a kind in the film, but it's one that assumes Providence will play a pivotal role.

The movie is rife with Biblical allusions; we even hear Birch reading Scripture aloud at one point, and at the end, Denning and Nelson clearly represent the new Adam and Eve, a theme familiar in nuclear war fiction. (There are other humans alive, however, as evidenced by the voice Birch briefly hears on the radio.) Birch comes off as a wise but stern patriarch-prophet, telling us he has planned for Total Destruction Day for ten years (in other words, since the first destructive use of the atomic bomb on Japan).

However, the movie paints a confused portrait of divine intervention. On the one hand, God's laws at work in nature create a life form that can thrive in a radiation-infested world—the mutants. As Denning declares in amazement, "A million years of evolution with one bomb!" But on the other hand, following the mutant's demise by uncontaminated rainwater, Nelson says, "Man created it [the bomb, the mutant] but God destroyed it." It would seem the Almighty is dealing cards from both sides of the deck.

Perhaps the movie's most interesting statement about the nuclear threat is found in the depiction of the Stage 4 mutant. The talented Paul Blaisdell created this monster on less than a shoestring. He nicknamed the triple-eyed creature Marty (he also affectionately nicknamed *The Beast with a Million Eyes*' puppet alien Little Hercules and *It Conquered the World*'s Venusian cucumber creature Beulah).[8] Blaisdell created many no-budget wonders for AIP movies, not the least of which is the amazing colossal six-foot hypodermic needle for *The Amazing Colossal Man*. As Bill Warren notes, this prop "is literally a giant hypodermic needle with giant holes for giant fingers, even giant cubic centimeters marked on the barrel."[9] (Yes, this may be ridiculous, but it's also fun.[10])

Blaisdell not only created Marty the Mutant, but he was also inside the monster suit. The design is curious—the skin appears to be asphalt, two tiny extra arms sprout from the shoulders, and the three-eyed face has a distinct Devil-like appearance, complete with scowl, hook nose and horns. Was the mutant intended to be a personification of humankind's presumptive nuclear sin, one vanquished, interestingly enough, by a baptism of holy water (the uncontaminated rain)? Or was Blaisdell just trying to come up with a suitably creepy creature? While the latter is the likeliest thesis, perhaps the mutant was unconsciously fashioned to be a malignantly evil gargoyle.

The budget only allowed for one fully transformed Stage 4 mutant. Interestingly, Dubov appears to stay in his Stage 2 form for almost two months without any further change; meanwhile, the Stage 4 mutant—presumably Nelson's boyfriend Tommy—must have changed almost immediately following the nuclear blasts, since it appears that both Nelson and Birch had been awaiting his imminent return just before the bombs fell. Also, though the protagonists worry that they too may change into mutants, they never reach Stage 2. This all implies that one's mutant status just after Total Destruction Day is the stage in which one remains for a considerable amount of time.

The movie clearly implies that the Stage 4 mutant mentally "calling out" to Nelson is what has become of her boyfriend Tommy. Yes, it does spirit away Nelson, but its intent does not seem murderous. Perhaps the Tommy mutant is watching over Nelson, and just longs to be with her due to their pre–World War III romantic relationship. In this sense, the Tommy-mutant is to be pitied, a pathos upon which the film subtly touches when Nelson says, "I feel so sorry for him. Strange I should feel that way."

Despite all this, Nelson does wind up with Denning as her significant other, and Birch lives long enough to see that his survivalist dreams will bear fruit via Denning and Nelson. The movie appears to say that even after a widespread nuclear war, there will still be hope. At the time, such an attitude appeared to be quintessentially American, though at the same time, atomic anxiety was just starting to eclipse that hope.

The Werewolf (Columbia, 1956)

Credits: Directed by Fred F. Sears; Screenplay by Robert E. Kent and James B. Gordon; Produced by Sam Katzman; Art Director: Paul Palmentola; Set Decorator: Dave Monstrose; Photography: Eddie Linden; Music Director: Mischa Bakaleinikoff; Sound: Ferol Redd; Editor: Harold White; Makeup: Clay Campbell; Assistant Director: Willard Sheldon.

Cast: Steven Ritch (Duncan Marsh); Don Megowan (Sheriff Jack Haines); Joyce Holden (Amy Standish); Eleanor Tanin (Helen March); Kim Charney (Chris Marsh); S. John Launer (Dr. Emery Forrest); George M. Lynn (Dr. Morgan Chambers); Harry Lauter (Deputy Ben Clovey); Larry J. Blake (Hank Dirgus); Ken Christy (Dr. Jonas

Gilchrist); James Gavin (Mack Fanning); George Cisar (Hoxie); Jean Charney (Cora); Jean Harvey (Ma Everett); Charles Horvath (Mugger); Don C. Harvey (Deputy); Ford Stevens (Reporter).

A Clover Production; black-and-white; 79 minutes; released in July 1956. Double-billed with *Earth vs. the Flying Saucers*. Available on DVD as a stand-alone or as part of the DVD set *Icons of Horror Collection: Sam Katzman* (with *The Giant Claw, Creature with the Atom Brain* and *Zombies of Mora Tau*).

"I want to cure a world," says one of the two mad scientists in *The Werewolf*. His method for bringing salvation to our planet seems bizarre, at best, but does explicitly draw upon 1950s fears of an all-out nuclear war. Overall, *The Werewolf* is a well-paced science fiction–horror film benefiting hugely from Steven Ritch's performance as the tormented werewolf.

Duncan Marsh (Ritch) is a car crash victim whom the madder of the two mad scientists has injected with (presumably irradiated) wolf serum. This causes Duncan to change into a werewolf when he becomes angry, and in the small town of Mountain Crest, he kills a mugger who tries to rob him.

Anguished, Duncan turns to the local doctor and nurse for help, but when they mention bringing in the law, he bolts. The local sheriff (Don Megowan) goes on the hunt for the werewolf, even enlisting the help of Duncan's wife and young son. Duncan subsequently turns himself in, but tells his wife and son that they must leave, because he doesn't want them to see what he has become. They reluctantly depart as the sheriff locks him in jail.

The two mad scientists, Morgan (George Lynn) and Emery (S. John Launer), journey to Mountain Crest, claiming they want to help Duncan; actually, they are planning to kill him so that he won't reveal anything about their unorthodox research. Under cover of night, Morgan and Emery overpower the lawman on duty and steal into Duncan's jail cell, Morgan intending to give their "patient" a lethal injection. Duncan, already in his wolf man state, brutally murders both men before escaping into the woods. The sheriff

Duncan Marsh (Steven Ritch), a lycanthrope for the atomic age, bears his pearly whites for the camera in Columbia's *The Werewolf* (1956).

enlists a posse to hunt Duncan down, and they shoot him to death. In traditional dying werewolf fashion, Duncan changes back to his human self.

As the tragic lycanthrope, Ritch perfectly captures the character's horror and anguish at what he has become, and though his death is inevitable, the viewer finds himself rooting for the beleaguered man. In *Scary Monsters* #20, Ritch told interviewer Paul Parla that at a preview showing of the film, "Many said they didn't want me to die and that I managed to touch a sympathetic chord in the audience."[11]

One problem with the film is that scientists Morgan and Emery don't suffer a dire enough fate. Yes, Duncan kills them, and we hear their horrible screams as he does so, but the protagonists don't find out that Morgan and Emery are responsible for Duncan's fate—they, not Duncan, are the villains, but no one knows this. (However, once the sheriff finds the syringe filled with a lethal injection in the jail cell, he might put two and two together and realize the doctors had intended to kill Duncan, not help him.)

The Werewolf's pseudo-scientific rationale for lycanthropy updated the supernatural explanations seen in past films such as 1941's *The Wolf Man*. For example, silver bullets aren't required to bring down our atomic age werewolf, just regular bullets. The full moon plays no role in his transformations—his emotional state fuels his metamorphoses, a matter of biochemistry.

This brings us to the two scientists' curious research. When Emery reads in the paper that Duncan, whom they had given a full injection of wolf serum, has killed, he says to his colleague, "Morgan, what have you done?"

Morgan replies, "'Done'? Accomplished is a better word, Emery." He then launches into a rant about why their research is necessary in the perilous atomic age in which they live: "Someday, the human race will destroy itself, not quickly but slowly.... Radiation creates mutants, monsters no longer human. They'll make the hydrogen bomb more powerful, then more powerful again, enough to change every person on Earth into a crawling, inhuman thing through fallout radiation."

However, using the wolf serum, Morgan says that he and Emery can "immunize ourselves from mutation and start a new world." To do so, wolf serum will be employed. Although Morgan doesn't specify that the wolf serum is irradiated, just as a viral vaccine contains an attenuated virus, so too must the wolf serum contain a radioactive substance.

Morgan paints the picture of a world in which he (and presumably other scientists) know that radiation turns humans into mutants. Thus, we can assume Morgan and Emery know of cases in which this has happened. This potentially mutant-ridden milieu is right at home amongst the other humanoid mutant movies of the 1950s.

Also, note Morgan's fatalism. He argues that an all-out nuclear war is inevitable, playing on the atomic fears of 1950s movie audiences. The world of *The Werewolf* is one in which nuclear war is as inevitable as tomorrow's sunrise. But why would wolf serum act as humankind's salvation from radiation causing mutation? Morgan doesn't give us a clue, and we are left scratching our heads. The fact that the wolf serum turns Duncan into a werewolf indicates that there must be some validity to the scientists' research; they can't be total wackos or they wouldn't have gotten any results.

On the other hand, the only people in the movie who speak of nuclear war are the two obviously evil scientists, and they literally create a monster. This implies that maybe it is best to go about one's normal business, as the protagonists do, than to fearfully prepare for a post–World War III mutant-infested world. Perhaps on an unconscious level, this could help assure viewers that it was okay to engage in conventional 1950s pursuits, such as attending movie theaters playing films like *The Werewolf*. After all, in the event of a nuclear war, like Bert the Turtle, we could always duck and cover.

World Without End (Allied Artists, 1956)

Credits: Screenplay and Directed by Edward Bernds; Produced by Richard Heermance; Art Director: David Milton; Set Decorator: Joseph Kish; Photography: Ellsworth Fredericks; Music Score: Leith Stevens; Music Editor: Neil Brunnenkant; Sound: Del Harris; Editor: Eda Warren; Special Effects: Milt Rice; Makeup: Emile LaVigne; Assistant Director; Don Torpin; Second Assistant Director: Ron Blair; Dialogue Director: Sam Peckinpah.

Cast: Hugh Marlowe (Dr. John Borden); Nancy Gates (Garnet); Nelson Leigh (Dr. Eldon Galbraithe); Booth Colman (Mories); Rod Taylor (Herbert Ellis); Christopher Dark (Henry Jaffe); Shawn Smith (Elaine); Lisa Montell (Deena); Everett Glass (Timmek); Stanley Fraser (Elda); William Vedder (James); Rankin Mansfield (Beryl); Strother Martin (Nihka).

Technicolor, CinemaScope; 80 minutes; released on March 25, 1956. Double-billed with *Indestructible Man*. Available on DVD (co-billed with 1958's *Satellite in the Sky*) and also as one of four features on a two-DVD set called *TCM Greatest Classic Films Collection: Sci-Fi Adventures* (with *Them!, The Beast from 20,000 Fathoms* and *Satellite in the Sky*).

In 1957, a space-time distortion sends a crew of four astronauts hurtling into the future. After escaping the distortion, their spaceship crashlands in a snow-covered area on an apparently unknown world. Soon enough, the astronauts discover they are on a suspiciously Earth-like planet. Upon discovering a graveyard with headstones written in English, the astronauts realize they are indeed back on Earth. But by the dates on the grave markers, they also realize they have been propelled several centuries into the future.

The astronauts encounter two giant (rubbery) spiders in a cave, and later hellacious multi-eyed humanoid mutants. Soon the astronauts also discover what appear to be the last remnants of the human race living underground, enjoying a high order of science and technology. The undergrounders' leader reveals that it is now 2508, and that in 2188, Earth suffered a catastrophic nuclear war. The multi-eyed humanoids who live above ground, called the Beasts, are the result of centuries of postwar radioactive mutation.

Astronaut Hugh Marlowe and his three companions soon learn that the underground males are more than content to passively exist as they have for decades, with no desire to live on the surface. Pacifists all, they see weapons and conquest as the very things that brought about the global nuclear war in the first place, so their society has no weapons, and in fact disdains them.

The underground women, beautiful and short-skirted, are attracted to the virile astronauts. Two of the astronauts find themselves likewise attracted to the females. Significantly, the underground women dress scantily in an apparent bid to interest the underground men who, unlike the women, do not dress to attract the females. The film implies that the underground women regard their male peers as soft, lackluster and unappealing. However, the astronauts perk up the women like a shot of Red Bull. When astronaut Rod Taylor parades about shirtless after taking a shower, one of the women gets a look at him and says, "My, you are so much more muscular than our men." Embarrassed, Taylor fends

1. All-American Aberrations: 1951–1959 (World Without End) • 31

Rod Taylor (holding the bazooka) fires at savage surface dwellers in Allied Artists' *World Without End* (1956). Left to right, Christopher Dark, Taylor, Hugh Marlowe, Nelson Leigh and, on the ground, Keith Richards (but not the Rolling Stones' Keith Richards).

off the compliment. The undergrounder woman continues to look him over, finally declaring, "I like it!"

Mories, a sour underground administrator, is jealous of Marlowe (whom he apparently believes has "stolen" his lady). He attempts to pin a murder on the astronauts but his villainy soon comes to light. In an attempt to escape to the outside world, he runs straight into the clutches of the Beasts, who quickly kill him.

Marlowe and his three twentieth century crewmates convince the underground men that weapons aren't so bad after all and that living on the surface would be grand. Sporting an underground-made bazooka, the astronauts attack the Beasts in order to free their non-mutant captives. There are too many mutants to take out with firearms and a bazooka, so Marlowe challenges the Beasts' chief to one-on-one, hand-to-hand combat. Quite unconvincingly, and far too easily, Marlowe dispatches the chief, thus becoming the new chief, and through an interpreter he orders the Beasts to depart. The last scenes of the movie show the undergrounders happily building above ground as the astronauts look on approvingly.

World Without End is enriched by its color CinemaScope photography and acceptable production values. However, it suffers from a comic bookish, simplistic script. The astronauts are right about everything 100 percent of the time, and the undergrounder leaders are wrong about everything all the time—that is, until the astronauts persuade the latter to adapt twentieth century American values.

The undergrounders' arguments against building weapons and fighting the Beasts are dismissed as craven and weak, whereas the astronauts' arguments for building weapons and establishing an above-ground presence are lauded as courageous and strong. But actually, one could mount a good argument supporting either viewpoint. After all, the underground leaders posit that the need for expansion and weapon-building is what led to the disastrous 2188 nuclear war, and there is merit in this assertion. Making no real attempt to understand this point of view, the astronauts immediately reject it. Yes, there are virtues to the astronauts' viewpoint as well: Without assertive advancement and societal expansion, humankind does tend to stagnate. Trying to maintain a passive status quo would, in the long run, not be a good prescription for the human race.

But look who's talking, er, writing: an American raised in the twentieth century sporting mainstream twentieth century American values! Politically, I am an independent; I try to weigh each issue on its own merits rather than submit it to a predetermined worldview. But I don't think the *World Without End* astronauts ever seriously consider the underground leaders' arguments for a pacifistic society.

World Without End would have been much more interesting and adult if the crux of the film had been the legitimate arguments for and against the current pacifistic civilization of the future becoming a more assertive society. Instead of being a dour-faced comic book villain, Mories could have championed reasoned ideas to counter the views of the astronauts, and vice versa. Such a story would have welcomed nuance, for both viewpoints battling it out in the movie would have sported merits and flaws. A compromise might have been interesting. Or perhaps some of the undergrounders might choose to ally themselves with the astronauts to build a surface civilization while another contingent of undergrounders might choose to go on beneath the earth as they have for centuries. Both sides could respect one another's decisions, and neither by default nor design would either side be depicted as villains.

But given the movie and its viewpoints as they stand, what does *World Without End* say about the nuclear threat? For one thing, it says humans will avoid nuclear war for an amazing 231 years. From 1957 through 2188, there apparently were no major nuclear wars, and presumably no minor ones either. But 2188's Big Blowout sets civilization back big time.

So how did humankind avert war for so long? We aren't told, but the movie implies it was probably due to deterrence, the need for each democratic nation to stay strong and hold the line against its totalitarian enemies, both sides maintaining a level playing field in terms of the balance of power. In addition, citizens were encouraged to stay strong and hold the line against defeatism.

In the movie, Hank, the astronaut who was married and had two kids, silently grieves over his knowledge that his family died centuries ago, so he will never see them again. His crewmates handle his predicament with a kind of muted sympathy that says, "Tough break, accept it and go on"—which is easy to suggest when it isn't your wife and two kids. But the suggestion appears to be that if one lost family members due to a nuclear war, one would grieve, yes, but should largely keep this mourning inside—just accept it and go on, because that's what Americans do. Or at least, it's what they should do. Isn't it? Some of you say yes, some of you say no. Welcome to the world of nuanced disagreement.

Regarding the mutants in the movie, what does their portrayal say about the nuclear threat? For one thing, it says that it could take hundreds of years before such mutants would reach the level of savagery seen in the film. It also suggests that mutants may not be just monsters. After all, the film reveals that some of the Beasts have children who do not sport misshapen skulls and multiple eyes. But if the mutants aren't just monsters on the same level as *Them!* or *Tarantula*, then does that mean there would be moral and spiritual issues involved in killing them?

We are told that a chief rules over the Beasts, and that a new chief assumes command if he is able to kill the old chief. Presumably, all their customs are equally harsh. They do have a rudimentary language, but we also find out they mistreat the non-mutants among them. At least one thing they seem to have going in their favor is that, unlike *The Time Machine*'s Morlocks, they are not cannibals.

Although the social and environmental effects of *World Without End*'s nuclear war lasted centuries, the film ends on an upbeat note. The human race is living above ground once more, the undergrounders' formerly sickly children have now become hardy youngsters who play with the freed Beast children, and the sky appears to be the limit. Indeed, one almost expects the cast to break out into song. Ethel Merman's "Everything's Coming Up Roses," anyone?

The Amazing Colossal Man (AIP, 1957)

Credits: Produced and Directed by Bert I. Gordon; Screenplay by Mark Hanna and Bert I. Gordon; Presented by James H. Nicholson and Samuel Z. Arkoff; Production Design: Bill Glasgow; Set Decorator: Glen Daniels; Photography: Joe Biroc; Music Score: Albert Glasser; Music Editor: Lloyd Young; Editor: Ronald Sinclair; Special Effects: Bert I. Godron; Assistant Special Effects: Flora M. Gordon; Makeup: Bob Schiffer; Assistant Director-Production Supervisor: Jack R. Berne; Assistant Producer: Henry Schrage; Second Assistant Director: Nate D. Slott; Property Master: James Harris; Sound Editor: Josef von Stroheim; Costumes: Bob Richards; Sound Recorder: Jack Solomon; Hair Stylist: Joan St. Oegger; Chief Set Electrician: Joe Edesa.

Cast: Glenn Langan (Lt. Col. Glenn Manning); Cathy Downs (Carol Forrest); William Hudson (Dr. Paul Lindstrom); James Seay (Col. Hallock); Larry Thor (Dr. Eric Coulter); Russ Bender (Richard Klingman); Lyn Osborn (Sgt. Taylor); Diana Darrin (Typist); William Hughes (Control Officer); Jack Kosslyn (Lieutenant in Briefing Room); Jean Moorhead (Woman in Bathtub); Jimmy Cross (Sergeant at Reception Desk); Hank Patterson (Henry); Frank Jenks (Truck Driver); Harry Raybould (Army Guard at Gate); Scott Peters (Sgt. Lee Carter); Myron Cook (Capt. Thomas); Michael Harris (Police Lt. Keller); Bill Cassady (Lt. Peterson); Dick Nelson (Sgt. Hanson); Edmund Cobb (Dr. McDermott); Paul Hahn (Attendant); June Jocelyn (Nurse Wilson); Stanley Lachman (Lt. Kline).

A Malibu Production; black-and-white; 81 minutes; released on August 28, 1957. Available on VHS.

Plenty of folks have had a field day mocking this low-budget 1950s AIP item, including the *MST3K* crowd. But others, such as *Keep Watching the Skies!* author Bill Warren, argue that the movie has its merits. Warren says it's "better than its effects and trappings, greater than the sum of its parts."[12]

Colonel Glenn Manning (Glenn Langan) waits in a trench with his troops for a plutonium bomb detonation. Something goes wrong, and the detonation is delayed. Meanwhile,

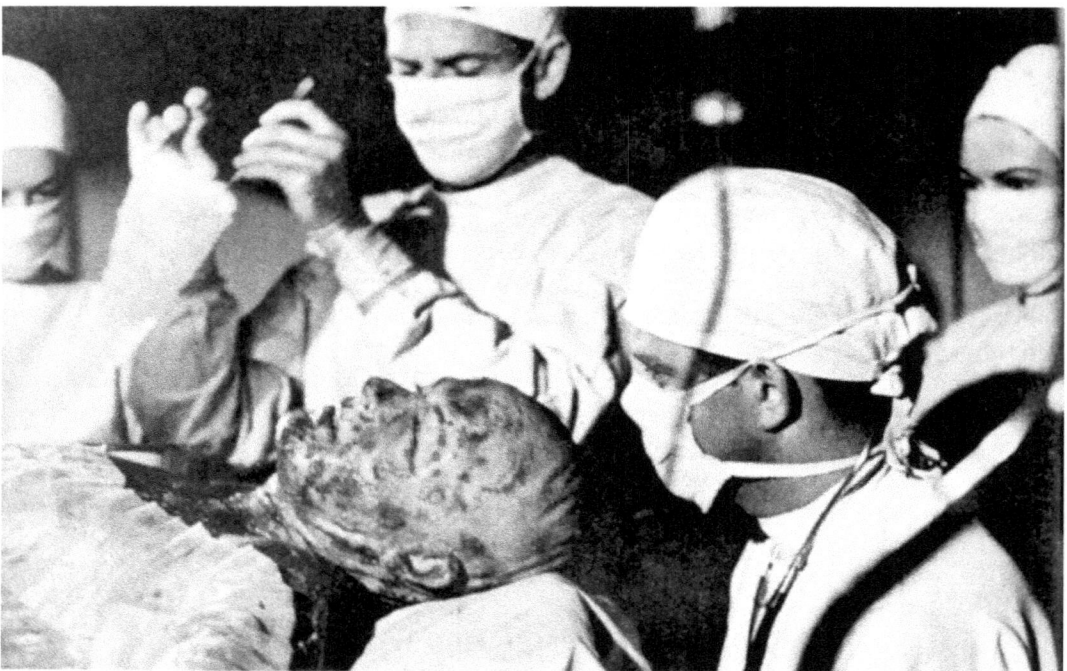

Dr. Paul Lindstrom (William Hudson, top middle) lays gauze over the horribly burned Colonel Glenn Manning (Glenn Langan) in *The Amazing Colossal Man* (AIP, 1957).

a civilian plane crashes in the blast zone. In an effort to rescue the pilot, Manning rushes out of the trench—and within seconds, the bomb goes off, searing the flesh from his body.

Inexplicably, Manning grows new skin, and also begins to grow at the rate of eight to ten feet a day. The Army takes him to the grounds of a remote hospital formerly used for military patients. There, his doctors discover that his heart isn't growing at the same rate as the rest of his body; this will affect his thinking. His fiancée Carol (Cathy Downs) tries to comfort him, but it's no good. Manning has become resentful about his fate.

Ironically, just as the doctors discover a way to stop Manning's growth and perhaps even shrink him back to normal size, Manning slips unseen into the Nevada desert, his thinking distorted by his oxygen-starved brain. In no time, he lumbers into Las Vegas, panicking local citizens and destroying city property.

In a helicopter, Carol and Manning's two physicians, Dr. Lindstrom[13] (William Hudson) and Dr. Coulter (Larry Thor), land in front of him, and the two medical men jab a six-foot hypodermic needle into his leg. Less than appreciative, Manning plucks it from his flesh and uses it like a dart on Coulter. Manning scoops up a screaming Carol and trots onto Boulder Dam. Lindstrom pleads with Manning to put Carol down, and after Manning does so, the military blasts him with bazookas and rifle volleys. Injured, Manning topples from the dam, plunging into the turbulent waters below.

Even by 1950s standards, this movie suffers from uneven (often just plain awful) special effects, which was a characteristic of most if not all of director-producer Bert I. Gordon's genre movies. Obviously fascinated by gigantism, Gordon directed several 1950s movies dealing with giant humans: *The Amazing Colossal Man*, its sequel *War of the Colossal Beast* and *The Cyclops*. Of the three, *Colossal Man* is easily the best.

Genre film scholars disagree about the film's merits. Back in the day (1965), *Castle of Frankenstein* #6 called the film a "[w]eak, foolish and unconvincing thriller." Latter-day Monster Kid scribes have accorded it more respect. For example, late horror movie scholar Tom Triman praised it in *Scary Monsters Magazine* #59: "A uniquely tragic and humanistic monster story … [that] has maintained its cult status as a memorable milestone of 1950s sci-fi cinema."[14]

As an unintentional polemic on nuclear testing, the movie gives all such detonations a failing grade. After all, the result of the plutonium bomb test is to turn Manning into an ever-growing mutant mushrooming (sorry) at the incredible rate of eight to ten feet a day. Just as Manning's growth is out of control, so too apparently is nuclear testing, or at least the potential effects of nuclear testing. Manning finds himself going mad: The atomic anxiety that gripped the American public in the 1950s becomes literal in his case due to the lack of blood reaching his brain.

Manning and his troops were being used as guinea pigs, the reason they are so close to the plutonium bomb's detonation tower. Of course, in the 1950s, real American soldiers were ordered to walk over ground on which a nuclear bomb had been detonated a short time earlier, obviously to see what effects the radiation would have on the troops.[15] Humane? Hardly.

Interestingly, an uncle of mine was one of those 1950s soldiers told to walk through a highly radioactive area after a nuclear detonation, and his wife and sisters swear that once he returned from his tour of duty, he had experienced a complete personality change. He died many years ago in his mid-forties. When his ex-wife contacted the VA about the possibility of his radiation walk contributing to his early demise, they refused to speak with her.

Given what happens to Colonel Manning, you have to wonder if the military might choose to intentionally expose soldiers to plutonium bomb radiation, thereby giving the army literally Kong-sized troops. With the treatments developed by Dr. Lindstrom and Dr. Coulter, the military could keep the plutonium-radiated soldiers from growing too big and thus prevent any mental impairment due to a slower-growing heart. Such gigantic soldiers could perform any number of tasks, and they could psychologically terrify normal-sized soldiers overseas. Not exactly an envious fate for the titanic American troops, of course.

But then, one major way in which *The Amazing Colossal Man* is a departure from *Day the World Ended* and *World Without End* is that the film ends unhappily. Manning doesn't get cured, he does go insane, and he dies—literally end of movie.

In *Day the World Ended*, Marty the mutant is not the main character, and the *World Without End* mutants are supporting characters. But *Amazing Colossal Man*'s protagonist is the title character, and traditionally, title monsters (such as King Kong) die at the end of their movies.

Manning is a tragic character. For risking his life to save another, the universe punishes him with the fate of unchecked growth. If he had simply stayed in the trench, or gone back when his commanding officer ordered him to do so over the loudspeaker, he and Carol probably would have gotten married as planned, had kids, and lived a long and happy life. But fate had something different in store for them. As Manning says at one point, "What sin could a man commit in a single lifetime to bring this upon himself?"

Actor Glenn Langan deftly brings the tortured Manning to life. Instead of facing

This poster for AIP's *The Amazing Colossal Man* (1957) promises spectacle the movie doesn't deliver. The fighter jets (not seen in the actual movie) *are* a nice touch, though.

his fate with a no-questions-asked stiff upper lip, Manning is embittered over the cards that life has dealt him. Though he laughs at his own darkly arch observations about his mutated status, his humor is devoid of comedy. As he notes, "I should never have lived through that blast."

This brings to mind that in an all-out nuclear war, it is often said that the lucky ones would die first. Those who live through an actual nuclear blast, such as many of the survivors of Hiroshima and Nagasaki, may eventually die from the bomb's effects—flash burns, radiation poisoning, cancer. Even when they don't die, they may still be physically scarred for life, emotionally and psychologically, if not spiritually. Certainly this is the case for Manning.

The Cyclops (Allied Artists, 1957)

Credits: Produced, Directed and Written by Bert I. Gordon; Associate Producer-Production Manager: Henry Schrage; Assistant Producer: Flora M. Gordon; Photography: Ira Morgan; Music: Albert Glasser; Editor: Carlo Lodato; Special Effects: Bert I. Gordon; Makeup: Carlie Taylor; Special Makeup Created by Jack H. Young; Assistant Directors: Harry O. Jones and Ray Taylor, Jr.; Animal Sequences: Jim Dannaldson; Properties: James Harris; Script Supervisor: Diana Loomis; Aeronautical Supervisor: Henry "Hank" Coffin; Sound Effects: Douglas Stewart; Snake Fight Supervisor: Ralph D. Helfer.

Cast: Gloria Talbott (Susan Winter); James Craig (Russ Bradford); Lon Chaney (Martin Melville); Tom Drake (Lee Brand); Dean Parkin (The Cyclops); Marlene Kloss (Newsstand Attendant); Manuel Lopez (Policeman); Vincent Padula (The Governor); Paul Frees (Voice of the Cyclops).

A B & H Production; 66 minutes; released on July 28, 1957. Double-billed with *Daughter of Dr. Jekyll* (which also starred Gloria Talbott, making for a Gloria double feature). Available on DVD.

Producer-director Bert I. Gordon's *The Amazing Colossal Man* and *The Cyclops* were both released in 1957, but *The Cyclops* was actually shot in 1955[16] (and released on July 28, 1957[17]) whereas *Colossal Man* was released on August 27[18] of the same year. While *Colossal Man* was somewhat ambitious in terms of theme, *The Cyclops* is a basic low-budget monster-on-the-loose programmer: The titular monster is only loose in a mysterious and remote region of rural Mexico.

To find her fiancé Bruce Barton, whose plane disappeared in Mexico, Susan Winter (Gloria Talbott) employs a crew of three: scientist Russ Bradford (James Craig), pilot Lee Brand (Tom Drake) and get-rich-quick schemer Martin Melville (Lon Chaney). After some wrangling with the Mexican authorities, which includes Martin decking a law officer, the quartet takes off in a plane, soon landing in the remote area in which Susan is certain Bruce's plane went down. The foursome discovers that the region is overrun with giant animals, ranging from a 12-foot hawk to dinosaur-sized lizards, two of which battle lethargically before them. There's also a house-sized arachnid (presaging Gordon's 1958 *Earth vs. the Spider*) which, despite its alarming proximity to the protagonists, doesn't attack them. (Perhaps it had recently consumed a giant fly?)

Eventually, the Cyclops, a 25-foot mutant, appears and spirits Susan to his literal Man Cave. When the men arrive, the Cyclops confronts them all; as he reaches for them, they cower in the back of the cave. The giant's countenance is severely distorted, one half a mass of scar tissue draped over the left side of the mutant's face, exposing upper and lower teeth, and the other half dominated by a huge, unblinking eye, hence the movie's title. The creature grunts, growls and bellows menacingly.

At Russ' urging, Susan speaks to the giant, and appears to be making some headway

Businessman Martin Melville (Lon Chaney, Jr.) appears tickled pink over the radioactive rock he's found in *The Cyclops* **(Allied Artists, 1957).**

until Martin stupidly shoots at the mutant. Enraged, the Cyclops kills Martin and, in perhaps the most unconvincing matte shot ever filmed, grabs Susan. However, a monstrous snake distracts the giant, and he deposits Susan on a huge rock before battling the super-sized serpent. Taking advantage of the situation, Susan, Russ and Lee hide in the countryside. An anguished Susan realizes that the giant is actually what's become of her fiancé Bruce Barton.

During the climax of 1957's *The Cyclops*, the title character (Dean Parkin) gets an eyeful in the worst way. This scene was trimmed in some TV showings of the film.

Our heroes try to leave in their plane, but they all run from the aircraft as the Cyclops approaches. Russ distracts the colossal creature and, running up a hill, creates a burning spear that he hurls into the giant's eye. Crying out, the blinded giant pulls out the spear as Russ, Lee and Susan hightail it into the plane. As they take off, it looks as though the giant's flailing arms may smash into their escaping aircraft, but they don't, and in the last shot, we see the plane soaring away as the title monster lies deathly still in the foreground.

Cheaper and less ambitious than *The Amazing Colossal Man*, *The Cyclops* plays like a dry run for Gordon's future humongous human movies: *Amazing Colossal Man*, its 1958 sequel *War of the Colossal Beast* (covered later in this chapter), 1962's *The Magic Sword* with its Cyclops-like ogre, and 1965's *Village of the Giants*, in which obnoxious titan-sized teenagers run roughshod over a small town.

The Cyclops has always gotten a less than warm critical reception. Bill Warren says, "This dreary disaster is one of Gordon's worst films in all respects."[19] In a similar vein, 1966's *Castle of Frankenstein* #8 called it a "[d]ismal, low-grade adventure." While obviously far less than first-rate, or even second-rate, *The Cyclops* definitely worked for me as a seven-year-old when I first beheld it on TV in 1963. I even found the monster scary due to its grotesque growls and its even more grotesque countenance. As Tom Triman said in *Scary Monsters* #59, "The film's single most startling element is Jack Young's spectacularly gruesome makeup for the title monstrosity, one of the most memorably nightmarish faces of 1950s science fiction cinema."[20] Amen.

Unlike other movie mutants created by fallout or a nuclear detonation, the Cyclops and the Mexican animals are oversized because of what Russ refers to as a "radioactive substance" in the vicinity. The villainous Martin establishes that uranium is present, but Russ appears to believe that something else—he mentions the possibility of thorium—

is causing the area's spectacular growth. In fact, he asserts that the Cyclops' "growth will never stop."

This begs several questions. If the mutant's growth—and that of the region's animal life—will never stop, how come none of them appears bigger than a dinosaur? Do they simply die or get killed by another mammoth animal before achieving Godzilla-like proportions? Also, if this radioactive substance has always dominated this region of Mexico, wouldn't someone else have stumbled upon it by now? And wouldn't some of them have returned to civilization and told of their amazing discovery?

On the other hand, the area's ability to mutate suggests that the menace of radiation can be found anywhere in the natural world, and can create monsters as fearsome as any spawned by man-made nuclear testing and fallout. In this sense, the movie may unconsciously imply that no one is safe from the menacing aspects of radiation. At one point, Martin asks Russ if they too will start to grow because of the region's radiation. This brings to mind another question: In however many years (decades? centuries?) that this area of Mexico has been hot, has no one ever wandered into the area and also become giant like Susan's fiancé?

But *The Cyclops* is not interested in logic, just in providing a low-budget scare show for kids, and in that area, it succeeds well enough. True, it does employ some pathos at the terrible fate of Susan's fiancé and her sorrowful reaction to this realization, but this theme becomes much stronger in Gordon's *The Amazing Colossal Man*, a movie that at least tries to say something. *The Cyclops* is basically only trying to say, "Boo!" with a Paul Frees snarl.[21]

From Hell It Came (Allied Artists, 1957)

Credits: Directed by Dan Milner; Screenplay by Richard Bernstein; Story by Richard Bernstein, Dan Milner and Jack Milner; Produced by Jack Milner; Art Director: Rudi Field; Set Decorator: Morrie Hoffman; Photography: Brydon Baker; Music: Darrell Calker; Sound: Frank Webster; Editor: Jack Milner; Special Effects: James H. Donnelly; Makeup: Harry Thomas; Assistant Director: Johnny Greenwald; Script Supervisor: M.E.M. Gibsone; Production Supervisor: Byron Roberts; Props: Ted Mossman; Wardrobe: Frank Delmar; Hair Stylist: Carla Hadley; Key Grip: Charles Hannawalt; Monster idea by Paul Blaisdell.

Cast: Tod Andrews (Dr. William Arnold); Tina Carver (Dr. Terry Mason); John McNamara (Professor Clark); Suzanne Ridgway (Kory); Robert Swan (Tano); Baynes Barron (Chief Maranka); Linda Watkins (Mrs. Mae Kilgore); Gregg Palmer (Kimo); Mark Sheeler (Eddie); Lee Rhodes (Norgu); Grace Matthews (Orchid); Tani Marsh (Naomi); Lenmana Guerin (Dori); Chester Hayes (The Tabanga).

A Milner Brothers Production; black-and-white; 73 minutes; released on August 25, 1957. Double-billed with 1957's *The Disembodied*. Available on DVD.

The Milner Brothers, producers of this low-wattage thriller, were taking no chances. *From Hell It Came* combines the supernatural with the science fictional, with the Milners possibly thinking that this approach would pull in two audiences—fans of traditional horror and fans of science fiction. But fans of either genre were probably disappointed with this tale of a vengeful tree monster (yes, you read right).

Taking place on a South Pacific island, the film opens with hapless native Kimo

(Gregg Palmer) pleading his innocence. But this is a non-starter with witch doctor Tano (Robert Swan) and Chief Maranka (Baynes Barron), who have ordered that a dagger be driven into Kimo's heart. Kimo's wife Kory (Suzanne Ridgway) has falsely testified against him, for she hopes to marry Chief Maranka. Before dying, Kimo swears he will return from the dead to get his revenge—definitely not a good sign for Kory, Tano and Chief Maranka in a movie called *From Hell It Came*.

American scientists Dr. Bill Arnold (Tod Andrews) and Professor Clark (John McNamara) toil to save the natives from a plague, as well as treat radiation burns, the result of a nearby atomic test. Some of the natives blame the Americans for recent deaths, claiming they are the result of "devil dust" (fallout), but the scientists' dialogue tells us that the amount of radiation the natives have received is negligible. Still, radiation plays a major role in Kimo's upcoming resurrection.

Via helicopter, a scientist named Terry Mason (Tina Carver) arrives to help the doctors treat the natives. Bill and Terry already know each other as friends, and the not-so-shy Bill makes it clear he wants to take their relationship to the next level. Terry is not so sure.

Meanwhile, a tree stump grows out of Kimo's grave mound. One of the natives alerts the American scientists about the bizarre stump, insisting it is the dead Kimo returning to life as a Tabanga, a vengeful tree creature. The scientists find that, amazingly enough, the scowling stump not only has a pulse and a heartbeat, but is also highly radioactive. Also, the dagger that killed Kimo sticks halfway out of the tree creature's chest.

The scientists dig up the tree creature and tote it to their lab, where its pulse weakens quickly. Terry, intent on saving this "new species," gives the Tabanga a shot of an experimental drug that has revived animals in a similar fragile state. Supposedly, the drug will take effect in eight hours. But the next morning, the lab, as well as the scientists' radio, have been smashed by you-know-who.

Wasting no time, the Tabanga finds two-faced Kory and pitches her into a quicksand pit. Next it kills Chief Maranka. Witch doctor Tano, frightened the Tabanga will come after him, leads the natives to build a pit into which the tree monster falls; they throw torches into the hole, assuming the Tabanga will go up in flames. It doesn't. But it does find and kill Tano. The glaring Tabanga (its eyes have only one mode: glare) continues to lumber about (sorry) as if it still means business. Maybe it is upset about the natives' recent attempt to burn it alive—apparently this didn't light its fire.

The scientists go on the hunt for the Tabanga. Terry inadvertently leans on the tree creature, which picks her up and begins carrying her off to parts unknown. All the while, Terry shrieks at the top of her lungs like any self-respecting scream queen wannabe.

Her colleagues decide that if a bullet forced the dagger to go all the way into the Tabanga's heart, the creature would die. So they start shooting. Predictably, one of the bullets hits the dagger, driving it deeper into the creature's chest. Finished, the Tabanga sinks into a quicksand pit, while a relieved and teary-eyed Terry falls into Bill's arms.

You may be wondering, "What the heck does that plot have to do with the nuclear threat?" Just this: Radiation was the catalyst that set the Tabanga's revenge in motion. When the scientists first examine the Tabanga growing out of Kimo's grave, their Geiger counter goes crazy, and one of them notes there is "radioactive material in this thing." A short time later, after the Tabanga receives the experimental drug and subsequently kills Kory and Chief Maranka, Terry is distraught. However, one of her colleagues says, "Don't blame yourself, Terry. The radiation dormant in the monster must have set off a chain reaction." This makes the Tabanga an atomic mutation, hence the inclusion of *From Hell It Came* in this chapter.

When I was in first grade, the local NBC affiliate had a Friday night program called *Science Fiction Theater*, which mostly played Allied Artists releases from the 1950s. At the end of each program, they would show a trailer for the following week's movie. I recall seeing the trailer for *From Hell It Came*, because the sight of the tree monster caused my older brother Frank to roll his eyes and say, "That looks so dumb!" Decades later, I am not inclined to dispute his appraisal.

In 1966, *Castle of Frankenstein* #8 had some pun-ishing fun in its *From Hell It Came* review: "[The Tabanga's] bark is worse than his bite, but he soon branches out, tearing people limb from limb." Groan-worthy to the max. However, the film isn't half as much fun as it sounds. When I watched it again for this book, I have to admit I was just waiting for it to end, and I have a pretty high fondness for low-budget monster movies.

The Incredible Shrinking Man (Universal-International, 1957)

Credits: Directed by Jack Arnold; Screenplay by Richard Matheson (from his novel *The Shrinking Man*); Produced by Albert Zugsmith; Art Directors: Alexander Golitzen and Robert Clatworthy; Set Decorators: Russell A. Gausman and Ruby R. Levitt; Photography: Ellis W. Carter; Music Supervisor: Joseph Gershenson; Sound: Leslie I. Carey and Robert Pritchard; Editor: Al Joseph; Special Photography: Clifford Stine; Optical Effects: Roswell A. Hoffman and Everett H. Broussard; Makeup: Bud Westmore; Assistant Director: William Holland; Hair Stylist: Joan St. Oegger; Trumpet Solo: Ray Anthony; Wardrobe: Jay A. Morley, Jr.

Cast: Grant Williams (Scott Carey); Randy Stuart (Louise Carey); April Kent (Clarice Bruce); Paul Langton (Charlie Carey); Raymond Bailey (Dr. Thomas Silver); William Schallert (Dr. Arthur Bramson); Frank Scannell (Carnival Barker); Diana Darrin (Nurse); Billy Curtis, Luce Potter (Little People); John Hiestand (TV Newscaster).

Black-and-white; 81 minutes; released on February 22, 1957. Available on DVD, either as a solo DVD or as part of Volume 1 of *The Classic Sci-Fi Ultimate Collection* (with *Tarantula, The Mole People, The Monolith Monsters* and *Monster on the Campus*).

In *The Cyclops*, the scientist states that the title character's "growth will never stop." In *The Incredible Shrinking Man*, lead character Scott Carey faces just the opposite dilemma: His shrinkage may never stop. But rather than this fate being a tragedy, the movie's luminous finale turns it into a spiritual triumph, quite unusual for any science fiction movie at any time, but perhaps especially so during the 1950s—and perhaps especially so during the height of the nation's atomic anxiety.

Penned by Richard Matheson, who wrote many wonderful scripts for the original *Twilight Zone* as well as numerous short stories and novels, *The Incredible Shrinking Man* begins with Scott Carey (Grant Williams) encountering a strange white mist at sea. Later, Scott fears he may be getting smaller, a notion his wife Louise (Randy Stuart) pooh-poohs. Eventually a doctor verifies that Scott *is* shrinking at an alarming rate. In the recent past, Scott was exposed to an insecticide, an event followed by the radioactive

1. All-American Aberrations: 1951–1959 (The Incredible Shrinking Man) • 43

A doll-sized Scott Carey (Grant Williams) struggles to keep his housecat Butch from making him lunch in *The Incredible Shrinking Man* (Universal-International, 1957).

mist at sea, and the doctor theorizes that this toxic combination has led to a "deadly chemical reversal of the growth process."

In a significant scene, Scott tries to convince Louise that she may have to leave him as his condition worsens; she responds that as long as he bears their wedding ring, her vows will remain true. At that moment, Scott's wedding ring slips off his finger. While perhaps too obvious, this action symbolizes the beginning of Scott's departure from our world and his descent into an unknown radiation-wrought realm.

Scott becomes embittered at his fate, and the media make him famous. When Scott is the size of a three-year-old, the doctors stop his shrinking. Scott finds solace with circus little person Clarice (April Kent), who gives him the will to live again. However, the shrinking process begins anew, and this sends Scott back home. Finally, he becomes so small he lives in a dollhouse, from which he emotionally bullies Louise. One night when she is gone, the family housecat attacks Scott. He escapes into the basement. Louise finds a shred of Scott's small, bloodied shirt in the living room and assumes the cat has killed him.

Scott's new world is the vast, barren landscape of his own basement. There, he secures food, uses a matchbox for a makeshift home, and encounters a deadly enemy: a spider, which, to Scott, is the size of a small car. Scott confronts the spider and kills it. By now he is so small that he can fit through the basement screen and step into the front yard, and it is there that he has his epiphany, a dawning realization of a majestic cosmos of which he is part. "To God, there is no zero," his voice tells us to the clanging of celestial chimes. "I still exist!"

Easily one of the best science fiction films not only of the 1950s but of any decade, *The Incredible Shrinking Man* achieved a high-water mark of excellence. By today's standards, many of the special effects are dated; for example, when Scott is matted onto sidewalks and such, he is overly bright and casts no shadow. But most of the visuals hold up quite well, most notably his harrowing battle with the spider. It's remarkable that this entire sequence was accomplished using optical and practical effects of 1957.

While the sequence with the housecat hunting Scott brims with excitement, it isn't always convincing. The cat screeches at Scott as though he is something abhorrent, not merely a mouse-sized animal; perhaps this is supposed to indicate that the cat senses something abnormal and disturbing about Scott. In another scene, Scott is straining to hold the basement door shut as the cat is trying to nudge its way through. That Scott could possibly be strong enough to hold the door against the *daikaiju*-sized cat is unconvincing, to say the least. But perhaps he somehow is supposed to possess a strength beyond his actual size, not unlike DC Comics' The Atom. The later sequence with the giant spider is more plausible—and more frightening.

More importantly, *Shrinking Man* sports an intelligent script populated by two characters—Scott and Louise—about whom the audience cares. Actors Grant Williams and Randy Stuart excel in their difficult roles. This is an adult science fiction movie; for example, though only implied, the film does subtly address the sexual tension between Scott and Louise as he continues to shrink. Scott's actions and reactions seem believable, and his adventures in the vast new continent of the family basement fascinate.

Also of note is Jack Arnold's savvy direction. Arnold, who directed several genre movies during the decade of carhops and drive-ins, was to 1950s science fiction what James Whale was to 1930s classic horror. Arnold's other directorial credits include 1953's *It Came from Outer Space*, 1954's *Creature from the Black Lagoon*, 1955's *Revenge of the Creature* and *Tarantula*, 1958's *Monster on the Campus* and *The Space Children* and 1959's *The Mouse That Roared*. They are all worthy items, but *Shrinking Man* represents the best of Arnold's fantastic oeuvre.

In terms of the nuclear threat, Scott encounters a radioactive cloud that Allen A. Debus likens to the actual H-bomb fallout suffered by the crew of the Japanese fishing boat *Lucky Dragon No. 5* in 1954.[22] This encounter with radiation profoundly changes Scott's world as well as his perspective. Not only does he face an increasingly changing environment as he dwindles, but also he suffers the shedding of his attachments to his former life. Eventually, he becomes detached, literally and figuratively, from Louise and from his brother Charlie.

Once exiled in the basement, Scott finds everything that once seemed so familiar and ordinary now alien and daunting. The new environment of the atomic age likewise changed our internal and external geography. Our former lives, free of the nuclear threat, were a stark contrast to our new post–Hiroshima existence. Now a sudden bright flash through the window might be lightning—or it might be a nuclear blast. Rainfall that once seemed pure might now harbor fallout that we could neither see nor feel nor smell, and storm sirens might indicate a tornado *or* imminent atomic attack.

Scott's radiation encounter not only changes his outlook, but literally his physical body as well. At first, this certainly seems to be a case of detrimental mutation, as unwanted as Colonel Glenn Manning's explosive growth in *The Amazing Colossal Man*.

The doctors strive to reverse Scott's diminution, and Scott and Louise hope for the best but fear the worst. And then the worst happens: Scott becomes so small that Louise can no longer realistically be part of his world even if she were to find him in the basement, which she doesn't. (Tellingly, she moves out of the house, a final declaration that she has moved out of Scott's life and that he now faces an unknown future stripped of all former attachments.)

Yet just when he should be overcome with despair at his lot, Scott instead takes glory in his dwindling state when he says, "And I felt myself melting." Marveling at his fate, he ponders just what he has become: "If there were other bursts of radiation, other clouds drifting across seas and continents, would other beings follow me into this vast new world?"[23] This seems to argue that Scott's mutation, and the possible mutations of others like him, might in fact bode well for humankind, perhaps resulting in the next step of evolution.

And while Scott's former "normal" life no doubt had meaning, it was probably an assumed meaning bolstered by culture, society and country. But his new life bursts with a new meaning Scott might never have known when he dwelled in the conventional world. He realizes there is more to life than our day-to-day customs, for as he feels himself "becoming nothing," he transcends earthly cares and experiences grace.

In essence, an encounter with the nuclear threat might literally bring one closer to his or her Maker. Thus, *Shrinking Man* ends with a ringing atomic optimism. Far from having been obliterated by radiation, Scott Carey has instead been blessed by it.

Attack of the 50 Foot Woman (Allied Artists, 1958)

Credits: Directed by Nathan Juran (as Nathan Hertz); Screenplay by Mark Hanna; Produced by Bernard Woolner; Executive Producer-Photographer: Jacques R. Marquette; Music Director: Ronald Stein; Sound: Philip Mitchell; Editor: Edward Mann; Makeup: Carlie Taylor; Props: Richard Rubin; Assistant Director: Ken Walters.

Cast: Allison Hayes (Nancy Fowler Archer); William Hudson (Harry Archer); Yvette Vickers (Honey Parker); Ken Terrell (Jessup); George Douglas (Sheriff Dubbitt); Roy Gordon (Dr. Isaac Cushing); Frank Chase (Charlie); Otto Waldis (Dr. Heinrich Von Loeb); Mike Ross (Tony/The Space Giant); Eileen Stevens (Nurse); Dale Tate (TV Commentator), Thomas E. Jackson (Prospector).

A Woolner Brothers Pictures Production; black-and-white; 66 minutes; released on May 19, 1958. Double-billed with *War of the Satellites*. Available on DVD, either as a solo DVD or as part of the DVD set *Cult Camp Classics 1: Sci-Fi Thrillers* (with *The Giant Behemoth* and *Queen of Outer Space*).

Famous as one of the all-time camp classics of twentieth century cinema, *Attack of the 50 Foot Woman* only partially lives up to its reputation. As Bill Warren notes, the actors acquit themselves well,[24] and he also rightly calls Allison Hayes and Yvette Vickers "virtues indeed."[25] However, for the most part, the special effects live up (or down, depending on your perspective) to expectations as some of the worst to emerge from the 1950s.

Rich heiress Nancy Archer (Allison Hayes) encounters a "satellite" (the movie's strange term for a UFO) and its 30-foot occupant on a deserted desert road. No one believes her, of course, and philandering husband Harry Archer (William Hudson) and his slut-bucket mistress Honey Parker (Yvette Vickers) see this as an opportunity to have

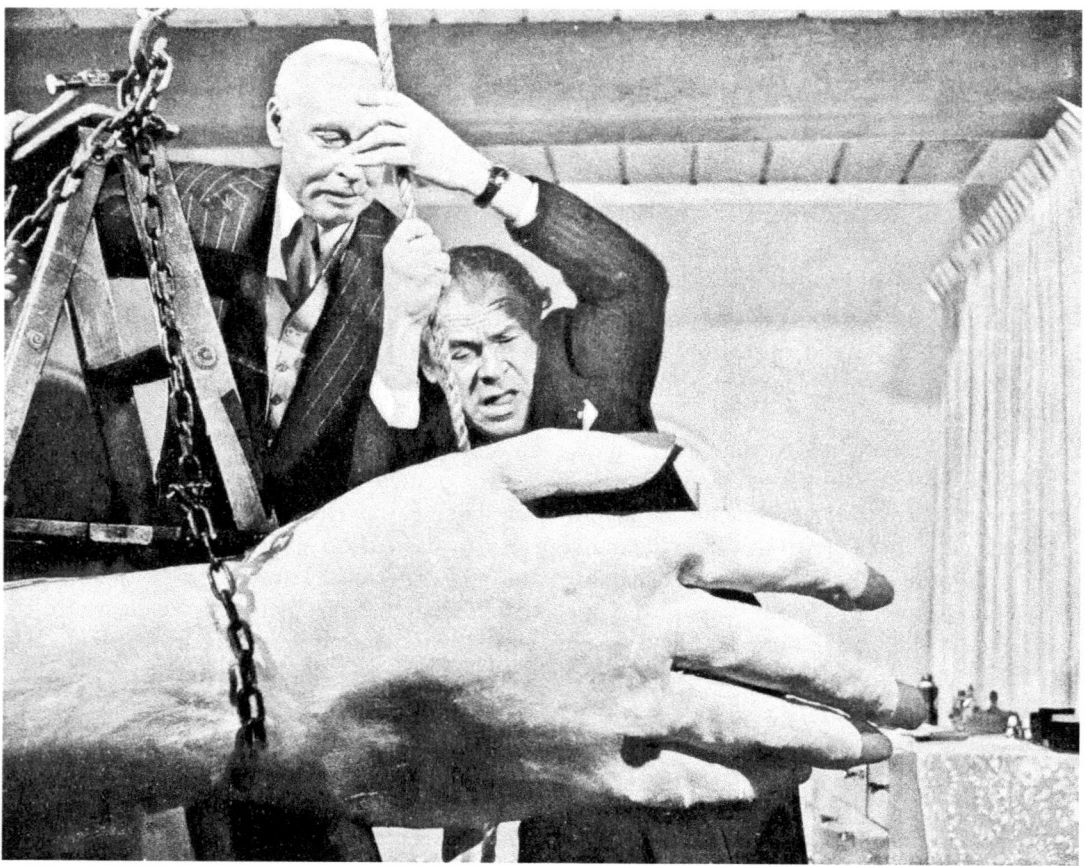

Dr. Cushing (Roy Gordon) and Dr. Von Loeb (Otto Waldis) struggle to secure the chain wrapped around Nancy Archer's giant hand in *Attack of the 50 Foot Woman* (Allied Artists, 1958).

Nancy tossed back into, as Honey calls it, "the booby hatch." (Nancy had recently been in a sanitarium.)

At Nancy's insistence, she and Harry go out looking for the "satellite." After a long search, they find it, and out walks the space giant, groping for Nancy's diamond; Harry shoots at the alien but hightails it out of there, leaving his screaming wife behind. Nancy reappears at her mansion, and Dr. Cushing (Roy Gordon) confines her to her bedroom. As he tells Harry, "There's some possibility she may have been contaminated. There's evidence of some kind of radiation."

We all know radiation is never a good thing in 1950s genre movies, even radiation from space, and just as Harry is sneaking up on Nancy in her darkened bedroom to give her a lethal injection, the nurse turns on the light. She and Harry are both astounded to see that Nancy has grown into a giant, though all we see is her colossal hand. (As many have pointed out, though Nancy is supposed to be 50 feet long at this point, she is still somehow lying in her bedroom in her normal-sized bed.)

The giant Nancy eventually bursts from the house, showering debris on her two doctors and nurse before heading for town, where Harry and Honey are mooning over each other as usual at Tony's Bar and Grill. As TCM host Robert Osborne said about the movie when it aired on TCM on June 16, 2011, the cheating lovers "soon find out hell hath no fury like a giant woman scorned."

In the low-budget rampage that follows, Nancy appears to change in size from shot to shot. Tearing the roof off Tony's, Nancy drops debris on Honey, killing the terrified mistress. She then picks up Harry, who appears to transform into a badly proportioned doll, and begins lumbering about again. The sheriff shoots at her repeatedly, hitting a nearby transformer. Electricity strikes Nancy and, her body aglow, she collapses to the ground, hubby Harry still gripped in her hand. As Dr. Cushing says, "She finally got Harry all to herself."

The special effects are poor, when not outright awful, but some believe this gives the film a certain charm. When I first saw this movie as a seven-year-old in 1963, I didn't realize the effects were bad. In fact, I thought the 30-foot space giant was *supposed* to be transparent.

The film was directed by Nathan Juran, a noted art director who in fact won a Best Art Direction Oscar for John Ford's 1941 *How Green Was My Valley*. Juran directed several genre films, including 1952's *The Black Castle*, 1957's *20 Million Miles to Earth* and *The Deadly Mantis*, 1958's *The 7th Voyage of Sinbad*, 1962's *Jack the Giant Killer*, and 1964's *First Men in the Moon*. He also directed 1958's *The Brain from Planet Arous* under the moniker Nathan Hertz, the same directorial *nom de screen* he chose for the likewise less-than-illustrious *50 Foot Woman*.

One could fault the film on any number of story points, but one thing I wonder is, what becomes of Nancy's 50-foot carcass after the film ends? Does it go to the Smithsonian Museum? Does the government take it to a secret research facility and perform an autopsy? Do Nancy's relatives claim it and have her buried in a 50-foot casket? Apparently her body was going to be preserved somehow, because in the early '60s, the Woolner brothers announced a sequel that that was to be filmed in CinemaScope and color, but it was never produced.[26] *Attack of the 50 Foot Woman* turned a nice profit in 1958—according to IMDb, its budget was $88,000 but its gross was $480,000—and apparently this is why the Woolner Brothers considered a follow-up.

Although radiation is involved in Nancy's gigantism, it is an otherworldly radiation that baffles the film's scientists. Dr. Von Loeb notes "the blue-green color around the scratches on her throat [caused by the space giant]. I would venture to say it's some sort of radiation which we in medicine have never touched upon." In this movie, you don't just have to worry about terrestrial fallout or a nuclear blast on Earth, you have to worry about radiation falling from the stars as well. It would seem 1950s audiences couldn't escape radiation's grip on the popular imagination. Still, unlike in the likewise radiation-as-gimmick genre flick *Creature with the Atom Brain*, *50 Foot Woman* features no emblematic atomic age signs of the times.[27]

However, it does appear to say something about gender issues of the day, given that this is the only American 1950s movie in which radiation turns a female giant. Otherwise, men are the monsters. Does this speak well or ill for the state of womankind in 1950s America? It suggests that just as in most movie genres of the "I Like Ike" decade, women played supporting and not primary roles in Hollywood's science fiction cinema.[28] After all, it was the era of *Father Knows Best*, not *Mother Knows Better*.

Frankenstein 1970 (Allied Artists, 1958)

Credits: Directed by Howard W. Koch; Screenplay by Richard Landau and George Worthing Yates; Story by Aubrey Schenck and Charles A. Moses; Produced by Aubrey Schenck; Production Designer: Jack T. Collis; Set Decorator: Jerry Welch; Photography: Carl E. Guthrie; Music: Paul Dunlap; Sound: Francis E. Stahl; Editor: John A. Bushelman; Electrical Effects: Richard Owens; Makeup: Gordon Bau; Assistant Director: George Vieira; Props: George Sweeney; Script Supervisor: Mary Yerke; Camera Operator: William T. Cline.

Cast: Boris Karloff (Baron Victor Von Frankenstein); Tom Duggan (Mike Shaw); Jana Lund (Carolyn Hayes); Donald Barry (Douglas Row); Charlotte Austin (Judy Stevens); Irwin Berke (Inspector Raab); Rudolph Anders (Wilhelm Gottfried); John Dennis (Morgan Haley); Norbert Schiller (Shuter); Mike Lane (Hans/The Monster); Jack Kenney (Assistant Cameraman); Franz Roehn (Cab Driver); Joe Ploski (Station Porter).

Black-and-white; CinemaScope; 83 minutes; released on August 20, 1958. Available in the DVD set *Karloff & Lugosi Horror Classics* (with *The Walking Dead*, *You'll Find Out* and *Zombies on Broadway*).

An atomic reactor brings a Frankenstein-created monster to life in this low-budget thriller, and for that reason, the film is included rather than excluded from our chapter on 1950s American humanoid mutants (and yes, I'm stretching the definition of "mutant" in order to include this monster, but better to err on the side of caution than chaos).

Having fallen on hard times, Germany's Baron Frankenstein (Boris Karloff) has rented out his castle and its grounds to an American troupe filming a TV special on Frankenstein's 230th anniversary (in this one, the famous mad scientist actually lived and created a real monster). The baron is less than excited about this turn of events, resenting the TV folks, but he needs their cash to fund his experiments, which involve acquiring a nuclear reactor to bring his monster to life. No one knows that this is what he's doing at night down in his secret lab—but remember, his real-life ancestor created a monster, so what do they *think* he's doing down there, constructing a Lego Logs cabin?

As the movie plods along, we witness the demise of a servant, an associate and two of the TV crew. Douglas Row (Donald Barry), the TV special's director, suspects foul play and contacts the police, who initially attribute it all to Row's imagination. By this time, the monster is carrying the TV special's pretty blonde actress down to the baron's secret lab. However, the monster sets the actress free, growling as it stalks the cringing baron in the lab before radioactive steam kills it, as well as the baron. All this build-up for the "big surprise" finale: The monster has the face of, heavens to Frankenstein remakes, *the baron himself!*

This undistinguished thriller wastes Karloff's talents, and he is clearly in this film purely for his 1958 marquee value. Remember, at this time, the syndicated *Shock Theater* TV package was circulating throughout the country, making Karloff known to many younger viewers who had never before seen his 1930s and 1940s horror films.

The best part of the movie is the opening, in which a monster (its face unseen) stalks a screaming young woman in the woods, finally catching her in a lake and strangling her. Then we hear from off-screen, "Okay, cut!" And we realize we've been had: Everything we just saw was part of the TV special. Which is unfortunate, because this opening radiates goose-pimply atmosphere to spare. In fact, on the commentary track for the

1. All-American Aberrations: 1951–1959 (Frankenstein 1970) • 49

At the atmospheric beginning of 1958's *Frankenstein 1970*, a screaming woman (Jana Lund) is menaced by a hulking monster (Mike Lane). But it's all a cheat: The viewer soon learns that the scene is part of a "film within a film" when the director says, "Cut!"

Warner Bros. DVD of *Frankenstein 1970*, Bob Burns says, "This is one of the greatest openings to a horror film I'd seen in years when I first saw this. I mean, this is really some creepy stuff here." Concurs Tom Weaver on the same commentary track, "I remember when I was a kid, this scene was almost unpleasantly scary."²⁹

This sequence was included in the movie's trailer as though it was part of the film's actual storyline, and in 1963, I saw this trailer on local TV. The monster stalking the girl knocked me out! I knew this was going to be one super-scary show. So when I sat wide-eyed in front of the TV when *Frankenstein 1970* aired, I was initially elated—but subsequently deflated when the director yelled, "Cut!" I felt I'd been ripped off.

After that great opening, the rest of the film offers little for either Gothic horror or atomic science fiction fans. It does manage a few nice moments. Bill Warren notes the scene in which the associate's eyes dissolve from the associate's sockets into the monster's.³⁰ But overall, this rates as one of the worst Frankenstein melodramas ever.

However, we do hear the word "radiation" a couple of times, and we see a radiation-suited guy checking the lab after the Monster's demise, his white coverall garb a '50s indicator of potential nuclear peril. Plus, of course, an atomic reactor brings the Monster to life.

Monster on the Campus (Universal-International, 1958)

Credits: Directed by Jack Arnold; Screenplay by David Duncan; Produced by Joseph Gershenson; Art Director: Alexander Golitzen; Set Decorators: Russell A. Gausman and Julia Heron; Photography: Russell Metty; Music Supervisor: Joseph Gershenson; Sound: Leslie I. Carey and Joe Lapis; Editor: Ted J. Kent; Special Photography: Clifford Stine; Makeup: Bud Westmore; Assistant Director: Marshall Green; Gowns: Bill Thomas.

Cast: Arthur Franz (Dr. Donald Blake); Joanna Moore (Madeline Howard); Judson Pratt (Lt. Mike Stevens); Helen Westcott (Molly Riordan); Alexander Lockwood (Gilbert Howard); Troy Donahue (Jimmy Flanders); Nancy Walters (Sylvia Lockwood); Phil Harvey (Sgt. Powell); Whit Bissell (Dr. Oliver Cole); Ross Elliott (Sgt. Eddie Daniels); Richard Cutting (Tom Edwards); Hank Patterson (Mr. Townsend); Anne Anderson, Ronnie Rondell, Jr., Louis Cavalier (Students).

Black-and-white; 77 minutes; released on October 22, 1958. Available either as a solo DVD or as part of Volume I of the DVD set *The Classic Sci-fi Ultimate Collection* (with *Tarantula*, *The Mole People*, *The Incredible Shrinking Man* and *The Monolith Monsters*).

This movie gives new meaning to the zinger "Put that in your pipe and smoke it," as irradiated blood that drips into the bowl of the lead character's pipe literally turns him into a monster.

This poster warns college guys and gals about a fiend on campus. It's not referring to the dean of students, but rather Arthur Franz as the *Monster on the Campus* (Universal-International, 1958).

Rin Tin Tin gone bad? No, Samson the normally gentle German shepherd after he's lapped up irradiated coelacanth blood in *Monster on the Campus* (Universal-International, 1958).

Scientist Dr. Donald Blake (Arthur Franz) is excited when a coelacanth from Madagascar is delivered to his lab at Dunsford University, USA. The fish was irradiated before shipment, and this leads to all kinds of problems. For example, a student's German shepherd that drinks some of the irradiated blood later turns savage, developing wolf-like fangs. The dog soon reverts to normal.

But even more problematic, the teeth of the coelacanth cut Blake as he moves the fish, and he also inadvertently dunks his hand in the bloody irradiated water. Soon enough, he turns into—what else?—the Monster on the Campus. While in this state, he kills a woman and demolishes his living room.

Next, an ordinary dragonfly nibbles on the coelacanth's carcass and later becomes a droning, two-foot terror. Blake kills the creature, and again showing he is not the most careful of scientists, accidentally lets some of the irradiated dragonfly's blood drip into his pipe bowl. After lighting up, he turns again into the destructive ape man, trashing the scientist's lab and killing a police officer.

Blake has a hunch about the coelacanth plasma and investigates, finding out that the coelacanth was treated with gamma rays before it was shipped to his lab. Once again, radiation "enhances" a prosaic substance (this time dead fish blood) and this results in retro-evolutionary physical mutations, happening in the case of the German shepherd, the dragonfly and Blake himself.

Realizing this, Blake retreats to a mountain cabin and deliberately injects himself with some of the fish plasma; he has cameras set up to capture the metamorphosis. Right on cue, he becomes the ape man, and true to the creature's cantankerous disposition, wrecks the cabin's interior. Once he ventures outside, his fiancée almost runs him down with her car, veering off the road at the last moment. The ape man carries her about, temporarily distracted by a forest ranger who is soon on the receiving end of the creature's ax. The fiancée runs back to the cabin, and soon Blake enters, once again his human self. She can't understand why the ape man was wearing his clothes.

The police arrive, along with the college dean, and Blake says he will lead them to the monster. In front of the dean, Blake injects himself with coelacanth blood and turns into the ape man. Though the dean yells at the police not to shoot, they do anyway, killing Blake, who reverts from the ape man back to his twentieth century self.

Monster on the Campus is an okay science fiction horror entry whose main claim to fame is having been directed by Jack Arnold (whose science fiction career is covered in the entry on *The Incredible Shrinking Man*). The movie starred reliable B movie lead Arthur Franz, who likewise appeared in *Flight to Mars* (1951), *Invaders from Mars* (1953) and *The Atomic Submarine* (1959). Franz brings a conviction to his role of Dr. Donald Blake, stereotypical as it may have been of 1950s monster movie scientists.

The film's nuclear threat element involves the gamma rays that "enriched" the coelacanth blood, leading to Blake's monstrous transformation. Also, Blake does say at one point, "Unless we learn to control the instincts we've inherited from our ape-like ancestors, the race is doomed." This probably implies that, in John F. Kennedy's immortal words, we must put an end to war before war puts an end to us, and the war alluded to is an all-out nuclear exchange. The fact that radiation releases Blake's primitive instincts implies that radiation might also release civilization's primitive instincts, resulting in literally grave consequences.

Terror from the Year 5000 (AIP, 1958)

Credits: Produced, Written and Directed by Robert J. Gurney, Jr.; Executive Producers: James H. Nicholson and Samuel Z. Arkoff; Associate Producer: Gene Searchinger; Scenic Design: Bill Hoffman; Properties: Henderson "Gus" Bockway; Photography: Arthur Florman; Sound Engineer: Bob Hathaway; Editor: Dede Allen; Makeup: Ralph Listz; Assistant Director: Jack Diamond; Script Clerk: Anita Hathaway; Production Supervisor: Beatrice Gurney; Production Coordinator: Mark Hanna.

Cast: Ward Costello (Dr. Robert Hedges); Joyce Holden (Claire Erling); Salome Jens (Nurse/Future Woman); Fred Herrick (Angelo); Beatrice Furdeaux (Miss Blake); Jack Diamond, Fred Taylor (Lab Technicians); Bill Downs (Bartender); William Cost (Dr. Blair).

A La Jolla Production; black-and-white; 74 minutes; released October 30, 1958. Double-billed with *The Screaming Skull*.

When was the last time you were hypnotized by the fingernails of a female mutant from the future? Well, cousin, that's too long.

Said mutant is the title menace in *Terror from the Year 5000*, a typical example of 1950s AIP programmer science fiction. Other movies have handled the time machine motif better, but this low-budget opus does benefit from occasionally imaginative touches and competent if unremarkable acting.

This arresting poster, typical of American International's sleek ad art, proclaims the title character in *Terror from the Year 5000* (1958) was "A Hideous She-Thing!"

Professor Howard Erling (Frederic Downs) and Victor (John Stratton) argue about how far to take their time travel experiments; they have been sending objects to the future, and someone has been transporting various trinkets back to them in a sort of time travel swap meet. Victor, who is financing the experiments, wants to push the project to its limits, but the more cautious Dr. Erling believes they should wait.

Enter Erling's friend Dr. Bob Hedges (Ward Costello). Bob receives a curious statue in the mail, and he is amazed to discover that it is from the future and highly radioactive. Investigating, he finds that Erline's daughter Claire (Joyce Holden) sent it to him, but didn't know it was radioactive. Bob accompanies Claire back to her father's island residence, a surprise visit that delights Erling but irritates Victor. Although Claire is engaged to the sullen Victor, in no time, she begins falling for Bob. Gotta have that love interest, gang.

One night Victor conducts a time travel experiment without Erling, and a hand reaches out from the time machine chamber, mangling Victor's arm. Reluctantly, Victor goes to a mainland hospital, where the doctor wants to keep him under observation. Erling, Bob and Claire decide to take in a movie, and not surprisingly, it is an AIP flick, namely *I Was a Teenage Frankenstein*. Afterwards, Bob imitates the Frankenstein Monster's halting gait, which Erling and Claire find hilarious. As Steve Martin once said, comedy isn't pretty.

Meanwhile, Victor leaves the hospital, gets drunk, returns to the island and ramps up the time machine. From the time machine chamber, out marches a screeching future woman in a sequined body stocking. Erling, Bob and Claire find Victor, who has been attacked by the future woman. Victor is in shock. The doctor tells the protagonists that he will send a nurse to the island.

Angelo (Fred Herrick), the Erlings' handyman, meets the future woman, who kills him. Later, the future woman also attacks the nurse, removing the latter's face and placing it over her own disfigured features. Posing as the nurse, she steals into Victor's room and explains that thousands of years hence, radiation has caused every fifth child to be born a mutant. The non-mutant leaders have exiled the mutants to separatist colonies, and it is into one of those colonies that Victor and Erling's time machine reached. Hypnotizing Victor, the future woman leads him to the lab, intending to take him into the future with her so that his "new blood" can end the plague of mutants in A.D. 5000.

Claire steals into the lab, realizes something isn't kosher and gets into a fight with the future woman. The latter's false face is ripped off in the struggle, and Claire reacts in horror at the futurian's real countenance. So does Victor, who says, "You're one of them. One of those freaks!" Erling and Bob burst into the lab, and Erling shoots the future woman. She tries to get into the chamber, but Victor rushes at her (whether to stop her or go with her isn't clear). The machine's high voltage electrocutes them both.

Later, Bob argues that they should help the future people in their plight. "After all," he says, "they are human beings." Erling says, "But there's another way. The future is what we make it…. Whether there'll be creatures like her depends on us." (Erling seems to ignore the fact that since the future woman did exist 5000 years hence, that future day of radiation poisoning apparently was not prevented.)

The movie's scant special effects are elementary. In the time chamber, something disappearing or appearing fizzes like a Fourth of July sparkler (which is probably what the filmmakers used). The makeup on the future woman, who is supposed to be hideous to behold, is less scary than homely. It's a bit unsettling that the characters keep making reference to the future woman as a "freak" and a "creature." None of them seems to realize how callous it is to react in horror to a disfigured face. People with facial deformities can't help it, not even people from the future, and they should be treated just like anyone else, not like monsters. But the movie is trying to make the point that the nuclear threat could usher in a horrendous future, and so uses heavy-handed attempts at physical shock.

The depiction of the future woman (Salome Jens) is interesting. The forceful manner in which she speaks, and her marching gait when she steps from the time chamber, are apparently attempts to make her seem foreign to our age. Also, she exhibits peculiar powers, the strangest her ability to hypnotize with her fingernails. In addition, she uses a life mask to "steal" the nurse's face and "wear" it over her own. (Seeing the nurse's blank face was unsettling to me as a kid.) Also, when the future woman first addresses the nurse, she speaks Greek, due to a Greek fraternity key sent into the future, and she is startled to learn that the nurse speaks English. This is an inventive touch.

Also inventive are the statues the future folk send back to the protagonists. In Greek, one of them reads, "Save us." (An effective moment to me when I saw this as a kid.) Also, the dead, multi-eyed cat mutation is disturbing and imaginative. Perhaps the film's best moment occurs when someone inside the time chamber smashes the plate glass portal, spider-webbing the glass. (Presumably, this was an act of the future woman.)

As for the present-day characters, they offer the usual. Of course, given that the perennially unpleasant Victor sports all the charm of a scorpion, you have to wonder why Claire got engaged to him in the first place. His death proves convenient for her and Bob, for now they can enjoy a romantic relationship without feeling guilty.

Though we never see the future world of 5000 years hence, we hear enough about it to make some sketchy assumptions. We don't know if there has been one nuclear war or several. One snatch of dialogue points to the twentieth century as being the turning point *vis-à-vis* the nuclear threat: As the future woman looks on, Claire tries to convince the mesmerized Victor to snap out of it. "Oh, Victor," she says, "you're all confused."

To which the future woman retorts, "It's you who are confused. Our history clearly records how the women of the twentieth century stood idly by while the atmosphere was contaminated and the children of the future doomed."

Interesting that women specifically are blamed, and perhaps the future woman's statement implies that women weren't independent or forceful enough in the first decades of the atomic age. On the other hand, the statement also implies that people in general indifferently let the nuclear threat grow. Certainly by the late 1960s, America's fears of worldwide nuclear conflict had abated, as borne out by the paucity of nuclear threat movies after the mid–1960s (although both 1968's *Planet of the Apes* and 1970's *Beneath the Planet of the Apes* point to a nuclear holocaust).

In the realm of nuclear threat movies, *Terror from the Year 5000* is a minor entry. However, it does seem sincere in its warning of a future Earth contaminated by atomic warfare. It also wants to be a respectable low-budget science fiction movie, and it partially succeeds. With some tweaking, it could have served as an episode of the original *Outer Limits*.

War of the Colossal Beast (AIP, 1958)

Credits: Produced and Directed by Bert I. Gordon; Screenplay by George Worthing Yates; Story by Bert I. Gordon; Presented by James H. Nicholson and Samuel Z. Arkoff; Art Direction: Walter Keller; Set Decorator: Maury Hoffman; Photography: Jack Marta; Music: Albert Glasser; Editorial Supervisor: Ronald Sinclair; Assistant Editor: Paul Wittenberg; Special Technical Effects: Bert I. Gordon; Assistant Technical Effects: Flora M. Gordon; Special Makeup Creator: Jack H. Young; Assistant Directors: H.E. Mendelson and John W. Rogers; Sound Editor: Josef Von Stroheim; Production Manager: Herb Mendelson; Property Master: Walter Broadfoot; Sound Mixer: Benny Winkler.

Cast: Sally Fraser (Joyce Manning); Dean Parkin (Col. Glenn Manning); Roger Pace (Major Mark Baird); Russ Bender (Dr. Carmichael); Rico Alaniz (Sgt. Luis Murillo); George Becwar (John Swanson); Robert Hernandez (Miguel); Charles Stewart (Capt. Harris); June Jocelyn (Mrs. Edwards); John McNamara (Neurologist); Loretta Nicholson (Joan); Raymond Winston (Arthur Lang); Jack Kosslyn (Newscaster); George Navarro (Mexican Doctor); Bob Garnet (Pentagon Correspondent); Stan Chambers (TV Announcer); June Burt (Laurie Edwards); Howard Wright (Medical Research Officer); George Alexander (Army Officer); Bill Giorgio (Bus Driver); George Milan (Gen. Nelson); Warren Frost (Switchboard Operator).

A Carmel Production; black-and-white; 68 minutes; released on July 30, 1958. Released in England as *The Terror Strikes*. Double-billed in the U.S. with *Attack of the Puppet People*. Available on DVD double-billed with *Earth vs. the Spider* as part of the *Samuel Z. Arkoff Collection Cult Classics* series.

In 1957, *The Amazing Colossal Man* did brisk box office business so, surprising no one, Colonel Glenn Manning returned in *War of the Colossal Beast*. However, it *is* surprising that AIP didn't release the film under its working title of *Revenge of the Colossal Man*; the title *War of the Colossal Beast* doesn't necessarily sound like a sequel. But according to Tom Triman, James Nicholson chose this title himself. Triman also said, "The studio's ad campaign made no mention that *Colossal Beast* was a sequel to *Colossal Man*."[31]

Manning survived the bazooka blast and fall from Boulder Dam and now resides in Mexico, but his countenance, or what's left of it, has become the stuff of nightmares. Shorn of flesh, the right side of his face exposes naked bone and lipless upper teeth, and a midnight-black socket yawns where his right eye should be. Jack H. Young's spectacularly grotesque Colossal Beast makeup, similar to the same work Young did on 1957's *The Cyclops*, ranks with the best of 1950s creature creations.

Manning's sister Joyce (Sally Fraser) convinces the authorities that her brother is living in rural Mexico; there, the protagonists discover the disfigured giant, sedate him and transport him to Los Angeles, where he is confined inside an airplane hangar. Attempts to help Manning regain his memory prove futile. Due to his potential menace, the authorities decide they will deposit him on a deserted Pacific island.

Manning escapes and, at Griffith Park, he holds a busload of screaming school kids over his head. Joyce convinces him to put the bus down. She appeals once more to Manning's memory, and this time he responds, hoarsely speaking her name. Despondent over his fate, he commits suicide by grabbing hold of high-tension wires that electrocute him.

Above: The Colossal Beast (Dean Parkin) appears down for the count, but rest assured he escapes soon enough in Bert I. Gordon's *War of the Colossal Beast* (1958).

Opposite: On this dynamic *War of the Colossal Beast* (1958) poster, youngsters are in peril, but in the actual movie, no kids fall out of the school bus.

Compactly made, *Colossal Beast* is a standard monster-on-the-loose thriller that takes a few stabs at pathos, but not to the extent of its better-made predecessor. The giant's suicide is shot in color, and as sparks fly and Manning screams, he turns from red to yellow before inexplicably disintegrating.

The script is sloppy in certain respects, primarily by featuring Joyce as Manning's sister even though in *Colossal Man*, his fiancée Carol (Cathy Downs) says he has no relatives. The film could have avoided this lapse by having Carol return for the sequel, but perhaps Downs was not available—or perhaps filmmaker Gordon thought no one would remember that Manning wasn't supposed to have any family.

Glenn Langan did not return for this sequel; instead, stuntman Duncan "Dean" Parkin plays Manning. So extensive is Parkin's makeup that no one would know if it was Langan anyway, and the Colossal Beast speaks only one word in the film, Joyce's name, otherwise growling and bellowing unpleasantly. Like its predecessor, *Colossal Beast* ends on a depressing note, once again with the giant's demise. This time, however, the death is self-inflicted. Manning may be the only 1950s giant monster to have actually taken his/its own life.

Actually, it's probably a good thing *Colossal Beast* comes off as a standard 1950s monster show. Had the script been better, the direction more sensitive, and the actor playing Manning articulate and lucid between his grunts and growls, the ending would have been more of a downer than it already is. However, as noted before, titular monsters must, as a rule, die in the end.[32]

This film, basically double feature fodder, reflects less the attitude of Americans regarding nuclear war than it does a monster movie following long-standing tradition. After all, plenty of non-nuclear men-who-turn-into-monsters also perish tragically, most notably Dr. Jekyll in 1931's *Dr. Jekyll and Mr. Hyde* and Larry Talbot in 1941's *The Wolf Man*.

Still, if read in the context of nuclear metaphor, Manning's suicide could reflect the gloomy prospects open to victims of nuclear testing: Face a life of misery and pain, or simply stop living altogether. As in *Amazing Colossal Man*, the effects of nuclear testing result in tragedy both for the victim and for his loved ones. With such hypothesizing, I may be "over-thinking" this movie, but as I wrote in the preface, perhaps symbolism works best when it isn't intended, especially in hindsight. You be the judge.

The Alligator People (Twentieth Century–Fox, 1959)

Credits: Directed by Roy Del Ruth; Screenplay by Orville H. Hampton; Story by Orville H. Hampton and Charles O'Neal; Produced by Jack Leewood; Art Directors: John Mansbridge and Lyle R. Wheeler; Set Decorators: Walter M. Scott and Joseph Kish; Photography: Karl Struss; Music: Irving Gertz; Sound: W.D. Flick; Editor: Harry Gerstad; Special Effects: Fred Etcheverry; Makeup: Ben Nyle and Dick Smith; Hair Stylist: Even Newing; Assistant Director: H.E. Mendelson; Production Manager: Herb Mendelson; Script Supervisor: Mary Coleman; Property Master: George Westernhiser; Costume Supervisors: William McCrary and Ollie Hughes.

Cast: Beverly Garland (Joyce Webster aka Jane Marvin); Bruce Bennett (Dr. Erik Lorimer); Lon Chaney Jr. (Mannon); George Macready (Dr. Mark Sinclair); Frieda Inescort (Lavinia Hawthorne); Richard Crane (Paul Webster); Douglas Kennedy (Dr. Wayne McGregor); Vince Townsend, Jr. (Toby); Ruby Goodwin (Lou Ann); John Mer-

Paul Webster (Richard Crane), medical patient turned Alligator Person, receives consolation from wife Jane (Beverly Garland) in *The Alligator People* (Fox, 1959). A veteran of genre movies of the 1950s, Garland enhanced any film in which she appeared.

rick, Lee Warren (Nurses); Bill Bradley (Patient); Dudley Dickerson (Porter); Hal K. Dawson (Conductor).

An Associated Producers Production; black-and-white; CinemaScope; 74 minutes. Released on July 16, 1959. Double-billed with *Return of the Fly*. Available on DVD.

The cynic's reaction to this quintessential 1950s title would probably be, "Can a movie called *The Alligator People* possibly be anything more than a hoot?" Most "civilians" would probably agree with the cynic, snickering before even seeing the film's first frame. But in truth, *The Alligator People* is a rather well-written, nicely directed, competently acted slice of 1950s science fiction-horror, only dropping the dramatic ball during the climax.

Under deep hypnosis, Jane (Beverly Garland), a nurse suffering from amnesia, recounts a fantastic story: In flashback, we see Jane and her husband Paul (Richard Crane), just married, having a wonderful time on a train until Paul receives an alarming telegram. He leaves the train at the next stop and disappears from Jane's life.

Jane searches for him and finally hopes she has tracked him down at a Louisiana swamp plantation called the Cypresses. The matron of the house rebuffs Jane, but Jane eventually discovers that Paul is a patient at the plantation's clinic. The skin on his face and hands has become alligator-like, his voice deep and guttural. Jane spies Paul in the mansion one evening, and follows him when he flees into the stormy night. The alcoholic plantation worker Mannon (Lon Chaney) saves Jane from a snake and takes her to his shack. There, he attempts to have his way with her, but Paul breaks in, beats Mannon up and rescues Jane. Mannon swears, "I'll kill you, alligator man!"

The Cypresses' Dr. Mark Sinclair (George Macready) explains to Jane that he thought he had discovered a miracle cure for people mangled in severe accidents, such as a plane crash that almost killed Paul. The treatment consists of injecting patients with an alligator hormone and then bombarding the patient with X-rays—this appeared to have healed Paul completely, thus the reason he ventured back out into the world and married Jane. But Sinclair discovered that the alligator hormone-radiation therapy was turning patients like Paul into humanoid reptiles. This had been the message in the telegram Paul received on the train, and the reason he had decided he could never again see Jane. But now that the truth is out and Jane knows, Paul insists that Sinclair submit him to a far more radical and untested treatment.

Sinclair bombards Paul with a combination of Cobalt 60 gamma rays and high-intensity X-rays. All seems to be going well—until drunken Mannon, still angry with Paul, bursts into the lab and goes berserk, shorting out sensitive lab equipment. Exposed far too long to the radiation, Paul turns into a literally alligator-headed monster. Mannon becomes entangled in the lab apparatus and is electrocuted.

Paul runs into the swamp, followed by Jane. Behind them, the lab explodes, presumably killing all within it. After battling an alligator, the gator-headed Paul falls into a quicksand pit that quickly sucks him under. A witness to this horror, Jane clutches her hands to her face and begins screaming.

Back in the present, once Jane's psychiatrist-boss brings her out of her hypnotic state, she again has no memory of these events. Since Jane appears to be living a happy life despite her amnesia about the traumatic episode at the Cypresses, the therapist elects not to tell her about it—a case of ignorance insuring bliss.

This intelligent film actually tries to flesh out the characters, and Beverly Garland gives a superlative performance as Jane. Garland starred in several '50s SFantasy films such as 1956's *Curucu, Beast of the Amazon* and *It Conquered the World* and 1957's *Not of This Earth*. Her strong performances were always a shot in the arm for any B movie, and her acting in *The Alligator People* is a welcome booster.

Though this film is better than most of its 1950s science fiction horror ilk, it's also less fun. Sinclair isn't a "mad scientist," simply a well-intentioned doctor who wants to heal badly injured patients. Paul's plight inspires sympathy, not horror, and until the gator-headed ending, he is an afflicted man, not an outrageously costumed monster. Everything ends unhappily, with Jane the only surviving protagonist. But it's equally unsatisfying when her psychiatrist-boss elects not to play back her story (he tape-recorded it during her hypnosis), leaving her ignorant of what happened; doesn't she have a right to know?

Every respectable Grade-B 1950s science fiction-horror flick had to have a monster, thus the gator-headed Paul. Obviously, kids would not be satisfied without a monster— I was a kid once and I know. For example, at a young age I saw Val Lewton's *The Leopard Man* (1943) on TV, fully expecting to see a were-panther at some point and profoundly disappointed when one never showed up.

As a pre-teen, I *liked* the look of the gator-headed Paul—it didn't seem overdone at all. In a 1960s issue of *Monsters Unlimited* I perused at the newsstand, I saw a full-page photo of the Alligator Man holding Jane, who is pulling away from him. At the time I thought this monster looked way cool, and I'm sure many 1960s Monster Kids felt the same. Nevertheless, the film's addition of a gator-headed monster seems almost tacked on, damaging the more adult, restrained approach attempted and largely achieved in *The Alligator People* prior to the climax. Indeed, as Jeff Rovin notes, "This well-made thriller was hamstrung by unconvincing makeup."[33]

This movie's dangerous radioactive substance is Cobalt 60. Although alligator hormones are employed in Sinclair's treatments, it takes radiation to bring about its short-lived curative effects. This is a case where radiation seems to be a good thing—until, of course, the long-term effects set in. Having irradiated alligator hormones turn patients into Alligator People implies that you could inject a patient with almost any reptile's restorative hormone, bathe the patient in radiation and, *voila*! Instant Gila Monster People, Horny Toad People or Coral Snake People.

Even though the use of Cobalt 60 at the end is a risk, it might have worked under ideal conditions; it's Mannon's interference that causes the treatment to go awry. Hence, apparently the proper, careful use of a radioactive substance may beget good results, but the reckless, random use of a radioactive substance will almost certainly beget disastrous results (monsterhood for Paul, death for others).

Prior to the final treatment, Paul says to Dr. Sinclair, "Who can know everything? You're not God, Mark," and he replies, "I feel as if I've been playing at it and been punished." This almost "universal scientist" angst over trying to accomplish a good that leads to a bad is how some American scientists, such as Dr. Robert Oppenheimer, felt about their contribution to the science that made the H-Bomb possible.[34] This line of thought was countered by scientists such as Dr. Edward Teller, who argued that America needed the H-Bomb for national security purposes.[35] Which of them was playing at being God? And which of them was punished for it?

The Hideous Sun Demon
(74 minutes; Pacific International, 1959)

Credits: Directed by Robert Clarke and Thomas Boutross; Screenplay by E.S. Seeley, Jr.; Original idea by Robert Clarke and Phil Hiner; Additional Dialogue: Doane R. Hoag; Produced by Robert Clarke; Associate Producer: Robin C. Kirkman; Art Direction: Gianbattista Cassarino [Richard Cassarino]; Photography: John Morrill, Vilis Lapenieks, Jr., and Stan Follis; Music: John Seely; Sound: Doug Menville; Editor: Thomas Boutross; Assistant Editor: Ron Honthaner; Makeup: Ben Sarino [Richard Cassarino]; Assistant Director: Tom Miller; Continuity: Deanie Follis.

Cast: Robert Clarke (Dr. Gilbert McKenna/The Sun Demon); Patricia Manning (Ann Lansing); Nan Peterson (Trudy Osborne); Patrick Whyte (Dr. Frederick Buckell); Fred LaPorta (Dr. Jacob Hoffman); Peter Similuk (George Messorio); Bill Hampton (Police Lt. Peterson); Robert Garry (Dr. Stern); Xandra Conkling (Susie); Donna King (Susie's Mother); Del Courtney (Radio Announcer); Pearl Driggs (Elderly Hospital Patient on Roof); David Sloan (Newspaper Boy); Helen Joseph (Nurse); Ron Honthaner (Police Officer Killed by Sun Demon); Doug Menville, Robin C. Kirkman (Police Officers); Tom Miller (Gas Station Attendant); Cass Richards [Richard

Cassarino] (Police Officer/Barfly/Guy on Beach with Kids); Deanie Follis (Nurse/Bar Customer).

A Clarke-King Enterprises Production; black-and-white; 74 minutes. British title: *Blood on His Lips* (making the monster sound as though it's a vampire). Released in August 1959; Premiered August 28, 1958, in Amarillo, Texas, at the Tascosa Drive-In Theater. This strikes a nostalgic chord with me because as a boy I lived in Amarillo, where I saw many drive-in features—but not this one.

We've seen that radiation supplied a pseudo-scientific rationale to update werewolves (1956's *The Werewolf*). *The Hideous Sun Demon* takes the notion of *The Werewolf* and goes it one better by flipping the "full moon" for lycanthropes into a "full sun" for the were-lizard of this low-budget programmer.

This movie is not as good as the aforementioned *Werewolf*, but it still has its adherents. It begins with the sound of a blaring alarm and a close-up of a sign reading "Atomic Research Inc." As orderlies wheel the victim of the radiation accident into a hospital, we hear a voiceover narrator mention two recently launched satellites and their amazing discovery. Says the narrator, "Newspaper headlines across the country told the world of a new radiation hazard from the sun, far more deadly than cosmic rays. An obscure scientist, my colleague Dr. Gilbert McKenna, had already discovered this danger from the sun. This is his story."

We learn that a lab accident exposed Dr. McKenna (Robert Clarke) to a new isotope, one that, according to his colleague, "never existed in nature before." McKenna exhibits no burns or other radiation-exposure symptoms, though he is initially unconscious. When the recuperating scientist is sunning on the hospital roof, this new isotope plus sunlight transform him into the were-reptile of the movie's title. This causes major personal and professional problems for McKenna who, feeling depressed over his fate, holes up in his house.

Were-lizard Robert Clarke moves in on the oblivious Nan Peterson in this publicity still for *The Hideous Sun Demon* (1959), which Clarke also produced and co-directed.

Later, he goes to a bar to take his mind off things. While there, he chats up Trudy (Nan Peterson), an attractive singer, and the two of them spend the night on the beach.

McKenna wakes up to see that the sun has risen, knowing that he may turn into the monster at any minute. He zooms home without waking up his overnight paramour. Ann Lansing (Patricia Manning), McKenna's lab assistant and girlfriend, finds him cowering in a closet. She convinces him to let a radiation specialist treat him. However, the deeply depressed scientist believes it will all come to naught. McKenna goes back to the bar to find Trudy. There, a big bruiser and a couple of other thugs rough up McKenna. Trudy takes him to her apartment to recover.

The next day, Big Bruiser shows up at Trudy's and forces McKenna at gunpoint to go outside, where the sun is shining. McKenna tells Big Bruiser this is a mistake, but the man won't listen. Once they are outside in the sun, sure enough, McKenna turns into the Sun Demon and kills Big Bruiser, to the horror of the screaming singer who witnesses the murder.

McKenna flees back to his house, where Ann, Dr. Buckell (Patrick Whyte) and the radiation specialist try to help him. The police arrive, and during McKenna's getaway he runs over a cop. (Story-wise, this makes it a cinch that McKenna can't live to the film's ending, which the viewer pretty much knows before even watching the film.) McKenna hides out in a refinery shed, where he meets a trusting little girl named Susie who goes back home to fetch him some cookies. (This mild attempt at pathos almost works.) Susie's mother grills her about her "new friend," and Mom frantically phones the police when she realizes the man must be the killer on the loose.

With the law in hot pursuit, McKenna again becomes the Sun Demon. He scales a gas storage tank as an officer chases him. At the top, the cop shoves a revolver against the Sun Demon's chest and fires twice, after which the monster plunges to his death below. As Ann weeps, Dr. Buckell says, "Perhaps you should cry. The rest of us can only hope that his life was not wasted."

To this final line of dialogue, Bill Warren quipped, "Many in the audience felt their time had been wasted with the movie, of course, and no wonder."[36] In 1966, *Castle of Frankenstein* #10 called it a "[t]errible film." Both are typical of the vigorous thumbs-down most reviewers give this movie, but it nevertheless has its supporters. For example, Jeff Rovin calls it an "effective and gritty film [boasting] an excellent monster costume."[37] Online, TellTale Mind gave it two and a half stars (out of five) and rated it as "a solid little science fiction film that never fails to entertain."[38]

I agree with the latter critique, for despite its budget-strapped production values, *The Hideous Sun Demon* has its virtues. While it is formulaic, it does attempt at times to rise above its budget and story level. Clarke gives a sincere performance, especially when we see him evincing unbridled angst in one scene, and the memorable lizard-man mask was, by '50s standards, inspired. Richard Cassarino created both the upper body costume and the mask and, for this job, he was credited on-screen as Ben Sarino. According to producer-director-star Clarke, Cassarino went by many "noms de screen."[39]

Since *The Hideous Sun Demon* is basically the atomic age version of *The Wolf Man*, just as Larry Talbot had to die for having spilled human blood, so too does Dr. McKenna. In *The Wolf Man*, a bite from a lycanthrope turns you into a werewolf, while in *Sun Demon* a "bite" from a radioactive isotope transforms you into a retro-evolutionary man-lizard. Just as Lon Chaney appealed to a descendant of Frankenstein to treat his lycanthropy, *Sun Demon* brings in a radiation poisoning specialist to work with McKenna. But how was this specialist going to treat the sun-cursed scientist—create a super-sunblock lotion? Have McKenna wear a sun-deflecting radiation suit during the daytime?

Confine him to a jail cell during the day and only release him at night? (Of course, in any of these cases, as Bill Warren has noted,[40] solar rays would still penetrate through these layers.)

The very first scene puts Radiation with a capital R front and center with the close-up of the Atomic Research Inc. sign. Also, the opening voiceover tells us that two space satellites have discovered a hitherto unknown form of solar radiation, yet its connection to McKenna's case and the new isotope with which he was working remains unclear. Is this "new radiation hazard from the sun" going to affect men and women in space only, or those of us here on Earth? Will scientists conduct further experiments on McKenna's "new isotope"? Will it in turn lead to more Hideous Sun Demons?

On one level, McKenna shares atypical radiation exposure symptoms with Colonel Manning of *The Amazing Colossal Man*. McKenna somehow inexplicably survives extreme exposure, as does Manning, but then they both appear to be okay—and then promptly start becoming monsters.

The movie implies that this "new isotope that never existed in nature before" is a bad thing. But can one make the leap from this line of dialogue and the film's subsequent events that the filmmakers are blaring a klaxon about radiation experiments? Maybe, maybe not. Still, those few words—"that never existed in nature before"—describe the splitting of the atom for much of the public. Prior to 1945, no one had ever seen an atomic explosion, and it certainly seemed unnatural enough (though of course it was brought about using natural principles). Likewise, the gigantic explosions resulting from H-bomb tests seemed new, unheralded in nature, yet our sun is basically a tremendous thermonuclear fusion reactor.

Make no mistake, in the world of *The Hideous Sun Demon*, radiation is scary stuff—but this is due to an *accident*, not due to the nature of radiation itself. Just as we must be careful with electricity, so too must we be careful with radiation lest it turn us into low-budget monsters. In this sense, the movie strangely implies something upbeat about radiation, namely that if one simply employs the proper precautions and protocols, there is nothing to worry about. Accidents, after all, occur only once every blue moon—or yellow sun.

The Best and the Rest

The best American-made humanoid mutant movies were made during the 1950s; the 1960s saw several as well, but none as good as, for example, 1957's *The Incredible Shrinking Man*. Even the 1950s' worst humanoid mutation film, arguably 1955's *Bride of the Monster*, is better than the worst 1960s example of this subgenre, inarguably 1961's *The Beast of Yucca Flats*. But remember that radiation-created humanoid mutants were new in the '50s. By the '60s, they had become somewhat shopworn. Put another way, if 1950s humanoid mutant movies were a Krispy Kreme doughnut fresh out of the oven, 1960s humanoid mutant movies were that same doughnut after it had been sitting out on the counter for three days. That said, it's time to turn to the decade that gave us the world's first alleged horror-monster musical—1964's *The Horror of Party Beach*. Don't say you weren't warned.

2. Mutations American Style

1960–1967

Bill Warren notes that by the early 1960s, traditional supernatural monsters were supplanting the 1950s science fiction mutants.[1] In the late 1950s, Britain's Hammer Films hit it big worldwide with *The Curse of Frankenstein* (1957) and *Horror of Dracula* (1958), and their color-saturated, blood-drenched horror movies continued to pack movie theaters well into the 1960s. Meanwhile, AIP's Roger Corman had for the most part deserted science fiction for a Gothic series of Edgar Allan Poe adaptations. Humanoid monsters were still a major presence in 1960s movies, but few of them were atomic in origin.

It wasn't that the public no longer feared the nuclear threat, but rather than the latter was finding expression in more serious American-made movies. These included low-budget efforts such as 1962's *Panic in Year Zero!* and high-profile dramas such as 1964's *Fail-Safe*. But 1960s cinema nevertheless did give birth to a handful of humanoid mutation movies tied to the nuclear threat, including 1961's infamous *The Beast of Yucca Flats* and 1964's far more palatable *The Time Travelers*.

Beyond the Time Barrier (AIP, 1960)

Credits: Directed by Edgar G. Ulmer; Story and Screenplay: Arthur C. Pierce; Produced by Robert Clarke; Executive Producers: John Miller and Robert L. Madden; Production Design: Ernst Fegté; Photography: Meredith M. Nicholson; Music: Darrell Calker; Music Editor: Gil Marchant; Sound: Earl Snyder; Editor: Jack Ruggiero; Special Effects: Roger George; Makeup: Jack P. Pierce; Hair Stylist: Corrine Daniel; Assistant Director: Leonard J. Shapiro; Production Supervisor: Lester D. Guthrie; Location Coordinator: W. L. "Pop" Guthrie; Camera Operator: Jack McCoskey; Script Supervisor: Shirley Ulmer; Properties: Joe Sullivan; Head Grip: George Fenaja; Costumer: Jack Masters; Photographic Effects: Howard A. Anderson Co.; Sound Editor: Don Olson.

Cast: Robert Clarke (Major Bill Allison); Darlene Tompkins (Princess Trirene); Arianne Arden (Major Markova); Vladimir Sokoloff (The Supreme); Stephen Bekassy (Karl Kruse); John Van Dreelen (Dr. Bourman); Boyd "Red" Morgan (The Captain); Ken Knox (Col. Martin); Don Flournoy, Tom Ravick (Mutants); Neil Fletcher (Air Force Chief of Staff); Jack Herman (Dr. Richman); William Shapard (Gen. York); James "Ike" Altgens (Secretary Patterson); John Loughney (Gen. LaMont); Russell Marker (Col. Curtis).

66 • Part I: Mutants

Miller Consolidated Pictures; black-and-white; released in July 1960. Available on DVD as a solo DVD or as part of the DVD set *Movies 4 You—Sci Fi Classics* (with *The Man from Planet X, The Time Travelers* and *The Angry Red Planet*).

Most nuke-spawned human mutants in the '50s and '60s resulted from direct exposure to nuclear tests or atomic fallout, but in *Beyond the Time Barrier*, a combination of nuclear testing and ecological disaster creates the mutants. This is novel, as ecology wouldn't became a major sci-fi movie theme for years to come. Otherwise, *Beyond the Time Barrier* is a typical time travel adventure.

Air Force test pilot Bill Allison (Robert Clarke) inadvertently breaks the time barrier (hence the title) and winds up in the year 2024. There, he discovers an advanced subterranean culture, most of whom are deaf-mutes. The Superior, leader of the under-earthers, and a few others can speak, and Allison demands to know what's going on, offering his captors only name, rank and country of origin.

Allison discovers that he is in the future (which the viewer has known all along). He is told that by 1971, nuclear testing had destroyed the protective layers of the upper atmosphere, exposing humans to potent cosmic rays. These radioactive beams created the mutants, and this event is referred to as "the plague," but presumably in the figurative or Biblical sense only, since a literal plague would be caused by bacteria or viruses.

While mutants run amok in the bottom right corner of the photograph, duplicitous Markova (Arianne Arden) turns the tables on Major Allison (Robert Clarke) in AIP's *Beyond the Time Barrier* (1960).

In any event, "the plague" killed half of the human race and has left almost all the rest sterile, save for the Superior's granddaughter, who naturally falls for Allison. Allison gets mixed up with other time voyagers—two from 1994, one from 1973—but eventually discovers they are all no-good-niks (none of them is an American, after all). The mutants escape "the pit" and terrorize the under-earthers while Allison struggles against the trio of treacherous time travelers. Almost everyone—including the Supreme's granddaughter—winds up dead except for Allison and the Supreme.

Using a formula devised by one of the now deceased 1994 time travelers, Allison returns to 1960. But jet lag obviously has nothing on time travel lag, as Allison now appears quite aged (the facial makeup causes him to resemble a Universal mummy). He warns the authorities about the oncoming plague, and the viewer assumes that due to two examples of corroborating evidence (the two 1994 time travelers are actual students in 1960), Allison's warning may be heeded.

The mutants in this film don't amount to much; their makeup basically consists of skull caps. In fact, several shots of "the pit" are actually scenes from a different movie, 1960's *Journey to the Lost City*. The fact that the "mutants" in these shots have hair plays hob against the presumed baldness of all 2024 mutants. As the latter run throughout the underground city babbling and carrying on like padded cell loonies, they are neither particularly frightening nor very convincing. In fact, they only appear in a small portion of the movie, most of which concerns itself with the melodramatic skullduggery involving Allison and the various supporting characters.

Probably accidentally, these mutants don't seem as far-fetched as those in most 1950s and 1960s genre flicks. They aren't multi-eyed savages, alligator-headed heroes or 50-foot giants. They are only slightly different physically than the non-mutants; in fact, much of their deformity appears to be mental.

As Bill Warren notes, the notion of having nuclear tests cause the destruction of the earth's ionosphere is more original than having a standard nuclear war.[2] However, Warren also finds this a gimmick on screenwriter Arthur C. Pierce's part to give him the kind of low-budget world he needed for the movie.[3] Warren is probably right. Again we have something nuclear (flashing radiation symbol please) linked with something catastrophic on a global level. It's as though, in the 1950s and 1960s, you couldn't have nuclear testing without the eventual flipside: nuclear disaster, probably in the form of an all-out war, but perhaps in the form of an ecological calamity as in *Beyond the Time Barrier*. Even if Pierce wasn't trying to criticize nuclear testing, this movie does so nevertheless.

The Beast of Yucca Flats (Crown International, 1961)

Credits: Written and Directed by Coleman Francis; Produced by Anthony Cardoza and Coleman Francis; Executive Producers: Roland Morin and James Oliphant; Associate Producers: Larry Aten and Charles Stafford; Photography: John Cagle; Music: Irwin Nafshun and Al Remington [according to Bill Warren's *Keep Watching the Skies!*, the music was actually prerecorded German music by Gene Kauer]; Sound Mixer: Titus Moody; Production Supervisor–Assistant Director: Austin McKinney; Camera Operator: Lee Strosnider; Makeup: Larry Aten; Publicity: Ted Charach.

Cast: Tor Johnson (Joseph Jaworsky/The Beast); Douglas Mellor (Hank Radcliffe); Barbara Francis (Lois Radcliffe); Bing Stafford (Jim Archer); Larry Aten (Joe Dobson); Linda Bielema (Wife on Vacation); Ronald Francis (Randy Radcliffe); Alan

Francis (Art Radcliffe); Anthony Cardoza (KGB Driver/Helpful Neighbor); Bob Labansat (Jaworsky's Bodyguard); Jim Oliphant (Husband on Vacation); John Morrison (KGB Passenger); Eric Tomlin (Driver Run Off the Road); Jim Miles (Jaworsky's Driver); Conrad Brooks (Man at Airfield); George Prince [Principe] (Man Who Reports Murder); Graham Stafford (Newsboy); Marcia Knight (Woman in Bed with Jim); Bob Carrano (Parachutist); Bob Calcagni (Plane Pilot); Lanell Cado (Woman Strangled in Opening Scene); Coleman Francis (Narrator/Gas Station Attendant/Man Buying Newspaper/The Beast's Roars).

A Cardoza Production; black-and-white; 54 minutes; released on May 2, 1961. TV title: *Atomic Monster—The Beast of Yucca Flats.* Available on DVD.

Tor Johnson—every Monster Kid Baby Boomer knows who he was—appeared in a series of bad movies, but this didn't mean he was a bad man or even a man without talent. For example, you figure Johnson's loved ones at the time of *The Beast of Yucca Flats* probably didn't regard the man as a "hoot." My guess is that Tor did his best in this phenomenally budget-strapped non-thriller, but he didn't have much to work with script-wise and received probably little if any help from director-writer Coleman Francis. In fact, this is probably the worst movie Tor appeared in, several rungs below even Ed Wood's 1955 *Bride of the Monster* (see previous chapter).

The Beast of Yucca Flats' tasteless opening, which features a large but unseen man strangling a woman to death in her bedroom, has nothing whatsoever to do with what follows. The actual (?) story is about scientist Joseph Jaworsky (Johnson) who possesses evidence that the Russians have already landed on the moon. As the omnipresent narrator tells us in his doom-laden voice, "Flag on the moon. How did it get there?" After Russian agents shoot at Jaworsky but miss, he hightails it into the desert. But as luck and convenient plotting would have it, a nuclear test explosion bathes him in radiation, and Jaworsky becomes the title monster. However, other than a desultory attempt at burn makeup on his face, he looks exactly the same as before.

"Shock waves of an A-bomb," the narrator tells us. "A once powerful, humble man reduced to nothing."

The bomb-mutated Jaworsky sneaks up on a guy having car trouble and kills him. Next, from the car's back seat, Jaworsky's arms reach into the front seat (how did he get into the back seat so fast?), strangles a woman in the passenger seat, and carries her to a cave. Again, the narrator: "A prehistoric beast in the nuclear age. Kill, kill just to be killing."

Another family has car trouble (this seems to happen a lot near Yucca Flats), and the father fusses over the auto as his two young sons go AWOL. Dad searches for them. Elsewhere, two police officers find Jaworsky's first victim. One of the officers hops aboard a plane with the intention to, as the narrator intones, "shoot first. Ask questions later." The patrolman takes the narrator's advice literally, for even though the officer has no idea what the killer looks like, he nevertheless begins firing repeatedly at the innocent father, who naturally runs as though his life depends upon it, because it does. That portentous narrator once more: "A man runs. Somebody shoots at him."

The father gets shot, twice, and goes down, apparently seriously hit, but he inexplicably recovers (maybe he is also a Yucca Flats mutant?) and runs to find his wife still standing beside their car. Saying he'll get help, he hops into the auto and speeds away, leaving his wife standing in the road with a stupefied expression on her face.

The two sons eventually encounter Jaworsky and run into a cave to hide. The Beast of Yucca Flats becomes cranky when he can't find them, hurls a big rock at nothing in particular, then promptly takes a nap. The boys escape. Jaworsky chases them, and soon he meets up with the two desert patrolmen. The Bomb-spawned mutant almost kills one of the officers, but the man's partner shoots Jaworsky several times in the back.

As the officers walk away from the dying Jaworsky, the narrator's last words are, "Joseph Jaworsky. Noted scientist." You expect the narrator to make some final somber observation about the guy, but like coherence in this movie, it doesn't happen. Jaworsky dies, but only after stroking a jackrabbit that hops onscreen out of nowhere for no apparent reason. *The End.*

The fact that nuclear testing could inform such a movie is itself amazing, as the film is vastly more bizarre than any atomic mutations spawned in Hollywood films of the '50s or any other decade one might care to mention.

Was the nuclear test that produces the Beast a gimmick, or was this movie trying to say something substantive? Bill Warren opines, "Just having someone turn into a monster because of an atomic bomb is hardly criticism of nuclear weaponry, but at least it's a faint perspective."[4] *The Beast of Yucca Flats* may not be a carefully constructed polemic indicting the nuclear threat, but the symbolism—the Bomb turning men into monsters, and certainly this could be true figuratively—can't be denied. Neither can the film's scoop that the Russians landed on the moon eight years before the Americans. Take that, NASA.

Most Dangerous Man Alive (Columbia, 1961)

Credits: Directed by Allan Dwan; Screenplay by James Leicester and Phillip Rock; Based on the Story "The Steel Monster" by Phillip Rock and Michael Pate (and, unbilled, Joseph Rock and Leo Gordon); Produced by Benedict Bogeaus; Photography: Carl Carvahal; Music: Louis Forbes; Sound Editor: Joe Kavigan; Editor: Carlo Lodato; Production Supervisor: Clarence Eurist; Wardrobe: Gwen Wakeling.

Cast: Ron Randell (Eddie Candell); Elaine Stewart (Carla Angelo); Debra Paget (Linda Marlow); Anthony Caruso (Andy Damon); Gregg Palmer (Lt. Bill Fisher); Morris Ankrum (Captain Davis); Tudor Owen (Dr. Meeker); Steve Mitchell (Carmen Devola); Joel Donte (Franscetti).

A Trans-Global Film; black-and-white; 82 minutes; released on June 28, 1961.

Gangsters and mushroom clouds may seem to have as much in common as politicians and hand grenades, but in *Most Dangerous Man Alive*, the wedding of atomic age science fiction and crime melodrama seems harmonious enough.

Eddie Candell (Ron Randell), former financial mogul unjustly accused of murder, escapes the police before they can lock him up. He happens to walk onto a nuclear testing site just as the bomb is detonated—don't you hate it when that happens? Candell survives (of course), and that's not all, for his flesh is now tough as steel. The film's obligatory scientific authority, Dr. Meeker (Tudor Owen), tells the none-too-happy police that Eddie has been exposed to Element X, "a new atomic element recently developed." Since Candell was at the detonation tower when the bomb exploded, the nuclear exposure "fused steel into the living tissues of the man."

The new and improved Candell doggedly seeks revenge against the creeps who sent him up the river. Now happily impervious to his enemies' guns, Candell's main quarry is Andy Damon (Anthony Caruso), who ousted Candell from his former financial empire.

Literal man of steel Eddie Candell (Ron Randell) hurls gangster Andy Damon (Anthony Caruso) to his death in *Most Dangerous Man Alive* (Columbia, 1961).

He also hunts for duplicitous Linda Marlow (Debra Paget), whose witness stand lies helped convict him. Candell kills sundry Damon henchmen.

Candell pursues temporary solace from Carla Angelo (Elaine Stewart), his heart of gold lady love. But he doesn't want her harmed, so goes it solo once more. Dr. Meeker shows Carla and the police the mutations that have occurred in animals exposed to the same blast that engulfed Candell; the scientist says that similar mutations could be happening to Candell, both on a physical and mental level, and that within 48 hours, he will start emitting deadly radiation.

Carla convinces Candell that Dr. Meeker can help him. Damon sets a trap for Candell at a brewery powerhouse, but the 10,000 volts of electricity don't faze Candell one iota. Triumphant, Candell speeds off into the countryside with Damon, Linda and Carla. Damon shoots and kills Linda, and Candell subsequently strongarms Damon.

Standing atop a hill and sounding a little like James Cagney in 1949's *White Heat*, Candell starts calling the police coppers before hurling Damon to his death. At this point the National Guard moves in with flame throwers. As twin gouts of flame assault Candell, the effects of Element X start to wear off. Eventually, Candell expires and turns into an ash silhouette, the wind blowing his dust vestiges hither and yon.

One major virtue of *Most Dangerous Man Alive* is the acting, particularly on the part of Elaine Stewart as Carla. She is utterly convincing as Candell's concerned girlfriend. She quit making movies not long after this one.[5]

Another acting plus is the great character actor Morris Ankrum, who appeared in a number of 1950s science fiction movies, most notably as the general who gets his brain vacuumed by space invaders in 1956's *Earth vs. the Flying Saucers.* In *Most Dangerous Man Alive,* Ankrum has a low-key field day as a no-nonsense police captain. While Carla is still with Eddie atop the hill, Ankrum tells the guardsmen, "Get your flame throwers ready."

"Captain," a concerned police sergeant says, "you can't use flame throwers with that girl up there!"

Replies Ankrum, "She made her own deal." Talk about hard-boiled.

As in so many of the old nuclear threat movies, a "new" radioactive element is the reason for the mutation, i.e., Candell's transformation from flesh into steel. This presumably means that any man touching steel who is simultaneously exposed to Element X's rays could also become well-nigh invulnerable. No doubt the U.S. military might use such knowledge to create thousands of soldiers impervious to gunfire. As for the deadly radiation these soldiers would eventually emit? Just a minor wrinkle to be ironed out—or so some military honchos would argue.

Candell is a budget-conscious atomic mutant, requiring minimal makeup. With the exception of one brief interlude, he also wears the same loosened necktie from the beginning of the picture when the nuclear blast envelopes him to his defeat at the end. Maybe that tie, and even his tattered clothes, are also infused with steel? Otherwise, why didn't the blast burn them away?

As for the nuclear threat, the movie echoes a frequent theme in American human mutant films when Dr. Meeker says, "Natural laws and balances no longer exist." In other words, the power, potential and mystery of the atom are limitless—who knows what it can do? Herein lies an uneasy American pessimism regarding the new atomic age into which we had been thrust.

Candell, like Colonel Glenn Manning and other mutants before him, becomes a monster and thus must die. But Dr. Meeker's final statement—"Nature has laws too and we can break only so many of them"—assures us that a balance will be maintained even in our uncertain atomic age. Instead of falling headlong into a bottomless nuclear pit, we will be rescued by Nature itself (and by implication a Supreme Power) pulling us back from the brink.

One interesting aspect of Candell's ongoing mutation is that he literally becomes cold-blooded, icy to the touch. Carla notes this with concern. Perhaps we as individuals likewise become colder as the potential horror of nuclear war fades into the background, the notion of thermonuclear conflict boring and passé as we convert bread and circuses into a myriad of twenty-first century hi-tech indulgences. Reality TV? Yes, please. Reality soul-searching? No thanks.

The Year 1962

No American-made atomic humanoid movies graced movie screens in 1962; however, the nuclear threat was alive and well in the notable low-budget movies *Panic in Year Zero!* and *This Is Not a Test.* Both offered a grim, non-mutant message on nuclear war, and are covered extensively in Chapter 8.

Monstrosity (a.k.a. *The Atomic Brain*) (Emerson Film Enterprises, 1963)

Credits: Directed by Joseph Mascelli; Screenplay by Vy Russell, Sue Dwiggins and Dean Dillman, Jr.; Associate Producers: Vy Russell and Sue Dwiggins; Produced by Jack Pollexfen and Dean Dillman, Jr.; Photography: Alfred Taylor; Music: Gene Kauer; Sound: Charles Knight; Editor: Owen C. Gladden; Special Effects: Space Age Rentals; Makeup: Lou Yates; Camera Operator: Ove Sehested; Production Coordinator: Kemp Niver; Dialogue Director: Bill Ashley.

Cast: Marjorie Eaton (Mrs. Hetty March); Frank Gerstle (Dr. Otto Frank); Frank Fowler (Victor); Erika Peters (Nina Rhodes); Judy Bamber (Beatrice "Bea" Mullins); Lisa Lang (Anita Gonzalez); Bradford Dillman (Narrator); Margie Fisco (Walking Corpse); Xerxes the Cat (The Cat).

A Cinema Ventures' production; black-and-white; 64 minutes; released in September 1963. Also known as *The Atomic Brain*. Available on DVD.

"Brain? Brain? What is brain?" asked the confused alien in the *Star Trek* episode "Spock's Brain." You may wonder the same thing after viewing this low-budget non-wonder. Some bad movies have their hearts in the right place, while their brains are in neutral. In *Monstrosity*, both vital organs appear to be misplaced.

The film opens with brooding narration (supplied by an unbilled Bradford Dillman

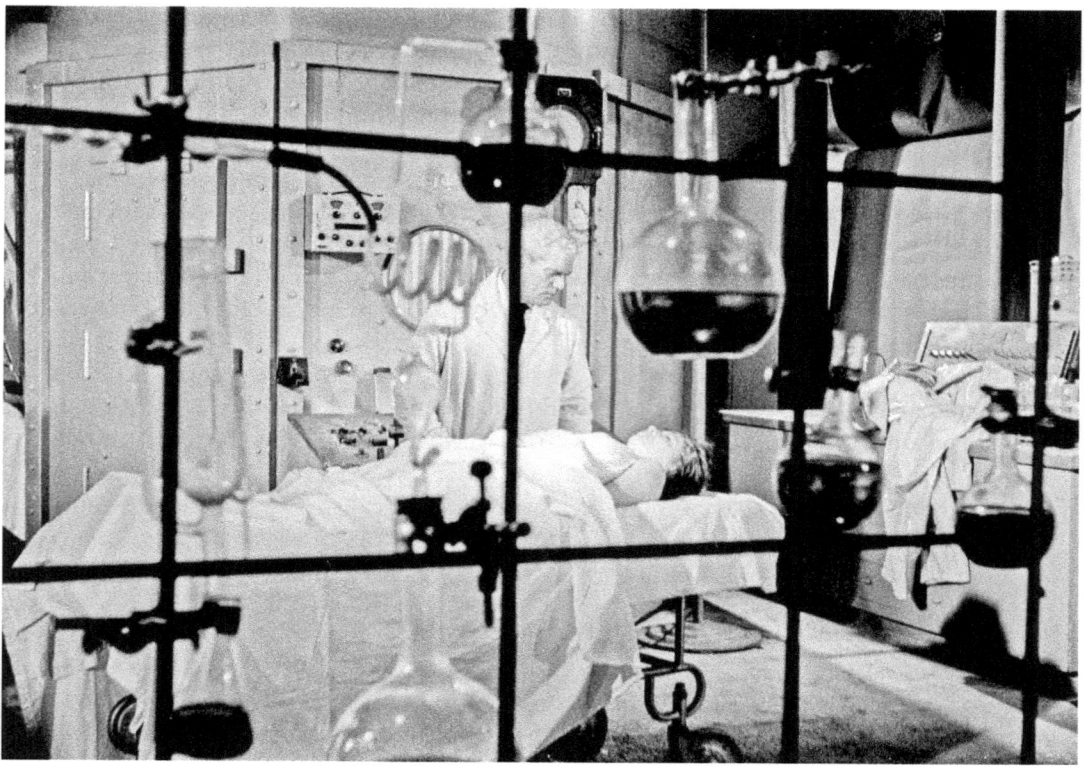

In his secluded lab, Dr. Otto Frank (Frank Gerstle) prepares to transplant the brain of Nina Rhodes (Erika Peters) into a rich old lady in 1963's *Monstrosity* (also known as *The Atomic Brain*).

of 1970s TV-movie fame), which we hear throughout the movie. Dr. Frank (Frank Gerstle) is performing brain transplants in the lab of a mansion, a procedure that requires the recipient's body to be basked in radiation in Dr. Frank's atomic reactor. Rich and aging Mrs. March (Marjorie Eaton) funds these experiments in the hope that the doctor will eventually be able to transplant her brain into the body of a beautiful young woman. However, most of his experiments have ended in failure.

One of Dr. Frank's botched experiments is Hans—Dr. Frank placed a dog's brain in the hapless handyman, resulting in the latter sprouting canine fangs, shaggy hair and a monstrous disposition. Hans is the titular *Monstrosity*, though viewers may feel that the real monstrosity is the film itself.

Mrs. March hires three young women from Europe to work as domestic help around the mansion: Nina (Erika Peters), Bea (Judy Bamber) and Anita (Lisa Lang). In reality, she is sizing them up to decide which of them will be the recipient of her brain. She even has them undress before her so she can see their bared bodies.

Upon spying a birthmark on Anita's back, Mrs. March says, "Hideous." She then gives Dr. Frank permission to do whatever he wants with her. He does just that, transplanting a housecat's brain into Anita's body. Immediately, Anita develops feline traits, including purring, meowing and hissing. With Anita now missing, brunette Nina and blonde Bea realize something doesn't add up. However, the mansion is guarded both by dog-man Hans and an electric fence, and Mrs. March's dutiful gigolo Victor (Frank Fowler) has cut the phone wires.

Bea is attacked by Anita and gets one of her eyes scratched out, proving blondes do not have more fun. Nina tries to help Anita, but the cat-woman winds up falling from the roof to her death. Dr. Frank sedates Bea. He also retrieves her dislodged eye, assuring Nina he will take care of her. Understandably, Nina is skeptical about Dr. Frank's brand of TLC.

With Anita dead and Bea disfigured, this leaves only Nina to be the recipient of Mrs. March's brain. Nina attempts to get Victor to help her and Bea escape. Mrs. March murders Victor, dashing Nina's hopes. Dr. Frank no longer trusts Mrs. March, clearly wondering if after the operation she will likewise kill him the way she did Victor. So instead of proceeding as planned, he deviously transplants Mrs. March's (apparently very tiny) brain into a housecat rather than into Nina.

Less than thrilled with the prospect of spending a lifetime prowling alleyways, the now feline but still nefarious Mrs. March seals Dr. Frank in his atomic reactor, which quickly kills him. Attempting to escape with Nina, Bea is electrocuted. Nina subsequently flees from the house just before it explodes. The cat (with Mrs. March's brain) follows Nina, the narrator telling us that it wants revenge.

Probably the best part about this film is its length, just a little over an hour. While not howlingly awful like *The Beast of Yucca Flats*, *Monstrosity* is still tough sledding. However, the actors are fairly good for this type of movie. Marjorie Eaton radiates wickedness as the ruthless Mrs. March—Margaret Hamilton has nothing on her. Judy Bamber's character Bea is supposed to be from England, but she often sounds more as though she just stepped out of the American South. Erika Peters probably fares best as Nina.

The transplantation business lacks basic logic. Once a cat's brain is inside Anita's body, she purrs just like a cat. How? Humans have no apparatus by which to purr. This gives the movie an almost supernatural feel, albeit it could still be classified as "science fantasy."

The film's nuclear threat element is minor, basically just that of atomic radiation being part of Dr. Frank's brain transplantation procedure. In this sense, Hans could be seen as a radiation-created mutant. Also, we see Dr. Frank don his radiation suit several times, and his atomic reactor kills him, leaving him a skeleton.

Monstrosity's story plays on themes as old as Universal's Frankenstein series—a scientist succumbs to the Dark Side to further his "mad" ideas. But what about the broader issue? Would brain transplantation be ethical? That, of course, is a gray matter. (Pun definitely intended.)

The Horror of Party Beach (Twentieth Century–Fox, 1964)

Credits: Produced and Directed by Del Tenney; Screenplay by Richard Hilliard; Additional Dialogue: Ronald Gianettino and Lou Binder; Associate Producer: Alan V. Iselin; Art Director: Robert Verberkmoes; Photography: Richard Hilliard; Musical Director: Bill Holcombe; Sound Recorder: Daniel Aldridge; Re-recording: Albert Gramaglia; Supervising Editor: Gary Youngman; Editors: Leonard De Munde, Richard L. Hilliard and David Simpson; Assistant Editors: Robert Rose and Mary Ann Miles; Assistant Directors: Daniel Walker and Wayne Tippit; Second Unit Photography: David Simpson; Camera Operator: Leonard De Munde; Production Coordinator: Ruth Freedman; Costumes: Dina Harris; Monster Costumes: Robert Verberkmoes; Still Photographer: Mary Ann Miles

Cast: John Scott (Hank Green); Alice Lyon (Elaine Gavin); Allan Laurel (Dr. Gavin); Eulabelle Moore (Eulabelle); Marilyn Clarke (Tina); Agustin Mayor (Mike); Damon Kebroyd (Lt. Wells); Monroe Wade (TV Announcer); Carol Grubman, Dina Harris, Emily Laurel (Girls in Car), Sharon Murphy (First Girl); Diane Prizio (Second Girl); The Del-Aires (Vocal Group); Charter Oaks Motorcycle Club of Riverside, Connecticut (Motorcycle Gang); Del Tenney (Gas Station Attendant); Daniel Walker (Drunk); Wayne Tippit (Drunk Killed by Monster).

Songs performed by the Del-Aires: "Drag" by Ronnie Linares and Gary Robert Jones; "Joy Ride" by Wilfred Holcombe and Edward Earl; "The Zombie Stomp" by Wilfred Holcombe and Edward Earl; "Wigglin' Wobblin'" by Gary Robert Jones; "You Are Not a Summer Love" by Wilfred Holcombe and Edward Earl; "Elaine" by Ronnie Linares.

An Iselin-Tenney Production; black-and-white; 78 minutes; released in April 1964. Working title: *Invasion of the Zombies*. Double-billed with *The Curse of the Living Corpse* (1964). Available on DVD with co-feature *The Curse of the Living Corpse*.

I include this hybrid of AIP's popular 1960s "Beach Movie" series and low-budget monster movies because radiation gives life to the creatures, and the movie unintentionally broaches the serious subject of nuclear waste.

A garbage scow dumps nuclear waste into the sea off the coast, said waste causing human skeletal remains on the sea floor to mutate into Beach Party Monsters (BPMs), basically Poverty Row versions of the Creature from the Black Lagoon. Young folks dance the day away on the beach until a BPM kills a girl, whose mangled body washes ashore. The BPMs next crash a sorority slumber party, but instead of a panty raid, this is a blood raid: The BPMs must have human blood to survive, though they indulge in killing any humans they encounter and subsequently leaving most of their mutilated corpses behind. (The gore, for the time, is fairly graphic.)

A monster on the prowl in *The Horror of Party Beach* (Fox, 1964). Note the strange hot dog–like protuberances in its mouth.

Before you know it, we hear of more killings—at one point, the film tells us that BPMs have murdered hundreds in the small coastal town. We also hear that Washington, D.C., authorities have been called in, but we don't seem to see them. Instead, it appears up to local college professor Dr. Gavin (Allan Laurel), his student assistant Hank Green

(John Scott) and local law enforcement to combat the creatures, while Hank's girlfriend Elaine Gavin (Alice Lyon) stands around looking worried. Inadvertently, the heroes discover that sodium is the BPM's Achilles heel.

While Elaine is measuring the radioactivity in a local body of water, BPMs appear. Hank and company arrive in time to pepper the aquatic monsters with sodium, putting an end to their menace as well as a merciful end to the movie.

One of the oddest aspects of this cult classic is the look of the BPMs. As many have noted, their mouths appear to be stuffed with hot dogs, which makes little sense. Are these tubes through which they suck human blood? The movie doesn't tell us, and certainly standard issue monster fangs would have been preferable to these comical Oscar Meyer protuberances. Also, the BPMs rolling eyes don't help their case. What were the filmmakers thinking when they designed

This *Horror of Party Beach* one-sheet's ad line "Weird atomic beasts who live off human blood!" implies that there are also *normal* atomic beasts who live off human blood. Today we call them politicians.

these monster costumes? In one scene near the end, the shots of the BPMs are speeded up, apparently a bid to make them seem scary. However, the herky-jerky results make the creatures appear as if they have stepped out of a 1920s silent movie

The story events likewise baffle. For example, although the local newspaper headlines scream of incessant monster killings, the residents of the town go about their business as though the deaths are no big deal. The film has firmly established that the BPMs attack at night, yet townspeople, especially young townspeople, trundle about at night as usual. Naturally, many become fodder for the Party Beach Horrors. With hundreds being killed, surely the National Guard would have been called in. Yet the movie portrays the besieged town as on its own, with local law enforcement providing little if any protection.

One troubling aspect of the film is the stereotypical portrayal of the African American housekeeper Eulabelle (Eulabelle Moore). She tells the characters innumerable times that "the voodoo" is responsible for the monster invasion.

Hank is ostensibly the hero, but he doesn't seem particularly pleasant. For example, at the beginning of the movie, Hank and his estranged girlfriend Tina (Marilyn Clark) are quarrelling at the beach. She softens and says to him in a conciliatory tone, "Oh, Hank, what's happened to us?" To which he curtly replies, "So when are you going to get it through your head that life isn't just all fun and games?" At another point in their argument, he says, "You just better stay out of my way." Tina may be immature, but Hank is a jerk.

Reviews of the film have mostly been unkind. *Castle of Frankenstein* #10 says this about the movie: "Imbecilic, third-rate bore." Similarly, a 1964 *New York Times* review by Eugene Archer quipped: "The question in *The Horror of Party Beach* is, Which is more horrible—the monsters or the rock'n'roll?"[6] Today, some Monster Kids look back on the film with fondness. In my own case, I remember reading through Jim Warren's photo story of *The Horror of Party Beach* in 1964; as a nine-year-old, I thought it looked great. But when I finally saw the movie on TV six years later, I felt let down.

Inadvertently, the movie sounds a nuclear warning, however faint, against indiscriminately dumping nuclear waste into the sea. In this case, the dumping created bloodthirsty monsters that killed hundreds. However, when Dr. Gavin and Hank discuss this dumping of nuclear waste from the university's reactor, neither seems the least bit outraged, but rather discuss it matter-of-factly. However, after all these murders, one assumes the university is in for some major lawsuits as well as criminal indictments.

Dr. Gavin tells us, "These creatures are human bodies kept alive by radioactive decay." Which presumably means nuclear waste dumping could result in more BPMs, not that anybody seems worried about this.

On the Dark Sky Films DVD of *The Horror of Party Beach*, producer-director Del Tenney notes that the movie and its co-feature, *The Curse of the Living Corpse*, played at a Dallas drive-in to brisk business. Initially, Twentieth Century-Fox had made only 50 prints, but after its Texan success, the studio made 500 prints that circulated throughout the country. Tenney calls *Horror of Party Beach* "a take-off on the Beach Party movies and the monster pictures."[7] In essence, *I Was a Teenage Gill Man*. Tenney also notes that the film was "what the audience needed at that point."[8] We can only hope there will not be another point at which audiences will need a movie like this.

The Horror of Party Beach is definitely a product of its day when drive-in exploitation movies were all the rage. It's like a time capsule of 1960s low-budget monster cinema.

The Time Travelers (AIP, 1964)

Credits: Written and Directed by Ib Melchior; Produced by William Redlin; Story: Ib Melchior and David Hewitt; Associate Producer: Don Levy; Art Director: Ray Storey; Photography: William Zsigmond; Music: Richard LaSalle; Sound: Leo Phillips, Jr.; Editor: Hal Dennis; Special Effects: David Hewitt; Makeup: Mark Snegoff; Assistant Directors: Clark Paylow and Lou Borzage; Script Supervisor: Hannah Scheel; Unit Manager: Tom Ramsey; Wardrobe: Phyllis Taylor and Ruth Weiss; Gaffer: Ernie Reed; Camera Operator: Leslie Kovacs; Legal Counselor: Donald E. Leon.

Cast: Preston Foster (Dr. Erik von Steiner); Philip Carey (Steve Connors); Merry Anders (Carol White); John Hoyt (Varno); Dennis Patrick (Willard); Joan Woodbury (Gadra); Dolores Wells (Reena); Steve Franken (Danny McKee); Berry Kroeger (Preston); Gloria Leslie (Councilwoman); J. Edward McKinley (Raymond); Margaret Seldeen (Miss Hollister); Forrest J Ackerman (Technician); Peter Strudwick (Mutant); Molly Glessing, Wayne Anderson (Androids).

A Dobil Production; color; 83 minutes; released on October 29, 1964. Working title: *Time Trap*. Double-billed with *Atragon*. Available on DVD in the set *Movies 4 You—Sci Fi Classics* (with *The Man from Planet X, Beyond the Time Barrier* and *The Angry Red Planet*).

You've probably heard the Chicago song "Does Anybody Really Know What Time It Is?" But when it comes to time hopping, does anybody really know what time it *isn't*? Take *The Time Travelers*: The four protagonists journey from the present day to 2071, then back to the present day, then ultimately wind up ... where?

At a college campus laboratory circa 1964, scientists Eric von Steiner (Preston Foster), Steve Connors (Philip Carey) and Carol White (Merry Anders) have opened a time window into the future. It shows a rocky, bleak tableau with no buildings or vegetation in sight. This naturally puzzles our heroes.

Happy-go-lucky handyman Danny McKee (Steve Franken) discovers that the portal is not only a window, but an actual door into the future, and he steps through it. Eric, Steve and Carol follow him, and before you can say "There's mutants in them thar hills," said mutants chase our four heroes into a cave. A force field saves them. Soon they meet the force field's creators—a group of scientists living underground.

Dr. Varno (John Hoyt), the leader of the undergrounders, reveals that the Earth of 2071 "is dying." The reason: a thermonuclear war. "The destruction was total," Varno says. "Earth, our home, our planet, is now just a burned-out, sterile slag in space." In addition, Varno explains that the undergrounders "are the descendants of a small group of far-thinking scientists and their families. We are the last normal human beings on Earth." The undergrounders' hope lies in a starship that will ferry them to an Earth-like planet orbiting Alpha Centauri.

Varno takes the protagonists to an android-construction center, a complex shown often throughout the film. Undergrounder Willard (Dennis Patrick) resents the time travelers. He calculates that the latter cannot blast off in the starship with the undergrounders because this would require time-intensive modifications to the craft that would put them behind schedule. The council votes on the measure, and Varno unhappily informs the protagonists that they indeed cannot share space on the starship.

Consequently, the time travelers decide they must recreate the time portal and journey back to 1964. While they work feverishly at their task, the undergrounders likewise toil to complete all the preparations for the starship, which must leave soon.

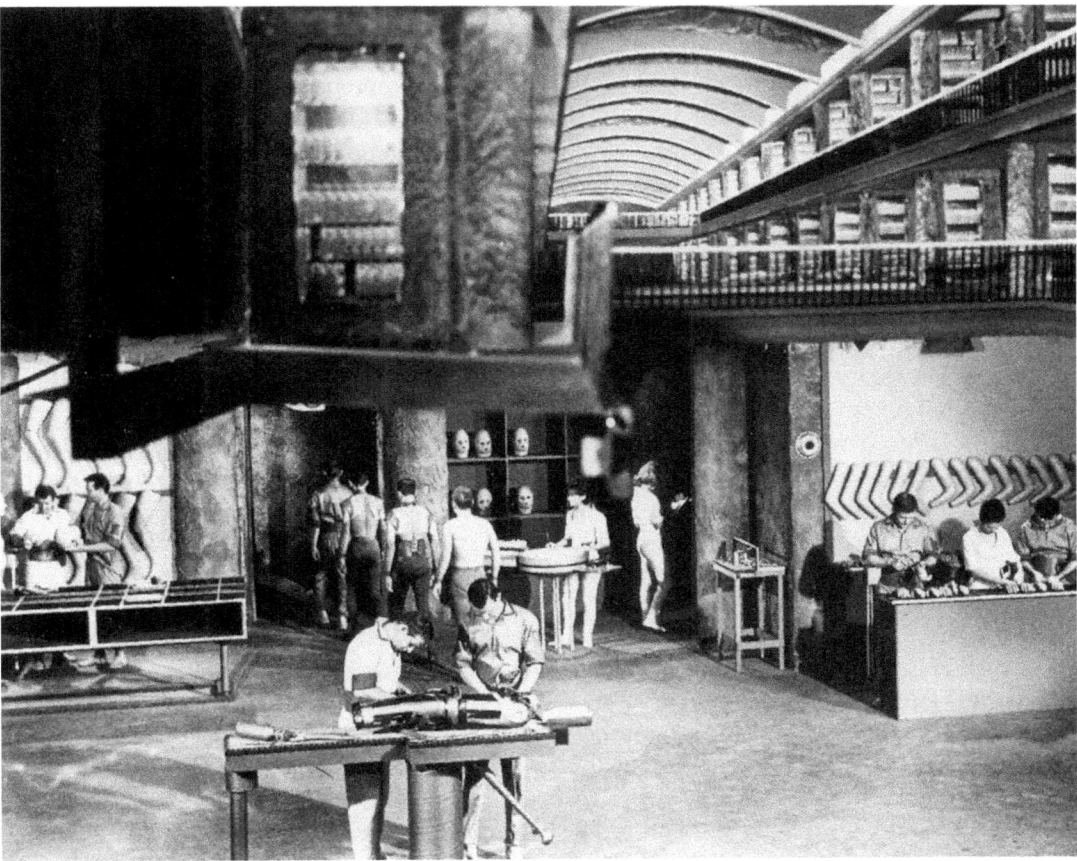

In the year 2071, underground factory laborers whistle while they work, creating more androids in AIP's ambitious *The Time Travelers* (1964).

With liftoff imminent, Varno notes that the force field generator's "power plant has been transferred to the ship," so the undergrounders' defenses are down. Just as undergrounder groups are boarding the starship, the mutants break into the installation's tunnels. A violent battle ensues between androids, mutants and undergrounders. During this fracas, the mutants make it to the starship area, causing a series of explosions that result in the starship's destruction.

The four protagonists, along with some of the undergrounders, escape through the time portal back to 1964 and disable the window so the mutants can't follow. However, when Eric, Steve, Carol and Danny rush into the lab, they see motionless versions of themselves—the scientists are frozen at the consoles, while the stock-still Danny leans against a wall. Eric says, "We've returned too far back in time," adding, "Somehow, we've disrupted the time flow. It's as if we were existing outside of time in … in limbo." Danny notices that his past self is moving incrementally. The time travelers determine that time is speeding by for them at a vastly accelerated rate.

Varno, who along with some of the other undergrounders has escaped with the time travelers, states that for them, they age "more than a year for every minute that goes by."

The time window is frozen at 100,000 years past 1964, and Eric cannot budge the machinery. With no real alternatives, the out-of-time protagonists, along with the undergrounders, step through the time portal into what appears to be total darkness. The darkness fades into a sunlit scene, and we see a long shot of the time travelers walking into an idyllic, Eden-like world. Then time begins again for the formerly "frozen" protagonists, and they repeat the events from the beginning when Danny first stepped into the time door all the way to all of them stepping into the darkened portal. The time sequence repeats again, and again, and again: They are caught in a never-ending time loop.

While time loops were a common science fictional device in 1964, the notion seemed fresh to me when I saw *The Time Travelers* at the age of nine in 1965, and I found the concept thought-provoking. I had seen one previous time loop story, *Twilight Zone*'s "Death Ship" (1963). But true to the spirit of *Twilight Zone*, "Death Ship" seemed like an unequivocal nightmare, whereas *Time Travelers* seemed more like a dream whose ending remained fuzzy.

Castle of Frankenstein #7 said of *The Time Travelers*, "Promising beginning and very imaginative ending almost compensates [*sic*] for the trite script, lurid treatment and poor performances in this weak grade-B fantasy." Methinks they doth protest too much. Yes, viewers had seen a similar future world in other science fiction movies, but the performances are all competent and the film features several imaginative touches beyond its opening and ending.

The film's screenplay, written by Ib Melchior (based on a story by Melchior and David Hewitt), does suffer from largely being a travelogue for the wonders of the future. Varno's guided tour appears to be a low-budget version of William Pidgeon's guided tour of the Krell machines in 1956's *Forbidden Planet*, but without the visual payoff. Hampered by a small number of sets and scant special effects, *Time Travelers* screams for a bigger budget. Still, the visual effects, such as the destruction of the starship in its crater launch pad, are not bad by 1964 standards. The aforementioned *Castle of Frankenstein* review cited the film's "[g]ood technical effects."

In addition to *Forbidden Planet*, the film also borrows from other 1950s science fiction movies. For example, the group of scientists living underground with bestial mutants on the surface smacks of *World Without End*'s (1956) future setup. Also, while toiling to complete accommodations for the starship's launch, the film employs motivational signs, such as "WORK! WORK! 4 DAYS, 15 HOURS TO DEPARTURE DAY." George Pal used this device in *When Worlds Collide* (1951).

Castle of Frankenstein #7 noted that in *Time Travelers*, "People of present enter future through time-warp and find same future as depicted in countless other films." Fair enough. However, "countless" is a bit of an overstatement, though similar future Earths can be found in *World Without End* and 1960's *Beyond the Time Barrier*. But borrowing general concepts such as time travel and a nuked-out future Earth isn't illegal or even unethical; fantastic cinema has always built on that which has come before. And *Time Travelers* does portray this familiar future Earth with welcome panache.

Director-screenwriter Melchior's approach is the reason for the film's aesthetic success. A prolific writer and no stranger to science fiction, Melchior was involved in a number of SFantasy projects in the 1950s and 1960s; he co-wrote the screenplays for 1962's *Reptilicus*, 1964's *Robinson Crusoe on Mars* and 1965's *Planet of the Vampires*. In addition

Opposite: **Emphasizing the "time portal" aspect of** *The Time Travelers* **(AIP, 1964), this poster teems with action.**

2. Mutations American Style: 1960–1967 (The Time Travelers) • 81

to *Time Travelers*, Melchior served as writer-director on 1959's *The Angry Red Planet*, best-known for its giant bat-rat-spider monster that menaces astronauts on Mars, as well as for its colossal one-eyed amoeba whose single eye rotates atop its gelatinous mass like a police car's spinning light.

Time Travelers often fumbles the ball in its attempts at "comedy relief." For example, Danny has become smitten with Reena (Dolores Wells), an undergrounder, who hands him a tray of android eyes. Danny looks into the camera and says, "Holy McKee, I thought I was giving her the eye." This breaking of the fourth wall is ill-advised and distracting. But the movie makes things worse by having a disembodied android hand grab Danny's behind. He pulls it off and places it back on the table, and it makes an "uh-uh" gesture with its index finger. Saints preserve us. But *Famous Monsters of Filmland* editor Forrest J Ackerman makes a welcome word play cameo. He is converting round metallic rings into squares. Willard says to him, "We're running low on liners. Do you think you can catch up?"

"Don't worry," Ackerman replies, "I'm keeping our spacemen happy, getting things squared away." For anyone familiar with the pun-heavy *Famous Monsters* of old, this is an admittedly silly but nevertheless golden moment.

While the sets in *Time Travelers* are sparse, the design of the androids is arresting. Their bodies resemble human bodies, but their heads sport a diamond shape with rounded edges, adorned only by an apparent speaker box (though we never hear the androids speak), two holes for ears on the sides of their heads, and distinctly human eyes. During the finale, the mutants mutilate one of the androids to startling effect: Though only its torso remains, its one arm keeps moving. Another fascinating shot shows a torched android gradually falling apart as it burns.

The Time Travelers' connection to the nuclear threat is vital. Due to its low budget, Varno shows the time travelers stock shots of nuclear blasts to depict the Earth's destruction. Despite the familiarity of the footage, it still sends a chill down one's spine, as an atomic exchange very well could have happened during the 1960s: The Cuban Missile Crisis could have turned into the Worldwide Nuclear War Crisis.

Tellingly, we don't know when the atomic war happened, although it is clear it was well before 2071. We also don't know who started it, or if it was in fact a mistake *à la* 1964's *Fail-Safe*. The destruction was global in scope. Indeed, the film's rocky, bleak landscapes could have been the long-term results of nuclear winter, though the latter didn't exist as a theory in 1964.

Varno tells us that the undergrounders are the only normal humans still alive in the world. But couldn't scientists in another country have likewise tunneled underground? The movie implies that the undergrounders cannot pick up any radio communications from anywhere else on the globe, and therefore Varno and his fellow scientists assume they are the last people on the planet.

Yet isn't it convenient that the only fully human survivors of the nuclear war are Americans—and indeed, white Americans at that? The future world depicted herein (and also in the similar *World Without End*) is no more diverse than a 1960s country club in the South. Apparently, all people of color bit the dust in Earth's final conflagration. However, I don't think the omission of African Americans, Hispanics or Asians in *Time Travelers* was intentional. But it would have been nice if at least a few of the survivors hadn't been Caucasian, and it might have been nice if a language in addition to English had been spoken. Gender-wise, *Time Travelers* fares better, in that Gadra (Joan Woodbury) is one of the council leaders. Nevertheless, it is a male—Varno—who is ultimately in charge. Paging Gloria Steinem.

Ethically, the undergrounders have made some stark (some might say questionable) decisions. The mutants are starving, yet the scientists do not share food with the unfortunates. Why? Because there simply isn't enough food to go around. Tellingly, when speaking of the mutants, Steve says, "They're hardly human, doctor."

But they certainly *look* human. Yes, they are bald (apparently the *de rigueur* style for post-apocalyptic mutants), but so was Yul Brynner. They also display facial disfigurations, but otherwise they look like people (though none of them seems to be female). But do mutants have to look like people, i.e., be implicitly "whole" (two arms, two legs, ten fingers, ten toes, etc.) to be considered human?

One interesting episode in the movie concerns Carol finding a half-mutant in one of the storage rooms. He has no toes, and only two fingers per hand. Warren wants to kill him, but Carol is shocked and won't have it. Steve, Eric and Varno enter the scene, and Eric suggests sending the unfortunate outside. Varno says, "He would not live long, Dr. von Steiner. He is not a mutant; he is not a human being. He belongs neither to us nor to them."

Willard insists, "He's a deviant!"

To which Carol replies, "He's a human being!"

That outburst is all it takes to persuade Varno that the half-mutant is indeed a human being, and apparently the undergrounders (or at least Carol) will tend to his needs. We never see this character again, so his ultimate fate remains unclear.

That the presumably enlightened Varno could so easily agree with the narrow-minded Willard about the half-mutant's human status suggests that the undergrounders have made moral compromises for years. That said, the movie does implicitly ask, "What is a human being?"

The mutants are simply too human-like to be thought of as monsters. One could argue that their brains have been mutated as well; thanks to generations of mutations, perhaps they are now hard-wired to be violent, possibly psychotic. But wouldn't this make them objects of pity, not of derision? Perhaps mutated psychopaths couldn't live alongside with non-mutants, but certainly the former shouldn't be looked upon as soulless ogres. *World Without End* somewhat "solves" this problem by having its mutants sport horrifically distorted faces, often with multiple eyes. But again, does one's physical appearance make one a monster? Fantastic cinema would seem largely to say, "Yes." And that is more chilling than the unmasking of any Phantom of the Opera.

Another way to look at the half-mutant sequence in *Time Travelers* is that in a post-nuke world, one must make hard choices. If there is only enough food for five people for six weeks, and five more people ask to partake of the food, should one let them? This is a choice faced by survivalist Paul Birch in 1955's *Day the World Ended*. His daughter Lori Nelson makes the choice for him by welcoming five strangers into their well-stocked home.

The post-nuke world of *Time Travelers* seems far removed from the optimism of 1950s entries such as *Day the World Ended*. Indeed, *Time Travelers* suggests that nuclear war might indeed usher in the end of the world, a finale without a happy ending. Yet what are we to make of the Eden-like world 100,000 years in the future? Could the planet have been terraformed by new "owners"? Or could this be the "new heaven and new earth" promised by Western Christianity?

Regarding the latter, it's interesting that religion either plays a major role in 1950s and 1960s American nuclear threat movies, or it plays no role at all. For example, both *Captive Women* and *Day the World Ended* are rife with religious allusions. But the same cannot be said for *World Without End* or *The Time Travelers*. Perhaps this is an issue considered too contentious to touch, yet it's true that in life-and-death situations, such as those that occur in nuclear threat movies, notions of God and the afterlife become important, even if one's reaction is simply to reject them. It has been said there are no atheists in foxholes, and while that isn't necessarily so, it probably is true that meaning becomes critically important when one's life or the lives of one's loved ones rest in the balance.

Though flawed, *The Time Travelers* is a thought-provoking example of low-budget 1960s science fiction cinema.

The Years 1965–1966

The years 1965 and 1966 saw no nuclear threat mutant movies. Indeed, by the 1960s, the threat of nuclear war became increasingly probable, and therefore, inherently unrealistic atomic age monsters almost totally disappeared from the cinematic landscape. One not-so-notable 1967 exception is *In the Year 2889*.

In the Year 2889 (Azalea Pictures, 1967)

Credits: Produced, Edited and Directed by Larry Buchanan; Screenplay by Harold Hoffman; Associate Producer: Edwin Tobolowsky; Production Coordinator: Joreta Cherry; Photography: Robert C. Jessup; Sound: Rex Cromwell; Special Effects: Jack Bennett; Dialogue Director: Annabelle Weenick; Assistant Cameraman: R.L. Buchanan; Gaffer: Robert Dracup; Key Grip: James Finley.

Cast: Paul Petersen (Steve Morrow); Quinn O'Hara (Jada); Charla Doherty (Joanna Ramsey); Neil Fletcher (Captain John Ramsey); Hugh Feagin (Mickey Brown); Max Anderson (Granger Morrow); Bill Thurman (Tim Henderson); Byron Lord (Mutant).

An Azalea Pictures production; released to TV (no theatrical release) by American International Television; 80 minutes. Available on DVD in a number of different packages; typical is *Horror from Hell Double Feature*, which pairs it with *Revenge of the Venus Fly Trap* (1970).

Great Caesar's ghost! Donna Reed's son is smoking cigarettes! I'm referring to *In the Year 2889* star Paul Petersen, who on *The Donna Reed Show* played son Jeff Stone during the program's seven-season run. In *Total Television*, Alex McNeil calls the series "[o]ne of the most wholesome sitcoms ever made,"[9] so naturally it's a shock to see Jeff, err, Paul smoking. Next thing you know, he'll be swilling root beer.

As *In the Year 2889*'s leading man, Paul was playing an adult role (hence the cancer sticks), and he's not bad. Unfortunately, the same can't be said for the movie. A remake of 1955's *Day the World Ended*, *Year 2889* offers the same storyline minus the intelligence and craftsmanship of Roger Corman's original. Also, though *Day the World Ended* is low-budget, it appears almost lavish compared to *Year 2889*'s almost non-existent production values.

Following a nuclear war, Captain John Ramsey (Neil Fletcher) and his daughter Joanna (Charla Doherty) dwell in a rural valley house stocked with provisions for three. Joanna's fiancé Larry doesn't show up, but five strangers do: Steve Morrow (Petersen), his brother Granger (Max W. Anderson), shady Mickey Brown (Hugh Feagin), his girlfriend Jada (Quinn O'Hara) and rancher Tim Henderson (Bill Thurman). The quintet quickly set up post-atomic residence, and this naturally creates friction.

Though frequently (and successfully) defied by his daughter Joanna, Ramsey runs a tight ship. But he still befriends Steve, who begins a romantic relationship with Joanna. Meanwhile, a mutant (presumably a mutated Larry) is stalking the survivors. Granger has become a half-mutant who eschews food and water, devouring radiation-rich meat only. Unhappy with the irradiated competition posed by Granger,

Joanna Ramsey (Charla Doherty) appears to be taking comfort from Mickey Brown (Hugh Feagin) in 1967's *In the Year 2889*. In the film, however, Joanna is repulsed by Mickey.

the Larry Mutant kills him. Mickey drowns Jada, and alcoholic Tim heads for the hills, stepping into a lethal radioactive mist. Ramsey tries to save Tim from the tainted vapors and sprains his ankle. Only Steve knows about Ramsey's contamination.

The Larry Mutant spirits Joanna away, with Steve in hot pursuit. Joanna and Steve stroll into a lake, where the Larry Mutant can't go. Non-contaminated rainwater falls, killing the Larry Mutant. Back at the house, Ramsey shoots Mickey, who was fixing to take a shot at the returning Steve. We then see a close-up—Steve and Joanna holding hands—and the screen reads, "The Beginning."

The abrupt ending suggests that the filmmakers ran out of money. Not that it matters. Among other things, despite the title that supposedly places the film in 2889, hundreds of years from 1967, nothing appears futuristic. Also, like so many other so-bad-they're-bad movies, the film drags. Worst of all, the mutant may rank as the poorest atomic mutant ever seen in an American science fiction movie. The skin looks fake, the teeth goofy, and the expression completely immobile. Compared to this threadbare monster, *Day the World Ended*'s acceptable mutant is an aesthetic masterpiece.

In addition to *Year 2889*, producer-director Larry Buchanan filmed several other 1960s remakes of 1950s AIP movies, including 1965's *The Eye Creatures* (a remake of 1957's *Invasion of the Saucer Men*), 1966's *Zontar, the Thing from Venus* (a remake of 1956's *It Conquered the World*), and 1967's *Creature of Destruction* (a remake of 1956's *The She Creature*). In all cases, the remakes are inferior to the originals. Buchanan specialized in low-budget films, his other opuses including 1966's *Mars Needs Women* and 1968's *It's Alive*, both starring a post–Disney Tommy Kirk.

Scary Monsters writer Jim Arena sent *In the Year 2889* star Paul Petersen a letter of appreciation for his performance, and Petersen gratefully responded with a two-page missive. Petersen wrote,

> To me the hilarious part was that so many of the actors took their roles seriously.... "What's my motivation?" and crap like that. Larry had a pat response to the motivation question: "Your salary!" ... I found myself moving lights, doing my own makeup, and helping with the makeup of others.... The simple fact is, I had a ball.... I think we took two and a half weeks to finish the movie ... and for all the ups and downs and curious beginnings, I had a grand time.[10]

In the Year 2889 plays out the same nuclear themes as *Day the World Ended*. The war has killed all but a remnant of humankind, and atomic mutations thrive in this new, radiation-contaminated planet. Steve's brother Granger represents an early stage of these mutants, whereas the dime-store Larry Mutant represents the final stage of mutation. Uncontaminated rainwater kills the mutated Larry, and by implication all other mutants. Presumably, Steve and Joanna will be the new Adam and Eve in this brave but not particularly new world.

Like *Day the World Ended*, the movie abounds with Biblical allusions, including the opening narration in which a thundering voice tells us, "The day of the Lord will come as a thief in the night, and the heavens shall pass away with a great noise, and the elements shall melt with fervent heat." Next, a radio announcer tells us that "the prophets [apparently a Judeo-Christian allusion] warned of this apocalyptic day." Indeed, the New Testament Scripture quoted above, 2 Peter 3:10, 12, sounded to many twentieth century Christians like an uncanny description of a nuclear war, and many believers saw this as proof that the Scriptures were indeed prophetic.

In the Year 2889 is basically a 1950s movie made in the 1960s. It begins in nuclear aftermath despair, but ends in standard 1950s American optimism. Completists may want to watch it once—others need not apply. But I was glad to read that Paul Petersen had a good time making this cheapie.

After the Year 1967

American-made atomic humanoid mutant movies were few and far between. There are exceptions, such as 1970's *Beneath the Planet of the Apes*, which in addition to the sentient apes features humanoid mutants with psychic powers. But for the most part, after the 1960s, American movie cinemas saw no more sun demons, monsters on the campus or beasts of Yucca Flats. A cinematic sub-cycle had ended, causing celebration for some, mourning for others, indifference by most.

However, via syndication packages, TV stations across America kept the atomic age humanoid mutant movies of the 1950s and 1960s alive and well. These films saw their "last hurrah" courtesy of TNT and AMC in the 1990s; nowadays, they have pretty much vanished from the television airwaves, but live on via DVD, and Blu-ray. The same can be said for two Japanese humanoid mutant movies, one from the 1950s, one from the 1960s, dealing with carnivorous radioactive liquid and A-bomb giants. Stay tuned for the next chapter for more details.

3. Rising Sun Terrors

1958–1965

What do a skyscraping Nipponese version of Frankenstein's Monster and a homicidal liquid monster have in common?

Plenty.

Japan is the only nation on Earth to have suffered an atomic attack, and this tragic history shaped the country's fantastic cinema of the 1950s and 1960s. According to Japanese movies, once humankind summoned the nuclear genie from its lamp, it could never force the genie back in.

This fatalistic thesis haunts a number of science fiction movies that Japanese studios released in the mid-twentieth century. And unlike their American counterparts of the same era, Japan's atomic age movies never leave the viewer with the optimistic feeling that "Gosh darn it, we can lick this atomic thing yet!" Instead, they leave the viewer with the pessimistic notion that gosh darn it, this atomic thing will lick *us* yet.

In this chapter, we shall examine the humanoid mutants depicted in Japan's *The H-Man* (1958) and *Frankenstein Conquers the World* (1965). "That's all?" you may be thinking.

Yes, but there are reasons for this small number. In the twentieth century, America was a big country with a legion of movie companies, whereas Japan was a small nation sporting only a handful of film companies. For example, in the 1950s, Toho generally released only one or two science fiction movies a year. This number didn't increase until the 1960s, but even then, most Toho science fiction movies involved giant monsters, not humanoid mutants. In fact, Chapter 6 covers 11 Japanese giant monster films relating to the nuclear threat. Nevertheless, the studio's one major Japanese nuclear mutant movie, *The H-Man*, packs enough of a horrific punch to equal several American mutant opuses.

The H-Man (released in Japan by Toho in 1957; released in America by Columbia in 1959)

Credits: Directed by Ishiro Honda; Screenplay by Takeshi Kimura; Story by Hideo Unagami (Kaijo?); Produced by Tomoyuki Tanaka; Art Director: Takeo Kita; Photography: Hajime Koizumi; Editor: Echiji Taira; Music: Masaru Sato; Sound: Choshichiro Mikami and Masanobu Miyazaki (Migami?); Production Manager: Teruo Maki; Assistant Directors: Koji Murata and Yoshio Nakamura; Lighting Director: Tsuruzo

Nishikawa; Special Effects Director: Eiji Tsuburaya; Special Effects Art Director: Akira Watanabe; Special Effects Lighting Director: Kuichiro Kishida; Optical Printing: Hiroshi Mukoyama.

Cast: Yumi Shirakawa (Chikako Arai); Kenji Sahara (Dr. Masada); Akihiko Hirata (Inspector Tominaga); Mitsuru Sato (Uchida); Koreya Senda (Dr. Maki); Yoshio Tsuchiya (Detective Taguchi); Yoshibumi Tajima (Detective Sakata); Eitaro Ozawa (Inspector Miyashita); Ayumi Sonoda (Emi); Toshiko Nakano (Okami); Yosuke Natsuki (Man); Kamayuki Tsubouchi (Detective Ogawa); Minosuke Yamada (Officer Wakasugi); Jun Fujiro (Nishiyama); Akira Sera (Yasukichi); Naomi Shiraishi (Mineko); Yo Kirino (Shimazaki); Hisaya Ito (Misaki); Shin Ohtomo (Hamano); Machiko Kitagawa (Hanae); Tetsu Nakamura (Chinese Gentleman); Yutaka Nakayama (An-chan); Senkichi Ohmura (Oh-chan); Shigeo Kato (Matsu-chan); Ko Mishima (Kishi); Kan Hayashi, Mitsuo Tsuda, Akio Kuama (Police Officers).

Japanese version: Color; TohoScope; 87 minutes; released on June 24, 1958. Japanese title: *Bijo To Ekatai-Ningen* (translation: *The Beauty and the Liquid People*).

American version: Color; scope; 79 minutes; released on June 3, 1959. Co-billed with *Womaneater*. Many dubbed voices provided by Paul Frees. Available on DVD (in both American-dubbed and Japanese-subtitled versions) on the three-DVD set *Icons of Sci-Fi Toho Collection* (with *Battle in Outer Space* and *Mothra*).

Should a fatal dose of fallout blanket the earth, will the H-Man take over the planet? This question forms the crux of *The H-Man*'s nuclear threat commentary. In the movie, radiation is not simply a gimmick to explain the presence of mutants, but rather a sober reality to spotlight a threat that may alter our very species and indeed the world as we know it.

Many have assumed that *The H-Man* is a version of 1958's *The Blob*. While it is true that the post–World War II Japanese excelled at assimilating Western culture, and it's likewise clear that the Land of the Rising Sun's *daikaiju* genre was inspired by both 1933's *King Kong* and 1953's *The Beast from 20,000 Fathoms*, *The H-Man* is an original.

Toho released *The H-Man* to Japanese audiences on June 24, 1958,[1] whereas Paramount released *The Blob* to American moviegoers on September 12, 1958.[2] (Released in 1956, Britain's blob-fest *X—the Unknown* beat both Japan and America to the punch, but didn't appear to have inspired either film, given that its creature is subterranean in origin.[3])

Having actually preceded *The Blob*, *The H-Man*'s connections to the American movie are purely coincidental, though the similarities are interesting. Chief among them, *The Blob* features a more benign late fifties atmosphere than *The H-Man*. The former features small-town Americana in all its cinematic wholesomeness, a hamlet whose worst offense is teenage hot-rodding. Even the adult authorities are good-hearted and mean well. Such is not the case with *The H-Man*, a far more adult movie than *The Blob*, even in terms of the graphic (by 1958 standards) melting of the H-Man's victims, clearly a reference to the horrific effects of nuclear weapons on humans.

Yes, the Blob absorbed hapless humans as well, but aside from the episode with the creature eating away the old man's hand, the film shies away from explicit carnage. (Of interest is an Internet still from the film showing the doctor in the throes of Blob absorption at his office window. Word is that the filmmakers found the scene too graphic, and thus cut it from the movie.)

Also, the special effects depicting the blob creatures are alike, though in *The H-Man*,

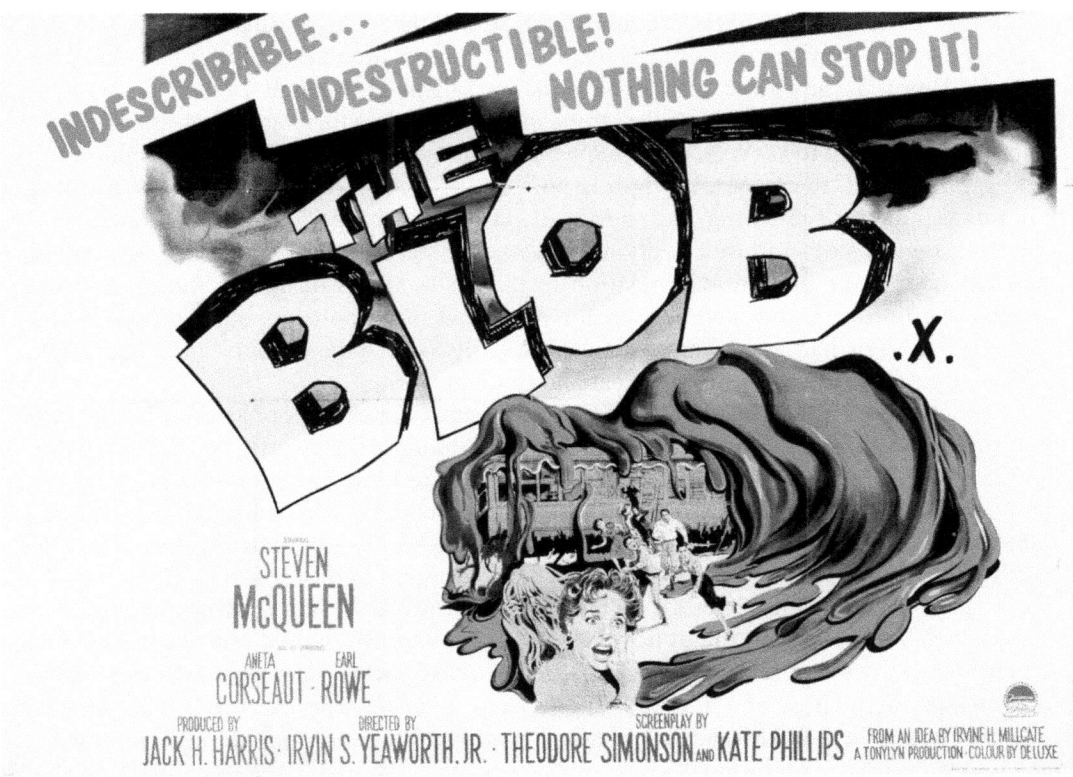

Many assume that *The Blob* (Paramount, 1958) was the inspiration for Toho's 1958 *The H-Man*. However, in reality, *The H-Man* was released in Japan before *The Blob* was released in America, meaning any similarities between the two films are coincidental.

the mutants often take on a bluish-green ghostly form, whereas the extraterrestrial goo in *The Blob* remains just that—a hunk of carnivorous ambulatory Jell-O, albeit one that changes color from green to red after it absorbs an unlucky victim. The H-Men likewise absorb their victims.

In addition, in *The Blob*, the authorities don't believe the hero and heroine—a young Steve McQueen (who went on to fame as a major movie star) and Aneta Corsaut (who went on to fame as school teacher Helen Crump in the 1960s sitcom *The Andy Griffith Show*). Likewise, in *The H-Man*, no one believes the hero (Kenji Sahara) or heroine (Yumi Shirakawa).

Gunfire has no effect on the creatures in either movie (recalling that wonderful '50s sci-fi movie tagline used in *The Creeping Unknown*'s ads: "Bullets can't stop it!"). Only elemental forces can defeat the monsters—cold (fire extinguishers) in *The Blob*, heat (flame throwers) in *The H-Man*. Both films end on a cautionary note; *The H-Man* implies more H-Men may be coming into the world, whereas *The Blob* ends with the frozen outer space organism dropped at the North Pole. Though neutralized, both menaces may return to terrorize humankind. (This literally happened when the American Blob returned in 1972's *Beware! The Blob* aka *Son of the Blob*.)

The titular creatures' origins, however, are quite different. The Blob hails from outer space, that great and mysterious "Other," perhaps speaking to America's 1950s paranoia and fear of the unknown. Many scholars have argued that alien invaders in 1950s Western science fiction movies represent the fear of Communist incursion, particularly from the Soviet Union. In this sense, unlike the humanoid aliens found in films such as 1951's *The Man from Planet X* and 1954's *Killers from Space*, the Blob is formless, faceless and mindless, existing only to survive, uncaring whether its food source is man or animal.

In contrast, the H-Man's origin is not "Other" at all. The creature is the result of humankind's nuclear testing, and specifically H-bomb testing. The film implies that such testing should stop, and indeed should have never started in the first place. Regardless of where a Westerner stood in relation to this issue, it has to be admitted that had a nuclear bomb been dropped on a major American metropolis during World War II— say, if the Nazis had atom-bombed New York City—our take on nuclear testing might have been different, or at the very least more nuanced.

Plot-wise, *The H-Man* involves the mysterious disappearance of Misaki (Hisaya Ito), a gangster involved in drug smuggling. The police assume that Misaki's girlfriend, nightclub singer Chikako (Yumi Shirakawa), knows where he is hiding; however, in reality, an H-man has "eaten" him off-screen. Chikako insists she doesn't know where Misaki is, but the police don't buy it. (One of the detectives boorishly attempts to get a peek at the attractive singer as she changes clothes in her apartment bedroom.)

Dr. Masada (Kenji Sahara), a young assistant professor researching the effects of nuclear fallout, posits to the police that a liquid mutant literally dissolved the missing gangster. Dr. Masada subsequently befriends Chikako, who confides that she herself has witnessed the melting of a human being (a nasty gangster who had brutally threatened her). Chikako and Dr. Masada are clearly becoming "an item," though in a chaste way.

Via flashback, in the Pacific Ocean we see the fate of a small Japanese ship blanketed with radioactive fallout from a nearby H-bomb test. The ship appears strangely deserted, but when another sea vessel's curious crew explores the boat, they discover an H-Man— or more precisely, *it* discovers *them*. The H-Men (there are more than one) kill three of the exploratory crew, while two others escape back to their vessel. In an eerie long shot, spectral H-Men glow on the ghost ship's deck.

Dr. Masada persuades skeptical Inspector Tominaga (Akihiko Hirata) that a liquid monster may be loose in Tokyo. For example, Masada shows the world-weary detective that a sufficiently high dose of radiation turns a normal frog into living slime.

Several H-Men attack the nightclub. One of the liquid monsters threatens a frightened Chikako, but she escapes unscathed. However, an H-Man does kill a gangster and a dancer. The criminal's bullets have no effect on the liquid mutant as it morphs into a spectral wraith and dissolves him. An H-Man also absorbs one of Tominaga's men. The inspector admits Masada was right. As Tominaga says, "We have to take care of H-Man before the drug gangs." No kidding.

Masada's elderly colleague Professor Maki (Koreya Senda) demonstrates that a frog mutated into an H-Frog can absorb a fellow frog (the latter literally bubbles away). This is the same process by which the humanoid liquid mutants "eat" non-mutated men and women. A detective says, "A liquid organism created by an H-bomb test with the mind of a human. I suppose you could call it an H-Man." The press runs with this catchy moniker, and newspaper headlines declare, "The H-Man Appears" and "H-Bomb Creates Another Kind of Human."

At a press conference, Professor Maki reveals that only fire or high-voltage electricity can stop the H-Men. The authorities marshal their forces with the intent to flood the sewers with gasoline and set them aflame, given that the H-Men hang out in the watery canals beneath the city. (They prefer to stay near liquid, hence the reason they often appear when it rains.)

A gangster kidnaps Chikako (by now clearly Masada's love interest) and forces her into the sewers while he recovers a cache of stolen heroin. An H-Man kills the gangster, and Masada rescues Chikako before the burning gasoline can reach her. H-Men try to escape from the blazing sewers, but flame throwers blacken them.

Professor Maki states that though the H-Men that had threatened Tokyo are now dead, other H-Men may come into the world. Ominous voiceover narration at the film's close states, "If this Earth were covered in radioactive fallout and humanity faced extinction, the next species to rule the Earth could very well be the H-Man." Not exactly a comforting bedtime story for little Susie and Johnny.

Richard Pusateri asserts that *The H-Man* is a form of film noir in his entertaining *H-Man* retrospective in *G-FAN* #34.[4] Indeed, *The H-Man* combines crime drama with science fiction horror and explores the seamier side of Tokyo nightlife circa 1958. Pusateri states, "*The H-Man* possesses an atmosphere of dread and fear.... There is the classic film noir sense of evil pervading every corner of every frame of every shot of every scene."[5]

However, the film lacks a femme fatale (which Pusateri acknowledges), though it does portray a dark world in which many of the police detectives are as crude and ethically challenged as the gangsters. Pusateri calls it a "gangster vs. 'bad cop' movie," noting its somewhat ambiguous morality. Also, unlike in film noir, the hero Dr. Masada is a genuine good guy bereft of a shady past, and while the heroine Chikako apparently has a checkered backstory, the implication is that she has inadvertently fallen in with gangsters due to her hapless romantic involvement with one of them.

Gloomy art direction enhances the film's dark atmosphere. Much of the movie occurs at night, some of it in the rain, and the darkly lit nightclub scenes practically swim in seediness. The female dancers, both scantily clad and boldly choreographed, evince an air of amoral misfortune. One can easily assume they wish they were dancing in a high-class musical instead of cavorting in a downbeat skin show.

The film's classic noir aspects initially overwhelm the movie's undeniable allusions to the nuclear threat, for the film's first two-thirds depict a sober crime drama in which the H-Man merely guest stars. This appears to be a peculiarly Japanese trait.[6] Although some 1950s American science fiction films did involve cops-and-robbers plots, such as 1955's *Creature with the Atom Brain*, the science fantasy-element was always front and center. But in a few Toho films, the crime drama element tended to dominate, most prominently in 1964's *Dogora, The Space Monster* (covered in Chapter 6) but also to some extent in 1960's *Secret of the Telegian* and 1962's *The Human Vapor*. These latter two films, along with *The H-Man*, comprise Toho's "human transformation" trio, all movies in which humans turn into homicidal mutants.

It isn't until the final third of *The H-Man* that the science-fantasy plot takes center stage, pushing the cops-and-robbers scenario into the wings. One wishes the entire movie had focused around the nuclear-created menace, but crime dramas were popular in Japan at the time, so Toho probably saw the melding of crime and science fiction as surefire box office dynamite.

Technically, *The H-Man* is one of Toho's best efforts from its much-heralded Golden Age. Visual effects director Eiji Tsuburaya's special effects shine. This time he is asked to conjure the illusion of the H-Men, both as blobs and as spectral wraiths. Of course, consummate professional that he was, the "Old Man" rallied to the task. (There is more on Tsuburaya's career in Chapter 6.)

To depict the melting of the monster's victims, Tsuburaya resorted to the simple but ingenious method of making life-sized balloons of characters called upon to melt. He then would let the air leak from the balloons while the deflation was filmed at high-speed.[7] This gave the appearance that a person was actually melting, aided by goo flowing from the imploding human. Perhaps the best example of this technique in the movie occurs when an H-Man assaults one of the police detectives in the nightclub. While tame today, this effect no doubt appeared startling to 1950s audiences.

When Columbia released the film on a double bill with *Womaneater* in 1959, it gave American kids the heebie-jeebies. In *Keep Watching the Skies!*, Bill Warren recounts that the movie terrified one of his cousins, who for years considered *The H-Man* "the scariest thing he ever saw."[8] To be sure, Toho aimed the film at adults, given its "mature audiences" storyline and racy (for the time) forays into nightclub entertainment. But the movie's English dubbing, while generally fair, probably put off most Western adult moviegoers, whereas North American kids no doubt waited impatiently through the "people plot" to get to the good stuff, i.e., the vivid H-Men attacks.

For years, the original Japanese-language version of *The H-Man* was unavailable to Western *kaiju eiga* (monster movie) aficionados. The Japanese version ran almost eight minutes longer than Columbia's Americanized version, and fans speculated that Columbia had trimmed certain effects shots. As a result, I was thrilled when, in 2009, Sony issued the original Japanese-language version of *The H-Man* with English subtitles to North America in its *Icons of Sci-Fi: Toho Collection* DVD set (the set also includes the Japanese language versions of 1959's *Battle in Outer Space* and 1961's *Mothra*, both also English subtitled and presented in anamorphic widescreen).

However, when the Japanese-language version of *The H-Man* reaches the point during which an H-Man attacks the nightclub dancer, my anticipation crumpled into disappointment. In the Japanese-language version, the film merely freeze-frames the stripper as green cartoon goo covers her. Not only was the scene not shocking, it was ineffective even by 1950s special effects standards. In this case, the result wasn't worth the wait, but this is the film's only disappointing visual effect.

More problematic is the movie's soundtrack. Behind the opening credits, we hear a bizarrely inappropriate military march. Masaru Sato, a frequent composer for Akira Kurosawa's films, scored *The H-Man*, and fortunately, following the off-putting opening march, the music accentuates the atmospheric goings-on, especially the horrific sequences. In addition, towards the end when flame throwers are burning the H-Men, we hear menacing low strings reminiscent of the sinister cello strains heard in 1957's *Quatermass II*. While the majority of Sato's *H-Man* score is good, one can't help but wonder what Akira Ifukube might have done with the film.

Regarding the notion of the H-Men being conscious and aware rather than mindless, Professor Maki hypothesizes that this is why the H-Men may have migrated to Tokyo. As he says, "If any of the victims' psyches are preserved, it's very possible that they tried to come to Tokyo." Such an idea is troubling. Does this mean the H-Men felt pain as the flame throwers fried them? Can they also feel sadness? Anger? Grief? Horror at what they have become? Do they regret having to absorb human beings, much as some vampires regret sucking the lifeblood from their victims?

Japanese film scholar Stuart Galbraith IV speculates that perhaps the humans eaten by the H-Men might themselves become H-Mutants.[9] If they do, then Misaki might have become an H-Man with his memories of and love for Chikako intact. Perhaps in liquid form, Misaki might have been watching over Chikako, thus killing the gangster in the sewers but leaving Chikako unscathed out of his continuing love for her. However, he would also no doubt consider the horror of what he had become, yet might not realize his state is due to Western H-bomb testing.

As for H-bomb fallout turning humans into H-Men, why doesn't this happen to all people exposed to H-bomb fallout? Apparently, only a sufficiently high dosage of radiation causes the transformation into one of the blob creatures. Professor Maki notes that the six men on the ship's deck received a huge dose of radiation, and thus morphed into H-Men, consuming their fellows quartered below deck. Also, the two sailors who investigated the ghost ship and survived now suffer from radiation sickness, yet neither turned into an H-Man, presumably because they didn't receive a high enough dosage.

The film also shows what happens when a non-human receives a high dosage of radiation, i.e., the frog turned into an H-Frog. This lab transformation implies that H-bomb radiation of sufficient magnitude can turn any animal into an H-Animal. Does this mean there were H-Fish? Or that had a feline been on the irradiated ship's deck, it would have become an H-Cat? Might there also be H-Dogs, H-Dolphins and H-Whales?

The film largely takes place at night, which is when the H-Men attack. The literally dark tone suits the film's subject—i.e., the dangers of H-bomb testing. Just as the H-Men can seemingly appear anywhere at any time, the nuclear threat can break out anywhere at any time.

The association of the H-Men with rain is interesting. One can't help but think of the Ray Bradbury short story "There Will Come Soft Rains" and Bob Dylan's "A Hard Rain's Gonna Fall." There is also the black rain that fell after the atom bombing of Hiroshima. Indeed, for the Japanese, post-nuclear testing rain could often mean environmental contamination. As Allen A. Debus notes in his well-researched article on the *Lucky Dragon No. 5* incident, "Rain falling over Osaka on May 17 [1954] registered 24,000 counts per minute!"[10] Indeed, both the rain and snow contained appreciable amounts of radiation.

The H-Man implies that in the '50s, the effects of radiation were mysterious and only dimly understood. Tweaking a Biblical adage, humankind was looking through a glass darkly. For example, scientists and governments knew that radiation exposure could cause minor mutations in offspring, that parents exposed to radiation might beget children with birth defects. But what might the long-term effects of radiation be, not only on the environment, but also on men and women?

True, in 1958, science knew that radiation did not create gooey human mutations that slithered through the Tokyo sewers. Quite the contrary, sufficiently high radiation killed you or gave you radiation sickness. Even if you lived after high exposure, or experienced a low enough exposure so as not to feel any immediate effects, cancer could later form in your body.

Instead, *The H-Man* operated in a kind of "code language" for the Japanese. In the film, radiation turns you into something horrible, something inhuman, something that will never be the same again. Radiation dehumanizes you, and once you've fallen under its influence, you can never be cleansed; a threshold exists from which there is no return to normalcy. This could have been a conscious or unconscious reference to the *hibakusha*,

The Japanese fishing trawler *Lucky Dragon No. 5* un-luckily received fallout from the March 1, 1954, Operation Bravo H-bomb test. (The entire crew got sick, and the radio operator died.) *The H-Man* alludes to this incident.

This mushroom cloud arose from the March 1, 1954, Operation Bravo H-bomb test. The explosion was the equivalent of 1000 Hiroshima A-bombs.

the Japanese survivors of the A-bombings of Hiroshima and Nagasaki. Certainly, these unfortunates felt a sense of contamination, of otherness.[11]

The *H-Man*'s irradiated sea vessel is a clear stand-in for the real life *Lucky Dragon No. 5*. This Japanese fishing boat was close enough to the Operation Bravo Bikini Atoll H-bomb test on March 1, 1954, to sustain substantial fallout from the blast; the crew became ill, and one later died. The vessel may or may not have been outside the test's danger zone, but the H-bomb explosion was far larger than the Americans had expected.

In Japan, many regarded this incident as a third nuclear attack on the island nation. In all fairness, the American government hadn't intended to afflict Japanese sailors with fallout, whereas the Hiroshima and Nagasaki bombings were intentional. Still, the U.S. refused to divulge the specifics of the Bikini Atoll H-bomb test to Japanese authorities, hence hampering the island nation's medical community from adequately treating the *Lucky Dragon*'s ailing sailors. Apparently, this was for security reasons, America fearing that revealing these secrets to Japanese doctors would tip off the Soviet Union about the H-bomb edge the U.S. believed it had over Russia. But at what point does national security trump humanitarianism to a 1950s ally like Japan? After all, Communists used the *Lucky Dragon* incident and America's response to it as proof that the U.S. cared little for Japan or its people and courted its favor for military purposes only.[12] To complicate matters, American H-bomb tests had irradiated much of Japan's tuna, which led to the Japanese authorities destroying it "by the ton."[13]

H-bombs were a major step above the previous atomic bombs. For example, the Operation Bravo blast was more powerful than a thousand Hiroshima-sized A-bombs. And the destructive capacity of the fusion weapon knew almost no limits. Perhaps this is why Toho did not produce a movie called *The A-Man* but instead one called *The H-Man*, for the advent of the H-bomb threatened the possible annihilation of civilization, or at least the deaths of millions if not billions in the face of a global thermonuclear war. Accordingly, the H-Men symbolized this limitless threat to humankind, of which there appeared no end. After all, just as the threat of the H-Men continues past the film's finale, the threat of H-bomb testing likewise continued past 1954. The narration at the end implies that we are all fated either to become H-People or to be consumed by them. What could be more fatalistic? Just as death knows no "do-overs," neither does nuclear testing.

Yet *The H-Man* remains fantasy. Indeed, the film is essentially two-faced, one side smiling and enticing audiences to enjoy the vivid delights of color-rich science fiction, the other side scowling and warning viewers to beware the all-too-real threat clicking away in Japan's Pacific backyard.

Speaking of the film's vibrant color, the opening scene of the H-bomb blast is scenic, just as the movie's blue-green H-wraiths are likewise picturesque. Beauty in the H-bomb? Why not? There is beauty in many of nature's dangers. A killer whale is beautiful until it bites your arm off; a Bengal tiger is lovely until it disembowels you; even Toho's Mothra is gorgeous until her winds whip you through a storefront window. As a young child, I witnessed nature's beauty in twin tornadoes about two to three miles from where I was standing; they appeared as breathtaking blue cones. Dangerous, yes, but also undeniably striking.

The literal translation of the Japanese title for *The H-Man* is *The Beauty and The Liquid People*. No doubt the beauty in question refers to the nightclub singer Chikako and perhaps the nightclub dancers. But it could also be an allusion to the film's menace, albeit unintentionally, or at least unconsciously.

The movie never mentions the United States, which on one level is not surprising, despite the fact that the U.S. was conducting the H-bomb tests in question. However, when the H-Man becomes front page news, Japan appears to face the nuclear-spawned menace alone, even though Professor Maki has noted that the liquid creatures could potentially threaten the world. Surprisingly, not even the United Nations helps. Given *H-Man* director Ishiro Honda's penchant for championing the U.N., and the fact that other nations joined Japan to defeat the extraterrestrial invaders in the previous year's *The Mysterians*, the international organization's absence in *The H-Man* baffles. Perhaps this indicates that Honda saw Japan as facing the nuclear threat (which actually existed) without assistance, yet when it came to fending off alien aggressors (which were fantasy creations), Honda could envision other countries joining the fight (as happened in 1959's *Battle in Outer Space*).

Regarding Toho's science fantasy takes on the nuclear threat, *The H-Man* is probably second only to *Godzilla* in terms of anti-nuke sentiments. *Godzilla* represents the large scale, macro effects of an H-bomb going off—Godzilla is what happens to the world crumbling around you in the wake of a nuclear holocaust. But *The H-Man* represents the small scale, micro effects—in other words, what personally happens to *you*.

The Americanization

As previously mentioned, *The H-Man*'s Americanization cut out eight minutes from the Japanese version, but basically left the movie intact. The English dubbing runs hot and cold, but the nuclear threat message comes across loud and clear. This may in part be because the film doesn't deal with large-scale carnage as did *Godzilla*; also, the film makes no allusions to World War II or to Hiroshima or Nagasaki. However, just as in *Godzilla*, there *is* a strong allusion to the *Lucky Dragon No. 5* incident in *The H-Man*, but this probably went over most American audiences' heads, especially the pre-adolescent and young adolescent crowd.

Frankenstein Conquers the World (Toho; Japanese release: 1965; American release by AIP: 1966)

Credits: Directed by Ishiro Honda; Screenplay by Kaoru Mabuchi (a.k.a. Takeshi Kimura); Written from a synopsis by Jerry Sohl; Based on a Story by Reuben Bercovitch; Produced by Tomoyuki Tanaka; Executive Producers: Henry G. Saperstein and Reuben Bercovitch; Photography: Hajime Koizumi; Music: Akira Ifukube; Editor: Ryohei Fujii; Art Director: Takeo Kita; Makeup: Rika Konna; Casting Assistant: Ai Maeda; Sound Effects: Sadamasa Nishimoto; Sound Mixer: Hisashi Shimonaga; Assistant Director: Koji Kajita; Special Effects Director: Eiji Tsuburaya; Special Effects Photography: Sadamasa Arikawa and Motoyoshi Tomioka; Special Effects Lighting: Kuichiro Kishida; Special Effects Production Design: Akira Watanabe; Special Effects Composition: Hiroshi Koyama; Optical Photography: Yukio Manoda and Yoshiyuki Tokumasa.

Cast: Nick Adams (Dr. James Bowen); Tadao Takashima (Dr. Kenichiro Kawaji); Kumi Mizuno (Dr. Sueko Togami); Yoshio Tsuchiya (Lt. Gawai); Koji Furuhata (Frankenstein Giant); Jun Tazaki (Okayama Police Chief Hideo Nishi); Susumu Fujita (Osaka Police Official A); Takashi Shimura (Hiroshima Doctor Examining Frankenstein's Heart); Nobuo Nakamura (Dr. Suga); Kenji Sahara (Okayama Police Officer Tadokoro/Submarine Crewman); Hisaya Ito (Osaka Police Official B); Yoshifimu Tajima (Submarine Captain Murata); Kozo Nomura (Reporter A); Haruya Kato (Tokyo TV Director); Ikio Sawamura (Elderly Man); Yoshio Kosugi (Defense Commander A); Noriaki Inoue (Young Man at Shirane Hostel); Keiko Sawai (Tazuko Toi); Noriko Takahashi (Young Woman at Shirane Hostel); Peter Mann (Dr. Reisendorf); Ren Yamamoto (Motoki); Yutaka Sada (Hospital Administrator); Kenzo Tabu (Newspaper Reporter); Shigeki Ishida (University Professor); Haruo Nakajima (Baragon); Yutaka Nakayama (TV Lighting Man A); Senkichi Omura (TV Lighting Man B/Oil Field Worker); Nadao Kirino (Police Inspector Okamoto); Yashiko Saijo (TV Camera Operator); Shin Otomo (Police Inspector Sugiyama); Sohichi Hirose (Shimizu Tunnel Worker); Junichiro Mukai (Fishing Village Police Officer); Toshihiko Furata (Village Farmer); Mitsuo Tsuda (Shimizu Tunnel Engineer); Hirohito Kimura (Reporter); Hideo Shibuya (Weekly Magazine Reporter); Yoshiko Miyata (Woman at Himeji Castle); Tadashi Okabe (Reporter B); Masaaki Tachibana (Reporter C); Rinsaku Ogata (Defense Commander B); Sumio Nakao (Frankenstein as Child); Kazuo Kumakura (Voice of Dr. Reisendorf in Japanese version); Goro Naya (Voice of Dr. Bowen in Japanese version).

Japanese version: A Toho Co. Ltd./Henry G. Saperstein Enterprises Production; color; TohoScope; 95 minutes: released on August 8, 1965. Japanese title: *Furankenshutain Tai Chitei Kaiju Baragon* (translation: *Frankenstein vs. Subterranean Monster Baragon*).

American version: Presented by James H. Nicholson and Samuel Z. Arkoff; color; scope; 87 minutes; released on July 8, 1966. Co-billed with *Tarzan and the Valley of Gold*. Originally announced as *Frankenstein vs. the Giant Devilfish*. The extensive cover story on the film in *Famous Monsters of Filmland* #39 (1966) included two photos of Frankenstein battling the giant devilfish. Available on DVD in both American-dubbed and English-subtitled versions.

Toho had already adapted King Kong into its kaiju universe (1962's *King Kong vs. Godzilla*) so perhaps it's not surprising that they chose to import an even more famous Western monster: Frankenstein. What is surprising, however, is that Toho blended the Frankenstein myth with its continuing nuclear threat commentary.

(A note for purists: Yes, we all know that Frankenstein is the name of the monster's creator, not the creation itself, but *Frankenstein Conquers the World* refers to the colossal creature in its film as Frankenstein, so I will do the same.)

So how does *Frankenstein Conquers the World* fit within the parameters of being a humanoid mutant wrought by the nuclear threat? In one of two ways: (1) After exposure to the 1945 A-bombing of Hiroshima, Frankenstein's living heart grew into a complete human being or (2) amidst the Hiroshima rubble, a waif devoured Frankenstein's living but irradiated heart. Either origin classifies the Japanese Frankenstein as a creation of the nuclear threat as embodied in America's A-bomb obliteration of Hiroshima.

Titled *Frankenstein vs. Subterranean Monster Baragon* in Japan, the film opens in 1945, as a Japanese submarine is transporting Frankenstein's living heart from Germany to Hiroshima. In response to a curious naval officer, a Japanese scientist (Takashi Shimura) explains that Frankenstein's heart "will never die" and that it can be used "to make soldiers who will never die from getting shot…. Eighty to ninety percent of the soldiers who die in wars could be saved." However, the Hiroshima hospital about to conduct research on Frankenstein's heart explodes in a nuclear blast, for it is August 6, 1945.

The film jumps to 15 years later, when American Dr. James Bowen (Nick Adams) is conducting research at a Hiroshima radio therapeutics center. Working with Dr. Sueko Togami (Kumi Mizuno) and Dr. Kenichiro Kawaji (Tadao Takashima), Dr. Bowen is conducting research to help the survivors of

Nick Adams was not ashamed to star in "mere" monster movies such as *Frankenstein Conquers the World* and *Invasion of Astro-Monster* (both 1965). A veteran of many TV shows and movies, he received an Academy Award nomination (Best Supporting Actor) for 1963's *Twilight of Honor*.

the 1945 Hiroshima bombing, many of whom are dying due to radiation-caused ailments.

He and Dr. Togami discover a strange, homeless adolescent boy and bring him to their facility. Dr. Bowen wonders why the boy isn't suffering from radiation poisoning but instead seems to be immune to radiation. When the boy grows into a giant, Dr. Bowen has him confined in an iron-barred cell. The scientists discover that the boy may be Frankenstein. One way to verify this theory is to cut off one of his arms or legs and see if it grows back. This suggestion horrifies Dr. Togami, who has developed a maternal sympathy for the A-bomb survivor.

Now three times bigger than a man, the boy-giant escapes from his cell, causes brief panic and flees into the countryside. In pulling loose from a tight chain, his hand is severed, and given that the (none-too-convincing) hand is still alive, the scientists realize that the boy really is Frankenstein. The authorities blame Frankenstein for local property damage, animal slaughter and human fatalities. But Baragon, a prehistoric monster, is actually responsible for the death and destruction.

Dr. Bowen, Dr. Togami, and Dr. Kawaji search for Frankenstein in the woods. Dr. Kawaji plans to blind and subdue the pitiable creature so that some of it will be left for his research after the army blows the A-bomb giant to bits. Baragon appears and threatens Dr. Togami, but it is quickly confronted by Frankenstein. After a long and arduous battle, Frankenstein kills Baragon.

Next, in the original theatrical version both in Japan and in the United States, an earthquake fissure swallows the arm-waving Frankenstein and the lifeless Baragon. However, Toho shot additional footage showing Frankenstein battling a giant octopus, hence the title *Frankenstein vs. the Giant Devilfish* that was reported in *Famous Monsters of Filmland* #39 in 1966. Two stills in the magazine showed Frankenstein battling the octopus, but by the time AIP released the movie to North America in the summer of 1966 as *Frankenstein Conquers the World*, all footage of Frankenstein's battle with the cephalopod had fallen to the cutting room floor.

Frankenstein's bout with the eight-armed creature was included on a Japanese laserdisc, and later on DVD. It is likewise included on the Media Blasters two–DVD set available in North America. Although the special effects in the

Nick Adams, left, as Private Mick Hellar in the "Bridgehead" episode of ABC-TV's *Combat!* (September 24, 1963), one of the many characters he played during his brief career. On the right is the series' star Vic Morrow.

sequence look fine—the octopus marionette is well-orchestrated and the battle energetic—this finale comes out of left field. Just after Frankenstein has tossed Baragon off a cliff, the giant octopus appears slithering over a hill no less! No mention has been made of this creature in the movie, and having it suddenly pop up out of nowhere is jarring, to say the least.

Though the Media Blasters DVD set claims to include the version of *Frankenstein Conquers the World* that AIP released to the U.S. in 1966, it actually cuts footage from the latter showing Frankenstein threatening a downed policeman and destroying two police cars. These scenes were cut from the Japanese version to make the monster more sympathetic, but were left in the AIP-released American version in 1966 to make Frankenstein seem more menacing, and were likewise intact in American 16mm TV editions of the movie. Now they have been unceremoniously exiled to the DVD's "Deleted Scenes."

Another interesting aspect of *Frankenstein Conquers the World* is its story genesis. In a Shinichi Sekizawa screenplay dated February 20, 1963, titled *Frankenstein vs. the Human Vapor*, the mutant from 1962's *The Human Vapor* was to have enlisted Frankenstein's help to revive his dead lady love.[14] Toho scrapped this idea in favor of pitting Godzilla against the Frankenstein Monster, hence screenwriter Kaoru Mabuchi turned in a screenplay for *Frankenstein vs. Godzilla* on July 3, 1964.[15] However, Toho chose Mothra as Godzilla's next monster foe in *Mothra vs. Godzilla* (a.k.a. *Godzilla vs. the Thing*, covered in Chapter 6). A new monster, Baragon, became the king-sized Frankenstein's opponent, and hence *Frankenstein vs. Subterranean Monster Baragon* was born.

Dr. Bowen proclaims the movie's Far Eastern Frankenstein is Caucasian, but the boy-monster is clearly Asian in appearance. (Perhaps Dr. Bowen needed to see a good optometrist.) Years earlier, driven by hunger, did the boy find Frankenstein's heart in the Hiroshima rubble and eat it? Or did the Monster's heart, bathed in A-bomb radiation, grow into a complete man? Richard Pusateri and J.D. Lees argue for the former, noting that Frankenstein's severed hand died due to lack of protein, and if this was so, then how could the Monster's heart have grown at all without a protein nutrient solution?[16]

Frankenstein Conquers the World works well as a Grade-B monster vs. monster epic. Akira Ifukube's outstanding music score matches the dynamics of each scene and sequence; for example, the quietly moody opening strains perfectly fit the otherwise almost completely silent sequence in the German lab. Likewise, his bombastic themes match the gigantic nature of Frankenstein as well as the man-monster's extended bout with Baragon.

Speaking of the latter, the movie features several good battle scenes between Frankenstein and Baragon; typical is a long shot of troops in the foreground, Frankenstein tangling with Baragon in the mid-ground, and a spectacular forest fire raging in the background, casting a crimson radiance upon the colossal combatants. Many of the effects work well, though some do not, even by 1965 standards. Special effects director Eiji Tsuburaya made some questionable choices, such as featuring an unconvincing miniature horse. Tsuburaya could have simply used a matte shot of a real horse, and when asked why he included a puppet horse instead, he said, "Because using a model horse was more fun!"[17]

Director Ishiro Honda, who took the film more seriously, said, "Frankenstein is not a monster.... This production was not simply a monster movie but a tragic story of science gone wrong."[18] Honda said he lost interest when Baragon shows up, preferring to demonstrate how Frankenstein was an outsider, and how difficult it would be for a giant man to adjust to our world.

Despite its monster-heavy story, *Frankenstein Conquers the World* is the only Toho *kaiju eiga* (monster movie) that directly took on the A-bombing of Hiroshima. In the opening scenes, we see an atomic fireball consume the city like a wildfire consuming a tumbleweed.[19] However, the movie spares us from the sight of Hiroshima's aftermath wreckage and seared corpses. Instead, the film leaps 15 years later into 1960.

But while we don't see ugly burn scars and the other physical ravages left in the wake of the Hiroshima bombing, the film does show us an American, Dr. Bowen, striving to help the victims of the bombing his country conducted. Motivated by guilt, Bowen clearly feels compassion for the victims of radiation poisoning, as well as the other deprivations and horrors the A-bombing of Hiroshima visited upon this metropolis. For example, the movie spotlights an orphaned adolescent girl whom we quickly understand is perishing due to radiation poisoning. From her hospital bed, she gives Dr. Bowen a pillow she has embroidered. When Dr. Bowen and his associates Dr. Tomagi and Dr. Kawaji are discussing the girl's case a short time later, Dr. Kawaji spots the pillow and says, "Did she die?"

Replies Dr. Tomagi, "It's worse than death." This observation must have stung Dr. Bowen, just as it would any American with a conscience.

Dr. Kawaji says, "Her parents were also killed by the A-bomb, weren't they?"

Dr. Bowen's two associates continue this line of discussion, to which Bowen finally says, "The story of Hiroshima is too tragic." This is like a confession for him, and perhaps by extension for all Americans. But he adds, "We must work to turn tragedy into eternal peace and happiness in the future." American optimism in the face of Japanese reality.

The movie could have vilified Dr. Bowen, thereby denigrating the United States for its controversial World War II bombings of Hiroshima and Nagasaki. Instead, the movie clearly offers an olive branch to Americans, just as it implies Japanese sorrow for its own country's wartime violence. The convivial professional and personal relationship between Dr. Bowen and Dr. Tomagi mirrors the growing friendship between each character's respective nation. When possible, director Honda championed international cooperation in his movies, so this theme would have harmonized with his own humanistic leanings.

The character of Frankenstein fancifully personifies the nuclear threat, but the latter is also shown to be all too real in the cases of the Hiroshima hospital's radiation poisoned patients. The same two-faced approach used in *The H-Man* prevails in this Japanese Frankenstein fable—the smiling side beckoning viewers to watch the big show, the frowning side daring viewers to behold unflinching reality.

Just as Frankenstein keeps growing in the film, so too did the nuclear threat in 1960s Japan. Caught between the superpowers, Japan faced the very real possibility of nuclear extermination, for which the atom bombings of Hiroshima and Nagasaki might have been a grim dress rehearsal. And just like the giant Frankenstein in the movie, the nuclear threat cannot be tamed, or "cured." Indeed, it is immortal, just as the knowledge that split the atom is immortal: According to Japanese science fiction cinema of the 1950s and 1960s, you can't put the atomic genie back into the lead-lined bottle.

Just as Frankenstein in this *kaiju eiga* adaptation represents science gone wrong, the same could be said for the creation of the nuclear weapon. Could any good come from a creature assembled from the parts of dead bodies, and could any good come from the splitting of the atom? Interestingly, the movie tentatively answers "Yes" to both queries.

102 • PART I: MUTANTS

A U.S. Air Force photograph of the mushroom cloud that billowed 20,000 feet above Hiroshima on August 6, 1945.

At the film's beginning in 1945, the Japanese scientist says that by discovering the secrets of Frankenstein's undying heart, medical science could quickly heal soldiers of what should be fatal injuries. An act of human hubris—the bringing to life of a man made of patchwork human parts—could perhaps ultimately result in restorative medicine.

Likewise, in 1960, Dr. Bowen notes that the tragedy of Hiroshima could lead to

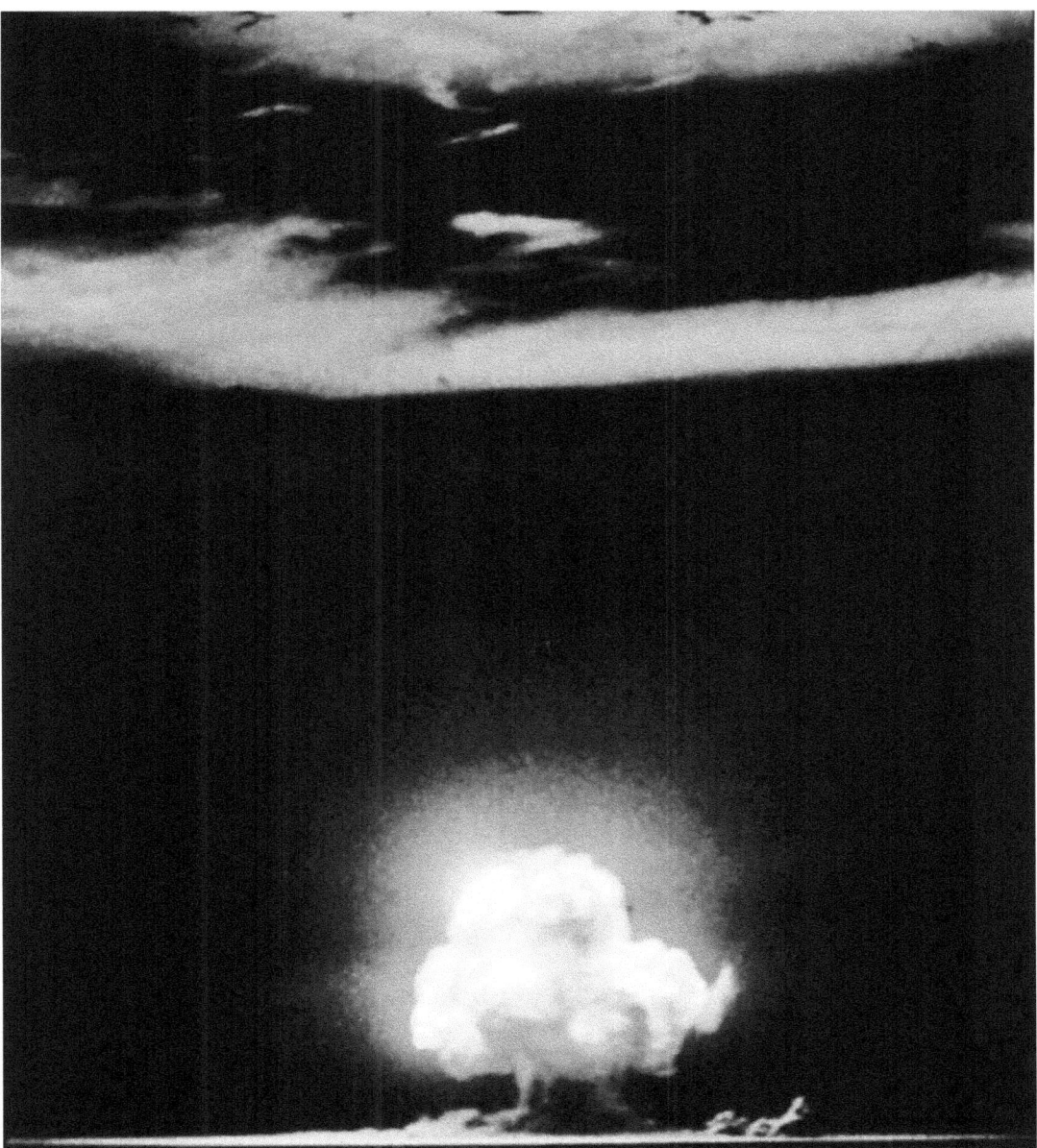

The world's first atomic bomb explodes in Alamogordo, New Mexico, on July 16, 1945, ushering in the atomic age. In the '50s, movies reflected this new nuclear era in films featuring human mutants.

breakthroughs in treating the victims of radiation poisoning. The operative word here is "could." In their research, Dr. Bowen and his associates appear to be at an impasse. However, with the introduction of Frankenstein in their midst, a boy-monster who not only can withstand a high dosage of radiation but actually thrive on it, Bowen's hope for radiation treatment breakthroughs is revived. But such hopes are dashed when the Frankenstein giant escapes and, blamed for Baragon's rural atrocities, is marked for execution by Japan's military.

This fanciful storyline somewhat parallels reality. While Japan maintained its fear of nuclear weapons, it nevertheless embraced nuclear power plants to provide its vast utility needs. This certainly seems to be a peaceful use of the atom, though its opponents claimed such technology was only a time bomb waiting to go off. Following the destructive tsunami that hit Japan in 2011, the subsequent catastrophe at the Fukushima nuclear power plant seems to bear out such predictions.[20]

The Americanization

At 87 minutes, the American version of *Frankenstein Conquers the World* is eight minutes shorter than the Japanese version. As mentioned previously, the American version includes scenes of Frankenstein behaving more violently—trashing a cop car, snarling at a downed police officer—than in the Japanese version. But the gist of the AIP-released version remained the same as the Japanese original.

Also, while the film's story championed friendship between Japan and America, the film's casting reflected this amity in reality. Nick Adams, who plays Dr. Bowen, was a hit on the set of *Frankenstein Conquers the World* and also the same year's *Invasion of Astro-Monster* (a.k.a. *Monster Zero*). He was a talented actor who had appeared in a number of American movies and TV shows, including the TV series *The Rebel* (1959–1961). Unashamed to be starring in "mere" monster movies, in 1965 Adams wrote an op-ed called "A Kind Word for Those Monster Movies" for the *Los Angeles Times*. His dynamic qualities may be somewhat understated in *Frankenstein Conquers the World*, but his enthusiasm for his craft, and the film, shines through.

Adams died under mysterious circumstances on February 7, 1968. His death was deemed a suicide due to drug overdose; however, some believe he may have been murdered. In addition to *Frankenstein Conquers the World* and *Invasion of Astro-Monster*, his other genre movies include 1965's *Die, Monster, Die!* and 1968's *Mission Mars*. He also appeared on TV's *Voyage to the Bottom of the Sea* in the 1964 episode "Turn Back the Clock" and on the original *Outer Limits* in the 1964 episode "Fun and Games."

Of Gelatin and Giants

In Japanese science fiction movies of the 1950s and 1960s, it's interesting that the nuclear threat only directly resulted in two humanoid mutations. H-bomb fallout created the slime monsters of *The H-Man*, radioactive creatures who in their liquid form bear no resemblance to human beings at all. In their mysterious blue-green wraith form, they are humanoid, but display no discernible eyes, nose or mouth. And their means of sustenance, absorbing men and women who subsequently melt, is revoltingly cannibalistic, as well as inhuman.

Frankenstein Conquers the World's A-bomb giant is clearly human, though his face becomes more monstrous as he grows. Unlike the H-Men, Frankenstein does not consume humans, though he does often seem ravenous, perhaps in part due to almost starving to death in the Hiroshima ruins, and in part because his rapidly growing body demands constant food for metabolic fuel.

In the previous two chapters, we have seen that giant atomic humans were not unusual in the States, i.e., 1957's *The Amazing Colossal Man* who returned for 1958's *War of the Colossal Beast*; 1957's *The Cyclops*; and 1958's *Attack of the 50 Foot Woman*. Another 1950s American giant, non-atomic this time, also appeared in Columbia's *The 30 Foot Bride of Candy Rock*, a 1959 spoof of 1958's *Attack of the 50 Foot Woman*.

No Hollywood mutants became unrecognizable blob monsters *à la The H-Man*. But when you X-ray beneath the surface, you see that American and Japanese humanoid mutant movies act on different sets of internal assumptions. The next chapter shines the spotlight on these culturally embedded distinctions.

4. Marty vs. the H-Man

1958

If *Day the World Ended*'s Marty the Mutant confronted the H-Man, who would win? Marty might sneer and claw at the latter's green goop, but the H-Man would simply envelope the asphalt-skinned mutant. In no time, Marty would implode, his body dropping to the ground as his insides gushed into the grass.

End of battle.

The H-Man would live on long after Marty had morphed into Jell-O, and this remains the key difference between Japanese and American humanoid mutants: American mutants were vulnerable and knew quick ends, but Japanese mutants, though temporarily defeated, remained a threat. This is even true for the A-bomb giant of *Frankenstein Conquers the World*. At the end of the movie after it appears Frankenstein has been vanquished, Dr. Togami asks, "Did Frankenstein die?" To which Dr. Kawaji responds, "No, Frankenstein will never die." And in the eyes of Japan, neither would the nuclear threat.

American and Japanese humanoid mutant movies enjoy similarities, but they also sport significant differences in terms of national identity, radiation perspective, and implicit worldview. We will examine each of these, followed by more specific comparisons of man-sized and king-sized mutants on both sides of the Pacific.

National Identity

Following World War II, America became a superpower, supplanting European nations as the major Western democracy. The U.S. had enjoyed victory over its World War II enemies, including Japan. In the 1950s, America's only serious atomic competition came from the Soviet Union, a fact that gave the U.S. government a greater urgency to stay ahead in nuclear arms research and testing.

On the other hand, the Land of the Rising Sun had lost the Pacific War to the Americans; while the U.S. basked in immediate postwar ascendancy, Japan collectively hung its head. Many of the island nation's cities—Tokyo among them—lay in charred ruins. And the atom bombings of Hiroshima and Nagasaki had not only shocked the Japanese and the world, but had ushered in the nuclear age with its attendant atomic anxieties.

American humanoid mutant films championed American supremacy; all were at least implicitly patriotic. In fact, the films rarely criticize American nuclear testing when

A three-eyed mutant (Paul Blaisdell inside his own monster suit) kneels over the unconscious Louise (Lori Nelson) in *Day the World Ended* (American Releasing Corporation, 1955).

it would have been easy to do so. For example, in *Day the World Ended*, Paul Birch tells Richard Denning that Operation Bravo had resulted in three animal mutations, a fact suppressed by the American government. Upon hearing this, Denning is neither shocked nor outraged; he doesn't say, "Good Lord, I can't believe the government withheld that information from the public!" Instead, he accepts such national secrecy matter-of-factly, as though the government *should* suppress controversial sociopolitical facts from the populace at large.

A real-life case of governmental cover-up concerned the anxiety felt by 1950s' Americans who lived "downwind" from domestic nuclear test sites. The Atomic Energy Commission (AEC) issued PR assurances to Nevada civilians that nearby nuclear testing was safe, though in reality, some of the AEC's own scientists contested this sweeping conclusion. The media even inadvertently colluded with the government on the issue of nuclear test fallout. For example, after a 1953 nuclear explosion in Nevada, CBS's Walter Cronkite—often hailed as "the most trusted man in America"—assured TV viewers that dust carried on the wind from the explosion was harmless.[1]

Concerning human guinea pigs, in *The Amazing Colossal Man*, the troops wait in trenches uncomfortably close to an intentional nuclear explosion, just as real American troops did throughout the 1950s as part of Operation Desert Rock. Does *Colossal Man*

The Colossal Beast (Dean Parkin) empties a bread truck for his daily rations in *War of the Colossal Beast* **(AIP, 1958).**

criticize the government for placing American soldiers in harm's way? Not directly. But movie scholar Kim Newman argues that "the independents [such as AIP, *Colossal Man*'s distributor] are actively anti-military."[2] Colonel Glenn Manning suffers severe psychological as well as physiological distress due to nuclear testing, leading both to insanity and death. Meanwhile, real-life troops ordered to march over radioactive hot zones suffered from lingering atomic anxiety, and some of them "quietly began to seek financial compensation for all sorts of maladies."[3]

However, *Colossal Man* was the exception (even for AIP), not the rule, in terms of implicit criticism of the military; as I mentioned, *Day the World Ended* endorsed government secrecy. However, it can't be denied that AIP's humanoid mutant movies *Terror from the Year 5000*, *Beyond the Time Barrier* and *The Time Travelers* paint a bleak picture of where all our nuclear testing and research may be taking us, with their mutants the inevitable result of the nuclear threat's end game.

Clearly, many in the military considered being a nuclear test guinea pig to be necessary and patriotic. On July 9, 1957, five military officer volunteers stood directly below a two-kiloton nuclear air burst 18,500 feet above their heads.[4] Instead of facing this event gravely, the officers exhibited a sense of humor by planting a sign next to them reading, "Ground Zero, Population 5." The men seem in high spirits both during and after the blast.[5]

How did Japan view American nuclear testing, as well as the nuclear threat per se? You won't find any direct answers in either of Japan's humanoid mutant movies, but *The H-Man* bristles with implicit criticism. As mentioned in the previous chapter, *H-Man*'s irradiated sea vessel is a clear stand-in for the *Lucky Dragon No. 5*. The film's Dr. Maki proclaims that the H-Men not only endanger Japan, but perhaps the entire world.

However, Dr. Maki never explicitly states that H-bomb testing in the Pacific should be stopped—and he also never mentions the United States. Of course, the American occupation of postwar Japan was still comparatively fresh in Japanese memory, and you figure Toho, a major Japanese company, did not want to antagonize America, now an ally. So while Dr. Maki tells the Rising Sun authorities that fire and electricity will kill the H-Men, he fails to address the core issue that brought the mutants into existence in the first place: America's nuclear testing.

Even *Frankenstein Conquers the World*, though released seven years later, doesn't explicitly criticize the U.S. for the atom bombings of Hiroshima and Nagasaki. True, in the film Dr. Bowen represents the U.S., but he puts a good face on the States. He is compassionate and implicitly guilt-ridden that his country atom-bombed Hiroshima and Nagasaki. One could argue that implicit criticism of the bombings is represented by the radiation-afflicted victims of Hiroshima in the hospital, such as the young girl dying from radiation poisoning, and also by the boy-monster Frankenstein, who tragically becomes a giant unable to live in our world. But again, no one explicitly mentions or criticizes America for the bombings.

Radiation Perspective

Did Americans in the '50s fear radiation? Yes, and the public's atomic age anxiety found expression in humanoid mutant movies. After all, among other monsters, radiation produced amazing colossal humans, sun demons and multi-eyed savages. Were these films an indictment of the then new nuclear age? Only partially.

For in each movie, the heroes have neutralized the threat at movie's end, even if this meant the mutant's death. The mutants in American films came into being largely through the *unintentional misuse* of radiation. If Colonel Glenn Manning had stayed in the trench, he wouldn't have become a brain-addled 60-foot giant. As another example, a nuclear accident turns Dr. Gil McKenna into *The Hideous Sun Demon*. Indeed, two American films—*Ma and Pa Kettle Back on the Farm* and *The Atomic Kid*—treat their radiation-created mutants as objects of breezy humor. As pointed out in Chapter 1, radiation turned out to be a source of spiritual awakening for *The Incredible Shrinking Man*'s Scott Carey. In addition, though the majority of the films featured a monstrous mutant or mutants, the latter's demise signaled the end of the menace—the nuclear threat had borne only temporary results resolved by the film's conclusion. (An exception is 1954's *Them!*, a film covered thoroughly in the next chapter. However, *Them!* does not concern humanoid mutations. Still, the reflective ending suggests that the nuclear menace is far from over, a spirit akin to that of Japanese nuclear monster films.)

Unlike the majority of their American counterparts, Japan's humanoid mutants of the '50s and '60s were anything but temporary. *The H-Man* ends with the warning that more H-bomb testing could lead to a plague of H-Men, and that a nuclear war could exterminate homo sapiens and enshrine the H-Man as the new dominant species. Clearly, the threat of the H-Man had not ended, given that nuclear testing continued. Also, *Frankenstein Conquers the World*'s A-bomb giant is still alive at film's end, his threat potential still a risk. Indeed, he is indirectly linked to the titular creatures of 1966's quasi-sequel *War of the Gargantuas*, one of whom is benign, the other baleful to the point of devouring hapless secretaries.

Implicit Worldview

In addition to national identity and radiation perspective, the humanoid mutant movies of America and Japan differ in terms of worldview. Indeed, some American humanoid mutant movies are overtly religious, such as *Day the World Ended* and *Captive Women*. The former, brimming with Biblical allusions, ends with the screen reading "The Beginning" as Richard Denning and Lori Nelson stroll arm in arm out of the rain-cleansed valley. *Captive Women* likewise features a hope-filled finale, and the movie treats Christianity reverently. Even the existential *The Incredible Shrinking Man* posits a purposeful cosmos.

The majority of American humanoid mutant movies don't discuss religion, but their milieu clearly implies that life has meaning, that some Higher Power is holding things together. Take, for example, the optimistic ending of *World Without End*. This buoyant finale almost makes the case that in the long run, maybe a major nuclear war wouldn't be so bad.

On the other hand, some American humanoid mutant movies end in tragedy. For example, through no fault of his own, *The Werewolf*'s Duncan March becomes a homicidal wolf man when angered. Instead of being cured in the end, he is killed. Because Duncan seems to be a good man, one who loves his family and is anguished by his current state, his death appears unjust. However, the two evil scientists who turned him into a werewolf suffer death as well, poetically at Marsh's lycanthropic hands.

Often the American humanoid mutant dies, but there are no villains to perish along with him. Examples include *The Amazing Colossal Man*'s Colonel Glenn Manning, *Monster on the Campus*'s Dr. Donald Blake and *The Alligator People*'s Paul Webster. All these are men of good will and sound character, yet each meets a tragic end, and each is accidentally mutated—none of them seeks out his post-nuke state. Indeed, two of them, Colonel Manning and Dr. Blake, are performing their respective jobs of army officer and college research professor when afflicted. They take a hit, and their cases smack of classic Greek tragedy and the inexorability of Fate.

However, while such movies feature tragic lead characters, the latter are one-off mutants. There is only one Amazing Colossal Man, one Monster on the Campus, one Alligator Person. Once they are dead, there won't be new mutants taking their place. Thus, the nuclear threat may lead to tragedy involving the innocent, but they are *temporary* tragedies, not to be duplicated. (The one exception could be the Colossal Man; perhaps other soldiers exposed to a plutonium bomb blast might likewise become reluctant giants. Or it could be that the Colossal Man had unique genes that allowed him to mutate, but the normal genes of other soldiers won't result in gigantism.)

In other words, even though accidents may happen, civilians can rest easy that for the most part, the authorities will handle the nuclear threat with a firm and just hand. The world still has meaning, structure and order. Even the tragic death of a Dr. Blake warns us all of the dangers of radiation exposure and the need to handle all such materials with the utmost care.

Despite this, it is intriguing that by the 1960s, American humanoid movies had, in contrast to their 1950s brethren, darkened. For example, consider Robert Clarke's grim fate in 1960's *Beyond the Time Barrier*. Also, 1964's *The Time Travelers* depicts a post-nuke world which will soon become uninhabitable, the reason the future people hope to pilot a starship to Alpha Centauri. This gloomy outlook is a stark contrast to the optimism found in *Captive Women*, *Day the World Ended* and *World Without End*: In all three films, there's hope for the world's redemption. But in *Time Travelers*, redemption no longer appears certain. Nevertheless, the ending in the Eden-like world we see in the time window gives the viewer hope.

In Japan's *The H-Man*, there is little ambiguity over worldview, as the film depicts a decidedly secular planet soaked in uncertainty. Here the characters exist in a seemingly capricious universe devoid of God or cosmic purpose. Yes, the protagonists survive to the movie's end, but one figures this has more to do with luck than Providence. Love may conquer all, as we see in Masada's rescue of Chikako, but are the lovers ultimately doomed due to future H-Man incursions into Japan? The movie answers with a troubling "Who knows?"

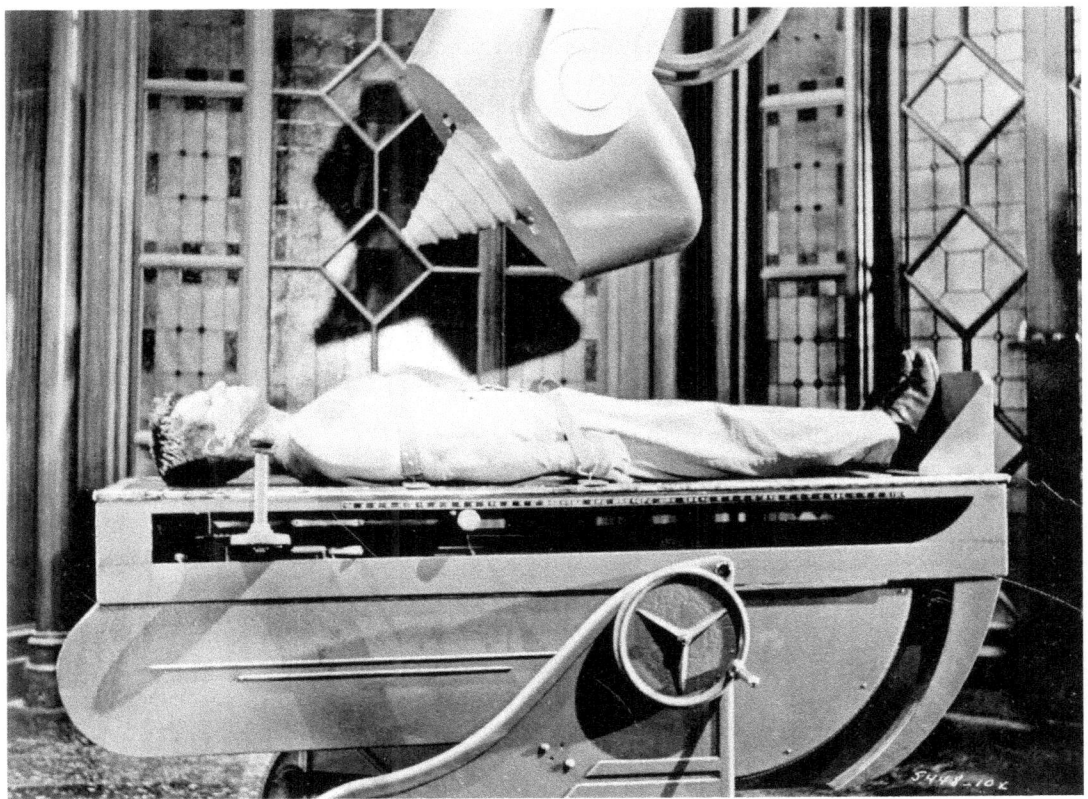

Paul Webster (Richard Crane) readies himself to undergo what he hopes will be his last radiation treatment in *The Alligator People* (Fox, 1959). It will indeed be his last—but with a result out of a nightmare.

Frankenstein Conquers the World features a friendlier worldview. There is still horror, such as that of the adolescent girl dying from radiation poisoning, which seems unfair, begging the question, "Would a benign cosmos allow such a thing?" Even the boy-monster's fate seems undeserved. But the film contrasts this bleak outlook with the compassion and optimism of Dr. Bowen and Dr. Togami.

The notion of amputating one of Frankenstein's arms or legs fills Dr. Togami with righteous indignation. Of course, what if Dr. Kawaji had suggested cutting off one of the boy-monster's little fingers instead of something so drastic as an entire arm or leg? No doubt Dr. Togami still would have objected, a protest born out of the fundamental worth and dignity of every human being—i.e., each human's intrinsic meaning.

Still, the atom bombings of 1945 darken *Frankenstein Conquers the World*'s overall outlook which even in 1960 (the year the movie takes place) were still exacting a heavy toll on the Japanese people.

Man-Sized Mutants

Comparing man-sized American humanoid mutants with the one Japanese example *The H-Man* yields a bowlful of differences contrasted against a thimbleful of parallels.

All 1950s and 1960s American man-sized mutants were clearly humanoid; unlike *The H-Man*, none were shape-changers. This was no doubt a budgetary necessity, but even in concept, the American mutants were more conventional than *The H-Man*. *Day the World Ended*'s Marty the Mutant, visited at the beginning of this chapter, is a good, representative example of American mutanthood, as exotic as man-sized mutants got in U.S. cinema.

In contrast to the solid, flesh-and-bone Marty, the H-Man is a boneless organic gel, though at times it appears as a ghostly blue-green wraith. Still, on an inhuman scale of one to ten, with one being the most human and ten the least, the H-Man would probably rank a nine in contrast to Marty's five. However, in its slime form, the H-Man would clearly rank a ten. The non-radioactive man-sized mutants in 1960's *Secret of the Telegian* and 1962's *The Human Vapor* likewise sport inhuman metamorphoses—the former becoming a transmitted signal, the latter a swirl of gas.

Meanwhile, Marty appears to have the normal human senses, represented by his hook nose, large ears, fanged mouth and three eyes. But even in its humanoid wraith form, the H-Man possesses no features at all. With no eyes, one wonders how it "sees." Perhaps it moves towards the heat signature emitted by humans.

Nutrition-wise, Marty ate irradiated meat apparently digested the normal way. But the H-Man absorbed its human meals whole, literally liquefying them. This is decidedly alien. Indeed, the H-Man is more akin to a protozoan than a mammal.

Marty appears to be male, for we know he was Tommy before Total Destruction Day's radiation mutated him. This implies that there would be female "Martys" as well. But true to its otherworldliness, the H-Man appears to be genderless. One assumes it reproduces members of its own kind via asexual reproduction, if it reproduces at all. Perhaps it is immortal and doesn't need to reproduce.

Pure rain, representative of baptism, kills Marty and by implication all the mutants like him. In addition, the rain ushers in a new birth for homo sapiens via Denning and

Nelson as a modern day Adam and Eve. Clearly, the mutant menace has ended, albeit unconvincingly.

Fire, representative of Hell, kills the H-Men during the blazing finale. However, because H-bomb fallout and testing continue, the H-Man menace hasn't ended. As the narrator ominously informs us, if H-bombs decimate humankind, the H-Man may be the new inheritor of the Earth.

King-Sized Mutants

But what about the giants that the nuclear threat produces in 1950s and 1960s American and Japanese humanoid mutant movies? As with man-sized mutants, the two nations differ in their depiction of cinematic titans.

For example, the American giants are clearly recognizable as enormous humans. Yes, both the Cyclops and the Colossal Beast sport hideous faces, but the pre-blasted Colossal Man and the 50 Foot Woman look normal from head to foot, even if Manning is bald (hey, so was Yul Brynner). Also, American giants appear well-fed and well-groomed (note the 50 Foot Woman's flawless makeup).

In contrast, the Japanese Frankenstein looks more like a traditional movie monster. At first, the A-bomb giant looks superficially man-like, but his face is malformed, and his countenance becomes more monstrous the larger he grows, i.e., the greater his (implied) threat becomes. Also, Frankenstein appears cadaverous, his limbs stick-like, almost as though he is starving, perhaps an intentional (or unintentional) reference to those who starved following the A-bombing of Hiroshima.

Then look at Frankenstein's two possible quasi-offspring, Sanda and Gailah in 1966's *War of the Gargantuas*. Both giants appear far more bestial than human, sporting scales, fur, fangs and misshapen faces. The Gargantuas are, in essence, "second-generation" representatives of the dehumanizing nuclear threat, whereas American A-bomb giants appear mostly human.

All American mutant giants go on a (low-budget) rampage. The Cyclops' violence is confined to the radioactive Mexican valley he inhabits. However, Colonel Manning stalks into Las Vegas, the 50 Foot Woman roughs up the local small town, and the Colossal Beast terrifies Los Angeles.

In addition, the Colossal Man, 50 Foot Woman and Cyclops each winds up holding its lover in its hand. Has the nuclear threat so contaminated the three giants that each will harm their beloved? In the case of the Colossal Man, no: Dr. Lindstrom talks the mentally disturbed giant into putting his fiancée Carol down. But even if he had harmed her, he was no longer the pre-plutonium bomb Glenn Manning, but a brain-dying Amazing Colossal Monster barely responsible for its actions, all thanks to nuclear testing.

Meanwhile, the Cyclops places his fiancée Susan on a boulder before tackling a giant snake. The one-eyed giant seems to recognize Susan, and she never appears to be in any danger. However, she is horrified at the monster her fiancé Bruce has become, and probably also feels guilty because he now repulses her. The 50 Foot Woman is in her right mind when she grabs her two-timing hubbie Harry. Does she plan to kill him? Something worse? We're never sure since both are electrocuted.

When it comes to aggression, Japanese goliaths both attack and defend. In *Frankenstein Conquers the World*, the A-bomb giant mostly seeks to stay out of the way of normal humans, though in the international version, he is more aggressive than in the Japanese version. He also takes a Kong-like shine to Kumi Mizuno, rescuing her from Baragon.

American titans—the Cyclops, Colossal Man-Colossal Beast and 50 Foot Woman—are all dead at the end of their movies (yes, the Colossal Man survived his Boulder Dam fall, but as the Colossal Beast, high-tension wires disintegrate him). Just as normal-sized humans are vulnerable, so too are red, white and blue nuked titans. Their threat ends with their demise, and the protagonists can go to bed untroubled.

However, Frankenstein is to some extent immortal. Although he is vulnerable to weapons, he can also re-grow limbs, and his heart will never die. Clearly, the nuclear threat lives on in Japanese king-sized mutants.

We opened this section by pitting Marty the Mutant against the H-Man. In a physical fight between the two mutants, the H-Man would win pseudopodium down. But what about an aesthetic duel? If you had to be an H-Man or a Marty, which would you choose? Many of us might opt for Marty, since at least he is not a cannibal, whereas the H-Man apparently must consume human beings. However, Marty has no hope of being reunited with his fiancée Louise. On the other hand, the H-Man who is Misaki might touch Chikako, thereby turning her into an H-Woman just as the H-Frog turned his fellow warty friend into an H-Frog. Could blobs know bliss?

From Mutants to Monsters

In our next section "Monsters," we move from humans to the strictly non-human results of the nuclear threat. These find expression in Bomb-revived prehistoric creatures and atomically mutated animal life, the latter mostly consisting of colossal "creepy-crawlies" (insects, arachnids, crabs). Here, the American and Japanese behemoths appear to have much in common—that is, until we look beyond their nuclear bomb origins.

PART II: MONSTERS

5. Red, White and Blue Behemoths

1953–1963

Bombs. Beasts. Bugs. Those three words sum up the atomic age non-humanoid monsters that crowded American movie screens during the 1950s. Bombs of the atomic variety blasted oceans and deserts. The bombs awakened beasts such as prehistoric monsters and gigantic cephalopods that attacked major cities. Nuclear radiation bloated bugs to titanic proportions, from ants to wasps to locusts. The "Big Bug" subgenre may be the 1950s' best-known form of American atomic age monster movie.

But fanciful though these films are, at their core they glow with the all-too-real atomic anxiety that gripped the nation during the "I Like Ike" decade. Maybe you didn't have to worry about giant ants infesting the L.A. storm drains, but you did have to worry about bombs falling on your town. And perhaps radiation swelling spiders to the size of Greyhound buses seemed far-fetched, but not the notion of fallout showering your neighborhood if you were downwind from a nuclear test.

The 1950s American atomic age films developed their own distinct iconography to coincide with current events, said images often including footage of real nuclear tests as well as characters in hazmat suits; soldiers running hither and yon; generals ordering tanks, trucks and jets into action; Geiger counters clicking away; and civil and military authorities racing against time. In addition, most of these movies were filmed in black-and-white and flatly lit, making them appear to be documentaries, thereby increasing their verisimilitude for 1950s moviegoers.

To today's audiences, these atomic age monster movies may seem quaint, their straight-faced narratives worthy of scorn *à la Mystery Science Theatre 3000*. But the films' sincerity is one of their major selling points, and while today it is fashionable to file nuclear war jitters under "I" for "Irrelevant," these movies, especially the best of them, may ultimately have the last laugh—or shudder.

The Beast from 20,000 Fathoms (Warner Brothers, 1953)

Credits: Production Design and Directed by Eugene Lourie; Screenplay by Lou Morheim and Fred Freiberger; Suggested by the *Saturday Evening Post* story by Ray Bradbury; Produced by Hal Chester and Jack Dietz; Associate Producer: Bernard W.

Courtesy of stop-motion animator Ray Harryhausen, the prehistoric Rhedosaurus makes an appearance on the New York docks in *The Beast from 20,000 Fathoms* (Warner Bros., 1953).

Burton; Set Decorator: Edward Boyle; Assistant Art Director: Hal Waller; Photography: Jack Russell; Music: David Buttolph; Orchestrator: Maurice de Packh; Sound: Max Hutchinson; Editor: Bernard W. Burton; Special Effects: Willis Cook; Technical Effects Created by Ray Harryhausen; Makeup: Louis Phillippi; Dialogue Director: Michael Fox; Assistant Director: Horace Hough.

Cast: Paul Christian (Prof. Tom Nesbitt); Paula Raymond (Lee Hunter); Cecil Kellaway (Prof. Thurgood Elson); Kenneth Tobey (Col. Jack Evans); Donald Woods (Capt. Phil Jackson); Lee Van Cleef (Corp. Stone); Steve Brodie (Sgt. Loomis); Ross Elliott (Prof. George Ritchie); Jack Pennick (Jacob Bowman); Ray Hyke (Sgt. Willistead); Mary Hill (Nesbitt's Secretary); Michael Fox (E.R. Doctor); Alvin Greenman, James Best (Radar Men); Frank Ferguson (Dr. Morton); King Donovan (Dr. Ingersoll); Merv Griffin (Voice of Radio Announcer); William Woodson (Radio Announcer); Roy Engel (Major Evans); Robert Easton (Deck Hand); Hugh Prosser (Doctor); Lee Phelps, Kenner G. Kemp (Police Officers); Ed Clark (Lighthouse Keeper); Richard Norris (Wilson); Joe Gray (Longshoreman).

A Mutual Pictures of California production; black-and-white; 80 minutes; released on June 13, 1953. Available on DVD as a stand-alone DVD and also as one of four features on the two-DVD set *TCM Greatest Classic Films Collection: Sci-Fi Adventures* (with *Them!*, *World Without End* and *Satellite in the Sky*). Also available on Bluray.

In the movies, there is a first time for everything, and *The Beast from 20,000 Fathoms* was the first time a nuclear explosion awakened a prehistoric monster. It also marked the first time stop-motion animator Ray Harryhausen brought a screen creature to life on his own; he had assisted Willis O'Brien with the stop-motion classic *Mighty Joe Young* (1949), but he went solo with *Beast*, and his star shone brightly.

Fittingly enough, the first of the atomic age giant monster movies begins with a nuclear explosion at the North Pole. The blast awakens a slumbering prehistoric monster, the Rhedosaurus, but only scientist Tom Nesbitt (Paul Christian) and his partner see it; the latter is killed, and no one believes Tom's tale of an antediluvian monster tromping about the Arctic.

Tom appeals to Dr. Elson (Cecil Kellaway), a renowned paleontologist, to mount an expedition to find the creature, but Dr. Elson finds Tom's story laughable. However, Dr. Elson's assistant, Lee Hunter (Paula Raymond), thinks Tom just might have seen something. She shows him a series of dinosaur sketches, and he identifies the Rhedosaurus as the prehistoric animal he saw. Subsequently, Tom tracks down the surviving sailor of a ship the monster recently sunk, and the seaman identifies the same sketch as Tom. This convinces Dr. Elson to launch a search. Lowered into the sea via bathysphere, Dr. Elson and a crewman discover the Rhedosaurus, which promptly dispatches them.

Next, the Beast attacks New York City, sending terrified citizens running through the streets. Why New York? It is in the area in which the monster's species spawned millions of years before. A night-time bazooka attack injures the creature. However, its spilled blood teems with a virulent pathogen that sends National Guardsmen to sick beds. This discovery rules out either artillery or flames killing the monster, as the particles could spread across the metropolis, killing thousands.

Tom hits upon the idea of shooting a radioactive isotope into the Rhedosaurus's neck wound, thereby killing it without any of its particles being scattered. Tom and a military marksman (Lee Van Cleef) ride to the top of a rollercoaster, a vantage point from which the marksman successfully fires the isotope into the wound. The rollercoaster inadvertently catches fire, and amidst a spectacular inferno, the Rhedosaurus dies.

The sight of a giant monster raging through a city wasn't new; this happened in both 1925's *The Lost World* and 1933's *King Kong*. However, the new element was the Bomb. Like the Bomb, the Rhedosaurus was dangerous, gigantic and destructive. Still, it was not invulnerable, and so its metaphorical significance only stretches so far. The theme posits that a scientific act of man—nuclear testing—provokes Nature to respond vengefully with the release of the Rhedosaurus, and in subsequent movies, the onslaught of giant ants, giant spiders, giant men, and so on. As an actress (Vera Miles) in the film's trailer says, "Who knows what waits for us in nature's no-man's land?"[1]

In *Beast from 20,000 Fathoms* and many of its progeny, the monster's intrusion into our world seems like an enemy sneak attack. In the movie, you get the impression the besieged New Yorkers weren't at all aware of the Beast's imminent invasion of their city. The monster had made its presence known in dribs and drabs—by sinking a ship, toppling a lighthouse, dispatching a bathysphere—but few pay attention to these omens. Monsters in subsequent films also gradually intrude into our world, finally climaxing in an invasion of a big city (if the budget allows).

Who should take care of these Bomb doppelgangers? Scientists and the military, of course. The public had faith in the latter, but they harbored ambivalence regarding the former. After all, eggheads had gotten America into this whole atomic age predicament

Terrified New Yorkers flee from Ray Harryhausen's prehistoric Rhedosaurus in *The Beast from 20,000 Fathoms* (Warner Bros., 1953) Harryhausen's stop-motion effects helped the roughly $200,000 movie gross several million.

in the first place—but they were also our most likely savior. In *The Beast from 20,000 Fathoms*, it's Tom, a scientist, who opines that the best method to dispose of the Rhedosaurus is to fire a radioactive isotope into its throat wound. It works.

It's ironic that it was a nuclear blast that gave the Beast life into our world, but a radioactive isotope that took its life. The implicit message: "Hey, Mr. and Mrs. Average Citizen, trust in good ol' American science to save the day!" Perhaps science could muster a defense against nuclear weapons—or perhaps not. Early in the film, Tom confesses concern over nuclear testing: "What the cumulative effects of these atomic explosions will be, only time can tell."

A fellow scientist replies, "You know, every time one of these things goes off, I feel as if we were helping to write the first chapter of a new Genesis."

To which Tom replies, "Let's hope we don't find ourselves writing a last chapter of the old one."

Though called science fiction, *The Beast from 20,000 Fathoms* and its successors dwell within the realm of science fantasy. For example, Dr. Elson finds the notion of a prehistoric monster having survived in a state of suspended animation for 100,000,000 years to be absurd—it wouldn't have had enough foodstuffs stored in its body to have stayed alive that long. Yet, the movie's events bear out this seeming impossibility. As Tom muses, who can say what the ultimate effect of nuclear testing will be? This was also a question mark in the minds of the public.

Director Eugene Lourie (who also helmed 1959's *The Giant Behemoth* and 1961's *Gorgo*) handles the panic scenes with an eye for detail; for example, we see a blind man fall to the street, and many of his fleeing fellows subsequently trip over him. The night sequences are atmospheric, no doubt benefiting from Lourie's talent at art design. The fiery finale in the amusement park brims with spectacle, courtesy of Lourie, but even more courtesy of animator Harryhausen. The animator endows the Rhedosaurus with a personality. A lively monster, it often moves like a housecat. For example, when it crushes the car, then scoots it with its foot, and also when it is cornered at night and thrashes its tail, its movements resemble those of a feline. As for its death throes, they are extravagant.

Speaking of the latter, Harryhausen noted in an interview, "Eugene Lourie said that I always make my monsters die like a tenor in an opera."[2] Harryhausen, of course, is the real star of *The Beast from 20,000 Fathoms*, for without his superlative effects, the movie wouldn't have become a runaway success. Estimates vary regarding the film's box office success, but Harryhausen said the film made millions.[3] Indeed, most sources indicate the movie took in between three and five million. Considering the film only cost about $200,000, that is a huge return on investment. No wonder a string of atomic age monster movies tripped all over themselves following in its wake.

Of course, few of them were buoyed by Harryhausen's genius. Revered by the industry and Baby Boomer Monster Kids, Harryhausen's name is synonymous with wonder. Throughout the '50s, his painstaking and time-consuming stop-motion model artistry gave us *It Came from Beneath the Sea* (1955), *Earth vs. the Flying Saucers* (1956), *20 Million Miles to Earth* (1957), *The 7th Voyage of Sinbad* (1958) and *The 3 Worlds of Gulliver* (1959). In 1963, he gave us his masterpiece, *Jason and The Argonauts*, featuring his magnificent sword battle between Jason's men and seven skeleton warriors. Also notable are *Mysterious Island* (1961), *First Men in the Moon* (1964), *The Valley of Gwangi* (1969), *The Golden Voyage of Sinbad* (1974), *Sinbad and the Eye of the Tiger* (1977) and *Clash of the Titans* (1981), his cinematic swan song.

Lavished with accolades and awards (including an honorary Oscar), Harryhausen frequently attended fan conferences and granted interviews. He passed away in 2013, but fortunately, he went to his grave knowing he had made a major impact on thousands (if not millions) of fans. In a pithy farewell, Mark Mawston—an acquaintance of Harryhausen's—perhaps sums up best the feelings fans had for Ray: "I, as well as the world of Monster Kids, [have] lost not just a genius but a great friend."[4]

The Magnetic Monster (United Artists, 1953)

Credits: Directed by Curt Siodmak; Screenplay by Curt Siodmak and Ivan Tors; Produced by Ivan Tors; Associate Producer-Art Director: George Van Marter; Set Decorator: Victor A. Gangelin; Photography: Charles Van Enger; Music: Blaine Sanford; Sound: Howard J. Fogetti; Sound Effects: Bill Naylor; Re-recording Supervisor: Joel F. Moss; Lighting Effects: Robert Jones; Editor: Herbert L. Strock; Special Effects Director: Harry Redmond, Jr.; Special Photographic Effects: Jack Glass; Assistant Director: Richard Dixon; Second Unit Director: Maxwell Henry; Dialogue Director: Michael Fox; Technical Radiation Advisor: Leonard Baurmash; Technical Electronics Advisor: Maxwell Smith.

Cast: Richard Carlson (Dr. Jeffrey Stewart); King Donovan (Dan Forbes); Jean Byron (Connie Stewart); Harry Ellerbe (Dr. Allard); Leo Britt (Benton); Leonard Mudie (Dr. Howard Denker); Byron Foulger (Mr. Simon); Michael Fox (Dr. Serny); John Zaremba (Chief Watson); Lee Phelps (City Engineer); Watson Downs (Mayor); Roy Engel (General Meehan); Jarma Lewis (Flight Attendant); Frank Gerstle (Col.

Willis); John Vosper (Capt. Dyer); William Benedict (Albert); Kathleen Freeman (Receptionist); John Dodsworth (Dr. Cartwright); Charlie Williams (Cabbie); Michael Granger (Kenneth Smith); Strother Marin (Co-pilot); Elizabeth Root (Joy); Juney Ellis (Spinster).

An A-Men Production; 76 minutes; released on February 18, 1953. The impressive special effects climax is mostly culled from the 1934 German film *Gold*. Poster and trailer tagline: "The thing that came alive!" Available on DVD and Blu-ray.

In most 1950s nuclear threat movies, the menace figuratively personified the Bomb, as the Rhedosaurus did in *The Beast from 20,000 Fathoms*. However, *The Magnetic Monster* is one case in which the nuclear threat is itself literally the menace: an unstable new element, the result of plausible nuclear experimentation.

Jeffrey Stewart (Richard Carlson) and Dan Forbes (King Donovan), "A-Men" who work for the OSI (Office of Scientific Investigation), look into a strange case of paramagnetism at a local hardware store. Everything in the store—clocks, appliances, keys—has become magnetized. Stewart and Forbes trace the source upstairs, where they find a dead man and an empty radioactive container.

The A-Men discover that nuclear physicist Howard Denker (Leonard Mudie) has made off with the missing radioactive element. On a commercial flight, the scientist attempts to escape with the hot contraband, but authorities order the plane to land. Dying from radiation poisoning, Denker tells Stewart and Forbes that the neo-element contained in his briefcase is the result of serranium having been bombarded with alpha particles for 200 hours. This unstable, newly formed "monster" has become magnetic and is growing. As Denker says, "It will reach out with its magnetic arms and grab anything within its reach, and kill it." These are his last words.

The deadly neo-element is moved to a college university's cyclotron, where it implodes, killing three scientists. Temporarily, the "magnetic monster" is not radioactive; the A-Men bombard a small sample of it with electrons, and this seems to work, quieting the "beast." However, the neo-element doubles in size every 11 hours, and it takes all the electrical power in the city to "feed" it so that it becomes sated.

In a last-minute bid to destroy the neo-element, which now threatens the world, Stewart and Forbes take it to an underground deltatron in Nova Scotia. In a spectacular display, the deltatron bombards the neo-element with massive amounts of electricity. At first, it appears that this last ditch effort has failed, but soon the magnetism fades, meaning that the experiment has worked—the neo-element has now been forced to split into two stable elements. The world is saved.

Entertaining as atomic age monster movies are, *The Magnetic Monster* is an attempt to depict a credible nuclear menace, envisioning a situation that might actually happen. In all facets—script, direction, acting—the film's approach is low-key. The OSI itself is an interesting organization, sort of an early *X-Files*, and it's too bad the movie's two scientific sleuths, Stewart and Forbes, didn't return for further adventures.

Producer and co-scripter Ivan Tors always tried for a low-key approach in his science fiction films, such as this one, *Gog* (1954) and *Riders to the Stars* (1954), as well as his 1950s TV series *Science Fiction Theatre*. Curt Siodmak, the director and co-writer, was also no stranger to genre material; among his other achievements, he wrote *The Wolf Man* (1941), *Frankenstein Meets the Wolf Man* (1943), *I Walked with a Zombie* (1943) and *Son of Dracula* (1943). In the 1950s, he moved from horror to science fiction, including

In *The Magnetic Monster* (United Artists, 1953), a different kind of "monster" film, the "creature" was a dangerous new radioactive element called serranium; agents of the Office of Scientific Investigation tried to halt the element's alarming growth.

this film, *Riders to the Stars*, *Creature with the Atom Brain* (1955) and *Earth vs. the Flying Saucers* (1956).

The film skillfully humanizes its lead, Jeffrey Stewart. For example, the repartee between Jeffrey and his wife lets us know that Stewart is a "regular guy" with feelings just like the rest of us. Richard Carlson's performance helps immeasurably, for Carlson was a personable actor who essayed the "visionary young scientist" in films such as *It Came from Outer Space* (1953) and *Creature from the Black Lagoon* (1954). Carlson was the co-star *and* director of *Riders to the Stars*.

Though *The Magnetic Monster* aspires to show us scientists (Stewart and Forbes) "as they really are," the "mad scientist" does make an appearance in the form of Dr. Denker, the nuclear physicist who created the menace. As Stewart says, "In nuclear research, there is no place for lone wolves." This sentence sums up the film's moral. In the hands of scientists constrained by the authorities (i.e., the government, university boards, etc.), the public had nothing to fear from nuclear experimentation. However, one did have to fear the rogues.

Low-key as it is, *The Magnetic Monster* depicts a menace that could affect the entire world. This played into the public's fear of the atom, and indeed, a scientific experiment that could imperil the planet was just science fiction—until the advent of the Bomb. Public fears grew with the testing of the hydrogen bomb, a force that magnified the nuclear threat from a destroyer of cities to a potential destroyer of worlds.

The Magnetic Monster also equates atomic research with forbidden knowledge. For example, when Stewart is bombarding a neo-element sample with electrons, the subsequent microscopic display causes him to say to his colleagues, "We're witnessing the secret of creation." Reality often symbolically attributed the atom to the province of God; for example, the nuclear test that took place in New Mexico on July 16, 1945, was code named Trinity as a direct reference to the Three-Persons-in-One Christian Deity.[5] However, movies like *The Magnetic Monster* attempted to assure us that scientists had this atomic thing well in hand. And they did—didn't they?

Killers from Space (RKO, 1954)

Credits: Produced and Directed by W. Lee Wilder; Screenplay by Bill Raynor; Story by Myles Wilder; Associate Producer: Fred M. Muller; Photography: William H. Clothier; Music: Manuel Compinsky; Music Supervisor: Alec Compinsky; Sound Recorder: George E.H. Hanson; Editor: William Faris; Makeup: Harry Thomas; Assistant Director-Production Supervisor: Mack V. Wright; Lighting: Jim James.

Cast: Peter Graves (Dr. Douglas P. Martin); James Seay (Col. Banks); Steve Pendleton (Briggs); Barbara Bestar (Ellen Martin); Frank Gerstle (Dr. Kurt Kruger); John Merrick (Deneb-Tala); Shep Menken (Major Clift); Jack Daly (Powerhouse Huard); Ron Kennedy (Sentry); Ben Welden (Pilot); Burt Wenland (Sergeant); Lester Dorr (Gas Station Attendant); Robert Roark (Guard); Ruth Bennett (Miss Vincent); Roy Engel (Police Dispatcher); Mark Scott (Narrator).

A Planet Filmways, Inc. production; black-and-white; 71 minutes; released on January 23, 1954. Available on DVD as a solo and in various collections, a typical case being the DVD set *Horrors from Space Collection* (with *Teenagers from Outer Space* and *Phantom from Space*).

5. Red, White and Blue Behemoths: 1953–1963 (Killers from Space) • 123

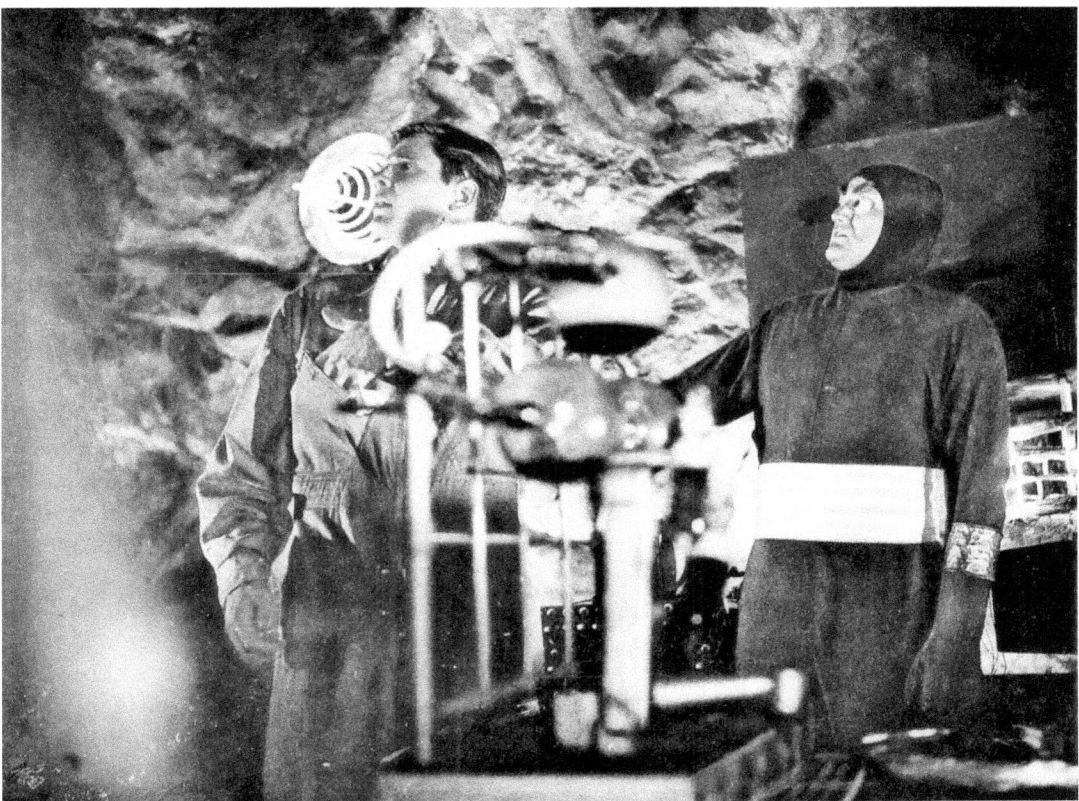

Dr. Doug Martin (Peter Graves, left) listens to extraterrestrial scientist Deneb (John Merrick) expound upon the wonders of Astron Deltan science in *Killers from Space* (RKO, 1954).

Some 1950s science fiction movies capture the holistic spirit of their times, and *Killers from Space* is one of them. This low-budget B film hits upon many public concerns of the day: the Red Scare, spies in our government, UFOs and atomic testing. The film itself is only average to sub-average; it has a few good ideas, and a couple of good scenes. Also, among '50s alien invasion films, in one way it is unique: This is the first theatrical American film in which aliens plan to use giant monsters to conquer the Earth.

After an atomic bomb test in Soledad Flats, Nevada, Dr. Doug Martin (Peter Graves) is making observations of the blast in a military jet. He and the pilot see something shiny reflecting on the ground far below. Abruptly, the jet nosedives, the pilot unable to alter the plane's headlong plummet.

Later, Colonel Banks (James Seay) tells Dr. Martin's wife Ellen (Barbara Bestar) that Dr. Martin wasn't found in the plane's wreckage, though he is almost certainly dead (the pilot's body was recovered). Surprising everybody, a dazed Dr. Martin shows up. He has no memory of what happened after the crash up until the point he staggered onto the base. In addition, though he has never had an operation in his life, he now sports a chest scar. This would seem to warrant intense investigation, but the authorities casually disregard it in the wake of Dr. Martin's amnesia. FBI agent Briggs (Steve Pendleton) suggests the memory-impaired Dr. Martin may be an imposter (i.e., a Red spy); however, fingerprint records show that the confused scientist is indeed the real Martin.

One night, Marten awakens from a restless dream and sees the image of two huge, staring eyes. This troubles him, and due to his erratic behavior and lack of memory, the authorities don't let him observe the next A-bomb test. This infuriates him.

Later, he inexplicably steals classified papers concerning the test and drives out of town, placing a message under a stone. Having trailed Martin, Briggs asks what's going on. But like any red-blooded, two-fisted American scientist, Martin knocks Briggs cold. The scientist then makes a run for it. The authorities put out an APB for him. Just before he crashes his car into a tree, Martin again sees the image of the two huge, staring eyes.

In the hospital, Dr. Martin is injected with sodium pentothal, after which he tells authorities an odd (to say the least) story. After the jet crash, he awakened to find himself in a cavern. Alien beings were operating on his chest; they have gigantic eyes and bushy eyebrows and wear black coveralls. The head alien tells Martin that he had died, but via advanced surgery, the extraterrestrials have brought him back to life. The alien also reveals that he and his otherworldly fellows are from a planet called Astron Delta, which orbits a dying sun. This forced the billion Astron Deltans to evacuate their planet and conquer other worlds (we see futuristic-looking miniatures of alien cities). But now the Astron Delta folks must find another new world—and Earth is ideally suited for their needs.

The head alien shows Martin orbital space platforms from which his compatriots will launch their invasion. He also reveals that humans have occasionally spotted the aliens as they have come and gone (the explanation for the era's flying saucer sightings). "Nothing can stop us," the alien boasts.

Alarmed, Martin makes a run for it through the cavern, jogging past multitudes of giant, rear-screen projected wildlife: spiders, insects and lizards. Laughing, the head alien tells Martin that these colossal creatures will serve as the aliens' conquering "armies." However, given that the aliens' route their electricity from the area's earthly power grid, Martin figures out the aliens' Achilles heel: "You're afraid of an overload," he says.

This puts the head alien in a snit, but he mesmerizes Martin, saying, "Listen and obey." The Killer from Space likewise tells him he will remember nothing, but that he will bring data from the next atomic test and place it under a particular stone. End of Martin's story told under the influence of truth serum.

The authorities think Martin is nuts. However, Martin has figured out that if he shuts off the electricity from the regional powerhouse, the aliens' cavern hideout will be, to borrow a phrase from 1935's *Bride of Frankenstein*, "blown to atoms." Like a man possessed, he hops in a car and speeds to the powerhouse. There he holds a hapless employee at gunpoint as Colonel Banks, Briggs and others look on. The employee protests that cutting off the power would cause a blackout for a hundred miles, but Martin remains adamant, so the man shuts off the juice. Soon, explosions rock the building—uncomfortably close atomic explosions that the characters see through a nearby window, though none of them seems worried about their alarming proximity to the blasts. Martin was right: Cutting off the power did destroy both the aliens and their horde of colossal bugs and reptiles. Thank God for red-blooded, two-fisted American scientist moxie.

But wait a minute. What about the orbiting space platforms? Can't the Killers from Space still attack from there? For having threatened a man at gunpoint, will Martin be arrested? Does the military face major lawsuits in the wake of this blackout?

When I first saw *Killers from Space* on TV in the mid–1960s, I didn't know what was coming, and when Peter Graves sees the images of the two huge eyes, I just knew that the aliens they belonged to would be scary stuff. Unfortunately, they weren't. But despite my disappointment at the look of the invaders, I liked the models of the planetary cities they had conquered, and also the scenes of Graves running past the seemingly endless parade of massive arachnids, giant grasshoppers, humongous horny toads and all the rest.

Director W. Lee Wilder was the brother of Billy Wilder, the filmmaker responsible for classics such as 1944's *Double Indemnity*, 1950's *Sunset Blvd.* and 1959's *Some Like It Hot*. W. Lee worked on decidedly humbler items such as 1953's *Phantom from Space*, 1954's *The Snow Creature*, 1957's *The Man Without a Body* and this movie. You have to wonder what Thanksgiving dinners were like with both Billy and W. Lee seated at the same table.

As previously mentioned, the aliens plan to use hordes of atomically enlarged bugs and lizards to conquer our planet. While a strategy unlikely to work, for 1954, it was novel. *Teenagers from Outer Space* (1959) featured aliens who planned to invade our planet with giant lobster-like creatures. In addition, the Japanese often employed this theme, first in 1965's *Monster Zero* (a.k.a. *Invasion of Astro-Monster*), in which Godzilla and Rodan battle perennial baddie King Ghidorah, and later in a number of further Godzilla adventures, including 1968's *Destroy All Monsters*, 1972's *Godzilla vs. Gigan*, 1973's *Godzilla vs. Megalon*, 1974's *Godzilla vs. Mechagodzilla* and 1975's *Terror of Mechagodzilla*. (Also, technically, 2004's *Godzilla: Final Wars*.)

As a period piece, *Killers from Space* involves the 1950s themes of Communist espionage in America and national security regarding top-secret atomic testing documents. Against his will, Graves becomes a spy for the Astron Deltans, and the movie implies that perhaps the Communist bloc has likewise mesmerized real-world Uncle Sam turncoats. The public's fear of the "other side" (i.e., the U.S.S.R.) getting its hands on nuclear data plays out in terms of the aliens acting as Soviet stand-ins.

This relates to the nuclear threat. After all, many feared that if the Soviet Union got the upper hand, they might start an atomic war with the U.S.; therefore, it was vital that America maintain a nuclear advantage. Was it? I don't know, but I do know that despite 1950s atomic jitters, World War III never happened, albeit for a multitude of reasons— one of them no doubt sheer dumb luck.

Suffering from flat direction and impoverished production values, *Killers from Space* is a typical low-budget science fiction item. Peter Graves does what he can with the role, but he was better in 1956's *It Conquered the World*. The other performances are competent but nothing special—my guess is the actors considered this just another day's work. And at the end of the day, *Killers from Space* is just another 1950s science fiction flick. Not that that's necessarily a bad thing.

Monster from the Ocean Floor (Lippert, 1954)

Credits: Directed by Wyott Ordung; Screenplay by William Danch; Produced by Roger Corman; Production Design: Ben Hayne; Production Manager: David Kramarsky; Photography: Floyd Crosby; Music: Andre Brummer; Sound: Roy Meadows; Sound Editor: Jack Milner; Editor: Edwards Sampson, Jr.; Microphotography by the Hancock Foundation; Makeup: Harry Thomas; Assistant Director: Jack Schachter; Monster Puppet: Bob Baker; Technical Advisor: Alfred Hanson.
Cast: Anne Kimbell (Julie Blair); Stuart Wade (Steve Dunning); Dick Pinner (Dr.

Baldwin); Jonathan Haze (Joe); Wyott Ordung (Pablo); Inez Palange (Tula); Roger Corman (Tommy—Dr. Baldwin's Assistant); David Garcia (Jose).

A Palo Alto Production; black-and-white; 64 minutes; released on May 21, 1954. Available on DVD as a stand-alone DVD or as part of various DVD sets, a typical case being *Creepy Creature Vol. 1* (with *Serpent Island*.)

This typical 1950s monster pic was the first movie produced by the legendary Roger Corman, thus its claim to science fiction fame. Also, it was one of the first genre films in which radiation created the menace, a concept that would soon become ubiquitous.

In the waters off the Yucatan Peninsula, commercial artist Julie Blair (Anne Kimbell) is swimming when she bumps into marine biologist Steve Dunning's (Stuart Wade) one-man mini-sub. She and Steve become the film's obligatory love interest. Stories about a monster off the coast intrigue June. Steve ridicules the notion, but Julie believes there might be something to it, and so she launches an investigation.

One night on the beach, a one-eyed, octopus-like creature emerges from the sea. After seeing it, Julie faints. After snagging a piece of the creature on a hook, she sends the specimen to Steve and his scientist friend Dr. Baldwin (Dick Pinner). They examine it and realize that it comes from an unknown amoeba-like species. Meanwhile, Julie has dived underwater to do more monster sleuthing. The cyclopean sea beast obligingly approaches her, and she freaks out. Steve arrives in time to smash the mini-sub into the creature's one eye, saving Julie's life.

The nuclear threat angle concerns the creature's origins. The monster first appeared in 1946, just after nuclear tests in the Pacific, so the protagonists surmise that undersea radiation from the tests created the thing. As low-budget 1950s creatures go, the puppet monster isn't bad. Its tentacles move well, and a paucity of close-ups adds to its effectiveness. Unfortunately, we never see the monster in the same scene as a person, much less attack anyone; Roger Corman said that the picture's $12,000 budget was too meager for process shots.[6]

While it would never be mistaken for a classic and often moves slower than a Southern drawl, *Monster from the Ocean Floor* is more or less professional. It's not a good movie, but it sports a few nice touches. In other words, completists—and that probably means the majority of you reading this book—owe it to themselves to catch this fledgling Corman item at least once.

Them! (Warner Bros., 1954)

Credits: Directed by Gordon Douglas; Screenplay by Ted Sherdeman; Adaptation by Russell Hughes; Story by George Worthing Yates; Produced by David Weisbart; Art Director: Stanley Fleischer; Set Decorator: G.W. Berntsen; Photography: Sid Hickox; Music Score: Bronislau Kaper; Music Director: Ray Heindorf; Orchestrator: Robert Franklyn; Sound: Francis J. Scheid; Sound Effects: William Mueller; Sound Editors: Lincoln Lyons and Dave DePatie; Editor: Thomas Reilly; Special Effects: Ralph Ayres; Ants Built by Dick Smith; Makeup: Gordon Bau and Henry Vilardo; Hair Stylist: Agnes Flanagan; Assistant Director: Russ Saunders; Second Assistant Director: Al Alleborn; Wardrobe: Moss Mabry and Marguerite Royce; Men's Wardrobe: Ted Schultz and Roe Ramsey; Stills: Jack Woods; Script Supervisor: Howard Hohler; Props: Robert Turner; Assistant Camera Operators: Ed Albert, William Ranaldi,

Robert Johannes; Second Camera Operator: Bill Schurr; Grip: Harold Noyes; Gaffer: Paul Burnett; Best Boy: Ed Rike; Boom Operator: Ora Hudson; Cable Man: William A. Thompson.

Cast: James Whitmore (Sgt. Ben Peterson); Edmund Gwenn (Dr. Harold Medford); Joan Weldon (Dr. Patricia Medford); James Arness (Robert Graham); Onslow Stevens (Brigadier Gen. O'Brien); Sean McClory (Major Kibbee); Chris Drake (Ed Blackburn); Sandy Descher (Little Girl); Mary Ann Hokanson (Mrs. Lodge); Don Shelton (Captain); Fess Parker (Alan Crotty); Olin Howlin (Jenson); Frederick J. Foote (Dixon); Robert Scott Correll (Jerry Lodge); Richard Bellis (Mike Lodge); Joel Smith (Ben's Driver); John Close (Voice of Pilot); William Schallert (Intern); Cliff Ferre (Man in Laboratory); Matthew McCue (Gramps); Grandon Rhodes (Doctor in Los Angeles); Waldron Boyle (Crotty's Doctor); Ken Smith, Kenner Kemp, Richard Boyer (Troopers); Joe Forte (Coroner Putnam); Wally Duffy (Airman); Fred Shellac (Attendant); Ann Doran (Little Girl's Psychiatrist); Willis Bouchey, Alexander Campbell (Officials); Norman Field (Five-star general); Otis Garth (Admiral); John Maxwell (Dr. Grant); Leonard Nimoy (Sergeant); Janet Stewart (WAVE); Dick Wessel (Police Officer); Dubb Taylor (Watchman); Russell Gaige (Coroner); Robert Berger (Sutton—Police Officer); John Berardino (Ryan—Police Officer); Mary Lou Holloway (Blonde); Harry Tyler, Oscar Blanke, Harry Wilson (Inmates); Eddie Dew, James Cardwell (Officers); Dorothy Green (Matron); Dean Cromer (Military Police Sergeant); Larry Dobkin (Engineer); Chad Mallory (Loader); Gayle Kellogg (Gunner); Booth Colman, Walter Coy (Reporters); Victor Sutherland (Senator); Charles Perry (Soldier); Warren Mace (Radio Operator); Jack Perrin (Army Officer); Hubie Kerns, Roydon Clark (Jeep Drivers).

Black-and-white; 94 minutes; released on June 19, 1954. Available on DVD as a stand-alone DVD and also as one of four features on the two-DVD set *TCM Greatest Classic Films Collection: Sci-Fi Adventures* (with *The Beast from 20,000 Fathoms, World Without End* and *Satellite in the Sky*). Also available on Blu-ray.

The late Carlos Clarens said, "Part brisk documentary, part outrageous fiction, *Them!* is probably the most successful example of its class."[7]

I disagree.

Them! is *unequivocally* the most successful example of its class, the finest big bug movie ever made. Some skeptics may consider that faint praise, but it isn't. *Them!* easily ranks among the Top Ten best science fiction movies of the 1950s, and those other chart-toppers include classics such as 1951's *The Day the Earth Stood Still*, 1953's *The War of the Worlds* and 1956's *Invasion of the Body Snatchers* and *Forbidden Planet*.[8]

Structured as a mystery during the first third, *Them!* begins with New Mexico police officers Ben Peterson (James Whitmore) and Ed Blackburn (Chris Drake) discovering a little girl wandering through the desert. She is mute and in shock; Ben and Ed soon discover the demolished trailer of the girl's parents. Ben and an ambulance attendant hear a weird, unidentified noise, after which the ambulance takes the shocked girl away.

After driving to a local general store, Ben and Ed find it has been wrecked like the trailer. They find the owner's corpse, his chest crushed. Ben leaves while Ed stays behind to keep watch—but he hears that same weird noise, and goes outside to investigate. Something off-screen kills him, something he shoots at to no avail, something that silences his scream as the desert wind howls in collusion.

FBI agent Robert Graham (James Arness), entomologist Dr. Harold Medford (Edmund Gwenn) and his scientist daughter Patricia "Pat" Medford (Joan Weldon) are

Dr. Pat Medford (Joan Weldon) and FBI agent Robert Graham (James Arness) are confronted by a giant mutated ant in the big bug classic *Them!* (Warner Bros., 1954).

brought into the case. With a whiff of formic acid (the kind found in ants), Medford brings the catatonic little girl back to reality, and she immediately starts screaming, "Them! Them!"

Out in the desert, Pat hears that same weird sound, which turns out to be the sound made by a gigantic ant, which attacks Pat. Ben and Robert come running and shoot the thing to death. Dr. Medford deems the almost nine-foot-long creature "A fantastic mutation probably caused by lingering radiation from the first atomic bomb" (at White Sands in 1945). Later, the ants' mound is discovered; in the hot noonday sun (the ants only come out at night), the protagonists bombard it with phosphorous, then drop cyanide into the nest to poison the colony.

Pat accompanies Ben and Robert into the nest. There, they have a harrowing brush with an ant that's still alive, but Ben kills it with a flamethrower. Once they are in the queen's egg chamber, Pat discovers that the eggs have hatched—and two winged princess ants (along with their male consorts) have escaped the nest. Dr. Medford and Pat fret over this development. General O'Brien (Onslow Stevens), in charge of the operation, says, "I don't get it. You two act like it's the end of the world." To which Dr. Medford replies, "Well, it could be."

In Washington, D.C., Dr. Medford shows assembled high-ranking authorities a film about ants, noting that the giant queen ants can produce multitudes of eggs, and therefore spread nests across the United States. Dr. Medford beseeches the Washington bigwigs to solve this dilemma. "Unless you solve it," Dr. Medford says, "unless these queens are located and destroyed before they've established thriving colonies and can produce

Heaven only knows how many more queen ants, Man, as the dominant species of life on earth, will probably be extinct within a year."

A nationwide search ensues, albeit cloaked in secrecy. The biggest lead is that of a Texan aviator named Crotty (Fess Parker), who has been confined to a mental ward because he insists he saw flying saucers shaped like ants. Though the doctor in charge of the facility contends that Crotty isn't crazy, Robert tells him to nevertheless hold the man indefinitely. Says Robert, "We'll send you a wire and tell you when he's well."

One queen ant establishes a nest on a ship at sea, and the vessel is quickly overrun by her lethal progeny. A naval ship fires upon the besieged vessel, sinking it. Ben and Robert discover that the ants have established another nest in the Los Angeles storm drains. A father died trying to save his two boys from the giant ants, and the protagonists believe the boys may still be alive in the storm drains. The authorities go public, stating that L.A. is now under martial law with a strict curfew due to the giant ants living beneath their city. At night, the military ventures into the storm drains; Ben, Robert, and Pat all ride into the tunnels in different Jeeps, reporting as they go. Ben discovers that the lost boys are alive, but ants have them trapped. Bravely, Ben rescues the kids and boosts both of them into a small tunnel that leads to the authorities. Before Ben can hoist himself into the tunnel, an ant kills him.

By this time, the soldiers are attacking the giant insects. Due to a cave-in, Robert gets cut off from the troops and is almost killed by a looming ant. But the military breaks

If you're picnicking in New Mexico, better have a bazooka handy in case these industrial-sized ants crash the party. A classic photograph from *Them!* (Warner Bros., 1954).

through in time to spray the monsters with gunfire. Robert, Pat, and Dr. Medford stand at the rim of the egg chamber, and the wise old scientist notes thankfully that none of the princess ants has escaped—they are still here drying their nascent wings. Flame throwers subsequently fry the would-be queens. As the oversized insects roast, Robert turns to Pat and says, "Pat, if these monsters got started as the result of the first atomic bomb in 1945, what about all the others that have been exploded since then?"

Dr. Medford: "Nobody knows, Robert. When man entered the atomic age, he opened a door into a new world. What we eventually find in that new world, nobody can predict."

Inspired by the success of 1953's *The Beast from 20,000 Fathoms, Them!* turned out to be a big moneymaker for Warner Bros. in 1954. The filmmakers handle the film in a sober, realistic manner; indeed, its overall presentation has much in common with the era's matter-of-fact police procedurals. Also, its idea of atomic mutations was novel in 1954, as *Them!* was the first of the "Big Bug" subgenre of radiation cinema. Hence, to audiences who swarmed to this movie in 1954, the premise and format were fresh.

The film handles its characters far better than the average atomic age monster movie. There is some nuance in the protagonists' personalities: Ben clearly feels responsible for his partner's death. He also has a dry sense of humor (as when he tells the train guy that Robert's interest in the sugar theft is due to a sweet tooth). James Whitmore is so good in the part that Bill Warren says, "When Ben the cop is killed at the end, children in the matinee audience at which I first saw *Them!* actually cried."[9]

In other character terrain, unlike most female scientists in '50s movies, Pat actually gets to take part in the action. Yes, this is after the usual "This is no job for a woman" prattle (from Robert, not Ben), but the point is that Pat does heroically descend into the ants' nest with the two male leads. While there, she is just as cool and professional as they are. Also, after she takes photographs of the queen's egg chamber, she forcefully orders Robert and Ben to burn it up. And at the end, she is riding shotgun in one of the Jeeps exploring the LA storm drains for giant ants.

Robert does something few male heroes did in 1950s American science fiction movies: He screams. Once a cave-in cuts him off from his comrades, an ant lunges for him, and like any of us, he shrieks in fear. This helps humanize him and allows the viewer to better relate to his heroics.

James Arness, who plays Robert, was no stranger to science fiction movies, having appeared as the alien invader in 1951's *The Thing from Another World*. His main claim to fame is the role of Sheriff Matt Dillon in the Western TV series *Gunsmoke* (1955–1975). Veteran actor Edmund Gwen (Dr. Medford) is probably best known as Kris Kringle in 1947's classic Christmas movie *Miracle on 34th Street*.

The filmmakers used several ant puppet heads, two head and forequarters, and two full-sized models to good effect. The models' greatest asset is that they are on the set "live" with the actors, and therefore realistically interact with them. Their greatest weakness: those legs. Though generally camouflaged by good camerawork, sometimes it is apparent that the legs aren't fully touching the ground and that the creature is not resting its full weight upon them. But this is a minor flaw, and one that probably didn't bother audiences—after all, *Them!* was nominated for the 1954 Oscar for Best Special Effects. (Walt Disney's *20,000 Leagues Under the Sea* won the award.)

Another minor problem with the ants: They don't completely look like ants. When I first saw *Them!* on a Monday night Late Show in 1963 at the age of eight, I liked the big bugs, but they didn't look like ants to me, especially those eyes. Fully acceptable as insect monsters, the titanic ants' physical differences from real backyard ants could be explained as the result of the mutation process that turned them into giants.

The film leaves many questions unanswered. We know the ants are about nine feet in length, and we are told there may be hundreds of them in the New Mexico nest. If that's the case, how could they find enough to eat? We are told they have gone carnivorous, but even in this case, surely it would take herds of cattle to satiate them. Likewise, when they are in the storm drains of L.A., what are they eating? Raids on food trucks or grocery stores would have been noticed. Also, the movie doesn't exploit one potential fear during the L.A. sequence, that the ants could be burrowing beneath your house—or burst up into it through the floor.

No revealed menace could have lived up to *Them!*'s eerie build-up in the first 15 minutes. For example, after the hospital intern has laid the catatonic little girl in the back of the ambulance, he and Ben hear a strange noise. Their backs are to the little girl, who sits up upon hearing the noise, her eyes wide and fearful. As the noise subsides, the girl closes her eyes and lies back down. Ben and the intern uneasily pass the noise off as desert wind—but no wind ever made a sound like that, which the audience knows all too well.

The menace of the ants parallels that of the nuclear threat; they are the strongest metaphor for atomic anxiety of any 1950s American monster movie. We hear that the ants multiply quickly, just as nuclear proliferation was multiplying quickly. Dr. Medford tells us that the ants could exterminate humankind in a year, just as nuclear weapons could exterminate humankind in a short time. And just as our triumph over the ants was in doubt, so too was our triumph over nuclear engagement. The film maintains a grim apocalyptic tone throughout. The ants are not a localized menace like the Rhedosaurus in *The Beast from 20,000 Fathoms*, but a global threat.

There's a potent line early in the film; after Ben and Robert kill the first giant ant. Dr. Medford says, "We may be witnesses to a Biblical prophecy come true: 'And there shall be destruction and darkness come over the creation, and the beasts shall reign over the earth.'" The film's closing lines (quoted above) echo this theme, in which Dr. Medford says the nuclear age has ushered humankind into a new world, one potentially fraught with danger and the unknown. Like the best of 1950s science fiction movies, his words evoke both a sense of wonder and a sense of unease—a beatific smile and a quiet shudder.

Despite occasional flaws in its depiction of the giant ants, *Them!* remains one of the best American monster movies ever made.

It Came from Beneath the Sea (Columbia, 1955)

Credits: Directed by Robert Gordon; Screenplay by George Worthing Yates and Hal Smith; Story by George Worthing Yates; Produced by Charles H. Schneer; Executive Producer: Sam Katzman; Art Director: Paul Palmentola; Set Decorator: Sidney Clifford; Photography: Henry Freulich; Music Conductor: Mischa Bakaleinikoff; Sound: Josh Westmoreland; Recording Supervisor: John Livadary; Editor: Jerome Thoms; Special Effects: Jack Erickson; Technical Effects Created by Ray Harryhausen; Assistant Director: Leonard Katzman; Unit Manager: Leon Chooluck; Makeup: Clay Campbell; Hair Stylist: Helen Hunt.

Cast: Kenneth Tobey (Commander Pete Matthews); Faith Domergue (Dr. Lesley Joyce); Donald Curtis (Dr. John Carter); Ian Keith (Admiral Burns); Dean Maddox, Jr. (Admiral Norman); Chuck Griffiths (Lt. Griff); Harry Lauter (Deputy Sheriff Bill Nash); Richard W. Peterson (Capt. Stacy); Tol Avery (Navy Intern); William Bryant (Helicopter Pilot); Del Courtney (Naval Assistant Secretary Robert David Chase); Roy Engel (Control Room Officer); Eddie Fisher (McLeod); Sam Hayes (Radio Newscaster); Jules Irving (King); Jack Littlefield (Aston); Rudy Puteska (Seaman Hall); Ray Storey (Reporter); William Woodson (Narrator).

A Clover Production; black-and-white; 78 minutes; released in July 1955. Double-billed with *Creature with the Atom Brain* (1955). Available as a stand-alone DVD and also as one of several features in DVD sets such as *Sci-Fi Creature Classics—4-Movie Set* (with *20 Million Miles to Earth, The Giant Claw* and *Mothra*). Colorized edition also available on DVD (the colorization was supervised by Harryhausen). Also available on Blu-ray.

In this opus, the heroine often uses the ABCs to express her views, which is only fitting for a movie that basically follows the ABCs of how to make a '50s monster movie. The special effects come courtesy of Ray Harryhausen.

In the Pacific, Commander Pete Matthews' (Kenneth Tobey) nuclear submarine encounters an unknown radioactive object that rams it; later, a chunk of it is found caught in the diving planes. The Navy commissions civilian marine biologists Lesley Joyce (Faith Domergue) and John Carter (Donald Curtis) to examine the chunk. Matthews, who is enamored with Joyce, sees to it that she is "drafted" to continue the investigation until she and her scientist friend Carter determine what kind of animal the flesh came from. Matthews makes a less-than-subtle move on Joyce, verifying that she and colleague Carter are not romantically involved. Gosh, where could this subplot be headed?

In *It Came from Beneath the Sea*, it isn't London Bridge that's falling down—it's the Golden Gate Bridge. Ray Harryhausen's six-armed cephalopod attacks the San Francisco landmark in this 1955 Columbia release.

When Joyce and Carter meet with government authorities, they explain that the chunk of tissue apparently came from a giant octopus. She and Carter theorize that radiation from H-bomb tests' fallout reached the bottom of the Mindanao Trench, irradiating an octopus. Surrounding sea life sensed its new "hot" status and kept out of its way, robbing the colossal cephalopod of its normal food sources. This forced the creature to the surface to find sustenance in the form of land animals and—yes, Virginia—people. Joyce says that it "hunted along the Japanese current," noting that part of a Japanese fishing fleet recently disappeared, implying that the octopus ate them.

Much to Joyce's dismay, the authorities don't buy the giant octopus theory. Then, faster than you can say, "Hey, doesn't that octopus only have six arms?" the marine monster attacks and sinks a tramp steamer. A surviving seaman tells a medico what happened, and for his trouble is quickly dispatched to a head shrinker. As a result, the other seamen clam up, and the one truth-telling sailor recants his tale. It's Professor Lesley Joyce to the rescue: Using her "feminine wiles," she persuades a survivor to admit that the ship really was attacked by a giant octopus.

The Navy orders a search for the octopus, which is lurking off the West Coast. Matthews and Joyce locate the beast. Subsequently, the authorities publicly acknowledge the mammoth cephalopod's existence. Given that the creature is expected to attack San Francisco, the military sets up defenses there; the Navy plans to fire a jet-propelled torpedo into the octopus's head, then electronically detonate the device.

The monster first attacks an electrified Golden Gate Bridge; however, the current eggs it on, so Carter cuts off the juice. Next, the gargantuan cephalopod begins to hoist itself up onto land, its tentacles destroying San Franciscan real estate as terrified citizens flee its wrath.

Army flame throwers drive the beast from the city. Below the surface of the Pacific, the sub fires a torpedo into the monster's head, but it grabs the sub and won't let go. Matthews uses plastic explosives in an attempt to *make* it let go, to no avail. Next, Carter fires a spear into the monster's eye, and the octopus thrashes wildly, freeing the sub. The embedded torpedo is exploded electronically, and the octopus is blown to bits.

But hey, what about Matthews and Carter? Not to worry, neighbor: They survived, of course. At dinner, Joyce once again gives Matthews the "ABCs" treatment, asking him if he would like to collaborate with her on a book called *How to Catch a Sea Beast* while good sport Carter looks on.

Frankly, I can relate to Carter more than I can Matthews. After all, let's face it, nice guys not only finish last, they also almost never get the girl. But on the positive side, the movie suggests that a man and a woman can be good friends (i.e., Carter and Joyce) without being romantically involved.

Which brings us to the supposed "new breed of woman" that Joyce says she represents. Yes, she assists in the investigation and search for the monster, but she doesn't get to engage in the movie's heroics. As a contrast, Dr. Pat Medford in *Them!* journeys into the ants' nest with the two male heroes, as well as into the dangerous, ant-infested L.A. storm drains.

That said, Faith Domergue endows Lesley with intelligence, beauty and believability. She appeared in several other genre movies, including *Cult of the Cobra* (1955), *The Atomic Man* (1956) and *This Island Earth* (1955). Although she never attained star status, she always gave good performances. For example, in *Cult of the Coba*, she is a were-snake who brings genuine pathos to her shape-changing character.

However, this film's take on femininity is cornball. Domergue employs sultry female "tricks" to persuade a sailor to spill the beans about having seen a giant octopus, and you just can't help but roll your eyes—not at her performance, which is good, but rather at this archetypal instance of 1950s female stereotyping.

As usual, Kenneth Tobey is dependable as the military hero. Tobey radiated a likable, albeit sometimes brusque charm. He excelled as the lead in 1951's *The Thing from Another World*, and he turned in good work in the previously examined *The Beast from 20,000 Fathoms*. His other genre films include 1957's *The Vampire* and 1983's *Strange Invaders*.

The real star of *It Came from Beneath the Sea* is the monster, right? Well, sort of. Actually, the real star is the man *behind* the monster, the brilliant Ray Harryhausen. Since I've already written extensively about him in the *Beast from 20,000 Fathoms* entry, I will keep my comments short.

Because *It Came from Beneath the Sea* was low-budget, Harryhausen built his monster octopus with only six tentacles, for this made the creature's stop-motion articulation less time-consuming and therefore cheaper. Once again, the master animator creates spectacular visuals, including the creature's attack on the Golden Gate Bridge and the Ferry Building. In addition to the main model, Harryhausen also animated a large, detailed tentacle for tighter shots.[10]

As the creature's tentacles grope through the downtown area, shattering windows, smashing masonry and squashing people, they function almost independently from the octopus, as though they are great blind earthworms in search of prey. Although the tentacles writhe throughout almost every monster scene, we rarely see the octopus's "face." However, the scene in which Carter swims in front of its immense, open eye, gives us a sense of its singular malevolence. (Too bad Carter's transparency somewhat spoils this scene.)

Tellingly, the movie links H-bomb tests and the monster. However, the H-bombs didn't awaken It, but rather irradiated the beast, sending It in search of food in more shallow waters. It's unclear whether the radiation is supposed to have increased the creature's size, but apparently not, since Joyce likens It to the ancient Kraken.

The movie's opening titles make a statement about the status of the nuclear threat in 1955: "Since the coming of the atomic age, man's knowledge has so increased that any upheavals of nature would not be beyond his belief." This obviously refers to the film's radioactive monster. In one way, this It is more believable than either giant insects or oversized arachnids—neither would be able to breathe if transformed into a giant. But an enormous octopus is another matter altogether; indeed, the largest known octopus was 30 feet across,[11] and the largest known squid was 43 feet across.[12] However, fallout radiation would probably kill a colossal cephalopod or make it sick, either possibility rendering the creature's menace moribund.

It Came from Beneath the Sea is giant monsterdom by the numbers, but when each intersection is packed with Ray Harryhausen magic, those numbers add up.

Tarantula (Universal-International, 1955)

Credits: Directed by Jack Arnold; Screenplay by Robert M. Fresco, Martin Berkeley; Story by Jack Arnold, Robert M. Fresco; Produced by William Alland; Art Directors: Alexander Golitzen, Alfred Sweeney; Set Decorators: Russell A. Gausman, Ruby

R. Levitt; Photography: George Robinson; Music: Herman Stein, Henry Mancini; Music Supervisor: Joseph Gershenson; Sound: Leslie I. Carey, Frank Wilkinson; Sound Editors: Joe Sikorski, Ed Sandlin; Editor: William M. Morgan; Special Photographic Effects: Clifford Stine, David S. Horsley; Assistant Directors: Frank Shaw, Cliff Reid; Makeup: Bud Westmore, Jack Kevan; Hair Stylist: Joan St. Oegger; Costumes: Jay A. Morley, Jr.; Dialogue Director: Irvin Berwick; Unit Production Manager: Norman Deming.

Cast: John Agar (Dr. Matt Hastings); Mara Corday (Stephanie "Steve" Clayton); Leo G. Carroll (Prof. Gerald Deemer); Nestor Paiva (Sheriff Jack Andrews); Ross Elliott (Joe Burch); Ed Rand (Lt. John Nolan); Raymond Bailey (Dr. Townsend); Clint Eastwood (First Pilot); Jane Howard (Co-ed Secretary); Billy Wayne (Murphy); Hank Patterson (Josh); Dee Carroll (Telephone Operator); Bert Holland (Barney E. Russell); Steve Darrell (Anfy Andersen); Tom London (Jeff—Miner); Edgar Dearing (Miner); James J. Hyland (Trooper Grayson); Vernon Rich (Ridley); Bob Nelson (Trooper); Ed Parker (Attendant/Eric Jacobs/Dr. Paul Lund); Bing Russell (Deputy); Ray Quinn (Trooper); Robert R. Stephenson (Warehouseman); Don Dillaway (Jim Bagny); Bud Wolfe (Bus Driver); Jack Stoney (Helper); Rusty Wescoatt (Driver).

Black-and-white; 80 minutes; released on November 23, 1955. Based on Robert M. Fresco's "No Food for Thought," an episode on *Science Fiction Theatre*. Available as a stand-alone DVD and as one of several features in the multi-DVD set *The Classic Sci-Fi Ultimate Collection Vol. 1* (with *The Mole People, The Incredible Shrinking Man, The Monolith Monsters* and *Monster on the Campus*).

If you say "tarantula" to your average Joe or Josette, they'll probably think of the hairy, three-inch arachnid. But if you say "tarantula" to your average 1950s monster fan, they'll probably think of the hairy, hundred-foot arachnid in Universal-International's answer to 1954's *Them! Tarantula* may be the quintessential 1950s Grade-B monster movie. Yes, it's that good—and that typical.

In the small town of Desert Rock, Arizona, Dr. Matt Hastings (John Agar) examines a man who has died of mysterious causes. Professor Gerald Deemer (Leo G. Carroll), who conducts experiments in his private lab far from town, declares the dead man—his assistant—to have expired due to acromegalia, but Matt doesn't buy it.

Later, in his home laboratory, Deemer inspects his lab animals which have been injected with a synthetic radioactive nutrient and are now several times their normal size. Of special interest is a four-foot tarantula in a glass cage. Another Deemer assistant, *also* affected with acromegaly, attacks the scientist and wrecks the lab, shattering the spider's glass cage. The oversized arachnid serenely creeps out the back door as Deemer and the assistant struggle. The assistant injects Deemer with the synthetic nutrient. But what about that spider...?

Matt drives Stephanie "Steve" Clayton (Mara Corday), the scientist's new assistant, to Deemer's place. Although at first kindly, Deemer becomes harsh as his face begins to change, the result of the radioactive nutrient. He orders Steve never again to bring Matt into the lab.

In the countryside, the titanic spider kills cattle, horses and humans. Deemer, in the last stages of acromegaly, tells Matt and Steve about his experiments and how his synthetic nutrient is unstable. Meanwhile, the authorities discover pools of white fluid around the dead animals, and Matt takes a sample to the nearby Arizona Agricultural Institute. There, a scientist tells Matt that the fluid is tarantula venom. Realizing that a giant spider is on the loose, Matt flies back to town, literally and figuratively (he owns a small plane).

Sheriff Jack Andrews (Nestor Paiva, left) confers with local doctor Matt Hastings (John Agar) about the strange events occurring in the Arizona desert in *Tarantula* (Universal-International, 1955).

In the meantime, the bigger-than-ever spider attacks Deemer's mansion, killing the scientist. A screaming Steve flees the house just as Matt fortuitously arrives to spirit her away, but the spider follows them.

At Matt's insistence, the sheriff calls in the state police. As Matt stops his car to confer with the cops, the spider creeps over a hill, wigging everyone out. Two patrol officers try (unsuccessfully) to hold off the monster with submachine guns as everybody else drives to town. Next, the protagonists place a large pile of dynamite in the spider's path; when it's detonated, the unharmed arachnid inexorably creeps forward.

Everyone drives into Desert Rock, which has otherwise been evacuated. Air Force jets arrive in the nick of time, firing missiles at the spider. No dice. And just as the spider has almost reached town, the jets plaster the arachnid with napalm, which sets it ablaze.

Whew!

Tarantula is an exciting little item, especially during the final 20 minutes. It's the kind of movie made to be watched in the den while scarfing down popcorn and cola. For example, when the state police and protagonists watch the titanic tarantula crawling towards them, the police captain tells two of his men, "You boys slow it down." Yeah, right, dude. As everyone else gets to race back to town, the two luckless cops spray the spider with machine-gun fire. Bad decision. As the spider relentlessly approaches, you find yourself yelling, "You idiots, hop in the car and get the deuce out of there!" Too late.

This wonderful poster for *Tarantula* (Universal-International, 1955) perfectly captures the spirit of 1950s giant monster movies. Artist Reynold Brown painted many excellent genre movie posters during his career.

One of them inadvertently floods the engine. Next thing you know, they have become tarantula chow.

Tarantula is one movie that most critics agree is top-rank fun. For example, the online TCM (Turner Classic Movies) entry for the film notes that Leonard Maltin gives it three out of four stars, and the online Rotten Tomatoes ranks the movie as 92 percent fresh. Even the hard-to-please *Castle of Frankenstein* wrote this about the film in 1965: "Taut, little grade-B sf-chiller. One of the best of the giant-insect [*sic*] films, this benefits from fast-paced Jack Arnold direction." As noted in the entry in Chapter 1 on Arnold's *The Incredible Shrinking Man*, the director was pivotal to 1950s science fiction cinema, and John Baxter declares *Tarantula* to be "one of his most accomplished films."[13]

Maltin's review notes the film's "convincing special effects." Now this is by 1950s standards, of course—no state-of-the-art animatronics or CGI sleight-of-hand here. But despite the movie's modest budget, the special effects crew members (including the redoubtable Clifford Stine) pay attention to small details. For example, they are careful to matte in the spider's shadow beneath the beast as it crawls across the countryside. Also, early in the film when the then dog-sized tarantula is imprisoned in its glass cage, we hear its legs squeak against the glass.

The film's most powerful sequence occurs about halfway through. At night, a herd of horses grows restless, and with good reason. As they whinny in fear, the massive tarantula creeps over a hill overlooking their corral. The eight-legged demon stops atop the hill's crest, coolly sizing up the small, terrified equines before moving in for the kill. Then the spider crawls into their midst and feasts.

A large spider prop was built for *Tarantula* and shows up in publicity stills, such as a famous (or maybe that should be infamous) one in which the arachnid appears to be floating amidst the clouds. But the prop is only used in a few scenes. Instead of the model, the moviemakers primarily relied on real tarantulas as their "stars." According to Bryan Senn and Lynn Naron, the crew used 60 different arachnids.[14]

Puffs of air moved the spiders about on the set. One remarkably good case of this occurs when the two state patrol officers begin spraying the spider with machine gun fire. As though it has felt the bullets, the spider turns *towards* them, no doubt buffeted in that direction by a jet of compressed air. (Of course, this implies the two officers probably would have been better off to leave the arachnid alone.)

As Dr. Matt Hastings, John Agar passes muster, and Leo G. Carroll turns in a solid performance as the tragic Professor Deemer. Baby Boomers probably know Carroll best as Mr. Waverly on the 1960s TV spy series *The Man from U.N.C.L.E.*, but he also shines in Alfred Hitchcock's *Spellbound* (1945). Meanwhile, Agar appeared in many genre movies throughout the 1950s, including *Revenge of the Creature* (1955), *The Mole People* (1956), *Daughter of Dr. Jekyll* (1957), *The Brain from Planet Arous* (1958), *Attack of the Puppet People* (1958) and *Invisible Invaders* (1959).

The nuclear threat element in *Tarantula* consists of Professor Deemer's synthetic nutrient, which a radioactive isotope triggers. Deemer is no mad scientist; he isn't out to hurt anyone. Quite the contrary, he hopes his synthetic nutrient can help feed starving millions as the worldwide population explodes. But the isotope renders the nutrient unstable, hence its effects on both himself and his two assistants, not to mention the arachnid. But the spider gets loose by mistake, not design. Still, the film implies that even nuclear knowledge used for good nevertheless goes awry. Deemer's experiments are conducted in secret, i.e., not "officially authorized." *Tarantula* posits that "lone wolf" scientists are bad for society, even if their motivations are good. The film implies it is better (intellectually and morally) to be regulated under the auspices of a major research institution and/or the federal government.

The spider symbolizes the Bomb, in that the arachnid is deadly and keeps growing, just as in real life the nuclear threat kept growing. Also, the bigger the arachnid gets, the harder it is to kill—and the greater the nuclear arms race escalated, the harder it became to control. However, the spider is killed, meaning the nuclear threat could likewise be put in its place by the authorities—in this case, the Air Force.

Along with many of its 1950s sci-fi brethren, *Tarantula* depicts an America awash in innocence and trust. For example, when Matt insists the sheriff phone the state police, he does so, and the state police don't balk and say, "A giant spider? Give me a break, pal." Instead, they show up as requested. Even the Air Force immediately believes the state police captain when he asks for jets armed with missiles and napalm.

At this time, movies still generally depicted social, religious and political institutions as trustworthy. Yes, there is more than a hint of Dudley Do-Rightism here, for we all know there were serious social issues simmering in the 1950s, and either intentionally or inadvertently, institutional America ignored many of them. For example, a white male in his seventies might remember the 1950s as a golden age—but an African American male in his seventies might recall that decade as more than a bit tarnished.

Still, the lack of irony in 1950s American science fiction films is somewhat refreshing. At its best, 1950s science fiction cinema evokes wonderment. Yes, too much wide-eyedness can distort discernment, but too much snarkiness can choke the soul.

Tarantula wants to entertain, not lecture, and for those open to its low-budget charms, it does just that.

The Phantom from 10,000 Leagues (American Releasing Corporation, 1955)

Credits: Directed by Dan Milner; Screenplay by Lou Rusoff; Story by Dorys Lukather; Produced by Jack Milner and Dan Milner; Photography: Brydon Baker; Music: Ronald Stein; Sound: Frank Webster; Editors: Dan Milner and David Wolfson; Special Effects: Dan Milner; Makeup: Ernie Park; Wardrobe: Frank Tate; Production Supervisor: Byron Roberts; Props: Ed Applegate; Assistant Props: Frank Lindsay; Stills: Bill Cary; Assistant Director: Earl Harper; Technical Advisor on Underwater photography: Alfred Hanson; Underwater Director–Associate Producer-Production Manager: Wyott Ordung; Gaffer: Charles Beckett; Grips: Chuck Hanawalt, Curley Jones; Camera Operator: Fred Kaifer; Assistant Camera Operator: Harry Young; Script Supervisor: Gordon Otto; Boom Operator: Bill Randall, Jr.

Cast: Kent Taylor (Ted Baxter aka Dr. Ted Stevens); Cathy Downs (Lois King); Michael Whalen (Prof. King); Philip Pine (George Thomas); Vivi Janiss (Ethel Hall); Rodney Bell (Bill S. Grant); Michael Garth (Sheriff); Helene Stanton (Wanda); Pierce Lyden (Andy); Wyott Ordung (Fisherman Victim); Norma Hanson (Scuba Diving Victim); Al Hanson (The Phantom/ Scuba Diving Victim).

A Milner Bros. production; black-and-white; 81 minutes; released in December 1955. Available on DVD as a stand-alone DVD and also in several multi-DVD collections, a typical example being *Attack of the Killer B's—10 B-Movie Collection*. Also available on Blu-ray.

If you were a kid growing up in the 1960s and 1970s, sometimes the monster in a science fiction movie made all the difference. If it was a cool monster, you could forgive any number of gaffes; if it was a lousy monster, forget it! And such is the case for *The Phantom from 10,000 Leagues* and its not-ready-for-scare-time creature.

On a beach, a man (Kent Taylor) who calls himself Ted Baxter (shades of *The Mary Tyler Moore Show*) and government agent Bill Grant (Rodney Bell) find a dead man and an upturned boat. The man and the boat are burned, but not by fire. In so many words, Grant tells Ted Baxter that he may be a suspect.

Professor King (Michael Whalen) of the Pacific College of Oceanography is secretly mutating aquatic animals, which include the title monster, the Phantom. He reveals to his inquisitive adult daughter Lois (Cathy Downs) that he is "working on breathtaking things, Lois. Great things." Speaking to Professor King's secretary Ethel (Vivi Janiss), Andy the janitor (Pierce Lyden) says the townsfolk believe the Phantom has killed three men.

With a Geiger counter, Ted learns that the dead man on the beach and the man's boat are radioactive. Grant again "runs" into Ted and tells him that he knows the truth: Ted Baxter is really Dr. Ted Stevens (I knew he didn't bear any resemblance to Ted Knight), a scientist who has written the controversial books *Biological Effects of Radiation on Marine Life* and *Nature's Own Death Ray*. Grant notes that in his lab, Ted "successfully activated the hydrogen isotopes in heavy water to form an atomic chain reaction. [Ted] called this development the first workable death ray." Uh-oh.

Close to the coastline, Ted explores underwater, discovering both a bright light and the Phantom. He escapes the latter. Next, encountering Lois on the beach, Ted implores her not to go swimming. (Naturally, Ted and Lois become an item.) Ted, certain that Professor King is involved with the Phantom, confronts the scientist. Says Ted, "There's a shaft of light coming up out of the ocean. I have reason to believe it's nuclear in character. Any object coming into contact with this light would be subject to extreme radiation. I believe this light killed three men." King pooh-poohs Ted's conjectures.

When Ted tells King that he and Grant plan to dive off the coast the next day, he is alarmed. But Ted and Grant perform their scheduled dive. We again see the Phantom and the bright light, though both men escape unscathed. George, Professor King's assistant, fires a spear from a spear gun at them, and later, George fires a spear into secretary Ethel's back, killing her—George plans to sell King's research to a foreign power, and Ethel knew about his scheme. (Yes, the plot is more convoluted than a multi-knotted rope.) Grant thinks King killed Ethel. But fingerprints on the spear and the spear gun prove that the murderer is actually George, who is quickly arrested.

Ted and King argue about the professor's experiments. King reveals that yes, there was a uranium deposit offshore that King took advantage of, creating both the "death ray" and the Phantom which guards the weapon. Ted insists that King destroy the Phantom and the death ray, but the conflicted professor asks for an hour to think it over. In the meantime, an offshore ship explodes; clearly, the death ray is to blame. Overcome, King takes several sticks of dynamite below the sea to destroy both the Phantom and the death ray. The Phantom grabs King, and the dynamite blows both (along with the death ray) to smithereens.

Trying to comfort Lois and apparently not worried about the radiation that has now contaminated the local waters, Ted says, "Nature has many secrets that man mustn't disturb. This was one of them." Then they walk down the beach arm in arm as Ronald Stein's melodramatic music swells.

When I caught this movie on TV in the 1970s, the Phantom's appearance was so unsatisfying, I almost changed the channel. It sports a poorly detailed body suit and an awkward, completely unconvincing dinosaur-like head. The creature's mouth moves up and down, but that's about it. Paul Blaisdell turned in far better work for probably half the cost.

The undersea "death ray" is ambiguous and at times inexplicable. The movie can't make up its mind whether it was the death ray or the Phantom that has killed three men. We see the Phantom overturn two boats, presumably to attack the passengers, but apparently it only dumps the latter into the sea so that the death ray can kill them. Why would it do this? Professor King's orders? Would the Phantom even be smart enough to take orders? And given its humanoid form, just what undersea animal was it mutated from?

Also, the death ray's power is erratic. It doesn't blow up the two boats we see overturned, but it completely obliterates an entire cargo ship. Among other things, this means that the ray would cut off once it reached the water's surface. Really? To be fair, in the movie Ted does say, "A weapon like this could destroy anything coming into contact with it ... once the chain reaction had started it could continue indefinitely, as a matter of fact keep becoming larger." But that still doesn't explain why it left the small boats intact but blew up the ship.

The Phantom serves little purpose in the story, and appears added almost as an afterthought. After all, 1950s science fiction movies needed at least one monster, and the Phantom fits the bill for this one, though I imagine kids who caught this film in 1956 were more than a little disappointed with the lackluster undersea ogre (it looks nothing like the sea serpent creature depicted on the poster). Aside from the monster, the movie's one special effect, that of the exploding ship, is actually quite good. In fact, it is so good, you have to wonder if this was actually stock footage from another movie. The actors are okay. Kent Taylor, who plays Ted, appeared in a number of movies and TV shows. Of interest to SFantasy fans are his appearances in *The Day Mars Invaded Earth* (1963), *The Crawling Hand* (1963) and *Brain of Blood* (1971).

As already mentioned, via dialogue the movie provides a detailed description of the atomic age experimentation that has led to both the Phantom and the death ray. The movie also makes it clear that people die due to this experimentation. So is the movie decrying atomic research? On the surface, it appears so. Professor King regrets the deaths he has indirectly caused, sacrificially destroying his lab and himself. In this sense, King is a little like *Godzilla*'s Dr. Serizawa who commits suicide so that no one will know the secret of the Oxygen Destroyer. At the end of *Phantom*, Ted indicates that regarding the danger of King's knowledge, "That's why he took his secret with him."

So nuke research is bad, *mon ami*? Not so fast. Like *Tarantula*, the movie actually argues that only *illegitimate* atomic research—that occurring outside conventional channels—is harmful. For example, Ted conducted an experiment similar to King's, but only on a small (albeit safe and authorized) scale. King, on the other hand, deigned to play God. Indeed, once King has trashed his lab, Andy the janitor spies a mutated turtle on the floor and asks, "What in the world is that? Do you mean to say that's one of God's creatures, professor?"

To which King replies, "No, Andy, that's one of man's follies, and I pray to God there'll never be another one." Clearly, King has scientifically trod where Man Should Not Go. By implication, America's Judeo-Christian mores should have constrained him, but King ignored them, and thus paid the price.

It might be a stretch to say that the Phantom itself symbolizes the Bomb. After all, it is only slightly larger than a man, and generally seems inept. The true menace here is that erratic death ray. Yet there is imagery that brings to mind the era's atomic anxiety. For example, when the cargo ship explodes, bright light flashes through King's window, similar to that a nuclear explosion would emit. We see King garbed in a radiation suit while conducting his experiments. And there are the radiation-burned bodies (we don't see the burns, the filmmakers apparently squeamish about this).

Finally, there is the Cold War subplot. George plans to sell Professor King's research to a Communist country. Secretary Ethel becomes aware of the scheme, hence the reason George kills her. This episode played into the paranoia of the era concerning atomic age national security and the need to be on the lookout for spies and double-crossers—even your own assistant (i.e., Professor King's George) might be a traitor. He might also be a stunningly inept murderer who leaves his fingerprints all over the murder weapon. Of course, this is fitting in a movie that itself can often be stunningly inept.

The Phantom from 10,000 Leagues is low wattage stuff. There is no light at the end of this tunnel—just a dead battery.

Attack of the Crab Monsters (Allied Artists, 1957)

Credits: Produced and Directed by Roger Corman; Writer-Associate Producer: Charles B. Griffith; Photography: Floyd Crosby; Music: Ronald Stein; Editor: Charles Gross; Makeup: Curly Batson; Set Decorator: Karl Brainard; Assistant Director: Maurice Vaccarino; Second Assistant Director: Lindsley Parsons, Jr.; Underwater Scenes Directed by Charles B. Griffith; Underwater Technician: Maitland Stuart; Chief Grip: Charles Hanawalt; Gaffer: Floyd Williams.

Cast: Richard Garland (Dale Drewer); Pamela Duncan (Dr. Martha Hunter); Russell Johnson (Hank Chapman); Leslie Bradley (Dr. Karl Weigand); Mele Welles (Prof. Jules Deveroux); Richard Cutting (Dr. James Carson); Beach Dickerson (Seaman Ron Fellows); Tony Miller (Seaman Jack Sommers); Ed Nelson (Ensign Quinlan-Crab Monsters); Charles B. Griffith (Tate).

A Los Altos Production; black-and-white; 62 minutes; released on March 3, 1957. Double-billed with Roger Corman's *Not of This Earth* (1957). Available on DVD as part of the set *Roger Corman's Cult Classics Triple Feature* (with *War of the Satellites* and *Not of This Earth*).

We've all heard, "You are what you eat," but according to this movie, you are what eats you.

This summarizes the theme of 1957's *Attack of the Crab Monsters*. For a low-budget B thriller, the movie sports an intelligent script, good acting and interesting implications. But for many, the hangdog (or should that be hangcrustacean?) look of the monsters negates the film's positive aspects.

An expedition consisting of six scientists arrive on a Pacific atoll to discover what became of the members of an earlier expedition, who have disappeared. Hank Chapman (Russell Johnson, the Professor on *Gilligan's Island*) tells two sailors stationed on the island that the eggheads are "here to study fallout effects at their worst." In regard to a recent H-bomb test, Hank says "A tremendous amount of radioactive fallout came this way. A great, seething, burning cloud of it sank into this area, blanketing the island with hot ashes and radioactive seawater." Doesn't exactly sound like an island resort.

5. Red, White and Blue Behemoths: 1953–1963 (Attack of the Crab Monsters) • 143

In the classic still from *Attack of the Crab Monsters* (Allied Artists, 1957), a giant crab gets ready to dine on Dr. Karl Weigand (Leslie Bradley).

The Navy plane that brought the group to the island takes off, and inexplicably explodes in mid-air. That night, physicist Dr. Karl Weigand (Leslie Bradley) reads aloud part of the previous group's journal, which tells of discovering a five-foot worm-like creature before the log abruptly ends.

That night, biologist Martha Hunter (Pamela Duncan) "hears" the voice of one of the previous expedition's scientists calling to her. Outside, she meets geologist Jim Carson (Richard Cutting), who has also "heard" the disembodied voice. Their investigation takes them to the rim of a newly formed pit. Via rope, Jim lowers himself into the pit, but an earthquake knocks Martha unconscious and sends the unseen Jim to the pit's bottom. We hear him scream but don't see what gets him.

While Martha and Dale Drewer (Richard Garland) stay in the expedition group's house, the others investigate the island's underground caves. One of the crab monsters trashes part of the house, destroying the radio. Now the entire group descends into the caves to investigate, but another quake causes a stalactite to fall from the cave roof and sever the hand of botanist Jules Deveroux (Mel Welles). Another giant crustacean attacks the two sailors stationed on the beach. The sailors' ghostly voices "call" to Deveroux, leading him to his doom at the claw of a crab monster. The crustacean-devoured Deveroux promptly "speaks" to his scientist friends, but knowing something's up, they ignore his entreaties.

That night the surviving scientists journey into one of the island's underground caves and confront a crab monster. Hank throws a hand grenade at the creature, which causes a stalactite to pierce the crustacean's brain. While it is disabled, Hank cuts off one of the monster's claws. A second crab monster attacks (apparently there are only two), and the protagonists flee back to their house.

Weigand explains that the radioactive fallout has mutated land crabs to gigantic proportions. These mutated crabs absorb the minds and memories of any human they devour; the voices the protagonists have heard calling them are their former companions now absorbed into a crab monster. Martha asks why their friends have turned against them. Dale answers, "Preservation of the species. Once they were men; now they are land crabs."

Dr. Weigand explains that the crabs are made of disconnected atoms that are negatively charged. A positive charge would destroy them, as it does the severed crab claw. The monsters also have the ability to make matter explode, hence the Navy plane that blew up and the earthquakes that are rapidly shrinking the island.

Martha and Hank place electronic transmitters outside a sleeping crab's lair, but it winds up chasing them. The crustacean corners Hank, Dale and Martha on what's left of the island. As it approaches, Hank manages to force a transmitter tower to crash onto the mutant crab. The electricity kills it—and Hank.

Dale says to Martha, "He gave his life," to which she replies mournfully, "I know."

Despite the film's lackluster crustaceans, *Attack of the Crab Monsters* (seen on a double bill with *Not of This Earth*) did brisk box office business in 1957. Although it only cost $70,000, the film grossed over a million dollars.[15]

Even many Baby Boomers find the crabs' appearance ridiculous and off-putting. For one thing, the crabs actually have human faces, complete with human eyes and eyelids! What was the designer thinking? Certainly eyes on stalks would have been more unnerving, as well as more accurate. Bill Warren reports that the script depicted the crabs as black shapes scuttling about, but of course, the actual crabs are light-colored and clumsy.[16]

Also, the crab creature's articulations often leave something to be desired, and their unnecessary roaring noises sound like some chump making unnecessary roaring noises in a recording studio. In one scene, we even hear a sleeping crab snore! But in their defense, in long shots, such as the one on the beach during the climax, the crab creature comes off okay. Producer-director Roger Corman said in an interview that he had two titles for the picture, *Attack of the Crab Monsters* and *Attack of the Lobster Monsters*. He asked his assistant which she preferred, and she said, "I like lobsters. I don't think it should be lobsters." So crabs it was.[17]

If one can look past those crabs (and if you're reading this book, you're probably the kind of fan who can), the movie has much to offer. *Apocalypse Movies'* author Kim Newman writes "*Attack of the Crab Monsters*, despite its ludicrous villains, is a decent, chilling little film."[18] Charles B. Griffith's script is smart and low-key, peppered with interesting dialogue. The characters are as lifelike as the short running time allows, and none of them is unpleasant in the slightest. Even the hinted "almost but not quite" romantic triangle of Hank, Martha and Dale depicts each of them as a decent person. This is a grown-up approach not always (some would say not often) seen in 1950s American science fiction movies.

The film even treats Martha, its one female character, with uncommon dignity for

Hank Chapman (Russell Johnson, left), Dr. Karl Weigand (Leslie Bradley) and Dale Drewer (Richard Garland, on the ground) confront a giant (offscreen) telepathic crustacean in *Attack of the Crab Monsters* **(Allied Artists, 1957).**

the era. When she and Hank are going to dive together to set up the electronic transmitters, none of the characters say, "This is no job for a woman," or any other such tomfoolery. They just accept her as an equal partner. But to be sure, the movie also has her say at one point, "About time I fixed us some food." Ouch.

The film does leave many questions unanswered. The only fauna on the island are normal-sized land crabs, seagulls and the two giant crabs. What happened to the other wildlife—did the radiation kill it? Also, we only see two giant crustaceans. Why didn't the radiation mutate all the land crabs on the island? And why didn't it have any effect on the seagulls? Like God, radiation apparently works in mysterious ways.

The film's connection to the nuclear threat is more textured than in most 1950s science fiction-horror efforts. For example, fallout has produced the complex crab monsters, creatures that sport unsettling intelligence, ruthless cunning and even sardonic humor, i.e., their taunting of the protagonists. Radiation has created a menace that in some ways is almost "Man Plus" as opposed to just another case of nature running amok in the form of big creepy-crawlies.

The crabs' intelligence makes them unique among non-human radioactive mutants in 1950s American movies. Their strangeness implies that the ultimate outcomes of the

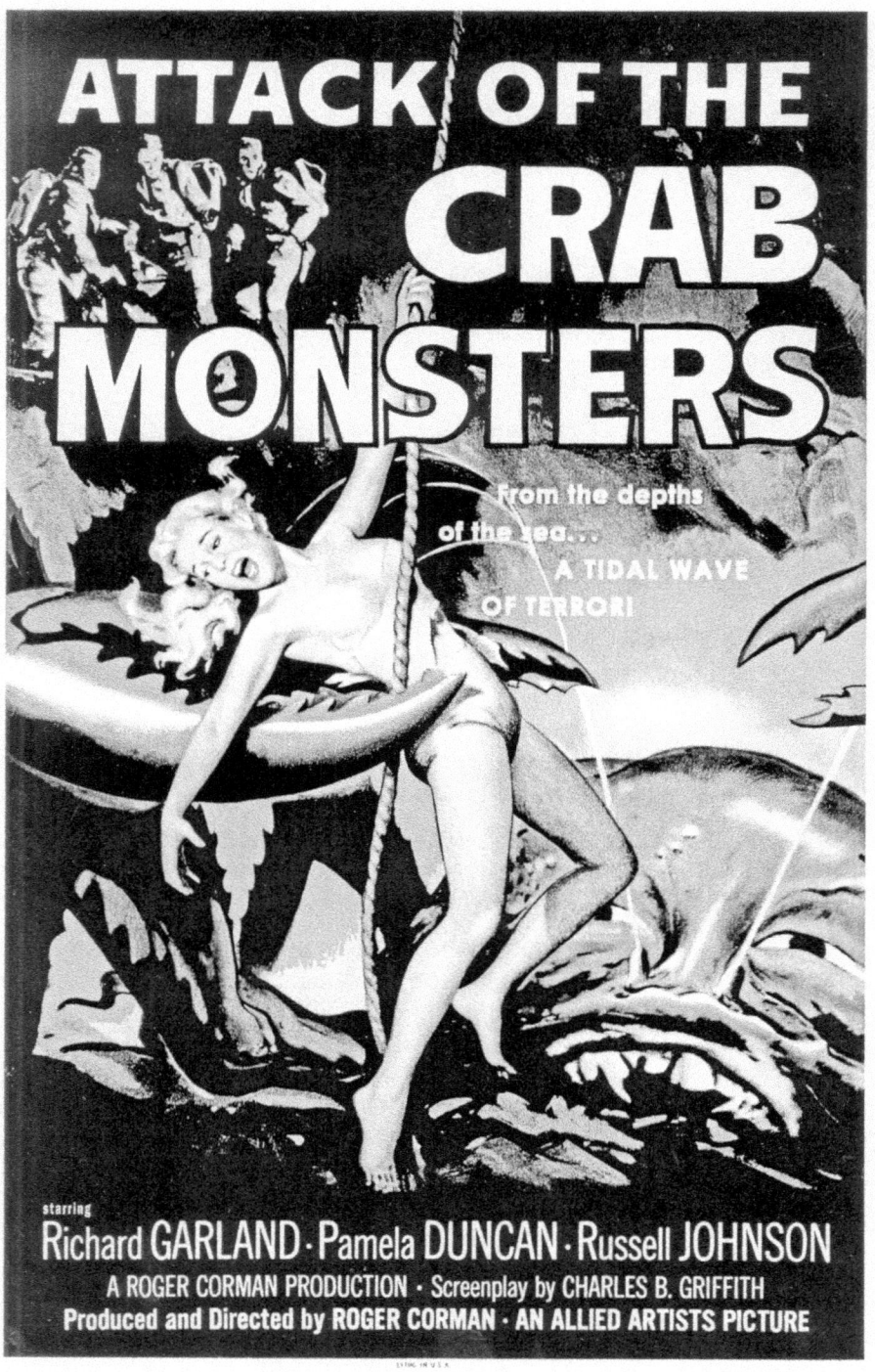

This *Attack of the Crab Monsters* (Allied Artists, 1957) poster should get plaudits for honesty in advertising for showing that the crustacean creatures do indeed have human-like faces.

atomic age are unknowable and perhaps dangerous in ways we might never imagine. Such a thought harkens back to Dr. Medford's disquieting observations at the end of 1954's *Them!*

And speaking of dire results, *Attack of the Crab Monsters* posits that once a crab eats a human, the human takes on new allegiances. As Dale says, their former friends have turned against them because the latter are now "land crabs." Apparently, moral absolutes do not determine our ethical worldview, but rather our current species. Courage, love, faith, loyalty—all disintegrate once one sports claws and ten legs.

In this sense, *Attack of the Crab Monsters* plays into the "loss of identity" subgenre of the 1950s, best exemplified by 1956's classic *Invasion of the Body Snatchers*. In the latter film, once you become a pod person, you have only the pod person instinct to survive—the transformation to podhood obliterates all other aspects of your personality. This appears to happen to the various characters who have now become one with the sentient crab monsters. One gets the impression that the characters don't mind the change—there is even a slight hint that they might enjoy it (i.e., their mordant sense of humor, as when Deveroux asks where the dead sailors are, and one of them replies, "We're right here, professor" as a crab claw clutches the scientist's throat).[19]

This could suggest that perhaps the nuclear threat can likewise absorb any one of us. Once "our side" trumps all other considerations, including the deaths of our own loved ones, we too have become a "new species." Certainly the presence of nuclear weapons in the 1950s, as well as today, merits complex reactions and approaches to their reality both in America and in the global community at large. In essence, there are no easy answers, though the far right and far left would have us believe otherwise. Nevertheless, if we let the nuclear threat devour us so that we serve it rather than it serving us, God help us all, each and every one.

Beginning of the End (Republic, 1957)

Credits: Produced and directed by Bert I. Gordon; Screenplay by Fred Freiberger and Lester Gorn; Art Director: Walter Keller; Set Decorator: George Milo; Photography: Jack Marta; Music: Albert Glasser; Music Editor: Morris McNaughton; Sound: Richard Tyler; Sound Effects: George J. Eppich, Douglas Stewart; Editor: Aaron Stell; Special Effects: Bert I. Gordon, Flora M. Gordon; Makeup: Steve Drumm; Assistant Director: Melville Shyer; Second Assistant Director: Wilson Shyer; Props: James Harris; Electrician: Austin Herrick.

Cast: Peter Graves (Dr. Ed Wainwright); Peggie Castle (Audrey Aimes); Morris Ankrum (Gen. John Hanson); Richard Benedict (Corp. Jim Matthias); James Seay (Capt. James Barton); Thomas Browne Henry (Col. Tom Sturgeon); Than Wyenn (Frank Johnson); John Close (Major Everett); Don C. Harvey (Guard at Lab); Larry J. Blake (Patrolman); Eilene Janssen (Teenage Girl in Car); Paul Grant (Teenage Boy in Car); Steve Warren, Frank Connor, Don Eitner (Observation Post Soldiers); Rayford Barnes (Chuck); Frank Wilcox (Gen. John T. Short); Douglas Evans (Norman Taggert); Hank Patterson (Dave); Patricia Dean (Red Cross Representative); Kirk Alyn (Bomber Pilot); Alan Reynolds (Insecticide Man); Lyle Latell (MacKenzie); Dennis Moore (Police Dispatcher); Hylton Socher (Frank); Richard Emory (Lieutenant); Alan Wells (Headquarters Sergeant); Bill Baldwin (TV Announcer); James Douglas (Army Sentry); Zon Murray (National Guard Sergeant); Bert Stevens (Col. Hill); Paul Frees (Voices).

An AB-PT Pictures Corp. production; black-and-white; 73 minutes; released June 28, 1957. Available on DVD.

They say imitation is the sincerest form of flattery, and if that's true, then filmmaker Bert I. Gordon must have worshipped at *Them!*'s altar. Yes, his *Beginning of the End* is that similar.

The film opens with two smooching teens in a car, buying it due to an unseen menace just outside Ludlow, Illinois. The authorities subsequently discover that not only has Ludlow been destroyed, but also that everyone in the town has vanished. This piques the curiosity of news reporter Audrey Aimes (Peggie Castle). However, the military won't let her past the town's roadblock. Sidetracking, she goes to a local USDA experimental station where she meets entomologist Ed Wainwright (Peter Graves) and his deaf-mute botanist assistant Frank (Than Wyenn). Audrey takes a gander at their giant radiation-produced tomatoes. Later, the military lets her take photos of the demolished Ludlow, whose destruction remains a mystery.

Audrey, Ed and Frank investigate a nearby, demolished warehouse. There they discover a giant locust, which promptly eats Frank. Ed realizes that the locusts must have devoured some of the giant radioactive tomatoes and subsequently turned giant themselves, attacking both the warehouse and Ludlow and eating every human in sight.

At first the military commander in charge doesn't believe Ed and Audrey, but his troops soon confront a platoon of giant locusts in the woods. Ed and Audrey go to Washington, D.C., where Ed tries to persuade the authorities that the local Illinois National Guard isn't enough to stop the locusts. The Army pits its full forces against the marching locusts, which are headed straight for Chicago.

Insecticide proves useless against the mammoth insects, and the Army's artillery is likewise ineffective. While hapless citizens flee in terror, the locusts swarm into Chicago. Once night falls, the big bugs become immobile; Ed explains that due to the chill of the night, the locusts shut down, but come morning, they will be hopping about, again ravaging the city.

Lt. General Arthur Hanson (Morris Ankrum) tells Ed that in the morning, the military will drop an A-bomb on the city. Ed theorizes that the right "locust call" for the monster insects would lure them away from Chicago into Lake Michigan. Hanson gives him until the break of day to prove his theory.

Ed does just that: A caged locust becomes agitated when it hears the right insect sound.[20] First, this broadcast sound summons the locusts to the building in which Ed's lab is located; then a boat in Lake Michigan blares the sound towards the city, causing the locusts to rush into the lake and drown. Audrey and Ed clinch in relief.

Most reviews of *Beginning of the End* are negative. The typical complaint involves the movie's visuals; for example, a 1965 *Castle of Frankenstein* declared that the film has "terrible special effects." It's true that most of the effects don't exactly pass muster, especially compared to previous big bug movies like *Them!* and *Tarantula*. For example, we can often see through the giant locusts. But a few of the effects really aren't bad. When the Army is battling the big bugs, there's a brief shot of a locust lunging at a soldier, and it works. Also far from terrible is a scene in which the locusts crawl up a building and one of them shatters the window of a woman brushing her hair.

Most big bug films (*Tarantula, Monster from Green Hell, The Black Scorpion*) used a large mockup of the critter's head in tight shots. But producer-director-effects creator

Soldiers fire upon an advancing horde of giant locusts in Bert I. Gordon's *Beginning of the End* (AB-PT, 1957).

Bert I. Gordon chose not to go this route. Too bad, because this would have improved scenes of the locusts fighting soldiers and attacking civilians at close quarters. Using real locusts caused Gordon headaches. After getting the okay to ship 300 male locusts to Los Angeles for filming, it turned out that the little beasties were voracious cannibals. By the last day of shooting, there were only 12 locusts left.[21]

Big bug films of the 1950s used *Them!* as their template, but perhaps none to the extent of *Beginning of the End*. We have the mysterious deaths, the monsters' signature sound, the educational film about the menace shown to authorities, and the dire predictions of global doom. At one point Ed says to Audrey, "We may be witnessing the beginning of an era that will mean the complete annihilation of man."

"Annihilation?" Audrey replies.

"Annihilation," Ed confirms, "the beginning of the end." Later in the movie, Ed says, "The time will come when the beasts inherit the earth." This amounts to a paraphrase of Dr. Medford's similar line in *Them!*

The Fred Freiberger–Lester Gorn script may be typical, but it really isn't bad. It even includes a couple of jokes: When soldiers are marching through the woods in search of giant locusts, one of them says, "Grasshoppers are good eatin'," to which his companion replies, "Yeah? Mustard or ketchup?"

If the movie's special effects had been better—say, if producer Gordon had enlisted low-budget effects wonder workers like Jack Rabin and Louis DeWitt—the film would no doubt enjoy a better reputation today. Also, stop-motion animated locusts might have been interesting, and they could certainly have interacted better with buildings and military equipment. Still and all, not all genre reviewers deride *Beginning of the End*. For example, Tom Triman called the movie "a gripping, scarifying science fiction shocker that once again explored the theme of radioactive mutation on a grand scale."[22]

Although Gordon used the nuclear threat to explain his monsters, this might have been mostly due to *Beginning of the End*'s determined replication of *Them!* Still, *Beginning of the End* does include Ed's formerly mentioned apocalyptic statements, and just as the giant locusts threatened annihilation, so too did nuclear weapons. Also, the movie makes clear that radiation can be dangerous stuff—for example, we are told that Frank lost his hearing and voice due to a radioactive accident. Later, when Ed jokes about his own scientific career being "a sheltered life," Audrey replies, "Sheltered? Look what happened to Frank."

The Monster That Challenged the World (United Artists, 1957)

Credits: Directed by Arnold Laven; Screenplay by Pat Fielder; Story by David Duncan; Produced by Jules V. Levy and Arthur Gardner; Underwater Unit Director: Paul Stader; Art Director: Jack Vance; Set Decorator: Rudy Butler; Photography: Les White; Underwater Photography: Charles S. (Scotty) Welbourne; Music: Heinz Roemheld; Sound: Charles Althouse, Joel Moss, B.F. Remmington; Editor: John D. Faure; Special Effects: Augie Lohman; Special Effects Design: Ted Haworth; Special Effects Photography: Robert H. Crandall; Makeup: Abe Haberman; Hair Stylist: Olga Collings; Assistant Director: Maurice Vaccarino; Production Assistant: Virginia Mazzuca; Dialogue Director: Harlan Warde; Casting: Kerwin Coughlin; Wardrobe Supervisor: Allan Sloane; Process Photography: Paul Eagler; Underwater Technical Advisor: Norman Bishop.

Cast: Tim Holt (Lt. Comdr. John "Twill" Twillinger); Audrey Dalton (Gail MacKenzie); Hans Conried (Dr. Jess Rogers); Barbara Darrow (Jody Simms); Casey Adams (Dr. Tad Johns); Harlan Warde (Lt. Robert "Clem" Clemens); Gordon Jones (Sheriff Josh Peters); Mimi Gibson (Sandy MacKenzie); Marjorie Stapp (Connie Blake); Jody McCrea (Seaman Fred Johnson); Robert Benevides (Seaman Morty Beatty); John Carlyle (Monster Victim); John Close (Deputy Larry); Michael Dugan (Clarke); William Forrest (Admiral Greenhouse); Gil Frye (Deputy Scotty); Dan Gachman (Deputy Brewer); Ralph Moody (Lock 57 Watchman); Joseph Hamilton (Lock Watchman); Charles Herbert (Boy with Morty's Cap); Byron Kane (Coroner Nate Brown); Ralph Littlefield (Gatekeeper); Dennis McCarthy (George Blake); David McMahon (Patterson); Milton Parsons (Lewis Clark Dobbs); Sarah Selby (Mrs. Simms); William Swan (Seaman Howard Sanders); Hal Taggart (Davis); Charles Tannen (Seaman Wyatt); Mack Williams (Capt. Masters); Eileen Harley (Sally).

A Gramercy Pictures production; black-and-white; 83 minutes; released in June 1957. Double-billed with *The Vampire*. Available on DVD as a stand-alone DVD or as a double feature with *It! The Terror from Beyond Space* (1958) as part of the *Midnite Movies* series. Also available on Blu-ray.

The title *The Monster That Challenged the World* sounds like a misleading AIP moniker for one of that company's humble '50s movies. Like some of those films, this entry's title *is* an exaggeration. But unlike some of those movies, this sleeper actually delivers the

Hans Conried, Harlan Warde, Casey Adams (in diving suit) and Tim Holt react to the appearance of a giant mollusk in *The Monster That Challenged the World* (United Artists; 1957).

goods seen on the movie's poster: a monstrous caterpillar-like creature, one of the best mechanical props of 1950s science fiction cinema.

An earthquake rocks the Salton Sea, and a naval boat rendezvous to pick up a skydiver turns into a nightmare, leaving three men dead. Lt. Commander John "Twill" Twillinger (Tim Holt) has just started his tenure as head of the naval experimental base; the men's deaths baffle him, especially since one of them died from a fear-induced stroke. Quickly, the authorities quarantine the Salton Sea and investigate the men's deaths, but this doesn't stop a young couple from taking a moonlight swim. What does stop them, however, is something below the water that pulls the screaming girl under. (Shades of *Jaws*.)

Two divers investigate, finding the girl's shriveled body; they also discover a huge white object that is hoisted up onto the boat. From an undersea cave, a large mollusk monster attacks the divers, killing one of them. Terrified, the other diver surfaces in hysterics. The monster rears up beside the boat, and Twill punctures one of its eyes with a boat hook, sending the shrieking monster back into the depths.

The white object turns out to be an egg laid by the monster. Dr. Rogers (Hans Conried) has it placed in a large vat of water in his lab, making sure the temperature is cold enough to prevent the egg from hatching. (That's what he thinks.) Dr. Rogers then relates his theory of the creature's origin: The recent earthquake exposed prehistoric mollusk eggs to radioactive water that the eggs absorbed, subsequently hatching. These monsters may escape to the ocean via the All-American Canal, and they could pose a major menace, for each of them can lay several thousand eggs. "Can you imagine," Dr. Rogers says, "an army of these things descending on one of our cities?" (Of course, any self-respecting Monster Kid could easily imagine this.)

The authorities go on the hunt for the creatures, putting every lock under surveillance. Twill becomes romantically acquainted with Gail MacKenzie (Audrey Dalton),

152 • Part II: Monsters

Dr. Rogers' widowed secretary. However, he is on hand when the remaining monsters are tracked down, and he and another diver plant explosives on the eggs, which obliterate them.

Remember that vat in the lab housing the mollusk egg? Gail's young daughter Sandy (Mimi Gibson) has turned up the temperature in the room to "warm up" one of the lab rabbits. This causes a monster mollusk to hatch from the egg, and the creature immediately menaces Gail and Sandy, cornering them in a lab closet. Twill uses a fire extinguisher to draw the creature's attention. This allows Gail and Sandy time to escape. Next, Twill scalds the monster with steam. Armed guards rush into the room and blast the squealing beast. Then Twill and Gail (and Sandy) stroll off to a happy ending, all thoughts of menacing monsters apparently having vanished.

The Monster That Challenged the World is a good example of Grade-B moviemaking at its best. The tone is low-key, the technical aspects professional, and the script relatively intelligent. For one thing, it allows the main characters to be somewhat rounded. Twill is a no-nonsense, by-the-book military man who gradually reveals a human side. Tim Holt makes the character believable. When he confronts the mollusk monster so Gail and Sandy can escape, he is terrified and shows it. This gives his Grade-B heroics a realistic human dimension.

The movie also allows one totally oddball character in the form of Mr. Dobbs, played with gleeful relish by Milton Parsons. Acting-wise, Audrey Dalton does everything she can with her widowed single mother character, and Mimi Gibson is credible as her daughter Sandy. Last but never least, the underrated Hans Conried ably brings to life the mild-mannered Dr. Rogers, a man who is both cordial and calm. The script allows him to

Gail MacKenzie (Audrey Dalton, left) screams in terror as a giant mollusk menaces her daughter Sandy (Mimi Gibson) in *The Monster That Challenged the World* (United Artists, 1957).

utter an interesting line: "Science fact and science fiction are not the same, not in the least."

Of course, it might have been more interesting if in this movie, Dr. Rogers had made a reference to actual science fiction monster movies of the day. This almost never happened in '50s SF movies; indeed, virtually every 1950s science fiction film occurred in a world in which there apparently were no 1950s science fiction movies. Dr. Rogers making a reference to *Them!* or *The Beast from 20,000 Fathoms* would have been a nice touch.[23]

The top attraction is the mollusk monster itself, and my guess is that this hydraulic ogre satisfied 1957 movie audiences. For the time, its articulation was state of the art, and I found the monster most convincing when I caught this film on a Saturday night Late Show in the mid–1960s. In fact, even my older brother Frank, a voracious science fiction reader who didn't always like SF movies, thought it was effective. As Barry Atkinson writes in *Atomic Age Cinema*, "Augie Lohman's mechanically operated giant mollusks-cum-caterpillars really leapt out of the screen."[24]

The atomic element in the film is slight. Nevertheless, Dr. Rogers identifies radiation as the agent that triggers the eggs to hatch, the atom once more creating a menace that, should it escalate (i.e., should thousands of eggs hatch hordes of mollusk-monsters), could threaten the entire country. But once again, it's science and the military to the rescue, implying eggheads and generals would likewise protect us from the nuclear threat.

As atomic age monsters go, few are as effective and creepy as *The Monster That Challenged the World*.

Monster from Green Hell (DCA, 1958)

Credits: Edited and Directed by Kenneth G. Crane; Screenplay by Louis Vittes, Endre Bohem; Produced by Al Zimbalist; Executive Producers: Jack J. Gross, Philip N. Krasne; Associate Producer: Sol Dolgin; Photography: Ray Flin; Music: Albert Glasser; Production Design: Ernst Fegté; Set Decorator: G.W. Berntsen; Music Editor: Robert Post; Sound: Stanley Cooley; Sound Editor: Charles Diltz; Special Effects: Jess Davison; Special Photographic Effects: Jack Rabin, Louis DeWitt, Irving Block; Stop Motion Animation: Gene Warren; Makeup: Louis Haszillo; Wardrobe: Joe Dimmitt; Script Supervisor: Doris Moody; Assistant Director: John Greenwald; Production Manager: Byron Roberts; Property Master: Robert Benton.

Cast: Jim Davis (Dr. Quent Brady); Robert E. Griffin (Dan Morgan); Joel Fluellen (Arobi); Barbara Turner (Lorna Lorentz); Eduardo Ciannelli (Mahri); Vladimir Sokoloff (Dr. Lorentz); Frederic Potler (Radar Operator); Tim Huntley (Territorial Agent); LaVerne Jones (Kuana).

A Gross-Krasne, Inc. production; black-and-white, some tinted sequences; 71 minutes; released in June 1957. Includes stock footage from 1939's *Stanley and Livingstone*. Double-billed with *Half Human* (1957), a poor Americanization of a Toho Abominable Snowman film. Available as a stand-alone DVD and also in several multi-DVD collections, a typical example being *Sci-Fi Classics Triple Feature, Vol. 2* (with *Devil Girl from Mars* and *Rocketship X-M*).

This threadbare tale of giant wasps in Africa has inspired many a critic to pen barbs such as "I really got stung on this one." But while *Monster from Green Hell* is not a good movie—and indeed, many find it one of the worst 1950s science fiction movies—it does have its merits, primarily the special effects of Jack Rabin, Louis DeWitt and Gene Warren.

Dr. Quent Brady (Jim Davis) stabs a giant radioactive wasp in the head in *Monster from Green Hell* (DCA, 1957).

To find out how weightless outer space affects Earthly organisms, scientists blast a test rocket into orbit, its payload consisting of spider crabs, guinea pigs, monkeys and wasps. The rocket goes awry and crashes in an area of Africa called Green Hell. Legend has it that Green Hell teems with monsters, and thanks to the downed rocket, now it does—giant wasps with useless wings that terrorize natives and wildlife alike. Prolonged exposure to outer space cosmic radiation has bloated the bugs to elephantine proportions.

Scientists Quent Brady (Jim Davis) and Dan Morgan (Robert E. Griffith) trek to Africa to find the downed rocket, for Brady believes mutated wasps are on the loose. Brady and Morgan form a safari that journeys on and on (and on) through an endless barrage of Hollywood stock footage. Our heroes encounter hostile natives, crippling dehydration, poisonous water, monsoon rains and tropical disease, and by this time the viewer may be forgiven if they have forgotten they are watching a monster movie.

Brady and Morgan finally reach the compound of Dr. Lorentz (Vladimir Sokoloff), only to learn that a giant wasp has killed the kindly physician. Lorna (Barbara Turner), the doctor's grief-stricken daughter, accompanies Brady, Morgan and a new safari to the heart of Green Hell. Naturally, our heroes confront the colossal insects, tossing explosives at the queen wasp. Undaunted, the understandably miffed monster corners the protagonists in a cave. Then a nearby volcano erupts. The subsequent torrent of lava kills all the wasps in an unsatisfactory special effects climax. After watching this dubious spectacle, Dan intones, "Nature has a way of correcting its own mistakes." Just as trite screenwriters have a way of magnifying theirs.

Jim Davis, best known for his role of Ewing family patriarch Jock Ewing on TV's long-running soap opera *Dallas*, does the best he can as the hero; indeed, all the actors struggle valiantly to make this movie work. But the leaden script and sluggish pace doom their efforts from the get-go. One of many scenes that doesn't work at all is that of the monsoon rains. A torrential downpour is supposedly inundating the characters, but they don't look as though they are getting wet—no doubt because they weren't! Scratches on the film are supposed to resemble raindrops. They don't.

Opposite, top: One of the giant wasps menacing Africa in DCA's *Monster from Green Hell* (1957). Gene Warren stop-motion animated the movie's big bugs. *Bottom:* As was so often the case in the '50s and '60s, this poster for *Monster from Green Hell* (DCA, 1958) promises more than the movie delivers.

But believe it or not, this movie begins fairly well. Albert Glasser's driving theme music evokes fond memories of Tarzan movies. Also, the first glimpses of a giant mutated wasp are effective. For example, we see a Godzilla-sized wasp appear on the horizon as hordes of natives flee in terror. Unfortunately, the monsters' sizes vary greatly throughout the film, not exactly helping our suspension of disbelief.

As with so many of its cinematic kin, this movie's major assets are the monsters themselves. These stop-motion bugs don't look much like wasps—as Bill Warren notes, they look more like beetles[25]—but their design is intriguing and their articulation proficient. As a kid, I would have loved these monsters. Alas, I didn't finally see *Monster from Green Hell* until I was in my early thirties.

In addition to the model bugs, a huge insect head prop occasionally pokes out of African foliage to sting a hapless native (yes, these mutated wasps inexplicably have stingers in their heads instead of their tails). Regrettably, due to the film's limited budget, the wasps enjoy scant screen time, but any Monster Kid at Heart will appreciate their fleeting moments.

There is little discussion of radiation or related topics; the message appears to be that prolonged exposure to cosmic radiation is a Bad Thing. But this movie cheerily posits that Nature will arrive at the last minute to save the day, i.e., the fortuitous volcanic eruption that kills the wasps. This is a stark contrast to Nature's wrath seen in such Japanese atomic age films as 1954's *Godzilla*, a topic explored more fully in the next chapter.

Attack of the Giant Leeches (AIP, 1959)

Credits: Directed by Bernard L, Kowalski; Screenplay by Leo Gordon; Produced by Gene Corman; Executive Producer: Roger Corman; Art Director: Dan Haller; Photography: John M. Nickolaus, Jr.; Music: Alexander Laszlo; Sound: Al Overton; Editor: Carlo Lodato; Assistant Director: John C. Chulay; Production Manager: Jack Bohrer; Props: Richard M. Rubin; Production Secretary: Kinta Zertuche.

Cast: Ken Clark (Steve Benton); Yvette Vickers (Liz Walker); Jan Shepard (Nan Greyson); Michael Emmet (Cal Moulton); Tyler McVey (Doc Greyson); Bruno Ve Sota (Dave Walker); Gene Roth (Sheriff Kovis); Daniel White (Porky Reed); George Cisar (Lem Sawyer); Joseph Hamilton (Sam Peters); Walter Kelley (Mike); Guy Buccola, Ross Sturlin (Giant Leeches).

A Balboa Productions film; black-and-white; 62 minutes; released in October 1959. Alternate title: *The Giant Leeches*. Available on DVD as a stand-alone DVD and also in several multi-DVD collections, a typical example being *Attack of the Killer B's—10 B-Movie Collection*.

This foray into atomically enlarged wildlife is so thick with Southern fried melodrama that it could have been called *White Trash Leeches*.

One night in the Florida Everglades, Lem (George Cisar) is startled to see the title menace in the swamp and takes a shot at it. Later, in a local hangout managed by Dave (Bruno Ve Sota), Lem's fellow rednecks ridicule his tale. Lem takes offense.

Long-suffering Dave appeals to his knockout vixen wife Liz (Yvette Vickers) to ease up on strutting her stuff in front of the men, but Liz finds Dave repulsive and lets him know it. When she goes for a stroll, she encounters Lem, now a sucker-scarred victim of one of the giant leeches; her screams bring game warden Steve (Ken Clark) and his girl-

5. Red, White and Blue Behemoths: 1953–1963 (Attack of the Giant Leeches) • 157

Heroes Ken Clark (at left) and Walter Kelley give those giant leeches what-for with their oars in *Attack of the Giant Leeches* **(AIP, 1959).**

friend Nan (Jan Shepard) to the scene. Steve reports the man's strange demise to Sheriff Kovis (Gene Roth), who immediately dismisses it.

Slut-bucket Liz sneaks into the woods to meet up with smooth-talking Cal (Michael Emmet)—they're having an affair, y'see. Dave catches them in the act and, with shotgun in hand, marches the terrified couple into the swamp. As they plead with Dave, giant leeches attack them and pull them underwater. When Dave tells the sheriff this story, the law officer doesn't believe him and locks him up. Alone in his jail cell, Dave hangs himself.

Two local yokels journey into the swamp to find the monsters, which drag them down to an underwater cave. There, the two hapless rednecks, along with Liz and Cal, scream and moan as the oversized leeches drain their blood—not quite enough to kill the luckless quartet, but just enough to weaken them so they can't escape. Obviously, the leeches have a lot in common with career politicians.

Meanwhile, Nan's father Doc Greyson (Tyler McVey) wants to dynamite the swamp to kill the creatures. Steve vetoes his idea because it might harm other underwater wildlife (shades of the EPA). Nevertheless, Doc drops a bundle of dynamite into the swamp, and the resultant explosion brings three corpses—those of Cal and his two redneck companions—to the surface; Liz, however, remains below. An autopsy determines that the corpses have been drained of blood, and the protagonists realize that Liz may still be alive.

At this point, Steve concurs with Doc about killing the creatures. He and his friend Mike (Walter Kelley) meet in a boat at the swamp while Doc, Nan, the sheriff and others look on. Steve leaps into the water, spears one of the leeches but loses his spear gun, then surfaces. Mike gives him another spear gun.

Liz's now lifeless body rises to the top of the waters; Mike hauls her corpse into the boat. Below the water, a leech attacks Steve, but Mike dives under and fends it off with a knife. In the boat, Steve and Mike quickly row to shore. Mike places dynamite on the swamp bottom, and once he is back on dry land, he tells Steve, "I used one hundred sticks at 40 percent. Ought to blow the bottom right off." Steve pushes the plunger, resulting in a huge explosion that apparently does indeed blow the bottom right off. Several dead giant leeches float to the surface, and the characters walk from the shore, assuming the monsters are dead. But wait a minute—what's that I hear? Why, it's the leeches' signature "sucker noises," indicating that the menace lives on.

Attack of the Giant Leeches is a minor science fiction horror item that wastes little time from start to finish (it only lasts 62 minutes). The leech monsters themselves are men in leech costumes, and to explain the monsters' arms, Lem notes that the creatures "had arms like a man." The costumes are occasionally effective, especially in the scene in which the leeches creep over the quartet of human blood banks in the underwater grotto, siphoning off a little blood here, a little blood there, indifferent to their victims' groans. As a kid, I found this sequence nightmarish, and it still holds up well today.

The leeches' whirring vocals are okay—after all, just as every Elvis imitator had to have a snarl, so every '50s mutant monster had to have a signature sound. However, we also hear the leeches roar like big cats, which is ludicrous. (However, even in *Them!* the ant that almost gets Pat Medford emits a mammalian roar when it's shot to death. Also in *Tarantula*, the title arachnid roars just as it's about to eat somebody.)

The story moves swiftly, and the main human drama spotlights the triangle of sincere Dave, scheming Liz and duplicitous Cal. These scenes, minus the leeches, would have been right at home in fare like 1958's *God's Little Acre*. Needless to say (but I'm saying it anyway), Dave is the only one of the trio who merits viewer sympathy.

Dave tells the sheriff he only meant to scare Liz and Cal, not for them to be killed, but the sheriff dismisses Dave's tale of swamp creatures. What remains unclear is why Dave hangs himself in his jail cell. He knows he didn't kill Liz and Cal, and the horror of the monsters themselves wouldn't be enough for him to commit suicide. Perhaps he is afraid he will be convicted of two murders he didn't commit. Or perhaps he feels guilty, thinking that if he hadn't forced Liz and Cal into the water, the leeches wouldn't have gotten them. Sadly, when Dave bows out of the film at the end of a rope, the storyline shoves Deep South melodramatics aside and becomes standard low-budget science fiction-horror stuff.

The actors all turn in professional performances, especially Bruno Ve Sota as the soul-torn Dave. Yvette Vickers also scores as his two-timing floozy wife, and Michael Emmet convinces as a craven opportunist willing to throw Liz to the vultures if Dave will spare his life. Everyone takes his and her roles seriously enough, and the ambience actually makes you feel as though this might have taken place in a Florida swamp, though of course, it didn't.

In *Scary Monsters* #20, Paul Parla interviewed Ross Sturlin, who played one of the leeches. At the behest of executive producer Roger Corman, Sturlin and actor Ed Nelson built the two leech costumes virtually from scratch—and speaking of scratch, because the inside skeleton of the leeches was a tangle of chicken wire, Sturlin and the other leech player, Guy Buccola, were often cut and poked inside the costumes.[26] Sturlin also noted that he and Yvette Vickers "had a ball," keeping the cast in stitches, revelry frowned upon by director Bernard Kowalski.[27]

When Doc and Nan discuss the creatures' possible origin, Doc opines, "Maybe the proximity of Cape Canaveral has got something to do with it ... they use atomic energy in their first stages of launching, not all of them have been successful."

Nan says, "You think if some animal life was close by, not close enough to be killed, but close enough to feel the effects of the radioactive energy that—"

"A mutation. A type of gigantism of some common animal."

In this scenario, unlike so many of the colossal insects and arachnids that infested 1950s movie screens, the giant leeches don't seem so large as to be impossible. They would be a nasty threat, but they would probably menace more poachers than law-abiding citizens, meaning that, ironically, the giant leeches might be good for the environment!

The talk of Cape Canaveral alludes to the heated space race of the day between the U.S. and the U.S.S.R. Russia seemed to be ahead, much to many Americans' dismay. The triumph of Sputnik in 1957 was a bitter pill for Uncle Sam to swallow, but of course the space race was far from over, and I think we all know who landed on the moon first. Unless, of course, you're one of those unbelievers who thinks the whole thing was filmed on a Hollywood sound stage. If so, I hope you like the Kool-Aid.

The Slime People (Donald J. Hansen Enterprises, 1963)

Credits: Directed by Robert Hutton; Screenplay by Blair Robertson and Vance Skarstedt (a.k.a. Joseph F. Robertson); Produced by Joseph F. Robertson; Associate Producers: Donald J. Hansen, Joseph F. Robertson; Photography: William Troiano; Music: Lou Froman. Sound: Rod Sutton; Editor: Don Henderson; Special Effects: Harry Woolman, Charles Duncan; Costumes: Tom Holland; Assistant Director: Herb Willis; Stunts: Bob Herron, Fred Stromsoe, Bob Miles; Lighting: George Breslaw; Camera Operator: James Crabe; Assistant Camera Operator: Pat O'Mara; Property Master: Mike Ezzes.

Cast: Robert Hutton (Tom Gregory); Les Tremayne (Norman Tolliver); Robert Burton (Prof. Galbraith); Susan Hart (Lisa Galbraith); William Boyce (Cal Johnson); Judee Morton (Bonnie Galbraith); John Close (Vince Williams); Edward Finch Adams (Man in Screening Room); Tracy J. Putnam (Dr. Timothy Brough); Bob Herron, Jock Putnam (Slime People).

A Joseph F. Robertson production; black-and-white; 76 minutes; released on September 18, 1963. Available on DVD as a stand-alone DVD and also in several multi-DVD collections, a typical example being *Creepy Creature, Volume 2* (with the same producer's *The Crawling Hand*).

Long before Bill Murray got slimed in the original *Ghostbusters*, there was *The Slime People*. These creatures don't slime you; they just run a spear through your chest. The reason for such antisocial behavior? It seems that our underground nuclear testing has disturbed their subterranean habitat, hence the reason they attack the surface world—and also the reason this movie is included in a chapter filled with otherwise giant monsters.

A TV news reporter and a scientist do characterize the Slimeys as "large," and a scientist likewise describes them with the adjective "prehistoric." But they are probably only about six and a half feet tall. However, (1) they are monsters (the movie treats them as decidedly subhuman) and (2) they do get riled up due to nuclear testing. The movie in which they appear probably riled up many a patron who paid to see it in 1963.

Experiencing air turbulence, news reporter Tom Gregory (Robert Hutton) lands his plane in a strangely deserted airport. He quickly runs into Professor Galbraith (Robert Burton) and his attractive daughters Lisa (Susan Hart) and Bonnie (Judee Morton). They inform Tom that Slime People have attacked L.A.; the army fought against them but lost. Now the Slimeys have built a huge wall (interchangeably referred to as a dome). Most of the citizens evacuated the city, but a few, like the Galbraiths, are trapped inside. (They were up in the hills when the Slimeys invaded.)

Tom and the Galbraiths trek to a local TV station and watch a broadcast film of the siege. On it, newscaster Vince Williams says, "The report of large, monstrous creatures roaming about the fog of our city and committing mass murder has been confirmed." In addition, the film reveals that the Slimeys have blanketed the city with fog, using a machine that thickens the mist to a wall (a.k.a. a dome). The Slime People's goal: lower the surface temperature so that they can live permanently above ground—presumably after they've killed off all the pesky humans.

Bonnie Galbraith (Judee Morton) finds herself in the unwanted clutches of a Slime Person in *The Slime People* (Donald J. Hansen Enterprises, 1963).

Tom attempts to broadcast live, but the power goes dead. Then the protagonists run into another building and seal the doors; there they meet stalwart Marine Cal Johnson (William Boyce), who quickly takes a shine to Bonnie, and vice versa. (You didn't think an apocalyptic crisis was going to interfere with budding movie romance, did you?)

Norman Tolliver (Les Tremayne), an eccentric writer with a pet goat, pooh-poohs the notion of Slime People, but decides to go with our heroes anyway, *sans* the goat. Professor Galbraith employs some chemicals against the wall, but to no avail. (By the way, the wall looks just like the side of a hill, presumably because it *is* the side of a hill.)

Slimeys doggedly pursue the protagonists, who take refuge in a butcher shop. By this time, Tolliver is a firm if quasi-hysterical believer in the Slime People, and he freezes in panic as Slimeys close in for the kill. Tom, Professor Galbraith, Lisa, Bonnie, and Cal flee into a locked freezer where, the professor figures out the Slimeys' weakness: salt. Cal and Bonnie go in search of same, but one of the Slimeys abducts Bonnie.

Tom and Cal hustle into the hills. There they find Bonnie near what Tom determines must be the Slimeys' "main headquarters." Tom clashes with a Slimey and bloodily spears it (which probably provoked a satisfied "Oooo!" from kids who saw this on 1963 drive-in screens). Tom, Cal and Bonnie also find the creatures' wall-making machine, which can barely be seen through the thick fog.

Next, the heroic trio retrieves Lisa and Professor Galbraith, who bring two buckets of salt to the wall; the scant amount of sodium chloride doesn't even come close to breaking it. Meanwhile, Tom and Cal engage Slimeys in hand-to-hand combat. Amidst the melee, Professor Galbraith hurls a spear into the wall-making machine, which explodes upon impact, destroying the wall. The fog lifts and the Slimeys start dying in droves. "Fresh air is killing them," the professor tells his companions. And a new day dawns for our intrepid heroes, as well as the unseen citizens of L.A.

Many reviewers revile *The Slime People* as one of the worst movies ever made, but this is by no means universal. For example, the website *B-Movie Central* gives the film 3½ out of 5 bees. And in *Scary Monsters Magazine* #17, Lawrence McCallum notes that the movie possesses "a crude virility that sets it apart from many of its type."[28]

The premise is interesting, and employs the subgenre of survivors fighting against an overpowering menace, also used in 1954's *Target Earth* and 1964's *The Earth Dies Screaming*, among others. However, the *Slime People* filmmakers lacked the cinematic savvy and an adequate budget to pull it off. The monster costumes are okay, but the direction is static, the pacing often monotonous, and the production values almost nonexistent. The actors acquit themselves decently, and the movie does remind one of a sporadically entertaining 1950s monster show.

Robert Hutton, who starred as Tom, also co-directed the movie. He'd already appeared in 1957's *The Man Without a Body*, 1958's *The Colossus of New York* and 1959's *Invisible Invaders*, in which he played second fiddle to John Agar. Character actor Les Tremayne, remembered by Baby Boomers as the no-nonsense General Mann in 1953's *The War of the Worlds*, likewise appeared in a number of other genre entries, including 1957's *The Monolith Monsters*, 1959's *The Monster of Piedras Blancas*, 1960's *The Angry Red Planet* and the 1967 telemovie *Creature of Destruction*. He usually essayed sober roles, but in *Slime People* he gets to kick up his thespian heels a bit as the pixilated author.

The only reference to the nuclear threat is the underground testing that has so displeased the Slime People, but we never see any footage (not even stock footage) of such tests, or of destroyed Slimey underground digs. The creatures evince intelligence, given that they have a machine that can thicken fog into a solid wall, yet their weapons are primitive spears. Of course, such inconsistencies aren't only found in low-budget 20th century genre items. For example, the aliens in 2002's *Signs* arrive in spaceships, yet act like cavemen.

Regarding the nuclear tests that have ravaged the Slime People's underground environs, it's odd that none of the characters even implies that maybe this was a bad thing for humans to do. No one at any point says something like, "Well, you can't blame them for being angry, but nothing excuses killing hundreds of innocent people."

But hey, I realize this is a monster movie in which the Slimeys are monsters and nothing more. Still, it's a shame the film, with its interesting premise, couldn't have had a bigger budget and a better director. Even then, it wouldn't have been a classic, but it might have been an exciting B adventure. As is, it's a tepid thriller at best—and a slow disaster at worst.

Almost Atomic

Having come to the end of this section on American atomic age non-humanoid monsters from the 1950s and 1960s, some of you are no doubt thinking, "Hey, what about *The Deadly Mantis*? *The Black Scorpion*? And heaven help us, *The Giant Claw*?"

While each of these movies featured giant menaces, none of them was directly linked to the nuclear threat. All three were released in 1957, a point at which the American giant monster movie was starting to wither on the cinematic vine. The plots had become highly ritualized, and perhaps to add a new wrinkle to the fossilized formula, natural causes rather than nuclear testing freed the titular beasts. For example, an ice avalanche unleashes the Deadly Mantis; a volcanic eruption unleashes a swarm of Black Scorpions; and the Giant Claw hails from outer space. However, like nuclear weapons, these 1950s monsters were giant and destructive, and thus are second cousins removed from full-fledged atomic age creatures such as Harryhausen's Rhedosaurus, Jack Arnold's Tarantula and or Roger Corman's Crab Monsters. Hence, the reason for this mini-section on American non-humanoid monsters that were *almost* atomic.

The Black Scorpion is a "group monster" film brimming with wonderful stop-motion animation effects by Willis (*King Kong*) O'Brien and Pete Peterson. The highlights include a giant trapdoor spider chasing a small boy (don't worry—the heroes save him), a group of scorpions attacking a train, and the "granddaddy" scorpion, the biggest of the bunch, battling tanks and helicopters in a Mexico City sports stadium.

Apocalypse Movies: End of the World Cinema author Kim Newman states, "*The Deadly Mantis* is a symbol for the Bomb all right."[29] And I am predisposed to agree with him. But *The Deadly Mantis* generally receives brickbats from genre critics; for example, the venerable Bill Warren calls it "one of the worst SF films made by Universal."[30] On the other hand, *Castle of Frankenstein 1967 Fearbook* wrote, "Typical grade-B monster-adventure, competently produced and directed." Realized via marionette techniques, the mantis looks pretty good, but alas, its movements are often sluggish and nothing like the lightning-quick attacks of an actual praying mantis. Also, its mammalian roar sounds ridiculous (although this was standard in Big Bug movies). *Deadly Mantis* still has its moments—the best is when the mantis crawls up the Washington Monument.

The Giant Claw gives new meaning to *Castle of Frankenstein*'s bad movie phrase "has to be seen to be disbelieved." The script and acting are okay, but the colossal bird-beast is ludicrous. Of course, it has become *de rigueur* to insult the creature, but you just can't help but wonder ... did the special effects guys know how foolish their monster looked? Did they care?

The Giant Claw was, up to this point, unique among American giant monsters in that it hailed from outer space. Again unlike its contemporary Western big beast brethren, it was a global threat, literally circling the planet and finally lighting in New York City,

Opposite: The giant praying mantis in *The Deadly Mantis* (Universal-International, 1957) may not be radioactive, but he (she?) is a clear stand-in for the Bomb.

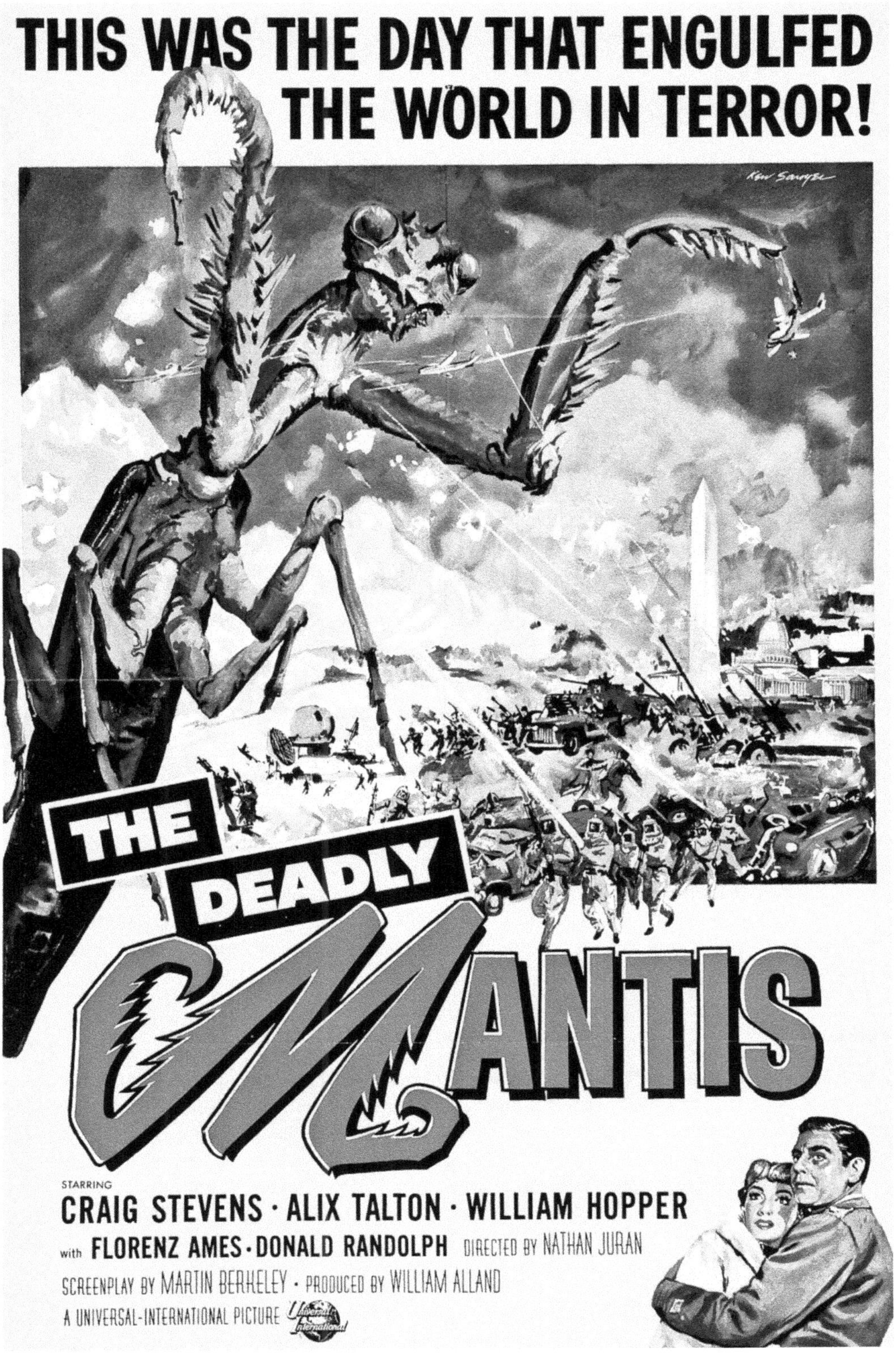

5. Red, White and Blue Behemoths: 1953–1963 (Almost Atomic) • 163

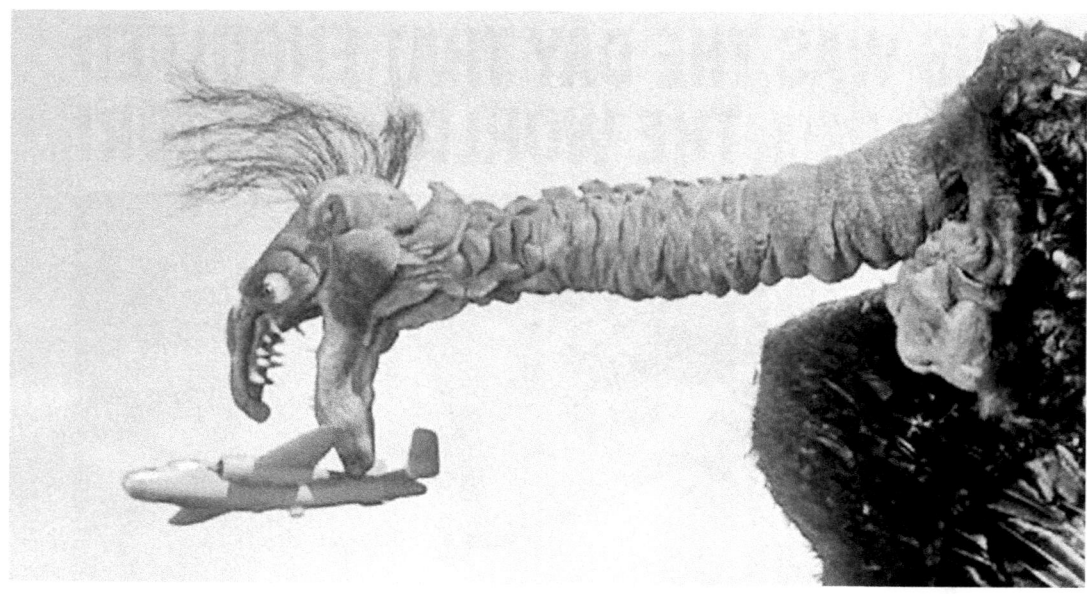

A great shot of perhaps the homeliest monster to grace American movie screens in the '50s: the fabulous and decidedly fan-famous *The Giant Claw* (Columbia, 1957).

where it destroys both the Empire State Building and the United Nations building (with a little stock footage help courtesy 1953's *The War of the Worlds* and 1956's *Earth vs. the Flying Saucers*). But never fear: Egghead Jeff Morrow develops a weapon that destroys the monster's force field, after which conventional weaponry sends the homely buzzard plunging into the sea.

THE BLACK SCORPION

An Amex Production; a Frank Melford–Jack Dietz Production; released by Warner Bros.; black-and-white; 88 minutes; released on October 19, 1957. Directed by Edward Ludwig; Screenplay by David Duncan and Robert Blees; Story by Paul Yawitz; Produced by Frank Melford and Jack Dietz; Music: Paul Sawtell; Special Effects: Willis O'Brien, Pete Peterson. Cast: Richard Denning, Mara Corday, Carlos Rivas, Mario Navarro, Carlos Muzquiz.

THE DEADLY MANTIS

Produced and released by Universal-International; black-and-white; 79 minutes; released on May 1, 1957. Directed by Nathan Juran; Screenplay by Martin Berkeley; Story by William Alland; Produced by William Alland; Music: William Lava, Irving Gertz, Henry Mancini; Special Effects: Fred Knoth; Process Photography: Clifford Stine. Cast: Craig Stevens, William Hopper, Alix Talton, Donald Randolph, Pat Conway.

THE GIANT CLAW

A Clover Production; released by Columbia Pictures; black-and-white; 75 minutes; Released in June 1957. Directed by Fred F. Sears; Screenplay by Samuel Newman and Paul Gangelin; Produced by Sam Katzman; Music Supervisor: Mischa Bakaleinikoff; Special Effects: Ralph Hammeras, George Teague, Larry Butler. Cast: Jeff Morrow, Mara Corday, Morris Ankrum, Louis D. Merrill, Edgar Barrier, Robert Shayne.

Of Beasts, Bugs and Behaving

Between 1953 and 1963, non-humanoid atomic monsters packed American movie houses and drive-ins. *Beast from 20,000 Fathoms* was the first but *Them!* proved to be the most influential, leading to a succession of colossal creepy-crawlies. However, while the menace might be terrifying, sometimes even apocalyptic, its reign of terror was temporary. The authorities always saved the day, primarily in the form of the U.S. military. Although sometimes eaten, sickened or squashed, Uncle Sam's finest marshaled on against the progeny of the Bomb.

Just as important as military intervention was governmental supervision; scientists should only conduct their experiments under the guidance of the authorities. Lone Wolf science produced monsters, Team Player science produced solutions. Also, national secrecy was paramount, for the Cold War stakes were high.

But in Japanese non-humanoid atomic age monster movies, the stakes extended far beyond statecraft, as we shall see in the next chapter.

6. Walking H-Bombs

1954–1967

In the English-dubbed version of 1955's *Godzilla Raids Again*, one Japanese character says, "Oh, banana oil!" Ludicrous, of course. But American wisdom smugly maintained that such absurd dubbing is typical of the absurdity of early Japanese monster movies as a whole.

This broad brush criticism might be news to *Village Voice* senior movie critic J. Hoberman, who wrote, "Gojira—Godzilla to us—is the great movie monster of the post–World War II period, in part because [director Ishiro] Honda seems to have conceived this primordial force of nature as a living mushroom cloud."[1] In other words, unlike America's Rhedosaurus, Japan's Godzilla wasn't just awakened by a nuclear weapon—he *was* a nuclear weapon.

This chapter explores Japanese monster movies dealing with the nuclear threat from 1954 through 1967. During their initial North American releases, films such as 1956's *Rodan* and 1961's *Mothra* actually received several good notices for their visual effects. To be sure, the special effects in the Japanese monster movies that we will explore herein were erratic but not "awful" as many contend today, and especially not in their 1950s cinematic context. In some cases, their effects are superior to their American counterparts—for example, compare the visuals of 1956's *Rodan* to those in 1957's *The Giant Claw*.

In "The Imagination of Disaster," a seminal essay on science fiction films written in 1965 by esteemed Western culture critic Susan Sontag, she wrote, "[Science fiction movies] by the Japanese director Inoshiro [*sic*] Honda and the American director George Pal are technically the most convincing and visually the most exciting."[2] And perish the thought if you think Ms. Sontag wasn't forthright in her opinions.

In addition, Japanese art had a penchant for sometimes being stylized. It didn't have to be realistic, just visually appealing or poetic. For example, in 1964's critically acclaimed Japanese fantasy *Kwaidan*, much of the art design is intentionally unreal. Among other artificial images, the "Woman of the Snow" sequence includes a painted sky filled with painted eyes "looking" at a woodcutter stumbling through the snow.

As for dubbing, the original Japanese studios, such as Toho, can hardly be held liable. And not all English looping was worthy of scorn—for example, the English dubbing in 1964's *Godzilla vs. the Thing* is generally intelligent and reasonably effective. With the exception of *King Kong vs. Godzilla*, viewers can watch (via American DVD and Blu-ray) each of the films in this chapter in its original Japanese-language version with English subtitles.

The image of Mike, the world's first hydrogen bomb explosion, detonated on Enewetak Atoll on November 1, 1952. It was followed by the giant monster boom in both America and Japan.

Three of the eight Godzilla movies examined in this chapter contain such minimal nuclear threat content—literally a handful of spoken lines—that I almost left them out. However, they do offer insight into Godzilla's shifting status from nuclear war omen to family entertainment icon. Consequently, the entries on *King Kong vs. Godzilla*, *Ghidorah, the Three-Headed Monster* and *Invasion of Astro-Monster* (a.k.a. *Monster Zero*) are brief. However, the five other Godzilla films examined herein—the first *Godzilla*, *Godzilla Raids Again*, *Mothra vs. Godzilla* (a.k.a. *Godzilla vs. the Thing*), *Godzilla vs. the Sea Monster* (a.k.a. *Ebirah, Horror of the Deep*), and *Son of Godzilla*—contain substantial nuclear threat content, so their entries are detailed.

Japanese *kaiju eiga* continue to this day, most recently with Toho's 2016 *Shin Godzilla*, which re-imagined the Japanese King of the Monsters for the 21st century. And it all began with a major financial risk for Toho Studios in 1954.

Godzilla, aka *Gojira* (Japanese release: Toho, 1954)

Godzilla, King of the Monsters (American release by Trans World Releasing Corp. and the Godzilla Releasing Company, 1956)

Credits: Directed by Ishiro Honda; Screenplay by Takeo Murata and Ishiro Honda; Story by Shigeru Kayama; Produced by Tomoyuki Tanaka; Executive Producer:

Iwao Mori; Music: Akira Ifukube; Photography: Masao Tamai; Editor: Yasnuobu Taira; Art Directors: Satoshi Chuko, Takeo Kita; Sound: Hisashi Shimonaga; Sound Effects Editor: Ichiro Minawa; Chief Assistant Director: Koji Kajita; Second Assistant Director: Susumu Takebayashi; Stunt Choreography: Haruo Nakajima; Special Effects Director: Eiji Tsuburaya; Special Effects Photography: Sadamasa Arikawa; Special Effects Lighting: Kuichiro Kishida; Special Effects Assistant Camera Operator: Yoichi Manoda; Mattes: Hiroshi Mukoyama; Special Effects Physical Effects (wire work): Fumio Nakadai; Special Effects Production Manager: Yasuaki Sakamoto; Special Effects Assistant Camera Operators: Sokei Tomioka, Hajime Tsuburaya; Monster Built by Teizo Toshimitsu; Special Effects Art Director: Akira Watanabe; Special Effects Technical Adviser: Fuminori Ohashi; Assistant Camera Operator: Yuzuru Aizawa; Lighting Technician: Choshiro Ishii; Lighting Assistants: Shinji Kojima, Shoshichi Kojima; Executive in Charge of Production: Teruo Maki.

Cast: Akira Takarada (Hideto Ogata); Momoko Kochi (Emiko Yamane); Akihiko Hirata (Dr. Daisuke Serizawa); Takashi Shimura (Dr. Kyohei Yamane); Fuyuki Murakami (Professor Tanabe); Sachio Sakai (Hagiwara); Toranosuke Ogawa (Shipping Company President); Ren Yamamoto (Masaji Sieji); Miki Hayashi (Diet Committee Chairperson); Seijiro Onda (Parliamentarian Oyama); Tsuruko Mano (Mrs. Sieji); Takeo Oikawa (Chief of Emergency Headquarters); Toyoaki Suzuki (Shinkichi Sieji); Kokuten Kodo (Old Fisherman); Tadashi Okabe (Professor Tanabe's Assistant); Kin Sugai (Senator Ozawa); Ren Imaizumi (Radio Operator); Katsumi Tezuka (Hagiwara's Editor); Kenji Sahara (Young Lover on the Sound); Keiji Sakakida (Odo Island Mayor Inada); Tamae Sengo (Mother); Haruo Nakajima, Katsumi Tezuka (Godzilla).

Japanese version: Black-and-white; 98 minutes; released on November 3, 1954. Japanese title: *Gojira*.

American version: A Trans-World (Embassy Pictures) release; black-and-white; 80 minutes; released on April 27, 1956. Released in Japan as *Kaiju-O Gojira* (*Monster King Godzilla*) on May 29, 1957.

American credits: Edited and Directed by Terry O. Morse; Screenplay by Al C. Ward; Produced by Edward B. Barison, Richard Kay and Harry Rybnick; Executive Producers: Joseph E. Levine, Terry Turner; Photography: Guy Roe; Sound: Art Smith; Set Decorator: George Rohr; Assistant Director: Ira Webb.

American cast: Raymond Burr (Steve Martin); Mikel Conrad (George Lawrence); Frank Iwanaga (Tomo Iwanaga).

Simply put, *Godzilla* represents the nuclear threat seen through the lens of cinematic science fantasy. Far more than just "another" giant monster movie, the original *Godzilla* tackles heady themes including nuclear testing, the arms race, the atom bombings of Hiroshima and Nagasaki, the fire bombings of Tokyo and the place of a postwar Japan in the then-new atomic age.

Most Baby Boomer Americans are probably familiar with the American version of the movie, 1956's *Godzilla, King of the Monsters!*, an international hit in the West during the 1950s. This Americanization featured Raymond "Perry Mason" Burr in the lead. It also played frequently on American television from the 1960s through the 1980s.

I first caught *Godzilla, King of the Monsters!* in 1972 on a Saturday night TV program called *Boo Theater*. Although I was past my "kid years"—I was 16—I still found the movie powerful and impressive. My mother watched it with me; she was a big *Perry Mason* fan, and she shook her head, saying, "I can't believe he [Raymond Burr] would be in such a thing." However, decades later when I was living and working as an adult in a different town, Mom told me she was channel surfing one night and came upon *Godzilla, King of the Monsters!* Fondly, she said it reminded her of me. So I guess you could say this Americanization of the 1954 Japanese film had come full circle in my life.

Of course, the original *Godzilla* released in 1954 to Japanese audiences featured no American stars and was in many ways substantially different than the Americanized version. Intended for the Japanese market only, this Toho film became a commercial powerhouse in Japan, selling 9.6 million tickets, and thus launching the entire Japanese monster movie genre. Also, the original *Godzilla*'s ambitions were almost as hefty as the monster itself.

The story: In the Pacific, something mysterious sinks a 7500-ton Japanese freighter, as well as another ship sent to investigate. Masaji (Ren Yamamoto), an exhausted and shell-shocked survivor, arrives on Odo Island, where there is a small fishing community. That night, the Odo islanders treat a team of Japanese investigators to a native dance intended to ward off the legendary Godzilla, a monster on whom the atoll's elder blames the recent disasters. A typhoon blows up from nowhere, during which an unseen Godzilla attacks, destroying 17 houses and killing nine people, including Masaji.

Best known for his long-running television shows *Perry Mason* and *Ironside*, Raymond Burr gave a sweaty immediacy to his role of reporter Steve Martin as he witnesses Tokyo's obliteration in 1956's *Godzilla, King of the Monsters!*

Paleontologist Dr. Yamane (Takashi Shimura), his daughter Emiko (Momoko Kochi) and seaman Ogata (Akira Takarada) sail to Odo Island to investigate. They find high levels of radiation in the ruins, as well as a trilobite and a giant footprint. Soon Godzilla appears, his head rising above a hill's crest to terrify the villagers as well as the investigators. The monster leaves behind a set of gigantic footprints trailing into the sea.

At the National Diet, Dr. Yamane states that Godzilla, some 165 feet high, is an amphibious prehistoric monster that lived deep undersea; H-bomb tests "destroyed its natural habitat," forcing Godzilla from his lair and resulting in the creature's recent ship attacks. Dr. Yamane contends that Godzilla should be studied, not destroyed; to his dismay, the Japanese Coast Guard sets off depth charges near Odo Island to kill the creature. However, the monster, still very much alive, soon appears in Tokyo Bay. The authorities seek Dr. Yamane's advice on how to kill the creature, to which he replies, "Godzilla was baptized in the fire of the H-bomb and survived. What could kill it now?"

Betrothed to research scientist Dr. Serizawa, Emiko plans to tell him that, because she and Ogata are in love, she will break the engagement. However, in his basement laboratory, Serizawa shows her the result of his research, which terrifies her. Serizawa swears Emiko to secrecy.

Godzilla surfaces and demolishes a major section of Tokyo's dock area before heading back to the sea. The authorities erect a huge electrical barricade around Tokyo in the hopes that it will electrocute Godzilla when he again attacks. Dr. Yamane and Ogata argue over Godzilla's fate. Says Ogata, "Godzilla's no different from the H-bomb still hanging over Japan's head." Dr. Yamane counters that the monster should be studied to determine how it managed to survive massive amounts of radiation.

Godzilla surfaces again, easily tearing through the electrical blockade, which doesn't deter him at all. Quite the contrary, he melts several of the electrical towers with his white-hot atomic breath. Next, he embarks on his *tour de force* destruction of Tokyo, obliterating buildings while using his nuclear breath to set huge sections of the city aflame. Japanese military jets attack Godzilla with a barrage of missiles, sending him back to sea—but of course, everyone knows he will return.

The next day, Emiko helps treat victims suffering from Godzilla's raid, including a young child whose mother has died. The human carnage causes her to break her promise to Serizawa, and she tells Ogata about Serizawa's Oxygen Destroyer which Emiko saw in operation in the scientist's basement lab; he used it to disintegrate an aquarium full of fish.

Ogata and Emiko plead with Serizawa to use the Oxygen Destroyer to kill Godzilla, but Serizawa refuses, contending that any public use of the Oxygen Destroyer will make politicians want to possess the super-weapon themselves, thereby imperiling the world. Ogata and Serizawa's war of words escalates into a physical fight, which Ogata loses. But on TV, in the aftermath of Godzilla's attack, a choir of schoolgirls sings a hymn for peace; their heartfelt plea persuades Serizawa to use the Oxygen Destroyer to stop Godzilla, but it can only be used this one time. As he burns his notes, Emiko sobs.

In Tokyo Bay, Ogata and Serizawa submerge beneath the sea, and soon they spot a resting Godzilla. As Ogata surfaces, Serizawa activates the Oxygen Destroyer—then severs his line so that he cannot be pulled up. As he sacrificially dies, he sees Godzilla's demise, from flesh to bones to nothingness. A somber and mournful Dr. Yamane notes that Godzilla probably is not the only one of his kind, and that if nuclear testing continues, another Godzilla will surface somewhere in the world.

No, this isn't exactly your traditional monster movie happy ending.

In 1946, director Ishiro Honda had seen the desolate A-bomb ruins of Hiroshima, and according to Stuart Galbraith IV, he "had long waited to somehow translate the apocalyptic horror of what he had seen to the screen."[3] *Godzilla* gave Honda that chance, and clearly, Godzilla's fiery destruction of Tokyo is a stand-in for the World War II atom bombings of Hiroshima and Nagasaki, as well as the fire bombings of Tokyo. The film even shows us Tokyo's burned and injured survivors in documentary-like footage, scenes that must have evoked chilling memories to Japanese audiences in 1954, just nine years after the end of the war.

In addition to World War II, however, Godzilla also pertained to more recent geopolitical matters, specifically the fate of the fishing vessel *Daigo Fukuryu* (*Lucky Dragon No. 5*), previously discussed in Chapter 3's entry on *The H-Man*. On March 1, 1954, the United States exploded an H-bomb at Bikini Atoll, a blast far more powerful than expected. Though 87 miles from the blast, the *Lucky Dragon No. 5*'s crew saw the flash of bright light in the west, several minutes later heard the blast. Soon fallout inundated their vessel. Suffering from radiation poisoning, the crew became ill, and the ship returned to Japan. Tragically, *Lucky Dragon No. 5* radio operator Aikichi Kubnoyama died on September 3, 1954. The Japanese largely saw this as a postwar atomic attack on the island nation, feelings bolstered by tons of radiation-bearing tuna that had to be discarded.

Godzilla begins with the vessel the *Eiko-maru* being blasted by a bright light that sets the ship afire, and the sequence spotlights the radio man as water gushes into the sinking ship. This was a clear allusion to the *Lucky Dragon No. 5* incident. Later in the film, when a woman complains of "atomic tuna," she is referring to the *Lucky Dragon No. 5.*

To Western audiences, Godzilla appears to be the villain in the picture. After all, personifying the Bomb as he does, Godzilla is destructive, radioactive and unstoppable, and his rampage turns Tokyo into an inferno. However, to Japanese audiences, Godzilla was both villain and victim. Japanese film critic Tadao Sato said, "Watching the film, we understand how Godzilla feels.... Its lair was destroyed, so it was roused to anger. It isn't particularly malevolent. Even children can understand how it feels. They can understand Godzilla's feelings."[4]

Several commentators have noted that Godzilla's appearance reflects H-bomb tests as not only having awakened the creature, but also having injured him. Bill Bussone writes that Godzilla "represents the horror of nuclear war. He himself is a scarred mutation whose blackened, scaly hide represents and indicates the horrible burns caused by atomic weapons."[5] Godzilla scholar Steve Ryfle recounts that at a screening of the film for cast and crew, writer Shigeru Kayama and *Godzilla* star Akira Takarada were saddened by the monster's demise.[6] As Takarada said, "We [humankind] were responsible for triggering Godzilla's violence."[7] Thus, as victim, Godzilla lashed out at Tokyo as punishment for humankind having injured him and having destroyed his home, but as villain, he obliterated Tokyo as a re-enactment of the atomic bombings of World War II. In this sense, some have seen Godzilla as representing the wartime United States.

Cinematically, it takes a super-weapon to knock out another super-weapon, thus Dr. Serizawa's dilemma whether to use the Oxygen Destroyer and thus risk other nations co-opting it. As David Kalat states in his lively Criterion DVD commentary on *Godzilla*, Serizawa faced "the impossible choice of doing right by your country and doing right by the human race."[8] He made his choice, but it included taking his own life. Perhaps the only parallel in 1950s American science fiction cinema is found in 1955's *The Phantom from 10,000 Leagues*, in which an undersea Dr. King destroys his nuclear death ray, a weapon of potential mass destruction, while at the same time destroying himself.

Godzilla's disintegration quashes any hopes Dr. Yamane may have had to learn Godzilla's secret for surviving irradiation. Perhaps Dr. Yamane's plea to study Godzilla symbolizes a call to study Japan to see how it survived irradiation in 1945 and thereafter. But just as Godzilla is an atomic distortion of the former animal, perhaps postwar Japan is a distortion of its former self, having embraced the Western mindset to the possible detriment of its cultural past. Perhaps like Godzilla, Japan too is villain (its World War II aggression) and victim (its postwar mutation into a materialistic Western society).

Many argue that *Godzilla* is Honda's finest film. Following in its wake, Honda directed the majority of Toho's science-fantasy films in the '50s and '60s, including 1962's *King Kong vs. Godzilla*, Toho's most lucrative monster movie and the one that truly started the Godzilla franchise in earnest.

Another key component to Godzilla's success: special effects director Eiji Tsuburaya. Smitten with 1933's *King Kong*, Tsuburaya had hoped to one day film his own monster movie, and he was given the chance with *Godzilla* (though his initial suggestion that Godzilla be a giant octopus was rejected). Originally, "The Old Man" (as Tsuburaya's crew nicknamed him) wanted to use stop-motion animation to bring Godzilla to life, but Toho deemed this method too expensive and time-consuming. So Tsuburaya opted for the man-in-a-monster-suit approach, a technique which would later be dubbed "suitmation." This technique brought almost all of Toho's following monster menagerie to life, including Anguirus, Rodan, Varan and King Ghidorah (a.k.a. Ghidrah).

Tsuburaya also relied heavily on miniatures, and *Godzilla* shows he and his crew in top form in the ⅟₂₅ scale recreations of Tokyo. Not all the miniatures work—for example, the helicopter on Odo Island is an obvious model. The weakest effects sequence is that of the jets attacking Godzilla; even by 1954 standards, it was subpar. But due in large part to the painstakingly detailed city models, Godzilla's Tokyo wrath brims with nightmarish spectacle.

Godzilla's evocative music score was composed by Akira Ifukube. As Peter H. Brothers writes, "Honda may have given the creature its mind and Tsuburaya its body, but Ifukube gave Godzilla its soul."[9] He also gave Godzilla its signature roar, using a resin-coated glove to rub a contrabass' strings to do so.[10] Ifubuke's music for Godzilla is so striking that it became Godzilla's signature theme forevermore, much as Agent 007 James Bond has his signature musical themes stemming from his first film *Dr. No*.

Director Honda said that *Godzilla* "represents only about 65% of what I wanted to achieve; maybe if we had a little more time, money, freedom, we could have gotten 100%."[11] In terms of accomplishment, his direction is as important to the film's power as the visual effects. As discussed above, *Godzilla*'s special effects are uneven, even by '50s standards, but Honda's direction rarely falters, and clearly represents the mark of a director who cared.

In my opinion, *Godzilla*'s finest sequence is perhaps its most understated: the schoolgirls offering a hymn for peace the day following Godzilla's destruction of Tokyo. As the camera pans past line after line of singing girls, this powerful combination of image, sound and solemnity, spiritual in scope, is moving even when removed from its cinematic context. It becomes all the more poignant as the catalyst that convinces Dr. Serizawa to use the Oxygen Destroyer.

Not everyone believes the first Godzilla exclusively represented dread of the atom. Composer Akira Ifukube said, "The tenor of the times was such that people thought Godzilla might be the symbol of the departed soldiers at sea."[12] This controversial concept, something of a sub-reading of *Gojira* by some, found concrete expression in 2001's *Godzilla, Mothra and King Ghidorah: Giant Monsters All-Out Attack*. However, few dispute that primarily, the first Godzilla was the nuclear threat made flesh. In a 1991 interview, Honda said, "Starting with Godzilla as the embodiment of fear of the atomic bomb, the three of us [Honda, Tsuburaya and producer Tomoyuki Tanaka] agreed we should tackle the film earnestly as if dealing with a factual subject."[13] So they did.

Although Godzilla would continue as a character icon for decades to come, even into contemporary times, his first film remains unique. As commentator Jon Inouye wrote in 1979, "[T]he Honda-Tsuburaya team would never again match *Godzilla* in terms of its moody stylisms [sic], its revealing visual summation of postwar feelings…. There can never be another *Godzilla*."[14]

The Americanization

Prior to 1956's *Godzilla, King of the Monsters!*, there had never been an English-dubbed monster movie mass-marketed to American audiences. But produced by American moviemakers, this is the version that grossed $2 million in the U.S. upon its initial run and went on to become an international hit throughout the West.

To make it commercial for the U.S. market, the 98-minute Japanese film underwent a number of changes that included dropping scenes not necessary to the plot. The biggest change was filming new scenes that established Raymond Burr as the movie's viewpoint character, journalist Steve Martin. (The comedian of the same name would not become famous until the 1970s.) Via clever editing, Burr interacts with body doubles of the actors in the Japanese film, leans on an acquaintance to translate Japanese so that many scenes wouldn't require dubbing, and keeps the film moving with his steady voiceover narrative. The American footage was about 20 minutes long, so when added to about 60 minutes of footage from the Japanese original, the film was 80 minutes long, a perfect length for an American double bill (and later for late-night TV).

Over the past two decades, the original Japanese version of *Godzilla* has become well-known in Japanese science-fantasy circles in the West, and some fans have accused the Americanization of deliberately watering down the anti-nuke sentiments of Honda's film. However, this seems unlikely.

For example, according to Richard Kay, one of the American version's producers, "We weren't interested in politics, believe me. We only wanted to make a movie that would sell. At that time, the American public wouldn't have gone for a movie with an all-Japanese cast.... We didn't really change the story. We just gave it an American point of view."[15] Although the Americanization does omit scenes specifically referring to Nagasaki, H-bombs and irradiated fish, it still makes it clear that nuclear testing is the culprit behind Godzilla's attacks.

The Americanization likewise re-structures the story's chronology, as it begins with an injured Burr stirring in the ruins of Tokyo, and his voiceover becomes a flashback leading up to Godzilla's raid on the doomed city. While it is true that the Americanization loses much of the original's characterization and contextual depth, Martin's narration during Godzilla's Tokyo pillage gives the film a sweaty immediacy. Also, Burr takes his role seriously despite the middling dialogue he is given, never playing down to the material. His earnestness helps to enrich *Godzilla, King of the Monsters!*, and no doubt played a significant role in its commercial success.[16]

Tellingly, the original's most striking set pieces, including all the key scenes with Godzilla, were left intact. In fact, during the argument between Ogata and Serizawa concerning the Oxygen Destroyer, the English dub allows Ogata to make a great comeback to Serizawa that doesn't appear in the original: "Then you have a responsibility no man has ever faced: You have your fear, which might become reality, and you have Godzilla, which is reality."

Peter H. Brothers did a good job of summing up the fans' estimation of *Godzilla, King of the Monsters!* when he noted, "[Director Terry Morse] paid Honda's film a great compliment by treating it with respect.... As such this international version titled *Godzilla, King of the Monsters!*, while not true to the letter of Honda's film, was still true to its overall spirit."[17]

Progeny of Godzilla

The 1953 American film *The Beast from 20,000 Fathoms*, covered in the previous chapter, inspired *Godzilla*. However, the Japanese took the nuclear metaphor in directions

In *Gorgo* (MGM, 1961), the monster was played by a man in a monster suit *à la Gojira*.

the Western film didn't attempt, and Toho's "atomization" of Godzilla made it a truly Japanese film.

The West "returned the favor" in 1961 with the spectacular *Gorgo*. Like Godzilla, Gorgo was gigantic, invulnerable to military weapons, and destructive, decimating a major city (London) in a *tour de force* display. Gorgo was likewise lashing out at humankind but, in her case, for the abduction and exploitation of her son. Also, the 200-foot Mama Gorgo and son were brought to life via suitmation, just like Godzilla, and the film made extensive use of intricately detailed miniatures, many of which Mama Gorgo trashes. Of interest is that both *Beast from 20,000 Fathoms* and *Gorgo* were directed by Eugene Lourie. Also of interest is that originally, *Gorgo* was set to take place in Japan.

Godzilla's success also inspired plenty of other Rising Sun *daikaiju*, most from Toho's stable—Anguirus, Rodan, Varan, Mothra, Dogora *et al*. Rival studio Daiei also got into the *kaiju eiga* act with 1965's *Gamera, the Giant Monster*, a series that resulted in seven sequels (eight if you count the 1980 pastiche *Gamera Super Monster*). In 1967, two other Japanese studios jumped on the *kaiju* wagon: Nikkatsu with *Gappa, the Triphibian Monster* (a.k.a. *Monster from a Prehistoric Planet*) and Shochiku with *The X from Outer Space*, featuring the endearing "chicken-monster" Guilala.

Godzilla's progeny likewise infested Japanese TV screens; for example, Japan Radio Pictures produced the four-part TV miniseries *Agon the Atomic Dragon* in 1964. But the most popular TV *kaiju* series was *Ultraman*, which debuted on July 17, 1966, enjoying an initial first run of 39 episodes. Although Ultraman himself was not a *kaiju*, he battled a host of oversized foes, including Baltan, Bemlar and Red King.

Although giant creatures had appeared in Japanese films prior to *Godzilla*, the King of the Monsters' debut film in 1954 gave birth to a franchise, and an entire Japanese genre. We focus the spotlight on many of Godzilla's cinematic cousins in the following pages.

Godzilla Raids Again (Japanese release: Toho, 1955)

Gigantis, the Fire Monster (American release: Warner Bros., 1959)

Credits: Directed by Motoyoshi Oda; Screenplay by Takeo Murata and Shigeaki Hidaka; Story by Shigeru Kayama; Produced by Tomoyuki Tanaka; Music: Masaru Sato (Japanese version only, though a few brief snatches show up in the Americanized version); Photography: Seiichi Endo; Art Director: Takeo Kita; Assistant Art Director: Teruaki Abe; Editor: Kazuji Taira; Sound: Masanobu Miyazaki; Sound Mixer: Ichiro Minawa; Special Effects Director: Eiji Tsuburaya; Special Effects Art Director: Akira Watanabe; Special Effects Lighting: Masao Shiroda; Special Effects Mattes: Hiroshi Mukoyama; Stunt Choreographer: Haruo Nakajima.

Cast: Hiroshi Koizumi (Shoichi Tsukioka); Minoru Chiaki (Koji Kobayashi); Takashi Shimura (Dr. Kyohei Yamane); Setsuo Wakayama (Hidemi Yamaji); Masao Shimizu (Dr. Tadokoro); Yukio Kasama (Koehi Yamaji); Seijiro Onda (Captain Terasawa); Sonosuke Sawamura (Hokkaido Branch Manager Shingo Shibeki); Yoshio Tsuchiya (Tajima); Mayuri Mokusho (Radio Operator Yasuko Inouye); Shin Otomo (Convict Leader); Shoichi Hirose (Convict); Senkichi Omura (Small Convict); Ren Yamamoto (Commander of Landing Craft); Takeo Oikawa (Osaka Municipal Police Commissioner); Junpei Natsuki (Convict); Haruo Nakajima (Godzilla); Katsumi Tezuka (Anguirus).

Japanese version: Black-and-white; 82 minutes; released on April 24, 1955. Japanese title: *Gojira no gyakushu* (*Godzilla's Counterattack*). Also known as *Godzilla Raids Again*.

American version: Black-and-white; 78 minutes; released on June 2, 1959. Release title: *Gigantis, the Fire Monster*. Co-billed with *Teenagers from Outer Space* (1959). Video title and current American title: *Godzilla Raids Again*.

American credits: Presented by Paul Schreibman; Editor: Hugo Grimaldi; Sound Effects Editor: Alvin Sarno; Music Editor: Rex Lipton; Visual Effects Production: Edward Nassour; Voice Actors: Paul Frees, Keye Luke, Leonard Stone, George Takei.

Just as a rose is still a rose by any other name, so too is Godzilla. Or perhaps that should be Gigantis. For reasons most commentators find inexplicable, Warner Bros. released 1955's *Godzilla Raids Again* in 1959 as *Gigantis, the Fire Monster*, a considerably altered version we shall discuss a bit later.

Both the Japanese and Americanized versions use the same plot. Cannery plane pilot Kobayashi (Minoru Chiaki) experiences engine problems over the sea and lands on Iwato Island. His fellow pilot Tsukioka (Hiroshi Koizumi) finds him, but shortly thereafter, they discover they are not alone on the rocky atoll: With astonishment, they watch Godzilla battling new monster Anguirus (a.k.a. Angilas) until both *kaiju* crash into the sea.

Once they are back in Osaka, the pilots identify Anguirus from a series of dinosaur illustrations; they also tell the authorities they saw Godzilla. But how? Godzilla perished at the finale of his previous film. Dr. Yamane (Takashi Kimura) notes that this must be another Godzilla, and that H-bomb tests must have revived both the new Godzilla and Anguirus. With the Oxygen Destroyer and its inventor gone, Yamane offers little hope, but does note that if Godzilla should appear near Osaka, flares might draw him away from the city.

Godzilla eventually does appear near Osaka, causing the authorities to order a blackout and a citywide evacuation. The military masses on the shore, and planes drop flares that lead Godzilla out to sea. All breathe a collective sigh of relief. Meanwhile, a group of escaped convicts crash a gasoline truck into an Osaka oil refinery. The raging conflagration lures Godzilla back to Osaka, and the spiny-backed Anguirus soon follows him onto the shore. The military opens fire—to no avail, of course.

Godzilla and Anguirus clash and carry their battle deep into the heart of the city, their bout culminating in the epic obliteration of Osaka Castle. Godzilla bites deeply into Anguirus' neck, drawing blood, then uses his atomic breath to fry his colossal combatant. Godzilla returns to the sea, leaving behind a smoldering Osaka that is, as the narrator of the Americanized version tells us, "a smoking cemetery filled with charred memories."

The fishing cannery that employs Kobayashi and Tsukioka moves its operation north to Hokkaido. As fate or convenient scripting would have it, Godzilla shows up there as well, sinking one of the company's vessels. Tuskioka spots Godzilla lumbering onto an icy island. Japanese military jets bomb the nuclear-spawned behemoth, but this tactic proves useless.

In a courageous if potentially questionable act, Kobayashi dives straight at Godzilla, whose atomic ray blasts his plane. Said plane crashes into a mountainside and explodes, sending a landslide of ice cascading onto Godzilla. Kobayashi's gesture shows the way to defeat Godzilla, and soon the military jets employ missiles to bury the King of the Monsters in an icy avalanche. Kobayashi's sacrifice was not in vain.

This story is more threadbare than a Mothra-eaten garment factory. As Stuart Galbraith notes, "The special effects work is often very good, but the script is poor and badly organized."[18] The superficial characters are almost incidental, and the movie's monsters take center stage. Not fatal, right? Well, it might not have been except for the film's wildly uneven structure: The big monster battle and city-razing take place long before the movie ends. Also, switching the locale from Osaka to Hokkaido results in an anticlimax. The story uses Kobayashi's suicide attack against Godzilla to lend poignancy to the tale, but this gesture seems forced and inorganic, quite unlike Dr. Serizawa's genuinely tragic fate in *Gojira*.

As many commentators have noted, *Godzilla Raids Again* was rush-released just a little over five months after *Godzilla*'s debut in Japan. The same fate happened with the 1933 *King Kong*, whose box office success resulted in the hasty release of the considerably less impressive *The Son of Kong*. Neither sequel is award-winning, but *Godzilla Raids Again* does have a slight edge given its spectacular destruction of a miniature Osaka by Godzilla and Anguirus.

The latter fight, fierce and animalistic, employs different camera speeds. At times, the monsters appear to be hyper-caffeinated, and at other times, uber–Valiumed. In *Japan's Favorite Mon-Star*, Steve Ryfle relates how one of three cameras filming the battling *kaiju* was set at low-speed rather than the usual high-speed required for giant monsters to move realistically as though they truly are massive. Apparently, Eiji Tsuburaya liked some of the low-speed camera work, hence the reason it alternates with high-speed filming throughout the monster bout.[19] (When I caught *Gigantis, the Fire Monster* on a Saturday night TV Late Show in 1966, I thought I had witnessed the greatest monster fight of all time.)

The movie's nuclear threat connection is far scrawnier than the muscular atomic associations found in the first *Godzilla*. *Godzilla Raids Again* tells us, "The hydrogen bomb test woke Godzilla and now, it awakened Ankylosaur.... He is also called Anguirus.... We are now under the greater threat than nuclear weapons [from Godzilla and Anguirus]." Certainly this invests the two creatures with the destructive capacity of the H-bomb, a notion backed up by the monsters' invulnerability to military weapons.

During Dr. Yamane's cameo, he tells the authorities, "I must say killing Godzilla is hopeless." The same could be said for the nuclear threat. At best, just as Japan was learning to live with Godzilla, humankind was learning how to live with the Bomb. Interestingly, Dr. Yamane says that Godzilla "becomes angry when he sees lights. We suspect it brings back memories of the hydrogen bomb testing." Just as such memories bring back Godzilla's brush with nuclear testing, so too did the sight of Godzilla bring back memories of Hiroshima and Nagasaki. Speaking of this, the heroine looks out her window at one point and sees the blazing Osaka in the distance, a mushroom-shaped cloud of smoke rising from the conflagration.

The majority of *Godzilla Raids Again* plays like a standard Japanese giant monster movie, if not its Western counterparts. Spectacle and action are the order of the day, not somber nuclear introspection. *Godzilla Raids Again* ends with the menace defeated but not destroyed, a fate quite unlike that of the vanquished giant monsters of Western giant monster films of the day.

THE AMERICANIZATION

Generally, I like to root for the underdog, and *Gigantis, the Fire Monster* is certainly the underdog of Americanized Godzilla movies. The mere contemplation of *Gigantis* blasts the average G-fan's blood pressure to hypertension emergency levels. But there is at least one good thing about the Americanization: It leaves the monster battles intact.

Although the plot is essentially the same, the Americanization stuffs the film with unnecessary and often awkward stock footage, not to mention non-stop narration that gives new meaning to the expression "Put a sock in it!" And if that wasn't enough, the dubbing rates among the worst ever foisted upon a Japanese monster movie, and that's really saying something. The American audio folks even seem confused by the monsters' roars, for at times, "Gigantis" sounds just like Anguirus! Needless to say, such sloppiness is *not* found in the Japanese original.

Worst of all is the "creation of the world" sequence, completely assembled by the American producers and featuring such "spectacle" as a cheap plastic dinosaur head popping up from a tabletop dry ice "lake." Other scenes were reportedly swiped from obscure genre flicks such as 1948's *Unknown Island*. As Godzilla scholar August Ragone notes, "This pathetic prehistoric sequence may account for the poor reputation these films have acquired in the West."[20]

Another oddity of *Gigantis* is that the American producers changed Godzilla's name to Gigantis. According to Steve Ryfle, producer Paul Schreibman (in a 1985 interview) boasted of changing the title to *Gigantis, the Fire Monster*, purportedly so people wouldn't confuse it with *Godzilla, King of the Monsters!*[21] But hey, *Godzilla, King of the Monsters!*

made money in the States, and certainly a follow-up could have cashed in on Godzilla's name. After all, in the '50s, *Creature from the Black Lagoon* begat two sequels, *Revenge of the Creature* and *The Creature Walks Among Us*. In addition, there was the *Amazing Colossal Man* sequel *War of the Colossal Beast* and the *Fly* sequel *Return of the Fly*. Also, *Godzilla Raids Again*'s morphing to *Gigantis, the Fire Monster* is ultimately ironic considering the long-running Godzilla series that blasted off from the early 1960s on.

Even when I first saw *Gigantis, the Fire Monster* as a preadolescent in 1966, it was evident that Gigantis was Godzilla, so I was totally baffled that everyone in the movie called him Gigantis. Hard as it may be to believe, the originally planned Americanization called *The Volcano Monsters* would have tried even harder to disguise Godzilla's identity. As David Kalat notes, *Volcano Monsters* would have been "a total remake, with only the special effects footage of the Japanese original to be used."[22] Even scenes of Godzilla firing his ray were to be excised. Penned by Ed Watson and the late Ib Melchior,[23] the script turned Godzilla and Anguirus into a supposedly ordinary Tyrannosaurus Rex and Ankylosaurus. Found dormant after a Japanese volcanic eruption, the monsters come to blows in San Francisco. Fortunately, this project ran out of gas before its engine could fire up.

Rodan (Japanese release: Toho, 1956; American release by Distributors Corporation of America, 1957)

Credits: Directed by Ishiro Honda; Screenplay by Takeshi Kimura and Takeo Murata; Story by Ken Kuronuma; Produced by Tomoyuki Tanaka; Music: Akira Ifukube; Photography: Isamu Ashida; Lighting: Shigeru Mori; Editor: Koichi Iwashita; Art Director: Tatsuo Kita; Assistant Director: Jun Fukuda; Sound: Masanobu Miyazaki; Special Effects Director: Eiji Tsuburaya; Special Effects Art Director: Akira Watanabe; Special Effects Lighting: Masao Shirota; Special Effects Opticals: Hiroshi Mukoyama.

Cast: Kenji Sahara (Shigeru Kawamura); Yumi Shirakawa (Kiyo); Akihiko Hirata (Dr. Kyuichiro Kashiwagi); Akio Kobori (Police Chief Nishimura); Yasuko Nakata (Female Honeymooner); Kiyoharu Onaka (Male Honeymooner); Minosuke Yamada (Colliery Chief Osaki); Yoshifumi Tajima (Izeki); Kiyomi Mizunoya (Otami); Rinsaku Ogata (Goro); Kiyoshi Takagi (Hospital Doctor); Fuyuki Murakami (Dr. Minami); Ren Yamamoto (Soldier in Jeep).

Japanese version: Color; 82 minutes; released on December 26, 1956. Japanese title: *Sora no daikaiju Radon* (*Rodan, the Monster from the Sky*).

American version: A King Bros. Production; color; 72 minutes; released August 1957. Advertised as *Rodan the Flying Monster*, but onscreen title reads simply *Rodan*.

American credits: Produced by Frank and Maurice King; English Dialogue by David Duncan; Editor: Robert S. Eisen; Voice Cast: Paul Frees, Keye Luke, George Takei, Les Tremayne.

The Four Tops sang about "Standing in the Shadows of Love," but in Rodan's case, he was standing in the shadows of Godzilla.

Plot-wise, the flying monster's debut film inherited many of *Gojira*'s story elements: reawakened gigantic prehistoric monster clashes with the military, destroys a major city, dies a noble death. However, unlike *Gojira*, *Rodan* (*Radon* in Japan) was filmed in color, featured two giant monsters (the two Rodans presumably being mates), and took a good part of its inspiration from 1954's *Them!*

6. Walking H-Bombs: 1954–1967 (Rodan)

Rodan combines two 1950s genres, big bug chillers and giant monster opuses. Its first third concerns the travails of a small coal mining community in Kyushu. Fights have broken out between miners Goro (Rinsaku Ogata) and Yoshizo (Jiro Suzukawa); next, one of the mining caves inexplicably floods. Yoshizo is found murdered, presumably by a knife wound to the head. Two miners and a police officer search the cave, until an unseen menace making strange squeaking noises kills all three. Goro's corpse turns up.

Shigeru (Kenji Sahara) attempts to comfort Goro's sister Kiyo (Yumi Shirakawa), but a giant, car-sized worm creature sporting lobster-like claws bursts into Kiyo's house. Shigeru and the police chase the monster up a hill, but their gunfire proves useless. The creature kills two more policemen before disappearing back into the mine, where more of the worm monsters lurk. Shigeru uses a speeding coal car to kill the monster, but the mine caves in, trapping the hero.

After a major earthquake, the authorities find a dazed and injured Shigeru, who suffers from amnesia. But the sight of a small bird egg hatching jolts his memory, and he recalls seeing a gigantic winged reptile hatch from a mammoth egg and proceed to devour the comparatively small worm monsters surrounding it.

A UFO appears in the skies over China, Okinawa and the Philippines. Faster than the speed of sound, it destroys a Japanese jet in pursuit. It later kills two young newlyweds. A photo from their camera shows the tip of the UFO's wing, which clearly belongs to a living animal. Also, horses and cattle have mysteriously disappeared in the area.

Dr. Kashiwagi (Akihiko Hirata), who has previously proclaimed that the worm monsters were prehistoric Meganulon, theorizes that the flying creature, with a wingspan of 257 feet, is a gigantic form of prehistoric Pteranodon. The scientist speculates that the creature "is the result of nuclear bomb testing. It not only has contaminated the ocean and the air, it's also had great effect on the Earth. This tremendous energy may have awakened Rodan from his 200-million-year-old sleep."

Rodan spars with military jets and destroys Sasebo Bridge. Next, it zooms over the city of Fukuoka at supersonic speeds, its gale force winds ripping buildings apart and sending busses spinning through the air. It lands, proves itself impervious to military tank volleys, and destroys a good deal of real estate while a second Rodan soars overhead, adding to the carnage. The two Rodans leave the city a flaming ruin. The authorities decide to attack the Rodans in their Mount Aso lair.

Due to warnings of potential volcanic eruption, the authorities evacuate the area, then proceed to pummel the landscape with missile fire, hoping to bury the two Rodans in their mountain den. Both winged monsters escape. To make matters worse, Mount Aso erupts, spewing smoke and lava. Apparently succumbing to the volcanic gases rising from the eruption, one of the Rodans slowly spirals to the earth. Subsequently caught in a lava flow, it appears helpless, shrieking in agony. Choosing not to leave its mate, the second Rodan settles beside its fellow *daikaiju* just as a lover might settle at the bedside of his dying beloved. Lethal flame and smoke envelope the primordial pair as the human spectators, visibly moved, watch in silence.

As *kaiju eiga* scholar Peter H. Brothers notes, at the end of *Them!*, one of *Rodan*'s chief inspirations, everyone is glad the giant ants are roasting, but "the Rodans' destruction would leave their spectators with decidedly mixed feelings."[24] Director Ishiro Honda's son Ryuji said that when he saw the film as a child, he cried.[25] This mirrors my own reaction upon seeing the film on TV as a six-year-old. Yes, at the time my older brother Frank scoffed, saying, "Yeah, they've killed hundreds of people, but we're supposed to feel sorry for them!" His argument was logical, but missed the inherent ambiguity and, yes, inherent paradoxes in many Japanese monster films.

Also, the Rodans' deaths are not so far removed from the poignant demise of 1933's *King Kong*, who had also caused a great deal of carnage. In fact, the Rodans' motivation seems to be simply to eat and survive, whereas Kong sometimes resorted to malicious squashing of natives underfoot and chewing them.

Why the Rodans decide to obliterate Fukuoka isn't clear—they don't seem to eat any of the people in the city. Couldn't they have just flown away before trashing the place? Maybe the jet attacks angered them, and they somehow knew that the tiny creatures milling about the steel and concrete jungle below were to blame. Or maybe they just obliterated Fukuoka because when you're a Japanese monster, that's what you do. Put another way, Japanese giant critters were not the rational monsters of the West: They were monster-gods whose motivations often defied logic.

In terms of spectacle, *Rodan*'s visuals compare favorably to those of similar Western giant monster movies of the time. Indeed, on its 1957 release in North America, several critics praised the effects.[26] As late as the mid–1970s, *Castle of Frankenstein* #24 proclaimed, "[I]t's the spcl fx dept., responsible, of course, for Rodan—and all other hardware, splashy effects, etc.—that takes all credits for a grand display (photographic effects by the redoubtable Eiji Tsuburaya)." Given that the original *Castle of Frankenstein* often castigated Japanese monster movies, this was an unexpected rave.

In contrast to the final two-thirds of giant monster action, the film's first third evokes a spooky feel. The deaths of the two miners and police officer, all murdered by an unseen something, are unsettling and eerie. And the Meganulon attack on the village is exciting, though the longer Japanese version allows us to see some of the creature's wire works. (This also happens with Rodan in a few scenes.)

Rodan attributes the hatching of the monsters' eggs to nuclear testing, but the movie also oddly makes this origin tentative. While Godzilla may have been a walking H-bomb, Rodan may not have been a flying ICBM. However, the tornadic winds that the Rodans whip up recall the blast effects of nuclear tests on structures such as houses, steel frames and other buildings. And just as a nuclear fireball basically just "stands" at the detonation site as the blast effects radiate out from it, Rodan basically just "stands" in the city as gale force winds radiate from its wings.

The Americanization

Rodan was English-dubbed and, unlike *Godzilla, King of the Monsters!*, the Western handlers did not insert new footage of Western actors. However, the Americanized *Rodan* does add a prologue featuring familiar (i.e., grainy) documentary footage of an H-bomb test, declaring such testing to be the reason for the subsequent appearance of the two Rodans. Interesting that the Japanese version suggests this as a probability only, whereas the Americanized version makes the connection airtight.

Also, the American distributors edited much of the film—shortening scenes, deleting portions of the soundtrack, inserting occasional stock music, and jumbling the sequence of events. For example, in the Japanese original, a rousing Akira Ifukube score accompanies the fighter jets attacking Rodan, but in the Americanized version, the music has been removed. Also, the Americanized version features the almost non-stop voiceover narration of Shigeru, whereas the original Japanese version contains no such narration.

Said narration was supplied by Keye Luke, probably best known to Baby Boomers as Master Po in the TV series *Kung Fu* (1972–1975).

Despite these changes, the spirit of the original Japanese *Rodan* remains intact. In fact, Luke's narration of the two Rodans' deaths moved me as a youngster, and while his words are perhaps a little heavy-handed today, they still achieve their effect.

Frank and Maurice King, the American version's producers, no doubt took note of *Rodan*'s success, for they would go on to produce 1961's spectacular giant monster opus *Gorgo*.

Mothra (Japanese release: Toho, 1961; American release: Columbia, 1962)

Credits: Directed by Ishiro Honda; Screenplay by Shinichi Sekizawa; Story by Takehiko Fukunaga, Shinichiro Nakamura, Yoshie Hotta, as published in *Asahi Shimbun*; Produced by Tomoyuki Tanaka; Music: Yuji Koseki; Songs: Ishiro Honda, Susumu Ike, Shinichi Sekizawa; Photography: Hajime Koizumi; Editor: Kazuji Taira; Art Directors: Teruaki Abe, Takeo Kita; Assistant Director: Samaji Nonagase; Sound Recordists: Shoichi Fujinawa, Masanobu Miyazaki; Lighting: Toshio Takashima; Special Effects Director: Eiji Tsuburaya; Special Effects Production Manager: Kan Narita; Special Effects Art Director: Akira Watanabe; Special Effects Photography: Sadamasa Arikawa; Special Effects Lighting: Kuichiro Kishida; Mattes: Hiroshi Mukoyama.

Cast: Frankie Sakai (Senichiro "Tsin-chan" Fukuda, aka "Bulldog"); Hiroshi Koizumi (Dr. Shinichi Chujo Nakazo); Yumi Ito, Emi Ito (The *Shobijin* aka "Little Beauties"); Jerry Ito (Clark Nelson); Ken Uehara (Dr. Harada); Kyoko Kagawa (Michi Hanamura); Akihiko Hirata (Doctor); Kenji Sahara (Helicopter Pilot); Seizaburo Kawazu (General); Takashi Shimura (News Editor); Yoshio Kosugi (Ship Captain); Yoshifumi Tajima (Military Advisor); Ren Yamamoto, Haruya Kato, Rinsaku Ogata, Ko Mishima (Ship Survivors); Tetsu Nakamura, Toshio Miura, Akira Wakamatsu, Osman Yusuf, Hiroshi Akitsu (Nelson's Henchmen); Shoichi Hirose, Toshihiko Furata (Dam Workers); Mitsuo Tsuda, Tadashi Okabe, Akio Kusama (Surveyors); Akira Yamada (Island Worshipper); Wataru Omae (Official); Koji Uno (Reporter); Takeo Nagashima (Island Dancers); Shigeo Kato (Dam Watchman); Hiroyuki Satake, Misuo Matsumoto (Police Officers); Kazuo Imai (Announcer); Haruo Nakajima (Head of Mothra Larva); Ed Keane (Rolisican Mayor); Harold Conway (Rolisican Ambassador); Robert Dunham (Rolisican Police Officer).

Japanese version: Color; TohoScope; 101 minutes; released on July 30, 1961. Japanese title: *Mosura* (a.k.a. *Mothra*). Working title: *Daikaiju Mosura* ("Giant Monster Mothra").

American version: Color; scope; 91 minutes; released on May 10, 1962. Alternate title (on some trailers): *Mothra, the Monster-God*.

American credits: Directed by Lee Kresel; Dialogue by Robert Myerson; Produced by David D. Horne.

In an American movie named *Mothra* circa 1961, you might expect radiation to have created the title creature. You might also assume the monster dies at the end, probably due to either military force or a weapon of super-science. However, Toho's *Mothra* turns each of these Western expectations on their respective Newtonian heads. The monster's origins remain unknown, the monster lives past the conclusion, and the monster is impervious to the movie's super-science weapon. Although radiation did not (apparently) give birth to Mothra, the nuclear threat does figure in the film.

The movie opens with a typhoon buffeting a commercial ship in the Pacific. The vessel runs aground, and some of the crew escape to nearby Infant Island, the site of both atom and hydrogen bomb testing by the mythical country of Rolisica. A rescue party is surprised to find the surviving crew unaffected by the island's radiation. When questioned, one of the crew men reveals that the island natives gave them a red juice to drink, and the authorities surmise that this protected them from radiation.

The island, according to Rolisica, is supposed to be uninhabited, hence the reason it was used as a nuclear testing site. But due to the presence of inhabitants, an expedition made up of Japanese and Rolisican scientists is formed to investigate. Oily Rolisican business tycoon Clark Nelson (Jerry Ito) is in charge of the expedition, much to the chagrin of the Japanese scientists, including Dr. Chujo Nakazo (Hiroshi Koizumi) and Dr. Haradawa (Ken Uehara). Tenacious news reporter Tsinchan "Bulldog" Fukuda (Frankie Sakai) has stowed on board the ship and joins the expedition's party, much to Nelson's dismay.

Garbed in radiation suits, the expedition finds the interior of the island to be unexpectedly lush with vegetation; apparently, the nuclear testing had no effect on the plant life; there is a hint that perhaps it actually invigorated it. Chujo discovers a cave with giant mold mutations and a vampire plant, which promptly attacks. A pair of foot-tall native women save Chujo. His fellow scientists are skeptical about his claim, but the next day they all encounter the tiny native women.

Nelson makes a play to kidnap the two fairies, prompting natives knocking rocks together to march from the jungle. Due to expedition pressure, Nelson has the girls released, which causes the natives to stand down. Once the expedition returns to Japan, Bulldog and the Japanese scientists have decided they will reveal nothing about the little women.

Nelson and his goons return to Infant Island, kidnap the miniature fairies and massacre many of the natives. Nelson exploits the *Shobijin* ("Little Beauties") in a lavish production called "The Secret Fairies Show" in Tokyo. Meanwhile, in caterpillar form, Mothra hatches from her Infant Island egg and makes for the sea, destroying an ocean liner and defying the efforts of the Japanese Self Defense Forces to stop it.

Nelson allows Chujo, Bulldog and photographer Michi Hanamura (Kyoko Kagawa) to see the two Shobijin in private. The fairies tell the protagonists that Mothra is journeying to Japan to rescue them and take them back to Infant Island. They also reveal they have no power to stop Mothra—the creature acts on instinct and will forge ahead even it if means unintended destruction. Nelson refuses to take the fairies back to the island, despite the lives that may be lost in the creature's implacable rampage.

Mothra destroys a dam, then enters Tokyo proper, bulldozing city blocks of real estate into heaps of rubble. The military's efforts to halt the monster's march prove futile. At this point, Rolisica insists that Nelson return the fairies to Infant Island, but he refuses, instead clandestinely boarding a flight to Rolisica and taking the fairies with him.

Mothra destroys Tokyo Tower and builds a cocoon. While the creature is dormant, Rolisica provides two atomic heat cannons (their newest super-science weapon) which blast the cocoon, wreathing the mammoth shell in flames. It appears that Mothra is dead—but upon hearing the fairies' song from faraway Rolisica, Mothra bursts from the cocoon, now an adult with a mammoth 820-foot wingspan.

Mothra attacks Rolisica's New Kirk City. Nelson tries to escape and guns down a police officer, but a fellow officer shoots Nelson, killing him. The authorities take the fairies to the city airport, where its Polynesian symbol is painted across the runways. Lured by the ringing of church bells, Mothra becomes more docile, lands at the airport and spirits the fairies back to Infant Island.

Different than its Western monster movie antecedents, *Mothra* moved the giant monster movie in a new direction. Peter H. Brothers wrote that the film "renewed and reestablished the genre [in Japan] with a permanency as strong as the giant caterpillar's silk."[27] Not only did its monster live past the finale, but it also is a well-intended creature who only attacked out of its mission to rescue the two exploited fairies. The monster has a motive: It doesn't just attack cities because That's What Monsters Do. Plus, the creature sports a kind of intelligence, an ingredient which would soon be sprinkled into all of Godzilla's 1960s movies, giving rise to the *"kaiju* comedy" baked into *King Kong vs. Godzilla, Ghidorah, the Three-Headed Monster* and *Invasion of Astro-Monster* (a.k.a. *Monster Zero*).

Speaking of comedy, some of the humans provide mugging on the level of a Jerry Lewis movie. As film scholar David Kalat writes, "*Mothra* makes no pretense at sophistication. This is a family picture with entertainment as its primary goal.... [It] never takes itself too seriously."[28] Jerry Ito essays bad guy Nelson as broadly as a heavy in a Three Stooges short. In his July 1962 review, *New York Times* critic A.H. Weiler wrote that the film's direction, acting, and dialogue "are clumsy and absurd." However, humor is in the eye of the beholder, and Honda apparently wanted to give the movie a light touch after his previously somber, often grim monster films. Honda was perfectly capable of providing restrained direction, highly evident in 1954's sober *Godzilla*.

One area in which *Mothra* unequivocally soars is its colorful and spectacular visuals. While rarely photo-realistic, the special effects are elaborate, eye-catching and fun. *Castle of Frankenstein* #4 gave *Mothra* a special recommendation and called it a "cleverly made SF movie. A monster picture with charm! ... Good color, trick effects." The previously mentioned *Times* review cited "some genuinely artistic panoramas and décor designs.... Several of the special effects shots are brilliant."

Opening in Japan on July 30, 1961, *Mothra* was, pardon the pun, a monster hit. It sold over nine million tickets, thus assuring that Toho was far from done with the giant monster format. In America, the film apparently did fair business. Of interest is the manner in which the American trailers advertised the movie. One offbeat trailer consists of black-and-white paintings and speaks of Mothra's "devastating death ray" (!) and posits the question, "Who is Mothra? What is Mothra? Why does all the world fear Mothra?" Another trailer, this one using scenes from the film, conceals Mothra's appearance, showing us only the larva form. The trailer asks, "What is the secret of Mothra?" One of the two title credits calls the film *Mothra, the Monster-God*.

This concealment of *Mothra*'s appearance in American trailers coincides with American International's advertising campaign for 1964's *Godzilla vs. the Thing* (a.k.a. *Mothra vs. Godzilla*). AIP hinted that "the Thing" was a monstrous creature, the newspaper ads showing tentacles writhing from behind a "Censored!" panel. The irony in both cases is that the adult Mothra actually sports a visually appealing appearance, hardly a hideous monstrosity at all.

Mothra's nuclear threat elements are minor, but still significant. At the beginning of the film, the Japanese fear of radiation is made clear by the fact that the rescuers assume that the ship's survivors will have succumbed to radiation poisoning. Indeed, a helicopter pilot expresses concerns about the amount of radiation through which the aircraft is flying. But the natives' special juice protects them from radiation sickness. Just as astonishing is that the Japanese-Rolisican expedition to the island discovers the interior to be verdant with vegetation. Due to its use as a nuclear testing site, one would expect the entire atoll to be blackened stubble, but instead it is almost as though the radiation has strengthened its plant life. Also, did the radiation give vent to the mutation molds that Chujo finds? Was it the origin of the vampire plant? Did it have an effect on Mothra's egg, i.e., did radiation cause the egg to grow larger, or the monster within to grow stronger?

The latter seems unlikely. When asked to describe Mothra, Bulldog says, "It's a dinosaur-like ... an ancient monster in Infant Island legends." The egg might have been ensconced in the temple for centuries, and apparently it was the fairies' kidnapping that caused it to hatch. But did radiation play a part in Mothra's hatching, or in the creature's tremendous size? Possibly, but we can't be sure.

However, one cannot as easily dismiss the abundant plant life, the mutation molds or the vampire plant. As the film unfolds, its early atomic anxiety elements give way to the fairy tale storyline and are soon forgotten. As we shall see, this playing down of the nuclear threat would become increasingly evident in the 1960s Godzilla series.

The Years 1962–1963

In 1962 and 1963, Toho produced an impressive five genre films: 1962's *Gorath* (released to the U.S. in 1964) and *King Kong vs. Godzilla* (released to the U.S. in 1963); and 1963's *Undersea Battleship* (a.k.a. *Atragon*, released in the U.S. in 1965), *Matango* (a.k.a. *Attack of the Mushroom People*, released to U.S. TV in 1965) and *The Great Thief* (a.k.a. *The Lost World of Sinbad*, released in the U.S. in 1965). Only *Matango* dealt with the nuclear threat, handling it in a tangential manner. Nuclear weapons are mentioned in *King Kong vs. Godzilla*, so it has a short entry in the "Almost Atomic" section at the end of this chapter. But we now turn our attention to an unusual *daikaiju* unabashedly created by nuclear radiation.

Giant Space Monster Dogora (Japanese release: Toho, 1964)

Dagora, the Space Monster (American release: AIP-TV, 1965)

Credits: Directed by Ishiro Honda; Screenplay by Shinichi Sekizawa; Original Story by Jojiro Okami; Produced by Tomoyuki Tanaka and Yasuyoshi Tajitsu; Line Producer: Shigeru Nakamura; Music: Akira Ifukube; Photography: Hajime Koizumi; Editor: Ryohei Fujii; Production Design: Takeo Kita; Sound: Fumio Yanoguchi; Sound Mixer: Hisashi Shimonaga; Assistant Director: Takshi Sano; Special Effects Director: Eiji Tsuburaya; Special Effects Photography: Sadamasa Arikawa, Motoyoshi Tomioka; Special Effects Lighting: Kuichiro Kishida; Special Effects Optical Photography: Sadao

Iizuda, Yukio Manoda, Yoshiyuki Tokumasa; Mattes: Hiroshi Mukoyama; Special Effects Art Director: Akira Watanabe; Special Effects Line Producer: Tadashi Koike.

Cast: Yosuke Natsuki (Inspector Kommei); Yoko Fujiyama (Masayo Kirino); Hiroshi Koizumi (Korino); Nobuo Nakamura (Dr. Munakata); Akiko Wakabayashi (Hamako); Jun Tazaki (Chief Inspector); Susumu Fujita (General Iwasa); Seizaburo Kawazu (Gangster Boss); Hideyo Amamoto (Maki); Haruya Kato (Sabu); Yoshibumi Tajima, Nadao Kirino, Akira Wakamatsu (Gangsters); Jun Funato (Detective Shinda); Hideo Shibuya (Reporter); Yasuhisa Tsutsumi (Police Official); Shoichi Hirose (Coal Field Man); Ichiro Chiba (Transport Company Man); Wataru Omae (Satellite Station Scientist); Tadashi Okabe (Police Officer); Yutaka Nakayama (Coal Truck Assistant); Keiko Sawai (Scientist's Assistant); Yutaka Oka (Transport Company Chief); Chotaro Togin (Coal Truck Driver); Takuzo Kumagai (Defense Corps Executive).

Japanese version: Color; TohoScope; 82 minutes; released on August 11, 1964. Japanese title: *Uchu daikaiju Dogora* (*Giant Space Monster Dogora*).

American version: Released to TV by AIP-TV; color; pan and scanned; 80 minutes; Released to TV in 1965. American TV title: *Dogora, the Space Monster*.

American credits: Executive Producers: James H. Nicholson, Samuel Z. Arkoff; Post-Production Supervisor: Salvatore Billitteri.

The stereotype of a 1960s Japanese monster movie: a man in a rubber monster suit stomps through a scale model of Tokyo. But Toho broke that stereotype more than once during the '60s, bringing several of its *kaiju* to life not through suitmation, but rather through sophisticated puppetry. Of those *kaiju*, perhaps the strangest is Dogora, a bizarre cross between an octopus and a jellyfish that is airborne. That's right—airborne.

Like *The H-Man*, *Dogora* mixes the gangster and *kaiju eiga* genres. However, Dogora seems to be more of a guest star in its own movie than the feature attraction. The film expends much of its running time depicting the adventures of a gang of jewel thieves, a "diamond G-Man" and the police, and amidst all this tomfoolery, Dogora gets short shrift.

In the film, Japanese TV satellites are mysteriously disappearing in orbit just over the island nation. They are crashing into one of several orbiting Dogoras, pulsating blue space blobs. The monster foils the would-be thefts of a gang of jewel thieves and baffles the authorities. Detective Komai (Yosuke Natsuki) meets up with Dr. Munakata (Nobuo Nakamura) and his pretty assistant Masayo (Keiko Sawai), as well as "diamond G-Man" Mark Jackson (Robert Dunham). Dr. Munakata has created artificial jewels that cause frustration for the jewel thieves and the police in a series of long and drawn-out cops-and-robbers sequences.

Komai, Masayo and her brother, Dr. Kurino (Hiroshi Koizumi), see Dogora sucking up coal and various metal structures from a factory. Indeed, Dogora is sucking up coal and diamonds worldwide. Dr. Kurino explains that Dogora "is a cell from space mutated by massive amounts of radiation.... There's a pocket of radioactivity in the atmosphere over Japan." We also discover that Dogora consumes carbon as an energy source, hence the reason it sucks up coal and diamonds. Dr. Munakata notes that if Dogora's appetite for carbon-containing substances (such as homo sapiens) grows, "it could mean the end of us all."

The giant, sky-faring jellyfish is impervious to conventional weapons. In the movie's best sequence, Dogora, perhaps irritated by all the artillery fire, uses its tentacles to uproot and demolish a suspension bridge in Kyushu. Missiles fired at the creature cause it to multiply, and soon there are dozens of smaller Dogoras bobbing through the skies. But the Dogoras turn out to be vulnerable to bee or wasp venom, which causes the creatures to turn into stone and plummet to earth. While the cops and jewel thieves trade gunfire by the seashore, helicopters dump parachuted packages of wasp venom above the Dogoras. Tank-treaded chemical cannons shoot wasp venom at the space monsters. In no time, they start dropping like bricks, one of them crushing the gang of fleeing jewel thieves. (Obviously, as they say, crime doesn't pay.)

Eiji Tsuburaya's effects team hits a home run with Dogora, for its articulations are perfect, with no trace of wires. It's also an inspired creation, a monster both alien and intriguing with its twisting tentacles and flowing body; its creepy heartbeat sound effects perfectly complement its innate weirdness. Unlike Godzilla, Dogora isn't interested in making the Japanese pay—it just wants to eat. Once all the coal and diamonds are gone, Japan may be the next entrée!

The movie's downfall is simply that we see too much of the jewel thieves and law officers and not enough of the monster. Intriguing publicity photos for Dogora show the creatures wrenching a passenger liner from the sea, derailing a train and trashing Tokyo Tower. Too bad these scenes don't appear in the actual movie.

Dogora is a result of atomic mutation, but the movie never really explains where the pulsating space blobs come from. Have they been in orbit all along? As for the pocket of radiation over Japan, could it have been a result of the Hiroshima and Nagasaki bombings? Or of more recent American H-bomb tests in the Pacific? The movie doesn't go there, but either or both of these explanations might have been on the screenwriters' minds.

Mothra vs. Godzilla (Japanese release: Toho, 1964)

Godzilla vs. the Thing (American release: AIP, 1964)

Credits: Directed by Ishiro Honda; Executive Producers: Tomoyuki Tanaka, Sanezumi Fujimoto; Screenplay by Shinichi Sekizawa; Photography: Hajime Koizumi; Art Director: Takeo Kita; Sound Recorder: Fumio Yanoguchi; Lighting: Shoshichi Kojima; Music: Akira Ifukube; Editor: Ryohei Fujii; Assistant Director: Koji Kajita; Special Effects Director: Eiji Tsuburaya; Special Effects Photography: Teisho (Sadamasa) Arikawa, Sokei (Mototaka) Tomioka; Special Effects Optical Photography: Yukio Manoda, Yoshiyuki Tokumasa; Special Effects Art Director: Akira Watanabe; Special Effects Lighting: Kuichiro Kishida; Special Effects Assistant Director: Teruyoshi Nakano; Special Effects Production Manager: Tadashi Koike.

Cast: Akira Takarada (Ichiro Sakai); Yuriko Hoshi (Junko Nakanishi [in American version called Yoka]); Hiroshi Koizumi (Professor Miura); Yu Fujika (Jiro Nakamura); Kenji Sahara (Jiro Torahata); Yoshifumi Tajima (Mr. Kumayama); Emi Ito, Yumi Ito (The *Shobijin*, or "Little Beauties"); Jun Tazaki (Newspaper Editor); Ikio Sawamura (Priest), Kenzo Tadake (Politician); Susumu Fujita (Military Commander); Yutaka Sada (School Principal); Miki Yashiro (Miss Kobayashi); Yoshio Kosuge (Infant Island Chief); Nobu (Shim) Otomo (Police Chief); Yasuhisa Tsutumi (Dock Police Officer); Ren Yamamoto (Captain of Small Boat); Akira Tani (Head of Fishermen); Kozo Nomura, Mitsuo Tsuda, Tadashi Okabe, Haruya Sakamoto (Military Officers); Terumi Oka (Waitress); Hideo Shibuya (Reporter); Kenzo Echigo (Soldier); Haruo Suzuki (Military Radio Operator); Haruo Nakajima (Godzilla); Senkichi Omura, Shiro

6. Walking H-Bombs: 1954–1967 (Mothra vs. Godzilla; Godzilla vs. The Thing) • 187

Tsuchiya, Takuzo (Jiro) Kamagai, Koji Uno, Yutaka Nakayama, Hiroshi Akitsu (Fishermen).

Japanese version: Color; TohoScope; 89 minutes; released on April 20, 1964. Japanese title: *Mosura tai Gojira* (*Mothra vs. Godzilla*).

American version: Presented by James H. Nicholson and Samuel Z. Arkoff; Re-recording by Titra Sound Corp.; color; ColorScope; 90 minutes; released on September 17, 1964. Release title: *Godzilla vs. the Thing*. Double-billed with *Voyage to the End of the Universe*, the Americanization of the 1963 Czechoslovakian film *Ikarie-XB1*. The sequence of Frontier Missiles firing on Godzilla was filmed for the American version and didn't appear in the Japanese release.

"Toho's monster makers reached the apex of the *kaiju eiga* genre with *Godzilla vs. the Thing*."[29] So declared stalwart G-fan Stuart Galbraith IV, and his fellow *kaiju* critics agree. For example, *G-Fan* editor J.D. Lees and author Marc Cerasini write, "In *Mothra vs. Godzilla*, all the best attributes of the Godzilla film converged into a seamless whole."[30] And distinguished G-scholar Ed Godziszewski gushes, "Overall, *Godzilla vs. the Thing* delivers everything that one can ask for in a giant monster film…. Toho hits its stride, with each member of the production team turning in some of their finest work."[31]

The film has also been a long-time favorite of Godzilla fans. In *G-Fan #24* (1996), a readers' poll (with a 1–10 scale, with 1 being poor and 10 being excellent) gave it a score of 8.49, ranking it the sixth best giant monster movie of all time. A subsequent *G-Fan* readers' poll in #105 (2014) gave the movie a score of 8.5, this time ranking it as the second best giant monster movie of all time, topped only by the 1954 *Gojira* original.

In addition to its entertainment values, Stuart Galbraith likewise notes, "The picture is surprisingly political."[32] Though it primarily fires salvoes at corporate greed and political corruption, it also takes aim at the nuclear threat. Arguably, it's the last Godzilla movie to do so effectively until 1984.

A tremendous hurricane leaves an industrial construction site in ruins near Nagoya. While investigating, photographer Junko (Yuriko Hoshi) discovers an odd Frisbee-shaped mass and shows it to her journalist mentor Sakai (Akira Takarada). Also, a monstrous egg appears in the bay and, once it's beached, Professor Miura (Hiroshi Koizumi) investigates it. Oily entrepreneur Kumayama (Yoshibumi Tajima) discourages any such investigation; he buys the egg from the nearby fishermen, for he and his even slimier partner Torahata (Kenji Sahara) plan to build an amusement park around the egg and charge admission to see it.

Mothra's twin fairies fruitlessly appeal to the two greedy men to return the egg to Mothra Island, for it belongs to the island people. Next, the fairies seek the help of Sakai, Junko and Miura, but though the trio is willing, they are unable to set the political machinery in motion to get the egg back to the island. Aloft atop Mothra's back, the fairies sadly depart.

The colorful object Junko found at the damaged industrial site turns out to be highly radioactive; Miura "decontaminates" Junko and Sakai, then the three trek to the place Junko found the object. Apparently having been buried beneath mountains of hurricane-packed soil, Godzilla rises from the earth, regally shaking the sand from his massive frame. In no time, the monster pillages Nagoya, climaxing in the elaborate destruction of Nagoya Castle.

A fellow reporter gives Sakai, Junko and Miura the idea to ask for Mothra's help in fighting Godzilla, and soon the trio are on a barren, lifeless atoll, what's left of Mothra

Island following nuclear tests from earlier in the decade. The islanders, including the twin fairies, refuse to ask Mothra to assist the trio, for Japan did not return the egg. Even worse, in a case of guilt by association, the island chief blames Japan for the nuclear testing that has devastated the once green atoll. A heartfelt plea from both Junko and Sakai convinces the fairies to ask for Mothra's help. Mothra benevolently obliges.

Meanwhile, seemingly guided by instinct to the site of a potential foe, Godzilla homes in on Mothra's egg and wrecks its colossal incubator. But have no fear, Mothra is here. The two monsters engage in a life-and-death struggle, with Godzilla ultimately winning.

While the military attempts to stop Godzilla with artificial lightning, the two fairies sing to Mothra's egg, causing it to hatch. Two larvae crawl from the egg's remains and soon they engage in "sniper" attacks, spraying Godzilla with their super-strong silk. Between sprays, they hide behind rock outcroppings to keep Godzilla's breath from blasting them. Godzilla quickly finds himself tightly bound in a silken straitjacket. Losing his balance, the radioactive *kaiju* crashes into the sea, sinking. Peace having been restored, the twin fairies depart on the twin larvae as the heroes bid them farewell.

For the most part, *Godzilla vs. the Thing* is a serious film, albeit one primarily designed to entertain. The battle between Godzilla and the adult Mothra is played straight. Eiji Tsubuaraya's effects for the battle work very well, including employing high speed photography and frame skipping, a technique which gives parts of the battle the look of having been filmed in stop-motion animation. However, one short sequence—a puppet Mothra pulling a puppet Godzilla's tail in long shot—fails to convince.

Tsuburaya's articulation of Mothra reaches its zenith in this film. From its twisting head to its lively legs to its graceful wings, the large-scale adult Mothra moves much like a real insect. The two twin larvae aren't bad, either. And Godzilla's design in this film ranks as one of his all-time best, with his sinister hooded eyes, flaring dragon cheeks, and sinuously snaking tail. This was the last time during Godzilla's original film series that he would function as the epitome of ill will, and he most assuredly looks the part.

Three sequences in *Godzilla vs. the Thing* spotlight the nuclear threat. When the protagonists first meet the fairies in the woods, Miura says (in the English-dubbed version), "I've heard of your island. Weren't atomic tests conducted there after the war?" The *Shobijin* sadly reply, "Yes, they were." Later, they add, "After the tests, Mothra Island completely changed. It became very ugly and unbearable." (The American version refers to Infant Island as Mothra Island.)

The Japanese-language version of the same scene contains an interesting nuance not found in the English dub. Miura asks the fairies, "Infant Island? Isn't that the island in the South where they tested the nuclear bombs?"

Note that Miura is blaming an unidentified third party—"they"—as opposed to the first person "we." Obviously, that third party is the United States, and it's intriguing that *Mothra vs. Godzilla* comes closer to identifying America than any Toho film during the period we are examining.

The film's second significant nuclear sequence shows Junko and Sakai standing in Professor Miura's radiation decontamination tubes, and a close-up of Junko shows her smiling and apparently making light of her partner Sakai's discomfort with the steam treatment. One would never find such a "light nuclear moment" in 1954's original *Godzilla*, or in any 1950s Toho genre film.

However, the Mothra Island nuclear threat sequence is humorless, as it should be.

Once they disembark from a seaplane, Sakai, Junko and Miura paddle a raft to Mothra Island (due to the radiation, presumably the plane's pilot didn't want to get any closer). Once the trio arrives on shore, they discover a bleak, lifeless tableau, not a shred of vegetation in sight. We see the skeleton of an unidentified animal, as well as a strange gray turtle—or is it a skeleton of a turtle? An atomic mutation? None of the above? The movie doesn't tell us, and the heroes don't seem to find the creature discomfiting.

While the original Japanese-language version and the English-dubbed version do agree in spirit with the ensuing dialogue, there are notable differences. First, let's examine a few lines from the Japanese-language version:

"What a desolate place!" Sakai exclaims.

Later, Miura says, "This must have been a beautiful green island at one time."

"Somehow," Junko confesses, "I feel responsible."

Sakai assures her this is a normal reaction, then soon notes, "Demonstrations against nuclear bombs don't make news any more. But not [sic] when you actually see something like this..."

As they walk inland, Miura says, "It is more cruel that people are forced to live in a place like this."

Natives spring out from the rocks and take the trio to their chief. The protagonists reveal their mission, but the chief refuses to help. Regarding Godzilla ransacking Japan, the chief says, "It's your own fault for playing with the devil's fire!" Here Japan is likened to be guilty of nuclear testing by association with the United States, even though the latter country remains unmentioned.

The chief later goes on to describe the island's living conditions since the atomic testing: "Since that day, this island has become a place of suffering."

Two things are interesting up to this point in the island sequence: One is that Mothra Island is in far worse shape in this film than Infant Island was in the original *Mothra*. Also, the sequence implies that America has done nothing to make restitution for its nuclear tests conducted at or near the atoll. It is likewise clear Japan has done nothing either, perhaps one of the reasons the natives blame the island nation as vigorously as they do the U.S.

Another interesting implication is that Mothra did not retaliate against either America or Japan for the atomic despoiling of her atoll. Hence, Mothra and her people did not seek revenge, despite the islanders' suffering. But they do crave justice.

Let's take a look at this same sequence in the English-language version. The sentiments are still anti-nuke, but betray interesting nuances. For example, shortly after Sakai, Junko and Miura land on the island, Miura says, "As a scientist, I feel partly responsible for this."

To which Junko replies, "All mankind is responsible."

Miura is given another interesting line when describing the island's desolation: "It's like the end of the world here." This calls to mind the bleak fate that could await the entire Earth and all humankind if the superpowers were to wage a worldwide thermonuclear war.

Sakai says, "Those who think of nuclear war should see this, eh?" Given *Godzilla vs. the Thing* director Ishiro Honda's anti-nuke stance, no doubt he would agree. The final portion of the Mothra Island sequence concerns the protagonists trying to talk the fairies into letting Mothra help Japan by fighting Godzilla. Junko and Sakai succeed in securing the mammoth insect's aid, but the dialogue leading up to this point again brims with nuclear threat implications.

In the English-language version, Junko appeals to the fairies and natives, telling them of Godzilla's wrath being visited upon Japan. "The monster is killing everyone—the good are being killed, as well as the evil. Are you going to let good men die alongside guilty men? You have no right to decide that—that right is sacred."

Her appeal in the Japanese-language version becomes broader and bolder: "There are good people among them [Godzilla's victims], but even the bad ones have the right to live. You may call it God's punishment, but all people are equal before God. God plays no favorites."

Interesting that in the American dialogue, the appeal is to spare the innocent, not the guilty, whereas the Japanese dialogue asserts that no one has the right to make value judgments when it comes to another person's life—that such a judgment can only be rendered by the Almighty. And although the English-dubbed dialogue implies it's okay for Godzilla to trounce the guilty, by implication, the guilty in the film may be the Americans! After all, we were the ones who with our atomic testing turned Mothra Island into a barren wasteland.

The entire Mothra Island sequence no doubt pleased director Honda, who in fact devised the protagonists' plea for brotherhood—it was not contained in Shinichi Sekizawa's screenplay.[33] It expressed Honda's own feelings regarding the nuclear threat, that the superpowers should break bread rather than rattle swords. Honda was probably gratified that Godzilla had at least partially returned to his serious atomic roots after 1962's monster bout free-for-all *King Kong vs. Godzilla*, a family movie emphasizing *kaiju* comedy and not social convictions. After all, it had been only ten years since the first *Godzilla*, and *Mothra vs. Godzilla* probably heartened Honda. It may have watered down Godzilla's nuclear subtext, but at least the latter had not yet evaporated entirely from the series.

Gamera, the Giant Monster (Japanese release: Daiei, 1965)

Gammera the Invincible (American release: World Entertainment Corporation, 1966)

Credits: Directed by Noriaki Yuasa; Screenplay by Niisan Takahashi, based on an idea by Yonejiro Saito; Produced by Hidemasa Nagata; Planning by Yonejiro Saito; Photography: Nobuo Munekawa; Sound: Toshikazu Watanabe; Sound Recorder: Riichi Watanabe; Lighting: Yukio Ito; Art Director: Akira Inoue; Music: Tadashi Yamauchi; Editor: Tatsuji Nakashizu; Production Manager: Hiroaki Kamijima; Assistant Director Shime Abe; Special Effects Photography: Yonesaburo Tsukiji; Special Effects Art Director: Akira Inoue; Special Effects Lighting: Mamoru Ishizaka; Composites: Kazufumi Fuji; Special Effects Assistant Director: Kiyoshi Ishida; Special Effects Production Manager: Kiyashi Kawamura; Monster Design: Ryosaku Takayama.

Cast: Eiji Funakoshi (Dr. Hidaka); Harumi Kiritachi (Kyoko Yamamoto); Junichiro Yamashita (Mr. Aoyagi); Yoshiro Uchida (Toshi Sakurai); Michiko Sugata (Nobuyo Sakurai); Jun Hamamura (Dr. Murase); Yoshiro Kitahara (Mr. Sakurai); Bokuzen Hidari (Eskimo Chief).

Japanese version: Black-and-white; DaieiScope; 78 minutes; released on November 27, 1965. Japanese title: *Daikaiju Gamera* (*Gamera, the Giant Monster*).

American version: A Harris Associates Presentation; black-and-white; Total-

6. Walking H-Bombs: 1954–1967 (Gamera, the Giant Monster; Gamera the Invincible)

scope; 86 minutes; released on December 15, 1966. American title: *Gammera the Invincible*. Released to VHS in 1987 (minus the Americanized scenes) with the title *Gamera*.

American credits: Directed by Sandy Howard; Executive Producer: Ken Barnett; Additional Scenes: Richard Kraft; Photography: Julian Townsend; Art Director: Hank Aldrich; Assistant Director: Sidney Cooperschmidt.

Songs: "Gammera Theme Song" written by Wes Farrell; arranged and conducted by Artie Butler; performed by The Moons.

Cast: Brian Donlevy (General Terry Arnold); Albert Dekker (Secretary of Defense); Dick O'Neill (General O'Neill); John Baragrey (Captain Lovell); Diane Findlay (Sgt. Susan Embers); Gene Bua (Lt. Clark); John McCurry (Airman First Class Hopkins); Mort Marshall (Jules Manning); Alan Oppenheimer (Dr. Contrare); Stephen Zacharias (Senator Billings); Walter Arnold (American Ambassador); Louis Zorich (Russian Ambassador); Robin Craven (British Ambassador).

The appeal of an impassioned Gamera fan: "I'm certain that no matter whether you see the original Japanese version or *Gammera the Invincible*, you will come away with a new-found respect for the Chelonian Kaiju's film debut!"[34] So declares Raul Cruz in *G-Fan* #83 concerning the oft-mocked giant Japanese turtle who breathes fire and walks on two legs. And flies.

Thanks largely to MST3K's unmitigated scorn, Gamera's eight pre–1990s movies have been derided more than the guest of honor at a Dean Martin roast. In addition, many giant monster fans regard Gamera as a second-rate Godzilla knockoff. Certainly his first film at times echoes the 1954 *Gojira*.

The movie opens at the North Pole, where scientist Dr. Hidaka (Eiji Funakoshi) is interviewing an Eskimo elder. Unidentified aircraft appear overhead, and soon American fighter jets give chase, demanding the unknown pilots identify themselves. An air fight breaks out, and an American missile strikes one of the nuke-carrying unidentified aircraft. It crashes, resulting in an atomic explosion that frees Gamera (he has two "m"s only in the American version *Gammera the Invincible*).

The giant turtle quickly dispatches a research vessel. Meanwhile, the Eskimo chief gives Dr. Hidaka a stone depicting "the Devil's envoy.... Gamera!" Just the mere mention of the name sends children and dogs scrambling for cover. As Count Floyd might say, "Ooo, scary stuff, kids!" Speaking of kids, the father of turtle-obsessed youngster Toschio (Yoshiro Uchida) has ordered him to free his pet turtle Pee-Wee. Gamera appears, frightening Toschio, his big sister and his father. Toschio foolishly runs up into the lighthouse, which Gamera promptly batters. Strangely, Gamera catches a falling Toschio and sets the boy down, an act that convinces Toschio that Gamera means no harm.

Next, in flat contradiction to Toschio's assurances that Gamera is a good guy, the *kaiju* attacks a geothermal power plant. Dr. Hidaka suggests high-tension wires might stop the titanic turtle, but like Godzilla in 1954, Gamera marches through them no worse for wear. The conventional military attack that ensues also proves useless.

Gamera, it seems, "eats" fire—you can just imagine the kind of five-alarm heartburn *he* must get. In addition, he is also immune to nuclear weapons; in fact, theoretically, he might thrive on them! Military aircraft bombard Gamera with an experimental freeze bomb that incapacitates the chelonian *kaiju* for ten minutes. During this time, explosions beneath Gamera send him tumbling down a cliff, and he lands on his back, presumably helpless as he wiggles his front and back legs.

Gamera attacks a Japanese geothermal power plant in 1965's *Gamera, the Giant Monster*, a film that saw stateside release in 1966 as *Gammera the Invincible*.

The scientists and the soldiers have a good laugh over the thought of the disabled Gamera starving to death. However, surprising everyone, Gamera pulls in his legs and head, and flame inexplicably blasts from his leg sockets. Soon he lifts off and goes spinning away into the night. Meanwhile, the U.S. and U.S.S.R. join forces to create Plan Z (designed to vanquish Gamera) on Oshima Island.

The Invincible One soon attacks Tokyo, destroying real estate left and right. Toschio's big sister loses track of him when he runs away to hide on a petroleum train car headed straight for Gamera (the kaiju eats oil), smiling all the while. An adult risks his life to save the foolhardy boy, who hides in a cargo shipment being ferried to Oshima Island.

The authorities use fire to lure Gamera to Oshima, but a sudden typhoon douses the flames. The above-ground installation is set ablaze to attract the turtle, but heavy rains extinguish the inferno. As though in collusion with the authorities, Oshima's volcano fortuitously erupts. Gamera does lumber onto the island, where he is quickly sealed in the nosecone of a rocket that blasts off for Mars—this is the Plan Z on which the superpowers have collaborated. Everyone is happy at the outcome, even Gamera-obsessed Toschio. Bye-bye, Gamera. (Until the sequels of course.)

As mentioned earlier, *Gamera, the Giant Monster* and *Gojira* have several characteristics in common. Both are black-and-white, both employ nuclear weapons to unleash the monster upon the world, both feature *kaiju* impervious to nuclear weapons, and both feature humankind's salvation through "superscience" (Plan Z in *Gamera*, the Oxygen Destroyer in *Gojira*). However, beyond those similarities, the films have little in common.

On this Japanese poster for *Gamera, the Giant Monster* (Daiei, 1965), the titanic turtle destroys a passenger train while, in the foreground, Kyoko Yamamoto (Harumi Kiritachi), Dr. Hidaka (Eiji Funakoshi) and Nobuyo Sakurai (Michiko Sugata) react in terror.

Director Ishiro Honda consciously crafted *Gojira* to be a warning against the deadly potential of nuclear weapons; in an interview, he said he "naively hoped that the end of Godzilla was going to coincide with the end of nuclear testing."[35] However, *Gamera* director Noriaki Yuasa had far less lofty ambitions for the flying turtle's debut movie. "For the first black-and-white film," he said, "the main goal was to make some money for the company."[36]

Gamera wreaks havoc in Tokyo in Daiei's *Gamera, the Giant Monster* (1965), a film that established the flying turtle's movie franchise. Gamera gave rival Toho's Godzilla series a run for its yen in the '60s.

The film's opening few minutes brim with Cold War tensions. With the crash of the unidentified plane in the Arctic and the explosion of its nuclear payload, atomic age anxiety takes hold. The nervous reporter asks Dr. Hidaki, "Why bother with this turtle business when World War III could be breaking out?" A crew member aboard the research vessel, apparently speaking for many of his fellow Japanese, says the nuclear tests "might change the Earth's axis. They're going to increase typhoons in Japan." Meanwhile, the commanding officer of a nearby American airbase nervously considers the volatile situation. If you removed the monster from the first few minutes, this introduction could be the beginning of a nuclear war movie.

But once *Gamera* hits its stride, it's basically Japanese Monster Movie 101. On this level, the film is not bad, though comparing it to *Godzilla* would be a little like comparing *Gilligan's Island* to *Lord of the Flies*.

Director Yuasa (who went on to direct six more Gamera films) did have more in mind that just a box office bonanza for Daiei: "Our real goal was to create a character that was the protector of children ... for them to know there's someone on their side."[37] Hence, the explanation for why Gamera catches Toschio and sets him gently on the ground. Even to casual viewers, Toschio is more than a tad annoying, but only Gamera understands the boy's outsider status, and in successive movies, Gamera would befriend many of Toschio's peers.

The Americanization

Just as the American distributor added Western-shot scenes to *Godzilla* to create the Americanized *Godzilla, King of the Monsters!*, so too did *Gamera*'s American handlers insert Western-shot scenes to create the Americanized *Gammera the Invincible*.

In the *Gamera* original, the amateur Western actors in the U.S. airbase scenes possessed acting skills that were, to put it kindly, less than inspired. Fortunately, the American company replaced these scenes with American-shot footage populated by professional actors, including Dick O'Neill as General O'Neill. An African American actor plays one of the Air Force sergeants, and he gets several speaking lines. Needless to say, the one thing you rarely (if ever) found in American and Japanese monster movies of the '50s and '60s was a black man, and he's a welcome touch of diversity.

Several scenes featuring Albert Dekker as the Secretary of Defense and Brian Donlevy as General Arnold were filmed, most taking place at the UN. (Donlevy is best-known to genre fans for his no-nonsense portrayal of Dr. Bernard Quatermass in 1956's *The Quatermass Xperiment* and 1957's *Quatermass II*, Dekker for 1940's *Dr. Cyclops*.) Although a Soviet and American ambassador bicker, the two superpowers agree to unite for Plan Z (we hear of this in the Japanese original, but don't actually see it). Then, when Gamera turns into a flaming Frisbee whizzing through the air, one of the incredulous scientists exclaims, "Look, an amazing adaptation!" A Darwinian understatement to say the least. Also, the Western scenes display Gamera as more of a worldwide menace than as a Japanese woe. At one point, an American at the U.N. says that if Plan Z doesn't work, "Gamera may well destroy civilization as we know it."

The English dubbing changes nuances in some of the scenes. For example, after Gamera falls flat on his back, no one in the English dub talks about him starving to death as they do in the Japanese version. Also, when the adult jumps aboard the train to rescue Toschio, he exclaims to the kid, "Are you nuts?" Obviously, viewers had been wondering the same thing! Another nice touch is the great Wes Farrell's theme song "Gammera! Gammera!"

And as for Cold War intrigue, in the American-shot North Pole airbase scenes, the president orders that the military be put on Red Alert. Fortunately, it's decided that the Soviet jets (an unnamed country in the Japanese original) really did accidentally go off course, and hence World War III is averted. Will we be so lucky next time?

Godzilla, Ebirah, Mothra: Great Battle in the South Seas (Japanese release: Toho, 1966)

Godzilla vs. the Sea Monster (a.k.a. *Ebirah, Horror of the Deep*) (American release: The Walter Reade Organization, 1967)

Credits: Directed by Jun Fukuda; Screenplay by Shinichi Sekizawa; Produced by Tomoyuki Tanaka; Music: Masaru Sato; Photography: Kazuo Yamada; Editor: Ryohei Fujii; Art Director: Takeo Kita; Assistant Director: Takeshi Sano; Sound Recorder: Shoichi Yoshizawa; Sound Effects: Hisashi Shimonaga; Lighting: Kiichi Onda; Special Effects Director: Eiji Tsuburaya; Assistant Special Effects Director: Teruyoshi Nakano; Special Effects Photography Directors: Sadamasa Arikawa, Mototaka Tomioka, Taka Yuki; Special Effects Lighting: Kuichiro Kishida; Special Effects Photography: Yoichi Manoda; Mattes: Hiroshi Mukoyama; Mechanical Effects: Fumio Nakadai; Stunts: Haruo Nakajima.

Cast: Akira Takarada (Yoshimura); Kumi Mizuno (Daiyo); Chotaro Togin (Ichino); Hideo Sunazuka (Nita); Toru Ibuki (Yata Kane); Akihiko Hirata (Red

Bamboo Captain Yamoto); Jun Tazaki (Red Bamboo Commander); Toru Watanabe (Ryota Kane); Ikio Sawamura (Elderly Slave); Pair Bambi (The "Little Beauties"); Hideyo Amamoto (Red Bamboo Naval Officer); Hisaya Ito, Tadashi Okabe (Red Bamboo Scientists); Kazuo Suzuki, Shoichi Hirose (Slaves in Canoe); Kenichiro Maruyama (Newspaper Reporter); Hideo Shibuya (Maritime Police Officer); Studio No. 1 Dancers (Infant Island Natives).

Japanese version: Color; TohoScope; 87 minutes; released on December 17, 1966. Japanese title: *Gojira, Ebira, Mosura: Nankai no dai ketto* (*Godzilla, Ebirah, Mothra: Big Duel in the South Sea*).

American version: Released to TV by the Walter Reade Organization in 1968; color; pan and scan; 82 minutes. Alternate title: *Ebirah, Horror of the Deep* (this was possibly a theatrical release title).

With this seventh entry in the long-running Godzilla series, the times were certainly a-changin' for the Big G. Gone were model cityscapes, replaced by more economical miniature jungles. The usual G-protagonists—scientists, reporters, detectives, military men—were supplanted by a thief, three teenagers and a resourceful Mothra Island native. And even the soundtrack at times took a turn for the atypical, such as the guitar-drenched beach music wailing incongruously as Godzilla fights a squadron of military jets.

But despite (or because of) these touches, many Godzilla fans regard this as one of the Showa series' best movies. For example, in his exuberant *Godzilla vs. the Sea Monster* retrospective in *G-Fan* #87, John LeMay writes, "Perhaps it's time *Sea Monster* is finally recognized as one of the 'better' Godzilla films."[38]

The movie was undeniably a departure for the Big G, and its slashed production values were certainly the shape of things to come for the next eight Godzilla opuses. But in one way, *Sea Monster* did look back to the Godzilla movies of the 1950s as well as *Godzilla vs. the Thing*: While its pulse may have been erratic, the heartbeat of nuclear warning was still thumping beneath *Sea Monster*'s colorful South Seas island exterior.

The story involves teenager Ryota's (Toru Watanabe) search for his missing brother Yata (Toru Ibuki), who was lost at sea. Through a series of misadventures, Ryota and two of his teenage friends wind up on a "borrowed" yacht commandeered by a professional thief (Akira Takarada). Soon the quartet is lost at sea, but wind up on Letchi Island, an atoll ruled by the evil Red Bamboo organization; said bad guys are forcing Mothra Island natives to do slave labor.

Daiyo (Kumi Mizuno), a native, escapes her Red Bamboo captors and partners with the four castaways. Breaking into the Red Bamboo installation, they discover that the base is a heavy water factory making nuclear weapons. The authorities almost catch the quartet, with all but one managing to escape. Ryota gets entangled in a rope attached to a big balloon that improbably "floats" him all the way to Mothra Island—where he finds his brother Yata!

Meanwhile, the protagonists have discovered Godzilla sleeping in a cave. Lightning awakens the slumbering behemoth, who promptly battles giant lobster Ebirah, the Red Bamboo mascot. The Big G later tangles with an unexplained giant condor, and takes an uncharacteristic shine to Daiyo.

Ryota and Yata arrive on Letchi Island, and soon they are helping the other protagonists take on the Red Bamboo. Meanwhile, Godzilla again fights Ebirah, this time decisively defeating the colossal crustacean. The enslaved Mothra Islanders escape their Red Bamboo captors, and soon everyone is busily building a raft as Mothra wings her way to the rescue. After a brief scrap with Godzilla, Mothra carries the raft of islanders and castaways far from the island, which is set to explode in a nuclear blast. The atoll does indeed go *blammo!* Did Godzilla escape in time?

Of course.

End of fairy tale.

Godzilla vs. the Sea Monster is a pleasant enough Big G entry, one that longtime adult fans as well as wide-eyed youngsters can enjoy. Save for a silly bit of volleyboulder, Godzilla's two battles with Ebirah are well-handled, as is his brief skirmish with the adult Mothra. Speaking of the latter, in a wonderful special effects shot, Mothra lands in the background while tiny natives in the foreground run towards her. This convincing shot gives a magnificent sense of scale. There is some other good matte work as well.

The Red Bamboo base is simplistic and poorly detailed, looking every bit like the model it is. The jets that attack Godzilla fare a bit better, as does the Big G's entertaining obliteration of same. Despite the hot-and-cold visuals, director Jun Fukuda keeps things moving along nicely.

Story-wise, the film infuses elements of then popular Beach Party youth movies and spy thrillers. The Red Bamboo certainly would have been at home in a Matt Helm movie. Likewise, the human action is very comic bookish—for example, in a scene where Takarada tosses a smoke bomb at Red Bamboo guards, they had plenty of time to shoot before being "blinded" by the smoke clouds, but of course they don't.

The nuclear threat figures into all this exuberant monster movie merriment in the form of the heavy water the Red Bamboo use to build nuclear weapons. The heavy water factory, a stand-in for the nuclear threat, serves as the impersonal "villain" of *Sea Monster* pointing to unspoken atomic mayhem. Obviously, the Red Bamboo will either use the nukes themselves or sell them to the highest bidder. They might even use them as weapons of nuclear terrorism.

John LeMay suggests that perhaps leakage from the Red Bamboo heavy water factory may have mutated Ebirah to be an oxymoronic king-sized shrimp.[39] In addition, LeMay suggests maybe the movie's giant condor drank some of this irradiated water, thus explaining its gargantuan proportions. A strong possibility is that the Red Bamboo deliberately exposed Ebirah to radiation to mutate him to become their crustacean watchdog.

By this time, despite still being radioactive, Godzilla's stature as "walking H-bomb" had been considerably diminished. Indeed, the two previous G films had morphed Godzilla into a hero-villain (with the emphasis more on the former than the latter) with a sense of humor. I don't know about you, but somehow I can't see a walking H-bomb dance a victory jig.

In *Invasion of Astro-Monster*, Godzilla and his pal Rodan have just whooped three-headed space dragon King Ghidorah on Planet X, and to celebrate the occasion, Godzilla indulges in a literal leaping dance known officially as the "jumping shie." Director Ishiro Honda didn't like the scene, but it nevertheless made it into the movie's final cut.[40]

Son of Godzilla (Japanese release: Toho, 1967; American release: The Walter Reade Organization, 1969)

Credits: Directed by Jun Fukuda; Screenplay by Shinichi Sekizawa and Kazue Shiba; Produced by Tomoyuki Tanaka; Music: Masaru Sato; Photography: Kazuo

Yamada; Editor: Ryohei Fujii; Art Director: Takeo Kita; Lighting: Eiji Yamaguchi, Shoshichi Kojima; Production Manager: Yasuaki Sakamoto; Sound: Toshiya Ban; Sound Effects: Minoru Kanayama; Assistant Director: Takashi Nagano; Special Effects Supervisor: Eiji Tsuburaya; Special Effects Director: Sadamasa Arikawa; Special Effects Art Director: Akira Watanabe; Special Effects Lighting: Kuichiro Kishida; Special Effects Optical Photography: Yukio Manoda, Sadao Iizuda; Special Effects Assistant Director: Teruyoshi Nakano; Stunt Choreography: Haruo Nakajima.

Cast: Tadao Takashima (Dr. Kusumi); Akira Kubo (Goro Maki); Beverly Maeda (Saeko Matsumiya); Akihiko Hirata (Fujisaki); Yoshio Tsuchiya (Furukawa); Kenji Sahara (Morio); Kenichiro Maruyama (Ozawa); Seishiro Kuno (Tashiro); Yasuhiko Saijo (Suzuki); Susumu Kurobe (Captain of Weather Plane); Kazuo Suzuki (Pilot); Wataru Omae (Radio Operator); Chotaro Togin (Navigator); Haruo Nakajima, Seiji Onaka, Hiroshi Sekita (Godzilla); "Little Person" Machan (Minya aka Minilla).

Japanese version: Color; TohoScope; 86 minutes; released on December 16, 1967. Japanese title: *Kaiju shima no kessen: Gojira no musuko* (*Monster Island's Decisive Battle: Son of Godzilla*).

American version: Released to TV by the Walter Reade Organization; color; pan and scan; 84 minutes.

Stuart Galbraith states that with *Son of Godzilla*, Toho "entered the kiddie market."[41] Certainly Toho designed Godzilla's son Minya (a.k.a. Manilla) to appeal to small fry. Genre critics often excoriate the diminutive *daikaiju*'s appearance. For example, Galbraith states that the atomic age tyke looks "like a cross between a tadpole and a badly deformed human fetus."[42] Certainly Minya looks nothing like Godzilla, though upon hatching from his egg, the reporter Goro instantly recognizes him as "a baby Godzilla." As David Kalat suggests, perhaps Goro needs an eye exam.[43]

Like the Big G's previous entry, *Son of Godzilla* makes use of a cost-cutting South Seas atoll, this time the supposedly deserted Solgell Island. A group of United Nations scientists, all Japanese and under the direction of Dr. Kusumi (Tadao Takashima), plan to conduct a weather experiment. Unwelcome reporter Goro (Akira Kubo) parachutes onto the island to investigate, but the scientists immediately give him the tasks of cook and custodian. A king-sized praying mantis skirts the camp one night. The island may be rife with other enormous multi-legged life forms. (It is.)

Dr. Kusumi reveals to Goro the nature of the upcoming weather experiment: Overpopulation will soon result in rampant mass starvation, but if weather control can turn infertile lands fertile, then starving millions could be fed. Goro is intrigued. When Goro insists he has seen a female on the island, no one believes him.

On the day of the experiment, Goro embarks on a search for the woman. The experiment, which consists of a freezing balloon detonated at 800 meters, silver iodide sprayed into the sky by two tall towers, and a radioactive capsule to be exploded at 1000 meters, commences. Electrical interference (actually Minya's mental "distress" call to Godzilla) causes the radioactive capsule to explode too soon, turning the island into a steamy inferno slashed by gales of hot rain.

The radiation and heat cause the Kamacuras (giant mantises) to become Godzilla-sized, and soon they pound on a huge egg, out of which hatches Minya, the son of Godzilla. Papa G shows up in time to rescue his hapless, balance-challenged offspring.

Meanwhile, Goro introduces the scientists to the female on the island, Saeko (Beverly Maeda), daughter of a Japanese archaeologist who died many years prior. Because of their wrecked island base, the scientists move their equipment, including a damaged radio, into Saeko's cave. When a jungle fever afflicts the scientists, Saeko leads Goro to a lake of red water that will heal them. Awakened, the giant spider Kumonga traps the protagonists in Saeko's cave. Kumonga also wraps Minya in a cocoon of its deadly silken webbing. Godzilla arrives to rescue his son and begins battling with the eight-legged *daikaiju*.

The experiment to freeze the island finally works, and (using the repaired radio) help is summoned to rescue the protagonists. As the temperature on the atoll plummets, thick snow carpets the landscape. Godzilla defeats Kumonga and sets the enormous arachnid on fire. Next, it appears the Big G is ignoring Minya as the latter clumsily plods after his gargantuan dad. But proving he is no absentee father, Godzilla turns and embraces his son as both are blanketed in wintry white.

Just as the submarine is rescuing the protagonists, Goro assures Saeko that Godzilla and son will hibernate beneath the snow, but will one day thaw out.

Son of Godzilla's visual highlights involve the Kamacuras and Kumonga. All are well-articulated marionettes under the direction of Fumio Nakadai. Kumonga will probably give the kiddies the shudders. In addition, the film boasts some nice matte work. No city destruction, of course, though Godzilla does stomp through the sparse U.N. island base (apparently he's attracted to a man-made structure the way a gold digger is attracted to a wealthy octogenarian).

The major problem with the film is its attempt to be both serious and silly. The human drama is handled straight, and is at times intense, with Akihiko Hirata realistically cracking up. This plays hob with Minya's pratfalls and Godzilla's anthropomorphic antics when teaching his son. Like Aerosmith and the Archies, the two elements simply don't mix.

Son of Godzilla depicts radiation as a strange substance that can result in disaster. For example, the prematurely bursting radioactive capsule causes both hellish storms and mutated animal life, i.e., the "gang" of marauding Kamacuras. The latter effect is only logical in the Toho kaijuverse of the 1950s and 1960s, when radiation had become firmly established as the catalyst for catastrophic mutations such as the H-Man, not to mention environmental devastation (for example, the atom-blasted Mothra Island in *Godzilla vs. the Thing*). In *Son of Godzilla*, the scientists are trying to harness the atom for good. Despite their benevolent intentions, reporter Goro has this interesting dinnertime conversation with Dr. Kusumi.

Goro: "Why must the experiment be conducted in secret?"

"Don't you see? If someone abused our system, they could also freeze the entire world. The results would be the same as a nuclear holocaust."

In other words, just like nuclear weapons—or just like Dr. Serizawa's Oxygen Destroyer—weather control could be used as a weapon of mass destruction. However, Dr. Serizawa was so distraught over the possible misuse of the Oxygen Destroyer that he obliterated both its plans and himself, its inventor. Although concerned over weather control's possible ill use, Dr. Kusumi appears to believe that its potential benefits (feeding millions who would otherwise starve) outweigh the risks (obliterating worldwide ecosystems). Thus, as long as weather control experiments and the technique's future use fall under the purview of the United Nations, all is well—we hope.

An interesting note on Dr. Kusumi's statement that weather control could "freeze the entire world": In essence, nuclear winter would cause the same thing. Nuclear winter would be irreversible, and though weather control's adverse effects are reversed on Solgell Island, could they be reversed over an entire continent, or over an island nation like Japan? *Son of Godzilla*, more concerned with escapist entertainment than speculation on the potential dire effects of weather control, keeps the subject at a "safe" comic book level, which for better or worse, indicates the path the Godzilla series had traveled in the 13 years since the original *Gojira*.

Almost Atomic

We now take a brief look at the Godzilla movies—*King Kong vs. Godzilla*; *Ghidorah, the Three-Headed Monster*; *Invasion of Astro-Monster*—that didn't qualify for full-fledged nuclear threat status since they only briefly discuss the issue. But these moments do have atomic age significance.

Like virtue in the U.S. Congress, the nuclear threat in *King Kong vs. Godzilla* is almost microscopic. Light-hearted merriment trumps soul-searching reflection. Plenty of human humor abounds, and so does "*kaiju* comedy." Godzilla "flaps" his arms, "laughs" at his monster opponent, and weaves and bobs—a major character transformation from the animalistic savagery the atom-spawned monster displayed in *Godzilla Raids Again*.

King Kong (he of the famed tacky gorilla suit and known by many fans as Toho Kong) likewise clowns it up, and Japanese audiences were delighted. In 1962, *King Kong vs. Godzilla* sold 11.2 million movie tickets in Japan, a significant increase over the original *Godzilla*'s 9.6 million. The film was a hit in the U.S. as well, boasting a 1963 movie gross of $2.75 million.[44] It firmly established Godzilla as a worldwide superstar and served as a springboard to his next 12 Showa era movies. Instead of assaulting King Kong with its blowtorch atomic breath, Godzilla should have been shaking the big palookah's paw, mainly because without Kong, there might have been no Godzilla series.

For readers who want details on *King Kong vs. Godzilla*, I suggest Steve Ryfle's *Japan's Favorite Mon-Star: The Unauthorized Biography of "The Big G"*; the second edition of David Kalat's *A Critical History and Filmography of Toho's Godzilla Series*, and Peter H. Brothers' *Mushroom Clouds and Mushroom Men: The Fantastic Cinema of Ishiro Honda*. *G-Fan Magazine* is another excellent source.

For this book's purposes, we will only focus on the minor nuclear threat aspects of the film. In the movie's American version, as Godzilla heads for Japan, reporters question the minister of defense about how the military will stop him. "Then," says one reporter, "you have discussed using the atom bomb?"

The defense minister responds, "Possibly, as a last resort."

Later in the film, after King Kong has broken through power lines and stomped into Tokyo, a reporter asks a government minister, "Sir, what about the atom bomb?"

The minister replies, "I am not ready to discuss it."

"But," the reporter says, "it's our only chance."

"We hope it is not."

"Why not?"

"Because we're not anxious to destroy Tokyo, that's why."

Moments later, reporters ask the defense minister the same question, and he says, "The atom bomb is ready and waiting. But first we must evacuate Tokyo and perhaps all Japan."

Sound like a disconnect among Japanese leaders? There's a reason for that. In the original Japanese version, the defense minister completely rejects the use of nuclear weapons as a means to defeat Kong and Godzilla.[45]

Why does the Americanization have Japanese leaders saying just the opposite? Probably because to 1963 Americans, nuclear weapons would be used as a last recourse against giant monsters. After all, to many Americans, nukes weren't necessarily bad in and of themselves, and the U.S. needed them to maintain an atomic parity with the Soviet Union.

But to the Japanese, the only recipients of nuclear attack, the question of the "goodness" or "badness" of atomic weapons was a non-starter. It would be like asking if a national famine was a good thing or a bad thing. No sane person would *choose* to have a famine. Thus, no sane person would likewise choose to use nuclear weapons; certainly this was the essence of *King Kong vs. Godzilla* director Ishiro Honda's views on the subject.

While *kaiju* comedy had suffused much of *King Kong vs. Godzilla*, *Mothra vs. Godzilla* had returned the King of the Monsters to his serious roots. Then was *King Kong vs. Godzilla* a one-off aberration?

Hardly. *Mothra vs. Godzilla* did fairly well at the box office, but sold only 3.5 million tickets, a major comedown from *King Kong vs. Godzilla*'s 11.2 million ticket sales. Thus, Godzilla series producer Tomoyuki Tanaka reasoned that a light tone was necessary henceforth to assure a successful Godzilla movie; special effects director Eiji Tsuburaya also favored more humor in the monster scenes. While this strategy worked in the short run, it arguably contributed to the Godzilla series' box office shortfalls in the 1970s.

Ghidorah, the Three-Headed Monster employs ample "monster humor" during its final third, particularly the "monster talk" scene during which Mothra "negotiates" with Godzilla and Rodan while the *Shobijin* translate for the human protagonists. Also noteworthy is a scene in which King Ghidorah blasts Godzilla in the backside. Suffice to say, the tone for the remainder of the 1960s and 1970s Godzilla series had been set.

In *Ghidorah*'s Americanization, a tight focus on the momentary nuclear threat issue reveals the minister of defense saying, "We cannot assume responsibility for authorizing the deployment and use of atomic weapons [to defeat the monsters]." In the Japanese version, the defense minister says, "Have all of you the courage to use nuclear bombs on Godzilla and Rodan? I don't think I need explain any more. My state of mind is to do man's best, then wait and accept God's will."

Just as in *King Kong vs. Godzilla*, *Ghidorah* views the use of nuclear weapons as forbidden. Of course, in this movie, King Ghidorah is considered a global threat. Of Venusian lineage in the Japanese version, Martian in the American, the film's prophet reveals that Ghidorah utterly destroyed the civilization on her world. Hence, when Ghidorah chose to attack North America, the U.S. would probably be only too happy to throw an H-bomb or two at the three-headed space dragon; the Soviet Union would have responded similarly. However, the combined trio of Godzilla, Rodan and Mothra send Ghidorah packing from the Earth, so the question of the monster's susceptibility to nuclear weapons remains unanswered.

As with *King Kong vs. Godzilla* and *Ghidorah, the Three-Headed Monster*, the nuclear threat amounts to only a few spoken lines in *Invasion of Astro-Monster* (a.k.a. *Monster Zero*), so we won't tarry long with this sixth entry in the Godzilla series. In the film, the Xians of the moon-like Planet X "borrow" Godzilla and Rodan to defeat King Ghidorah, who is plaguing them. The Earth monsters succeed, but—*surprise!* It was all an Xian ruse. Actually, they plan to use Godzilla, Rodan *and* King Ghidorah to destroy the Earth unless we submit to Planet X rule pronto. This doesn't sit well with anyone, especially impassioned astronaut Nick Adams, a hero so intense he could burst a blood vessel at any moment.[46]

But not to worry: The humans' science releases the monsters from Xian control, after which Godzilla and Rodan tussle with Ghidorah once again, climaxing with all of them crashing into the sea. However, only Ghidorah emerges from the waves. So is Godzilla history? Not as long as he kept Toho in the black, and *Invasion of Astro-Monster* sold a healthy 3.78 million tickets in Japan.

In the American version, when the authorities are discussing how to defeat Godzilla, Rodan and King Ghidorah, Dr. Sakurai (Jun Tazaki) tells astronaut Fuji (Akira Takarada), "The military men want to use all our nuclear weapons and then resist them [the Xians] to the bitter end."

Fuji replies, "We'll be wiped out by the radioactivity."

The Japanese version basically agrees:

"What is the decision of the Defense Council?" Fuji asks.

Dr. Sakurai replies, "Nothing yet. The Defense Force insists on using our hydrogen bombs to resist."

"We can't live with that massive radioactivity," Fuji says.

This represents an interesting shift from *King Kong vs. Godzilla* and *Ghidorah, the Three-Headed Monster*, in which Japanese leaders reject nuclear weapons outright. But in *Invasion of Astro-Monster*, the Japanese military is apparently endorsing the use of nuclear weapons as a last resort. However, the context implies that non-military Japanese leaders disagree with their militaristic peers. (Interestingly, this seems to parallel the then conflicting nuke attitudes between many civilian leaders and military generals in America.)

KING KONG VS. GODZILLA

Produced and released by Toho; color; TohoScope; 98 minutes; released on August 11, 1962. Directed by Ishiro Honda; Screenplay by Shinichi Sekizawa; Produced by Tomoyuki Tanaka; Music: Akira Ifukube; Special Effects: Eiji Tsuburaya. Cast: Tadao Takashima, Mie Hama, Kenji Sahara, Yu Fujiko, Ichiro Arishima.

AMERICAN VERSION

Released by Universal-International; 91 minutes; color; scope; released on June 3, 1963. Produced by John Beck; Directed by Thomas Montgomery; Written by Paul Mason, Bruce Howard; Music Supervisor: Paul Zinner. Cast: Michael Keith, Harry Holcombe, James Yagi.

GHIDORAH, THE THREE-HEADED MONSTER

Produced and released by Toho; color; TohoScope; 92 minutes; released on December 20, 1964. Directed by Ishiro Honda; Screenplay by Shinichi Sekizawa; Produced by Tomoyuki Tanaka; Music: Akira Ifukube; Special Effects: Eiji Tsuburaya. Cast: Yosuke Natsuki, Yuriko Hoshi, Hiroshi Koizumi, Takashi Shimura.

American Version

Released by Continental and the Walter Reade Organization; color; scope; 85 minutes; released on September 29, 1965. English dialogue by Joe Belluci; Post-production Consultant: Ray Angus.

Invasion of Astro-Monster

Produced and released by Toho; color; TohoScope; 96 minutes; released on December 19, 1965. Directed by Ishiro Honda; Screenplay by Shinichi Sekizawa; Produced by Tomoyuki Tanaka; Music: Akira Ifukube; Special Effects: Eiji Tsuburaya. Cast: Nick Adams, Akira Takarada, Kumi Mizuno, Jun Tazaki.

American Version

Released by Maron Films; color; Tohoscope; 92 minutes; released on July 29, 1970. Double-billed with *War of the Gargantuas* (1966). Original movie release title: *Monster Zero*. Later re-titled *Godzilla vs. Monster Zero* (sorry, Rodan—you didn't quite merit a title credit).

Going back to basics and 1954's *Gojira*: a shocking confession: After having watched the uncut Japanese-language version of the venerable monster's first film for the first time, I was impressed, but not bowled over, and in many ways, the movie didn't seem all that different from the Americanized *Godzilla, King of the Monsters!* In fact, I kind of missed Raymond Burr. (In my defense: I had probably seen the Burr version at least 20 times before I first beheld 1954's *Gojira*). While I appreciated the Japanese version's political content, I did not realize I had witnessed a masterpiece that many Japanese film critics consider one of the best Japanese movies ever made.[47] Perhaps unconsciously, I could hold the film at arm's length—after all, I was a citizen of the country that had dropped the atomic bomb, not a resident of the country that had suffered its wrath.

Fortunately, I do have several sensitive bones in my overfed red, white and blue body, and I was and have always been sympathetic to what must have been a nightmare of horrendous proportions for the Japanese in 1945. (As a child, I remember my brother Frank telling me that when the A-bomb was dropped on Hiroshima, oblivious schoolchildren were performing calisthenics. I inwardly shuddered at how horrible it must have been for them, and I have never forgotten that unsettling meditation.)

The more I read about the first *Godzilla*, the more I realized why, for the Japanese, it was more than a mere "monster movie." My sympathy turned to empathy, and as I watched the original Japanese film again and again and still again, my cup runneth over with enlightenment.

I came to understand how, after all, *Gojira* and *Godzilla, King of the Monsters!* are two very different albeit complementary sides of the same atomic coin, the latter the product of the same American mores that had given life to *The Beast from 20,000 Fathoms, Tarantula* and *It Came from Beneath the Sea*, among others. It is in that spirit that we turn to a comparison and contrast of how the Japanese and American atomic age monsters gave substance—and controversy?—to the nuclear threat.

7. Honda vs. Harryhausen

True or false: Japanese monster movies of the 1950s took their cues from Western monster-on-the-loose epics, but they marched to the beat of a different drum. (If you answered "false," please consult the ample literature in this book's bibliography.)

On the surface, 1953's *The Beast from 20,000 Fathoms* and 1954's *Godzilla* appear to be cut from the same cake—that is, until you take a bite. Then you will find each offers a dissimilar taste, sharing some ingredients, yes, but sporting others as different as vanilla and cocoa. The *Beast* slice will inspire you to keep a level head, but the *Godzilla* piece will provoke you to wake up and smell the Strontium-90. I will primarily use these two creature feature classics to demonstrate how American and Japanese atomic age monsters differ in terms of scope, invulnerability, significance and mortality in their metaphoric embodiments of the nuclear threat. I will refer to other Eastern and Western monster movies as well..

American giant monster movies often feature solo menaces geographically localized in scope, such as *The Beast from 20,000 Fathoms*, 1955's *Tarantula* and 1955's *It Came from Beneath the Sea*. *Beast*'s Rhedosaurus may squash a few cars, eat a few police officers, and trash a few New York buildings, but there's no possibility of the creature becoming an international or even a national menace. In other words, the Beast may have rocked the Big Apple, but Cleveland was still sitting pretty. Likewise, *Tarantula*'s hundred-foot arachnid is confined to terrorizing the locals (mostly livestock) around Desert Rock, Arizona, and while *It Came from Beneath the Sea*'s colossal cephalopod ravages the West Coast and sinks some ships, it mostly sets its sights on San Francisco. (Some of you are saying, "Yeah, but what about *The Giant Claw*? It was no localized monster!" We'll get to her soon enough—yes, *her*. After all, she did lay an egg—in more ways than one.)

But what about Japanese solo monsters of the same period? In his first film, Godzilla menaces Japan, yes, but due to the monster's invulnerability, he could easily become a worldwide terror, a beast without borders. Certainly *Godzilla, King of the Monsters!* regards Godzilla as a potential threat to human civilization. As Steve Martin watches Godzilla demolish Tokyo, he says, "I'm saying a prayer, George, a prayer for the whole world." Then, after the monster's death, Burr says, "The whole world could wake up and live again."

The two Rodans are likewise formidable. The Americanized version has one of the Japanese authorities fretting, "If they're not killed, they'll take over the Earth!" Mothra becomes a true international despoiler of both Japan and Rolisica (the 1961 film's surrogate United States). And *Gammera the Invincible* proclaims the titanic turtle's worldwide potential for destruction. As the Japanese ambassador in the film's American trailer states, "Plan Z is the hope of the world." In essence, solo Japanese movie monsters were generally

Ray Harryhausen's cephalopod besieges San Francisco in *It Came from Beneath the Sea* (Columbia, 1955).

harbingers of the global Apocalypse, whereas solo American movie monsters were usually localized Armageddons, symbols perhaps of a "limited" nuclear war.

In other words, the U.S. could easily contain the nuclear threat and, according to the subtext of American monster movies, did just that during the '50s. For example, the government ramped up Civil Defense to quell American jitters about a potential nuclear war. Were the "Russkies" to drop a nuke on St. Louis, Americans could duck into the nearest Civil Defense shelter. Or better still, citizens with means could build their own bomb shelters to protect their families during a nuclear conflict, waiting in their cramped refuges until the authorities gave the "all clear" to come out.

Yes, our military had everything well under control, and in the event of an atomic war, we would come out on top. After all, Curtis LeMay, commander of Strategic Air Command in the 1950s, had his "Sunday punch" waiting in the wings, which was no less than throwing our entire nuclear arsenal at the Soviet Union "at the shortest possible notice."[1] He also pined for a single bomb powerful enough to obliterate Russia entirely.[2]

However, Japanese atomic age monster films assert that neither militaries nor governments could contain the nuclear threat; for Japan, bigger bombs and "Sunday punches" found personification in the many *daikaiju* that routinely attacked the island nation. Japan's solo monsters are inexplicably invulnerable to conventional military weaponry. Tanks, jets, artillery—Godzilla brushes them all aside. However, a mere torpedo kills *It Came from Beneath the Sea*'s giant octopus; similarly, simple napalm barbecues *Tarantula*'s colossal spider, and a radioactive grenade (exotic but still conventional) takes out the Rhedosaurus in an ironic touch. Indeed, in this case, "good" atoms triumph over "bad" atoms. This echoes President Dwight D. Eisenhower's 1950s Atoms for Peace campaign that promoted the allegedly peaceful uses of the atom, such as nuke-generated electricity. But no atomic reactors were necessary to deliver the Beast's slayer. It was traditional physics in the form of a rifle that shoots the isotope into the monster's open wound.

But when it comes to Japanese solo monsters, it takes super-science to save the day, such as the Godzilla-disintegrating Oxygen Destroyer, a weapon of mass destruction perhaps deadlier than the H-bomb. Super-science likewise appears in *Mothra* in the form of the atomic heat cannon; Rolisica provides Japan with two of these radar-dished H-bombs on wheels, but their combined attempts to figuratively swat Mothra come to naught. And as for Gamera, the film establishes that not only would nuclear weapons not harm the monster, but would most likely nourish it! (Shades of 1957's *Kronos*.) Consequently, super-science in the form of experimental freeze bombs besiege the beast, albeit unsuccessfully. Since there is no way humankind can kill Gamera, super-science in the form of Plan Z saves the day by blasting the indestructible *kaiju* into outer space. Unlike their giant Western counterparts, Japanese monsters such as Godzilla, Mothra and Gamera resist conventional weapons.

How? Simple. Just as you can't kill a nuclear explosion, you can't kill Godzilla, a personification of a nuclear explosion. Godzilla scholar Steve Ryfle quotes an interview with director Ishiro Honda in which Honda said, "If Godzilla had been a big ancient dinosaur or some other animal, he would have been killed by just one cannonball. But if he were equal to an atomic bomb, we wouldn't know what to do. So, I took the characteristics of an atomic bomb and applied them to Godzilla."[3]

Indeed, Japan's atomic age movie monsters display an invincibility reserved for gods and acts of nature; they represent the freed nuclear genie in all its unassailable independence. While Godzilla, Rodan, Mothra and Gamera represented the destructive powers of nuclear weapons, the Rhedosaurus, Tarantula and It stood for nukes in small case, i.e., not the Bomb but rather the bomb.

But then there's *The Giant Claw*. As noted in Chapter 5, this big bird threatened the world, resisting all conventional weapons thanks to a force field that even protected the monster from nuke attack! As the film's worried general says, "We have tried every weapon in the arsenal of the mightiest armies on Earth. They have proven worse than useless. Atomic, hydrogen weapons capable of wiping cities, countries off the face of the Earth are completely ineffective against this creature from the skies." Move over, Godzilla!

But just as Dr. Serizawa's Oxygen Destroyer overcame Godzilla, so Jeff Morrow's mu-meson cannon disrupts the Claw's force field, allowing conventional weapons to finish her off. This shows a nuance between the Claw and her colossal Japanese cousins: Godzilla and company don't need a force field, because somehow their unvarnished selves are able to withstand military attack, no matter how intense. But once the Claw loses her equivalent of a soldier's body armor, she's toast.

Aside from the Claw, when it comes to global menace, what about American "group monsters"? *Them!*'s giant ants threaten the planet, with Dr. Medford predicting human extinction in a year if the insects aren't stopped. The same goes for the bloated locusts of *Beginning of the End*. Both films root around in the soil of American anxiety concerning life after the Bomb. *Them!* brims with spooky foreboding about humankind's potential post-nuke fate, employing Biblical prophecy to drive home the point. Copycat *Beginning of the End* does the same with its talk of a time "when the beasts inherit the Earth." However, these two films are atypical of American group monster films. For like their solo American monster counterparts, the creepy-crawly group menaces in *Attack of the Crab Monsters*, *The Monster That Challenged the World*, *Monster from Green Hell* and *Attack of the Giant Leeches* are localized only. Bill Warren argued that this is one of the qualities that makes *The Monster That Challenged the World* seem plausible.[4] American atomic

"Kill one and two take its place!" screams a fleeing woman. The ants in *Them!* (Warner Bros., 1954) multiplied, not unlike nuclear arms. The ants on the poster are much bigger than in the film, and even sport bloodshot eyes.

One of Bert I. Gordon's giant locusts on a Chicago roadway in *Beginning of the End* (AB-PT, 1957).

age monster films usually strive to be plausible, albeit a "movie reality" plausibility only. Yes, these creature features definitely had their pseudo-scientific feet planted firmly on the ground.

For while American atomic age monsters of the '50s are presumably scientific in nature—present-day organisms mutated by radiation or prehistoric animals awakened by it—their science collapses upon a closer inspection. In *Them!*, Dr. Medford appears to be a brilliant entomologist, yet he never brings up the fact that due to the square cube law, ants simply could not grow to the size of Army trucks, because they would be able neither to move nor to breathe. This same law of physics would likewise apply to the multi-legged menaces of *Tarantula* and *Beginning of the End*.

However, *Them!* is intelligent in one respect concerning radiation. It wasn't a single nuclear test that turned these ants into giants; Dr. Medford explains that for years, the ants have been breeding into the giants they are today, one of the reasons they hadn't been discovered sooner. However, the majority of American atomic age monsters need only one dose of radiation and *presto change-o*—instant Goliath. Yes, in cases like *The Amazing Colossal Man*, *Attack of the 50 Foot Woman* and *Tarantula*, the mutants grow a bit day by day, but they still needed only one bite from the atomic apple to set the growth process in motion. In these movies, radiation may sound "scientific," but it is actually tantamount to magic.

As for the first monster awakened by a nuclear explosion, *The Beast from 20,000 Fathoms*' redoubtable Rhedosaurus, paleontologist Dr. Elson sensibly scoffs at the notion that any animal could survive millions of years in suspended animation after having been flash-frozen. After all, what was its body metabolizing all this time? But to Elson's amazement, he discovers that the Rhedosaurus did survive, thawing out none the worse for wear thanks to a nuclear blast. Another problem is the creature's plague-producing bacteria. Since it evolved in a time before hominids walked the earth, it is highly unlikely that any bacteria it carried would affect modern humans. But plot-wise, it needed its diseased blood to prevent the Army from simply blowing it to smithereens in the people-packed metropolis of New York.

Yet despite these pseudo-scientific plot contrivances, the film's trailer has an actor (Paul Picerni) saying, "Impossible? Unbelievable? Fantastic? But I tell you it could happen." Then the narrator kicks in with this amazing claim: "Yes, it could happen, for various authorities believe that buried somewhere under the polar icecap in a state of suspended animation are the awesome creatures, the leviathans that roamed the earth at the dawn of time, and under certain conditions, a nuclear explosion could free one from an icy tomb." You have to wonder who these "various authorities" were. Probably the PR boys at Warner Bros.

Yes, in all American atomic age monster films, scientists speak knowingly to their colleagues—as well as to the movie audience—but much of their science concerning the atom wouldn't fly in the average 1950s Romper Room. Scientists like *Them!*'s Dr. Medford and *Beast*'s Dr. Elson give these movies a veneer of plausibility, but that's all it is, and please pay no attention to that man behind the curtain.

Speaking of plausibility, Japan had its own "group monsters" in the period we're examining, and they almost seemed credible. Rodan's meganuron are sturdy (one resists point blank gunfire) but still ultimately vulnerable to conventional physical forces, such as the speeding coal car that kills one of them. In terms of their only relative invulnerability, these prehistoric worm creatures are probably the most "realistic" monsters in Japanese atomic age genre films. Perhaps not coincidentally, they are also the creepiest.

But giant Japanese solo monsters are decidedly non-plausible—indeed, they are virtually mystical in their defiance of the laws of physics. For example, the Odo Island elder speaks of their island deity Godzilla, claiming the lack of female sacrifices to the monster is the reason for its rage. Likewise, the Eskimo elder in Gamera warns of the giant turtle's sinister legend. As for Mothra, she acts as her atoll's deity, and her two tiny fairies suggest that a heavy dose of mysticism figures into her identity, with radiation perhaps playing a minor (or not-so-minor) role.

Also, these same Rising Sun monsters exhibit "superpowers." Godzilla spews his atomic breath; Gamera breathes fire; Rodan sprays an unidentified vapor-like ray in its debut film; and Mothra employs her silken webbing as a weapon, using it, for instance, to cocoon Godzilla (in 1964's *Godzilla vs. the Thing*) and a short time later, King Ghidorah (in 1964's *Ghidorah, the Three-Headed Monster*).

In the case of Godzilla, its weapon has been "transposed" from a fairy tale context to a science-fantasy milieu. For example, instead of simply breathing fire, Godzilla shoots his radioactive ray, which immediately seems more contemporary. (Director Ishiro Honda came up with the idea of Godzilla's ray as a means of making radiation visible.[5])

When it comes to the super-winds generated by Rodan and Mothra, science-fantasy supplants science reality. When Rodan zooms over Fukuoka, his supersonic slipstream

The Rhedosaurus rages through New York City on this poster from *The Beast from 20,000 Fathoms* (Warner Bros., 1953).

rips the city apart. But in reality, his flight over the city doesn't look all that fast and wouldn't be powerful enough to cause such damage. Even more telling, when he simply stands in urban ruins and casually flaps his wings, he generates winds violent enough to obliterate buildings. But in reality, his wing flaps would hardly produce any wind at all. Also, when he flies, what is one to make of his vapor trail? And for that matter, how does he create the sound of a jet engine when he flies? None of this would work in science reality, but it works readily enough in science-fantasy. (Mothra is in the same boat. Her flight over New Kirk City would neither have demolished skyscrapers nor sent a major suspension bridge crashing into the sea.)

In contrast, with the exception of the Giant Claw, American atomic age monsters sport no superpowers and are less mystical than a Richard Dawkins Fan Club. The Rhedosaurus is nothing more than a dinosaur that a nuclear blast has awakened; it merely has size, strength and petulance going for it. Tarantula is an average hairy eight-legger that Gets Real Big. And It is a six-armed cephalopod stirred from the ocean depths by H-bomb tests. None of these monsters sports a legendary pedigree. (However, again, the Giant Claw is the exception as she both sports a superweapon—her antimatter force field—and linkage to a legendary monster.)

When it comes to urban destruction—that time-honored ritual of every giant monster movie that has the budget to provide a model city—American monsters have naturalistic motives only. The Rhedosaurus attacks New York because this is the site of its

Why did the *Tarantula* (Universal-International, 1955) cross the road? To find hapless new victims, of course.

ancient spawning grounds. It attacks San Francisco in search of food. And Tarantula likewise pillages the countryside simply to sate its enormous appetite. Even the Giant Claw circles the globe searching for food for her soon-to-be hatchlings (whose eggs are destroyed by the protagonists).

But Godzilla's attack on Tokyo is irrational, for Japan's capital city is neither a spawning ground nor a source of nourishment for the creature. Instead, Godzilla deliberately singles out the city for one purpose—to vent its rage. The filmmakers intended these scenes to evoke memories of the atomic bombings of Hiroshima and Nagasaki, as well as the fire bombings of Tokyo; the combined death toll in these three cities was a staggering 210,000. Godzilla is lashing out at Tokyo as a representation of humankind, angry over the H-bombs that have awakened and scarred the creature. By implication, the atomic wrath he visits upon Tokyo awaits us all.

Godzilla's debut film is not afraid to dwell on the human toll of pain and suffering the monster causes. For example, in the scenes of burned and injured victims of Godzilla's wrath receiving medical care, a doctor uses a Geiger counter to determine the amount of radiation a young Japanese girl has received, and he shakes his head to Emiko, indicating that the girl will not survive. There is no such analogous scene in any American atomic age monster movie. True, in *The Beast from 20,000 Fathoms*, we see troops recovering from the plague the Rhedosaurus has brought to New York, but these scenes are not explicit, nor do any children die. When a monster threatens a child in an American atomic age movie, he or she is always saved in time, as in *The Black Scorpion* and *The Monster That Challenged the World*.

However, the first *Godzilla* was willing to show children in jeopardy and even imply their deaths. In addition to the fatally irradiated little girl, there is also the mother sheltering her two young offspring from Godzilla's fiery destruction of a department store, and their deaths occur off-screen. The mortality of the young implies that the nuclear threat doesn't just menace adults, but likewise endangers children, even infants, but there is little or nothing the Japanese can do about it. Meanwhile, in American films, the take-charge Yanks can and do defend children from the nuclear threat.

Another characteristic of Japanese atomic age monsters is that their attacks often seem providential. Certainly this is true in the case of the first Godzilla, and could arguably be the case in *Godzilla Raids Again*. Mothra attacks Tokyo and New Kirk City because Nelson and his goons have kidnapped the fairies, her wrath more focused and rational than Godzilla's rage, but still divinely appointed. After all, the Japanese version of *Mothra* implies that the prayers of New Kirk City residents influence the giant moth to settle down and land at the airport. Not only that, orthodox Christian priests lead these prayers!

However, in American atomic age monster movies, the monster attacks are just random acts of nature, not the meting out of divine will. Now these acts are due to humans tampering with nature *vis-à-vis* the Bomb, meaning we are to blame. But in *Them!*, for example, there are no indications that a Supreme Being has mobilized the giant ants in the Southwest to teach us human beings a lesson. Similarly, the Rhedosaurus isn't out to punish anyone—he's simply foraging for grub and a mate. Godzilla, on the other hand, appears to seek divinely appointed vengeance on Tokyo due to humankind "playing with the fire of the gods."

American monster films tend to be relatively optimistic, while Japanese monster films tend to be relatively gloomy. In the U.S. giant monster films, the menace is soundly defeated in the end, usually due to good old American know-how—or good old American napalm or radioactive isotopes. And once the Rhedosaurus is killed, no one frets that nuclear tests might awaken more such behemoths.

But in Japanese monster films, the menace is rarely defeated. In the case of Godzilla, he *is* destroyed, but only due to a super-weapon. However, the Oxygen Destroyer's creator takes his own life to keep the world safe from the weapon. Dr. Yamane notes that if nuclear testing continues, more Godzillas may come into the world—a prophecy borne out in *Godzilla Raids Again*.

Meanwhile, the limited wrath of U.S. creatures implies that the limited nuclear tests in the Pacific and in America are completely under control. But Japanese monsters are localized only in one sense, in that they primarily menace Japan, as indeed did the nuclear threat. The hapless island nation sits smack dab between the Soviet Union and the U.S., so could easily fall victim to any escalating nuclear conflict between the superpowers. But we have also seen that Japanese movie monsters, like the nuclear threat, implicitly imperil the entire planet, whereas American movie monsters usually do not.

Also, who are the good guys in American atomic age monster movies? Primarily the military, of course, followed in a close second by those tweed-jacketed egghead scientists, the FBI and the police—in other words, the authorities. Who ultimately exterminates the giant ants in *Them!*? The U.S. Army. Who defeats It? Navy commander Kenneth Tobey. Who takes out Tarantula? The U.S. Air Force led by Clint Eastwood. The message from the Pentagon: We have this atomic thing well in hand, America. But did they?

My hat is off to all the men and women in uniform for their valor and service to America, past and present. But I think the motives of some American military leaders during the 1950s were questionable. For example, General Curtis LeMay spoke of deliberately goading the Soviet Union into starting World War III since the U.S. allegedly had the nuclear advantage.[6] And in the 1950s, military brass ordered our troops to march across radioactive test sites upon which nuclear bombs had just exploded. Was this to see how such a hot zone might affect American soldiers as a "dress rehearsal" for combat under World War III battle conditions?[7]

Japan never tested nuclear weapons, and thus never exposed its men in uniform to radiation. But even if the country had possessed nuclear weapons, and had chosen to test them, its leaders probably would not have exposed any Japanese citizen, civilian or military, to a nuclear blast. After all, the island nation possessed a collective fatalism concerning atomic weapons.

This fatalism played out in the country's atomic age monster films not just in terms of civilian casualties, but also in its victimization of the average military man; you have to wonder how many hundreds of Japanese soldiers needlessly gave their lives in attempts to combat the indestructible *daikaiju*. After all, the first *Godzilla* establishes the monster's invincibility, yet in *Godzilla Raids Again*, *King Kong vs. Godzilla* and *Godzilla vs. the Thing*, the military again rolls into action in a suicidal attempt to halt the *daikaiju*'s swath of destruction.

The military is generally helpless against giant monsters in Japanese atomic age films. To defeat the second Godzilla in *Godzilla Raids Again*, the JSDF buries the Big G in ice, simply because they cannot kill him. Rodan is done in not by Japanese missiles and artillery, but rather by Mother Nature (an erupting volcano). Mothra stalwartly resists all military efforts to halt her progress, and she's alive and free at the end of her debut film. And because the military can't even touch Gamera, the solution is to send him to Mars on a rocketship! This symbolizes how the Japanese military was likewise helpless in the face of the nuclear threat, which simply could not be defeated, just as Japanese atomic age monsters could not be defeated.

And note how in American atomic age monster films, the menace is almost always dead at the end, as opposed to Japanese atomic age monsters who marshal on past the finale. In fact, only one American atomic age monster movie resulted in a sequel: *The Amazing Colossal Man* begat *War of the Colossal Beast*. Again, said films imply America could take care of any nuclear crisis, and was in fact doing so.

But Japanese atomic age monsters appeared in sequel after sequel. For example, in the 1950–1967 period this book examines, Godzilla appeared in eight movies, Rodan three, Mothra four and Gamera three. The latter kept coming back for more because, like the nuclear threat, they couldn't be stopped. They represent the nuclear genie with fangs and claws and wings and scales, a Pandora's Box nightmare seemingly multiplying at will, just as the superpowers continued to escalate their arsenals of nuclear weapons. The Japanese couldn't stop giant monsters any more than they could stop the superpowers' arms race.

Also, Japanese giant monsters were subjective in nature, as opposed to their objective American counterparts. American giant monsters were generally actual biological beings enlarged by the atom or awakened by it. But Japanese movie monsters were fantasy creations even before the atom affected them. There never was a species of Godzilla, Anguirus, Rodan, Mothra or Gamera (granted, there never was a Rhedosaurus or Giant Claw either). And note how each of these Japanese monsters has a name, as though it is an actual character, whereas American giant monsters (with the exception of giant humans) remain nameless. Indeed, the nuclear threat was impersonal to Americans of the 1950s, for aside from our troops who marched across radioactive hot zones, our country had never personally faced the Bomb's wrath, hence the reason for the detached nature of American giant monsters.

However, the nuclear threat embodied in the atom bombings of Hiroshima and Nagasaki haunted the Japanese in the 1950s and 1960s, an apprehension exacerbated by 1954's *Lucky Dragon No. 5* incident. The nuclear threat was very personal to the nation's civilians, for it found form in the *hibakusha*, survivors of the atom bombings who epitomized the nuclear dread that had contaminated the nation's psyche. Americans who watched the scenes of burned and injured Japanese victims in *Godzilla, King of the Monsters!* could remain disconnected, but for the Japanese, this was the ghost of nuclear horrors past—and the ghost of possible nuclear horrors to come.

Another contrast between Japanese and American giant monster movies of the 1950s involves the depiction of radiation. Radiation altered (as in Godzilla's case) and/or awakened Japanese monsters, but it rarely turned them giant, for they were already behemoths. (The exceptions include the title monster from *Frankenstein Conquers the World*, the mantises in *Son of Godzilla* and possibly Ebirah and the Giant Condor in *Godzilla vs. the Sea Monster*.) However, in the majority of American giant monster movies of the 1950s, radiation is the force that enlarges rather than awakens animals and humans. This implies that radiation takes something natural (men, women, bugs) and bloats it into something unnatural. In Japanese films, radiation awakens a sleeping, quasi-mystical *kaiju*—something quite unnatural already—and sets it loose upon the world in an atomic context. In such films, the monster is not generally a "bad guy"; for example, in the first *Godzilla*, the Japanese regard the monster's disintegration with mixed relief and sadness. Likewise, the death of the two winged monsters in *Rodan* deliberately evokes sympathy. But in American giant monster films, the monster's passing, save for the cases of giant humans, is regarded as an unequivocal victory. None of the characters in *The Beast from 20,000 Fathoms* sheds a tear upon the Rhedosaurus's demise. (Director Eugene Lourie's daughter was quite upset that her daddy had killed the monster,[8] but Lourie atoned for this sin by directing *Gorgo*, a movie in which both the monster and its titanic mother escape unscathed at the end.)

American movies of the '50s expressed concern about nuclear secrets falling into the wrong hands, i.e., Communist hands. Yet in *Godzilla*, Dr. Serizawa fears not that the Oxygen Destroyer will fall into the wrong hands, because *any* government's hands would be the wrong hands. He assumes, cynically perhaps, that one or more governments would use his weapon to gain a geopolitical advantage—it wouldn't be a matter of *if* but *when*. *Godzilla* implies that it isn't a matter of *if* nuclear weapons will be used again, but *when*. However, *The Beast from 20,000 Fathoms* implies that if nuclear weapons are ever used again, it will be a surgical application that will cleanly and simply finish off the "bad guys." So even if there was a *when*, Americans need not be troubled.

Perhaps *troubling* is the best word for Japanese and American giant monster films in the 1950–1967 period. In the movies of both countries, the immense monsters personified the fear of the ongoing nuclear threat. However, Japanese giant monsters were invulnerable, defying the power of the government or military to stop them, and these unconquerable colossi implicitly threatened the entire world. Thus, the Japanese saw these beasts as embodying the outcome of the nuclear threat as inevitably ruinous on a global scale.

However, the military always triumphed over American giant monsters, dispatching them with relative ease. Spencer Weart notes in his book *The Rise of Nuclear Fear* that, when it came to nuclear weapons in the 1950s, "the word 'control' was on every [American] tongue."[9]

Nevertheless, when it came to the nuclear threat, American giant monster movies sometimes possessed a disquieting undercurrent of unease; one immediately thinks of Colonel Glenn Manning and his anguished plea, "I don't want to grow any more." Even more disturbing is the open-ended finale of *Them!* Would more giant ants, spiders, locusts and other creepy-crawlies pop up across the U.S. thanks to nuclear testing? Would more soldiers exposed to nuclear blasts grow into psychologically tormented giants? Would more prehistoric monsters awakened by nuclear tests threaten major American coastal cities with destruction and plague? As Dr. Medford says at the end of *Them!*, "When man entered the atomic age, he opened a door into a new world. What we eventually find in that new world, nobody can predict."

Unlike their Japanese counterparts, American atomic age monster movies held out hope that we would learn from our mistakes. For example, *Tarantula*'s radioactive growth nutrient accidentally led to the spider's super-sized wrath. But next time, science could be more cautious, thus using the atom to feed the world under carefully controlled conditions rather than terrorize the Southwest under lax laboratory protocols. American atomic cinema posited that if scientists worked together under the auspices of the authorities rather than separately under their own authority, the atom need not herald the end of the world at all; instead, we could learn from our errors and create a better, stronger future.

Speaking of strong: Although American giant monster cinema opened like gangbusters in 1952, the year of *King Kong*'s highly successful re-release, by 1960 the cycle had played itself out. (One exception is 1965's *Village of the Giants*, but it was chemicals, not the atom, that produced the film's titanic teens.) Commercially, there wasn't anywhere for the "objective" giant American monster genre to go, largely because it possessed no continuing monster characters. Also, one could argue that American fears over a possible nuclear exchange with the Soviet Union peaked in the early 1960s, especially during 1962's Cuban Missile Crisis. Consequently, the giant monster as a metaphor for the nuclear threat no longer cut it. America was now ready to behold the atomic genie unmasked, as we shall see in the next chapter.

PART III: MUSHROOM CLOUDS

8. Twilight's Last Gleaming

1951–1964

In the 1950s, mutants and monsters glowed brighter at the box office than a uranium mine, thus the reason most American nuclear threat movies featured atomic ogres. The ad art could always exploit the monster, thus reeling in both preteens and teenagers. An example is the poster of 1955's *Day the World Ended*, which prominently features its three-eyed mutant.

"Pure" nuclear threat movies were harder to sell, and by pure, I mean movies whose "monster" was the nuclear threat itself, i.e., pre-aftermath or post-aftermath depictions of a nuclear war. *Day the World Ended* might fascinate a nine-year-old thanks to its mutant, but 1951's *Five*, in which nary a mutant or monster can be found, might bore him silly. For this reason, American studios produced relatively few pure nuclear threat movies between 1951 and 1967. The majority of the ones that *were* made appeared in the late 1950s and early 1960s.

A couple came out in the early 1950s, and we will first direct our attention to these: the first (*Five*) philosophical, the second (*Invasion U.S.A.*) histrionic.

Five (Columbia, 1951)

Credits: Produced, Directed and Written by Arch Oboler; Photography, Editing and Production Assistance through arrangement with Montage Films by Sid Lubow, Ed Spiegel, Louis Clyde Stoumen, Arthur L. Swerdloff; Music: Henry Russell; Orchestrator: Charles Maxwell; Music Editor: Betty Steinberg; Sound: William Jenkins Locy; Special Sound Effects: Gus Bayz; Poem "Creation" Written by James Weldon Johnson; Editor: John Hoffman; Cinematographic Consultant: Louis Clyde Stoumen; Executive Secretary: Geraldine Klancke.

Cast: William Phipps (Michael); Susan Douglas (Roseanne); James Anderson (Eric); Charles Lampkin (Charles); Earl Lee (Oliver Barnstapler).

An Arch Oboler Production; black-and-white; 93 minutes; released in April 1951. Available on DVD.

What if after a nuclear conflict, you were one of the only five people left alive? This happens in director-writer-producer Arch Oboler's *Five*,[1] the first film to depict the aftermath of a nuclear war. For that reason alone, it is significant. (Some might point to 1950's

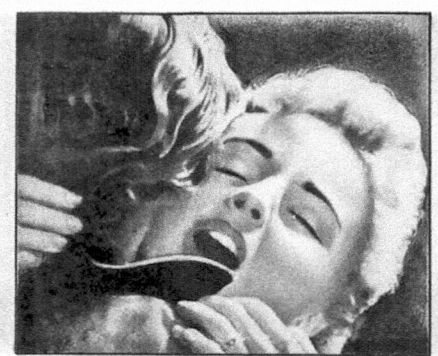

This poster captures the tensions between the last five people on Earth after a nuclear war in producer-writer-director Arch Oboler's *Five* (Columbia, 1951).

Rocketship X-M as being the first American film to depict a post-aftermath world, but its world in question was Mars, not Earth.)

Five begins with a literal bang—a thundering music score accompanying stock footage of nuclear explosions. Dark, radiation-saturated clouds pass over major cities including London, Moscow and New York. Next, the film spotlights Roseanne (Susan Douglas), a pregnant survivor who stumbles through the countryside until she finds a house occupied by fellow survivor Michael (William Phipps). They bond, and she travels with Michael to a country store. There, in a touch of irony, a posted sign says, "Be back in five minutes." In addition, they find a laundry detergent called "Atomic Suds," which Michael angrily flings aside.

In a Jeep, two more survivors arrive at Michael's, Charles (Charles Lampkin) and Barnstaple (Earl Lee). Charles worked as a bank doorman, and Barnstaple worked at the bank as well; he suffers from radiation poisoning. Michael, Susan and Charles take Barnstaple to the beach at his request, where they find a man named Eric (James Anderson), a disagreeable type who survived a plane crash into the sea. Barnstaple expires on the beach.

Michael and Charles plant seeds in a field and find a generator, but Eric offers no help whatsoever. Eric also shows himself to be a racist. Roseanne gives birth to her child. Eric talks her into agreeing to go to the city with him, where Roseanne believes her husband may still be alive. Before Eric leaves, he kills Charles.

In the city, Roseanne finds skeletons everywhere, including that of her husband. She wants to go back to Michael's, but Eric informs Roseanne she is his and that he has no intentions of letting her go. They struggle and his shirt is torn, revealing radiation sores on his chest. Howling hysterically, he stumbles away.

Susan doggedly walks back to Michael's house, but her baby dies on the way. She and Michael may be the last two survivors on the planet. As we see them standing side by side, the movie ends with the hope-filled words of Revelation 21.

Some critics have accused *Five* of being long-winded, pseudo-artsy and far-fetched. Bill Warren wrote, "*Five* might be considered the first science fiction Art Film, in the worst senses of the term."[2] According to *Castle of Frankenstein* #9 (1966), "Arch Oboler's atomic destruction drama has fascinating appeal despite 'preachy' moments.... See it." While the film is overly talky and somewhat slow, I agree with *Castle of Frankenstein*: In addition to its flaws, the film does have its virtues.

However, plausibility isn't one of them. For example, when the holocaust happened, Michael was in New York City and Eric at the top of Mount Everest. That they would happen to meet with the only three other survivors in California is less probable than a politician fulfilling all of his campaign promises. The coincidence asks too much of the viewer, and if one reads into this divine intervention to get these five together, then the movie becomes less science fiction than science-fantasy. There's nothing wrong with the latter, but *Five* makes no allusions to God herding the characters under one roof.

One oddity is that major cities such as Moscow and New York are still standing amidst the atomic onslaught, albeit choked by radioactive clouds. Does this mean Earth experienced a limited nuclear war instead of an all-out atomic conflict? If the latter had occurred, you would assume the major cities in the U.S. and U.S.S.R. would be heaps of rubble. Instead, the film suggests that most people die due to radioactive contamination.

Even though *Five*'s opening employs stock footage of nuclear explosions that would soon become commonplace in 1950s films, the combination of the first atomic explosion to the accompaniment of the dramatic music score is effective, as are the brief scenes of the clouds floating across the world. The constant background screaming also adds to the grim effect, and 1951 movie audiences must have found this alarming.

The film also scores points when Eric and Roseanne trek into the city, for there they encounter dozens of clothed skeletons. These scenes evoke an empty desolation, climaxed by Roseanne finding what's left of her husband and weeping over his remains.

Five wants to be the equivalent of an air raid siren, warning moviegoers of the atomic horrors that may lie ahead. It strains for credulity, but winds up with fantasy. Also, the relatively upbeat finale begins well with Roseanne, tears streaming down her face, walking up to Michael in the cornfield and saying, "I want to help you." This is much stronger, and more credible, than if she had said, "Michael, I love you."

However, then the music swells and we see the partial text of Revelation 21, which speaks of a new beginning in which there is "no death" and "no tears." Given all the grimness we've witnessed, including the recent death of Roseanne's baby, this assurance of a new Heaven and a new Earth promises too much, though no doubt the intention was to leave the viewer with a sense of hope to temper the film's overall gloominess.

Five set the tone for the ending of almost all American nuclear threat movies throughout the '50s and '60s. In virtually every case, there is a sense of hope at the movie's finale, sometimes as flag-waving as the ending of *Panic in Year Zero!* but generally to the level of *Five*, in which a couple lives to begin a new day.

It is significant that Charles, one of the five survivors, is an African American. Most science fiction films during the 1950s include no characters of color at all, so Arch Oboler wins points for diversity long before it became standard in Hollywood.

Invasion U.S.A. (Columbia, 1952)

Credits: Directed by Alfred E. Green; Screenplay by Robert Smith; Story by Robert Smith, Franz Spencer (a.k.a. Schulz); Produced by Albert Zugsmith, Robert Smith; Associate Producer: Peter Miller; Executive Producer: Joseph Justman; Art Director: James W. Sullivan; Set Decorator: John Sturtevant; Photography: John L. Russell, Jr.; Music: Albert Glasser; Sound: Frank McWhorter; Editor: W. Donn Hayes; Special Effects: Rocky Cline, Jack Rabin; Makeup: Harry Thomas; Production Manager-Assistant Director: Ralph E. Black; Dialogue Director: Robert Bice.

Cast: Gerald Mohr (Vince Potter); Peggie Castle (Carla Sanford); Dan O'Herlihy (Mr. Ohman); Robert Bice (George Sylvester); Tom Kennedy (Tim); Wade Crosby (Congressman Arthur V. Harroway); Erik Blythe (Ed Mulfory); Phyllis Coates (Mrs. Mulfory); Aram Katcher (Factory Window Washer); Knox Manning (Television Newscaster); Edward G. Robinson, Jr. (Radio Dispatcher); Noel Neill (Airline Ticket Agent); Clarence A. Shoop (Army Major); John Crawford (Man in Bar); Richard Eyer (Mulfory's Son); Franklyn Farnum (Man from Omaha); Joseph Granby (U.S. President); Ethan Laidlaw (Russian Sea Captain); Jack Lomas (Wise Guy in bar); Renny McEvoy (Military Guardsman); Jack Carr, Frank Mills (Plant Workers); Jack Reitzen (Russian Invader); William Schallert (Newscaster).

An American Pictures production; black-and-white; 73 minutes; released on December 10, 1952. Poster tagline: "It will scare the pants off you!" (quote from columnist Hedda Hopper). Available on DVD.

Five doesn't concern itself with who started the nuclear war, but *Invasion U.S.A.* makes the culprit clear: the Soviet Union. Though the film never mentions the nation's name, it includes plenty of tip-offs that clearly point to the U.S.S.R. Certainly, 1952 audiences had no doubt about who the Enemy was.

The film introduces us to six characters in a New York City bar: journalist Vince Potter (Gerald Mohr), socialite Carla (Peggie Castle), industrialist George Sylvester (Robert Bice), rancher Ed Mulfory (Erik Blythe), Congressman Arthur (Wade Crosby) and "forecaster" Mr. Ohman (Dan O'Herlihy). Several of them are grousing about talk of a universal draft in which every civilian would have to commit both his or her career and his or her business interests to the U.S. military.

A TV news broadcaster announces that enemy aircraft have been spotted over Alaska. The Enemy quickly takes over several American airports, from which they launch a nationwide attack on the country. This includes using atomic bombs; the U.S. retaliates by bombing Russia.

Rancher Ed and industrialist George fly to San Francisco, and shortly after they arrive, the Enemy begins to bomb the city. Back in the Big Apple, despite the cataclysmic events overtaking America, Vince and Carla are falling in love. Meanwhile, the "People's Army" quickly overtake George's factory. When he fights backs, Enemy soldiers shoot him to death. San Francisco is now under Enemy control.

In Arizona, Ed meets his wife and kids just as the Enemy has atom bombed Boulder Dam; the resulting flood drowns him and his family. Next, New York City is A-bombed, but despite extensive damage and 30,000 dead, Vince and Carla survive, more in love than ever. Atomic war may be just the thing for budding romance.

Enemy troops invade Washington, D.C., and massacre a number of Congressman, including Arthur. Vince and Carla meet again in her apartment, albeit accompanied by two Enemy soldiers. One of them tries to force Carla to drink; Vince intervenes on her behalf, and the soldier shoots him to death. Then the boorish People's Army soldier paws Carla, but she jumps out the window of her high-rise apartment rather than be raped.

Just when you think things can't get worse … they get better. Suddenly we're back to the bar in the movie's first scene and it turns out that Mr. Ohman mass-hypnotized the characters (yeah, right). The protagonists have now seen the light. For example, industrialist George declares he is going to have his tractor factory make tank parts, and rancher Ed says, "I'm in on this too." Carla indicates that she is going to the nearest blood bank, Vince beside her all the way.

First, the mass hypnosis bit: Yes, it is preposterous, and as "It Was All a Dream" scenarios always are, it's a cheat. But it's interesting that although Mr. Ohman only made Vince and Carla think they had started a romance, they still have those feelings for one another. Relationship hypnosis to unite two might-be lovers? Sounds like it might have commercial potential. There should definitely be an app for that.

Second, the presentation: The film mostly consists of stock footage, much of it military. While some of it is interesting, it invariably distracts the viewer from the plight of the protagonists. On the other hand, Jack Rabin supplies a handful of original special effects, and they're not half-bad for the time. For example, the atom bombing of New York City, a mixture of a superimposed nuclear explosion over New York and the use of miniature buildings, proves effective, as does a quick shot of the smoldering ruins of what's left of Manhattan Island.

Third, the vignettes: A handful of these actually work. Of course, the sequences with Ed and George's fates are over the top, but a low-key set piece at an airline ticket counter generates genuine pathos, especially when a ticket agent has to tell a customer that flights to her hoped for destination have been permanently cancelled. In another quietly effective scene, Vince and Carla discuss the war, and she expresses disbelief that such a thing could be happening. For me, this recalls my own thoughts on September 11, 2001. It seemed incredible that terrorists had hijacked passenger planes and flown them into the World Trade Center, with another hitting the Pentagon, and a fourth plane crashing in a rural area before it could reach its destination, thanks to a heroic group of Americans.

Like many Americans, I figured there might be more terrorist mayhem to come. At work, a colleague (incorrectly) said that a fifth passenger plane had crashed into Seattle's Space Needle. Given what had actually happened already that day, it didn't sound farfetched. Likewise, if World War III had broken out in the 1950s in the limited nuclear war scenario of *Invasion U.S.A.*, no doubt Americans like Carla would indeed react in disbelief, anxious over how it would all play out.

Fourth, the theme: Were the filmmakers truly fearful of a Communist sneak attack, or was making a movie depicting such an event just good business? If the latter was the motive, producer Albert Zugsmith cleaned up. According to IMDb, *Invasion U.S.A.* cost only $127,000 (not surprising considering all the stock footage) and grossed $1.2 million. But if alerting audiences to the Communist threat was the motive, even partially, the film's strident tone would have alienated anyone who wasn't already a true believer.

The enemy sets off an A-bomb in *Invasion U.S.A.* (Columbia, 1952). Although the identity of the aggressors remains unnamed in the movie, it is obviously the Soviet Union.

The Enemy soldiers are sneering and nasty, with an apparent policy of "shoot every American on sight." Even if one believed Soviet leaders were evil to the core, that mentality wouldn't hold true for the nation's soldiers, who probably weren't much different than American soldiers. As is, *Invasion U.S.A.* is propaganda of the most pandering sort.

Despite the rampant use of atomic bombs, the film isn't terribly interested in the after-effects of nuclear explosions on people, despite the fact that we see New York blasted. We rarely see casualties, though certainly showing radiation-burned civilians might ramp up the movie's anti–Communist slant. On the other hand, showing American victims of atomic bombs might cause viewers to think about the actual repercussions of using nuclear weapons in war, making audiences less prone to buy into the movie's tone of "Hey, World War III is inevitable anyway, so let's get it started already!"

However you view it, *Invasion U.S.A.* is an interesting time capsule of the anti–Communist passions that gripped many Americans during the 1950s.

Teenage Cave Man (AIP, 1958)

Credits: Produced and Directed by Roger Corman; Screenplay by R. Wright Campbell; Executive Producers: James H. Nicholson, Samuel Z. Arkoff; Editor: Irene Morra; Photography: Floyd Crosby; Production Manager: Maurice Vaccarino; Art Director: Dan Haller; Costume Design: Marjorie Corso; Music: Albert Glasser; Sound: Herman Lewis, Philip Mitchell; Assistant Director: Jack Bohrer; Title Design: Bill Martin; Property Master: Karl Brainard.

Cast: Robert Vaughn (The Boy); Darah Marshall (The Blond Maiden); Leslie Bradley (The Symbol Maker); Frank De Kova (The Villain); June Jocelyn (The Symbol Maker's Wife); Jonathan Haze (Curly-haired Boy); Beach Dickerson (Fair-haired Boy/Man from Burning Plains/Tom-Tom Player/Bear); Ed Nelson (Blond Tribe Member); Robert Shayne (Keeper of the Gifts); Marshall Bradford (Keeper of the Third Gift); Charles Thompson, Joseph H. Hamilton, Barboura Morris, Stephanie Shayne (Tribe Members).

A Malibu Production; black-and-white; Superama; 65 minutes; released in July 1958. Double-billed with *How to Make a Monster* (1958). Available on DVD on a double feature with 1957's *The Saga of the Viking Women and Their Voyage to the Waters of the Great Sea Serpent*.

Robert Vaughn strikes a pensive pose as the title character in AIP's *Teenage Cave Man* (1958).

This film's title suggests images of an adolescent Fred Flintstone sporting sideburns, but it actually stars pre–*Man from U.N.C.L.E.*[3] Robert Vaughn as a thoughtful youth pushing the boundaries of his tribe's mores.

The Boy (Vaughn) longs to know what lies across the river, but his tribe forbids members from crossing it. Legends say dangerous animals teem in the land across the river, and even worse, the God That Gives Death with Its Touch dwells there. Vaughn talks some of his young comrades into crossing the river with him; there they see various dinosaurs, and one of Vaughn's friends (Beach Dickerson) dies in the "sinking earth" (quicksand).

His friends return to the tribe, but the Boy stays and confronts the God That Gives Death with Its Touch—and lives to tell the tale. When the Boy returns to the tribe, the Villain (Frank De Kova, and yes, his part is called "The Villain") points out that, according to the Law, the Boy must be put to death. The Keeper of the Law (Robert Shayne) instead decrees that the Boy will be figuratively dead to them until he reaches manhood. Eventually the Boy takes a mate, and all seems well for a time.

But the Boy's wanderlust compels him to cross the river yet again. Incensed, the Villain leads tribesmen to follow the Boy to kill him. The Boy again confronts the God Who Gives Death with Its Touch, but this time he makes peaceful gestures to the creature. The Villain kills the God, and in turn the Boy kills him. It turns out the God was actually an ancient human wearing a radiation suit. The Boy takes a book from the human; it's filled with pictures from the twentieth century.

We then hear the human explain, via an apparent diary entry in the book, that he was one of 23 scientists left alive after a worldwide nuclear holocaust. Both animals and

The Villain (Frank de Kova, left) battles the Boy (Robert Vaughn) while tribesmen look on in *Teenage Cave Man* **(AIP, 1958).**

men were mutated by the blast (stock footage from *Day the World Ended* and *The She-Creature*), and the scientist developed extra longevity. Formerly, his suit was radioactive, hence the reason he killed with his touch, but "the radiation has worn away these long, long years."

James Robert Parish and Michael R. Pitts peg this one about right when they say that, among producer-director Roger Corman's '50s efforts, *Teenage Cave Man* is "one of the most beguiling plotwise and poorest in production values."[4] Bill Warren notes that, at one point, the hunters kill "the phoniest-looking bear in cinema history."[5] Corman said the movie was filmed under the title *Prehistoric World*, and he was shocked when he saw that AIP had released it as *Teenage Cave Man*, apparently due to the company's major successes with *I Was a Teenage Werewolf* and *I Was a Teenage Frankenstein*.[6]

Teenage Cave Man is intended as a cautionary tale, but it isn't until the last few minutes that its nuclear threat connection becomes evident. The nuclear war apparently literally bombed the world back to the Stone Age, something SAC commander General Curtis LeMay said the U.S. should do to Russia. The scientist's closing words are, "Retaliation added to retaliation until all traces of man's works had been wiped from the face of the Earth." In other words, once a nuclear war got started between the superpowers, it would not be limited, but would inevitably escalate to catastrophic levels.

The final voiceover is not from the scientist, but rather an objective narrator who tells us, "This happened a long time ago." He then notes how all this led up to more war. "Will it happen again? And if it does, will any at all survive the next time? Or will it be the end?"

As far as being a serious post-aftermath tale, due to its minuscule budget and fanciful touches (i.e., dinosaurs reappearing after the Big One), *Teenage Cave Man* just misses the mark.

On the Beach (134 minutes, United Artists, 1959)

Credits: Produced and Directed by Stanley Kramer; Screenplay by John Paxton; Based on the Novel by Nevil Shute; Music: Ernest Gold; Photography: Giuseppe Rotunno; Editor: Frederic Knudtson; Production Design: Rudolph Sternad; Art Director: Fernando Carrere; Makeup: John O'Gorman, Frank Prehoda; Hair Styling: Jane Shugrue; Production Manager: Clem Beauchamp; Assistant Director: Ivan Volkman; Sound: Walter Elliott; Sound Engineer: Hans Wetzel; Special Effects: Lee Zavitz; Stunts: Carey Loftin, Harvey Parry, Dale Van Sickel; Auto Race Photography: Daniel L. Fapp; Wardrobe: Joe King, Eva Friend; Script Supervisor: Sam Freedle; Property Master: Art Cole; Chief Gaffer: Allen Grice; Camera Operators: Ross Wood, Robert Wright; Technical Advisor: Vice-Admiral Charles A. Lockwood U.S.N.; Royal Australian Navy Liaison: Lt. Commander A.A. Norris-Smith.

Song: "Waltzing Matilda": Music by Marie Cowan; Lyrics by A.B. Paterson.

Cast: Gregory Peck (Comdr. Dwight Lionel Towers); Ava Gardner (Moira Davidson); Fred Astaire (Julian Osborne); Anthony Perkins (Lt. Peter Holmes); Donna Anderson (Mary Holmes); John Tate (Adm. Bridie); Harp McGuire (Lt. Sunderstrom); Lola Brooks (Lt. Hosgood); Ken Wayne (Lt. Benson); Guy Doleman (Lt. Comdr. Farrel); Richard Meikle (Davis); John Meillon (Yeoman Ralph Swain); Joe McCormick (Ackerman); Lou Vernon (Bill Davidson); Kevin Brennan (Dr. Forster); Basil Buller-Murphy (Sir Douglas Froude); John Casson (Salvation Army Captain); Paddy Moran (Stevens—Wine Steward); Grant Taylor (Morgan); Harvey Adams (Sykes); Jim Barrett

(Chrysler); C. Harding Brown (Dykers); Keith Eden (Dr. Fletcher); Stuart Finch (Jones—Radio Operator); Frank Gatliff (Radio Officer); Katherine Hill (Jennifer Holmes); Audine Leith (Betty); Peter O'Shaughnessy (Jorgensen Associate); Rita Pauncefort (Elderly Woman); John Royle (Senior Officer); Jerry Ian Seals (Fogarty—Sonar Operator); Peter Williams (Prof. Jorgensen); Carey Paul Peck (Boy).

A Lomitas Production; black-and-white; 134 minutes; released on December 17, 1959. Available on DVD and Blu-ray.

If you could choose only one movie that every human being should see, would it be *On the Beach*? Probably not. A sensation in its day, the movie premiered in multiple world capitals on December 19, 1959 and trumpeted the tagline "If you never see another motion picture, see *On the Beach*." But lo these many years later, only Baby Boomers and film fans seem to remember this message-heavy movie. On the other hand, plenty of folks—even many young whippersnappers—have heard of "mere" 1959 commercial movies such as *North by Northwest* and *Ben-Hur* and might have even seen them.

But no one can deny that *On the Beach* believed it had something vital and profound to say to 1959 audiences. It wastes little time establishing its premise: Over an Australian radio, we hear a newscaster say, "The atomic war has ended, but the prime minister reports no proof of survival of human life anywhere except here [Australia]."

The *Sawfish*, a U.S. nuclear sub, sails into Melbourne, where, Captain Dwight Towers (Gregory Peck) meets with naval authorities about embarking on a reconnaissance mission to the north to check radiation levels. In town, he stays with level-headed Lt. Peter Holmes (Anthony Perkins) and his distressed wife Mary (Donna Anderson). At a party, Dwight encounters both booze-guzzling Dr. Julian Osborn (Fred Astaire), who helped build the Bomb, and free-spirited Moira Davidson (Ava Gardner), who feels an immediate attraction to Dwight. But the talk at the party turns into a heated debate about the world's current predicament: Australia has only five months before radiation will wipe out every man, woman and child on the continent. Julian says, "The background level of radiation in this very room is nine times what it was a year ago!"

Mary breaks down, insisting there must be hope, and flees from the party, followed by understanding husband Peter. Meanwhile, hard-drinking Moira becomes acquainted with Dwight. At one point she says, "You look married."

"Oh, I am," he replies in the present tense. "My wife's name is Sharon." As he talks about his two young sons as though they too are still alive, Moira silently pities him, for his family and everyone else in America is dead.

The next day, Peter, Mary and Julian lounge on the beach with Dwight and Moira, who frolic together. But Dwight unthinkingly refers to Moira as Sharon, his wife, which causes everyone to look down in embarrassment.

Knowing he will soon be shipping out on the *Sawfish*, Peter pulls some political strings to obtain suicide pills to leave with Mary, for he may not return in time for the end, and he doesn't want her and their child to experience the agony of radiation poisoning. Peter tries to explain to Mary that if he is away when the time comes, she must take a pill and give one to their baby; she will have none of it. Meanwhile, Dwight tries to explain to Moira that he can't control his denial of his family's demise, and their relationship appears to have ended.

The next morning, the *Sawfish* sails for the Arctic Circle, but discovers that even there, the air is rife with deadly radiation. At their next stop, San Francisco, the sub's

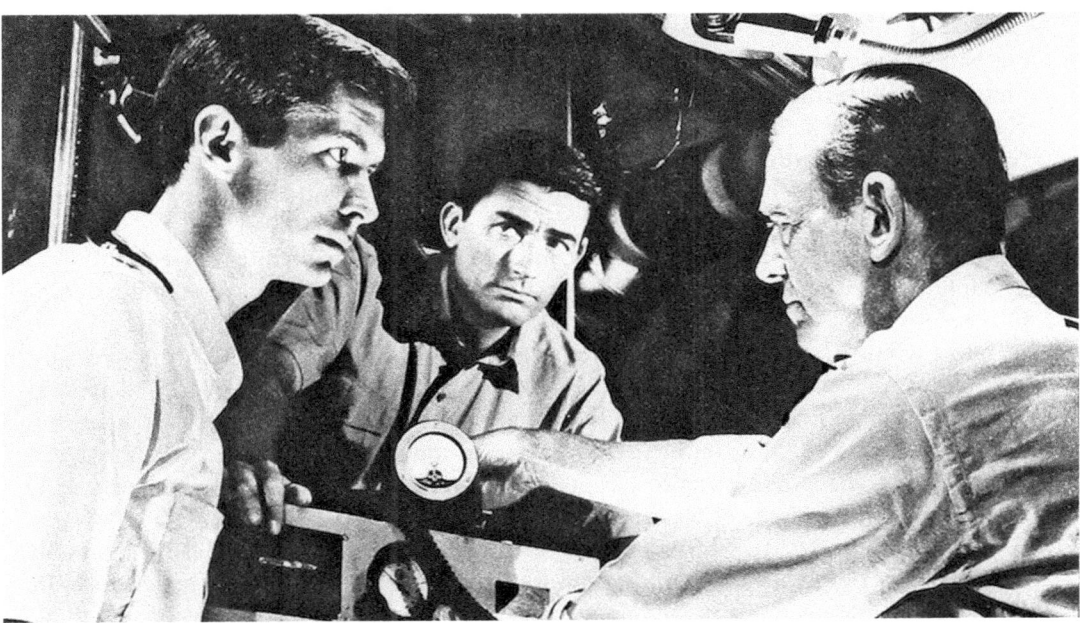

Safe inside a submarine, Lt. Peter Holmes (Anthony Perkins), Comdr. Dwight Towers (Gregory Peck) and Julian Osborn (Fred Astaire) contemplate the high radiation reading found in the Arctic in *On the Beach* (United Artists, 1959).

periscope shows a total lack of life or even bodies in the City by the Bay. Swain (John Meillon), a crew member whose hometown is Frisco, leaves the ship and swims for shore; Dwight orders him back, but he ignores his commanding officer. The next morning, via periscope, Dwight talks to Swain and tells him to take it easy, even though they both know Swain will die within days.

Next stop is San Diego, from which a bizarre Morse code message has been sent for weeks. A radiation-suited crew member investigates in a hydroelectric power plant, only to find the code was a case of a window shade persistently yanking a soda bottle. The crew member returns to the sub and it sails back to Australia, mission accomplished. Dwight and Moira finally have a romance. Julian takes part in a reckless car race—we see several vehicles crash and burn. Julian wins, later killing himself in his garage via the Ferrari's exhaust fumes. Peter manages to convey the reality of Australia's grave situation to Mary, and she accepts the inevitable. The *Sawfish* crew votes to return to America to die, and as their commander, Dwight feels duty-bound to sail with them. One of the last scenes shows a Salvation Army Band assembly over which a banner reads, "There is still time ... brother."

During the closing minutes, we see the banner again, only this time the streets are empty, and the sledgehammer musical cue makes it clear that This Is the Movie's Message.

On the Beach is a well-made film. The acting on all fronts is more than capable, though Gardner never really sounds Australian, and Astaire certainly doesn't sound British. However, the romance between Gardner and Peck works—it is pure Hollywood "love interest," but the actors make their characters and their motivations seem real, and their final scene together is touching.

One of the film's vignettes is likewise powerful. Gruff Admiral Bridie (John Tate) has barked orders to his dutiful young assistant Lt. Hosgood (Lola Brooks) for years. But on their last evening on Earth, the admiral shares a drink with the deferential Hosgood. He gently asks why there have been no young men. "They never asked me," Hosgood replies. "I guess maybe it was the uniform."

"They're blind," the admiral says. "Blind world." You wish he would—or could—say more.

The movie spares the viewer any scenes of characters lapsing into lethargy, followed by euphoria, leading to coma and death, the three stages following ingestion of the suicide pill.

But when it comes to stirring emotions, albeit gloomy ones, the film's strongest moments take place in the lifeless environs of San Francisco and San Diego. Cinematographer Giuseppe Rotunno's masterful lensing of these scenes is deliberately hazy, but only subtly so, to cue the viewer that these once familiar cities have now become urban graveyards. In the film's closing scenes of deserted Australian streets, the cinematography again takes on the same eerie aspect.

Is *On the Beach* art, or is it commerce? After all, most of the movies in this book, especially the ones with literal monsters, were clearly out to make a buck; several were quality productions, made by people who cared, but none of their filmmakers had illusions of being another Ingmar Bergman.

Certainly *On the Beach* played it safe in many ways, not the least of which is featuring typical Hollywood situations. For example, when the lovely Gardner is strolling to the docked *Sawfish*, aware of her effect on men, all eyes of the male crew are fixed upon her. Once she vanishes into the conning tower, Peck tells the sailors, "Relax!" Which they do—cue audience chuckle. It's a nice, audience-pleasing scene, but some might find it too hackneyed for a movie that wanted to motivate the viewer to do no less than save the planet.

Indeed, Jack Sheehan probably speaks for the movie's harshest critics when he calls the film "a $4 million soap opera endeavoring to qualify as cinematic art ... a lucrative venture masquerading as social consciousness."[7] Certainly the fact that the movie featured big-name movie stars speaks to its commercial ambitions. Including a typical Hollywood romance (albeit a well-crafted one) was also a case of hedging its bets. But if, in 1959, you believed humankind was on the edge of extinction due to the nuclear threat, and you wanted to do your part to make this clear to as many people around the world as possible, would you target the art house or the downtown cinema? Producer-director Stanley Kramer made a career off commercial "message pictures," such as 1958's *The Defiant Ones* and 1967's *Guess Who's Coming to Dinner*, so you assume he at least believed his movies might help to push society in the right direction. This certainly appeared to be his aim for *On the Beach* in 1959.

However, his aim was shy of a bulls-eye. For example, the film never shows us anything messy. We hear of radiation poisoning, but we don't see any of its unpleasant effects. Granted, seeing an extra or two pocked with sores and puking their guts out would have been repellent, but it would have also been memorable, and realistic. As is, *On the Beach* is simply too antiseptic for its own good.

Also, in San Diego and San Francisco, where are the bodies? The movie offers the idea that people preferred to die at home, but not everyone would do so—there should be some bodies in the streets. And if the radiation dosage was high enough fast enough

This poster for *On the Beach* (United Artists, 1959) puts the emphasis where it should be in a movie about atomic annihilation—on the love interest.

(surely some bombs would have exploded very close to San Diego), some human beings almost certainly would have died in the open.

Another criticism is that a nuclear war in 1959 would not have killed all human life on Earth. However, this appeared largely to depend on one's political persuasion. Conservatives would tend to note that a nuclear war would "only" kill several million people, as if that were a perfectly acceptable number of casualties. On the other hand, liberals would tend to assert that nuclear war would kill everyone, and anybody who said there would be any survivors at all was a traitor to the cause of world peace. Obviously, the point is that nuclear war would cause human casualties and destruction on an unprecedented level, as well as perhaps end civilization, and this is the essence of the movie's warning.

A more widespread criticism of *On the Beach* refers not to its message, but to the reaction of the surviving Aussies. All of them seemingly accept the coming extinction of humankind with a stiff upper lip. But while most folks would remain civil, certainly at least a few would be given to looting, murder, rape and other atrocities, especially as the end grew near.

The movie tells us that Australia has five months before the radioactive winds hit, and the Australian government seems to shrug its collective shoulders and dispense suicide pills to spare the populace the agonizing death of radiation poisoning. But in five months, surely the government could build a well-stocked underground shelter where dozens if not hundreds of Aussies could live for a period of time while waiting for the surface's radioactivity to reach safe levels. This might be a long shot, but with the literal extinction of humankind hanging in the balance, any shot would be worth taking.

In addition, the film treats the dispensing of the suicide pills matter-of-factly, and it appears everyone will be taking them. But surely not everyone would agree to do so. Some Christians and Jews would have religious objections to killing themselves. Others might simply refuse to give up without a fight. But in the world of *On the Beach*, the only response possible to the coming extinction of the human race is dignified acquiescence.

I hadn't seen *On the Beach* for many years before watching it again for this book, and given some of the harsh criticism the film has garnered, I fully expected to find it wanting. Instead, I found it a well-made end of the world drama undeserving of its often tarnished reputation.

The World, the Flesh and the Devil (MGM, 1959)

Credits: Directed and Written by Ranald MacDougall; Story by Ferdinand Reyher; Based loosely on M.P. Shiel's 1902 novel *The Purple Cloud*; Produced by George Englund, Harry Belafonte; Executive Producer: Sol C. Siegel; Music: Miklos Rozsa; Photography: Harold J. Marzorati; Editor: Harold F. Kress; Art Directors: Paul Groesse, William A. Horning; Set Decorators: F. Keogh Gleason, Henry Grace; Costumes: Kitty Mager; Makeup: William Tuttle; Hair Stylist: Sydney Guilaroff; Assistant Director: Al Jennings; New York Assistant Director: Robert H. Justman; Sound: Franklin Milton; Special Effects: Lee LeBlanc, Matthew Yuricich; Special Mechanical Effects: A. Arnold Gillespie.

Cast: Harry Belafonte (Ralph Burton); Inger Stevens (Sarah Crandall); Mel Ferrer (Benson Thacker).

8. *Twilight's Last Gleaming: 1951–1964* (The World, the Flesh and the Devil) • 231

Ralph Burton (Harry Belafonte) finds himself alone in an eerily deserted New York City in *The World, the Flesh and the Devil* (MGM, 1959).

A Sol C. Siegel-Harbel Production; black-and-white; CinemaScope; 95 minutes; released in May 1959. Available on DVD.

The last surviving man and woman on Earth becoming the new Adam and Eve? Nothing new, of course. However, what happens when there are two last men on earth, but only one last woman? Such is the dilemma raised by *The World, the Flesh and the Devil*.

For several days, mine inspector Ralph Burton (Harry Belafonte) is trapped underground. At first, he hears what he assumes are rescuers digging to save him, but the sounds stop abruptly and do not re-commence. On his own, a determined Ralph escapes to the surface, only to discover there are no people anywhere. He finds two newspapers, their headlines reading "U.N. RETALIATES FOR USE OF ATOMIC POISON" and "MILLIONS FLEE FROM CITIES! END OF THE WORLD."

Ralph drives to New York City, but still finds no people, just empty cars, empty streets, empty buildings. At a radio station, he plays back the tape of a broadcaster's final minutes on the air: "Tons of radioactive dust released into the upper atmosphere, circling the Earth, sodium isotope, half life 53 hours, deadly for about five days, no defense against it." Ralph is devastated.

Once he overcomes his shock, Ralph becomes playful in this brave new world where he appears to be the only player. He takes two store mannequins to his apartment, gives them names and talks to them. When he tosses a mannequin to the street, he hears a woman scream. It is Sarah Crandall (Inger Stevens), who thinks the mannequin was a real person.

Ralph and Sarah meet, talk and begin a friendship; she explains that she was in a decompression chamber, the reason she lived through the five days of atomic poison. Ralph is African American and Sarah is white, and they uncomfortably discuss the race issue, with Ralph explaining that her expression "free, white and 21" may mean nothing to her, but it means plenty to men and women of color.

Ralph and Sarah attempt to carry on. Ralph throws Sarah a surprise birthday party, and although it at first goes well, the race issue again clouds their relationship. Ralph has picked up short-wave chatter from Europe, meaning there are other people alive.

As if to punctuate that reality, Ben Thacker (Mel Ferrer) sails into New York Harbor, and Ralph and Sarah flag him down. Ben is ill, but Ralph nurses him back to health. From this point on, Ben clearly wants Sarah for himself and sees Ralph as an unwanted rival. Ralph resigns himself to the apparent reality that Sarah and Ben will now become an item while he remains alone.

Ben tells Sarah he wants her. Frustrated by her indecision, he tells Ralph to arm himself. Ben stalks Ralph with a rifle, the weapon's sharp reports echoing throughout the empty streets. Ralph also acquires a rifle, but he finds himself in front of the U.N. building, and decides he will live the Biblical Scripture engraved on the structure that refers to beating swords into plowshares. He tosses away his rifle and confronts Ben unarmed. Ben, frustrated, flings away his own gun and stalks off.

Sarah runs down to meet Ralph; she begs him not to go and takes his hand. She then calls out to Ben to wait, and when she and Ralph catch up to him, Sarah takes Ben's hand. The trio walks into the dawn as the words THE BEGINNING fill the screen.

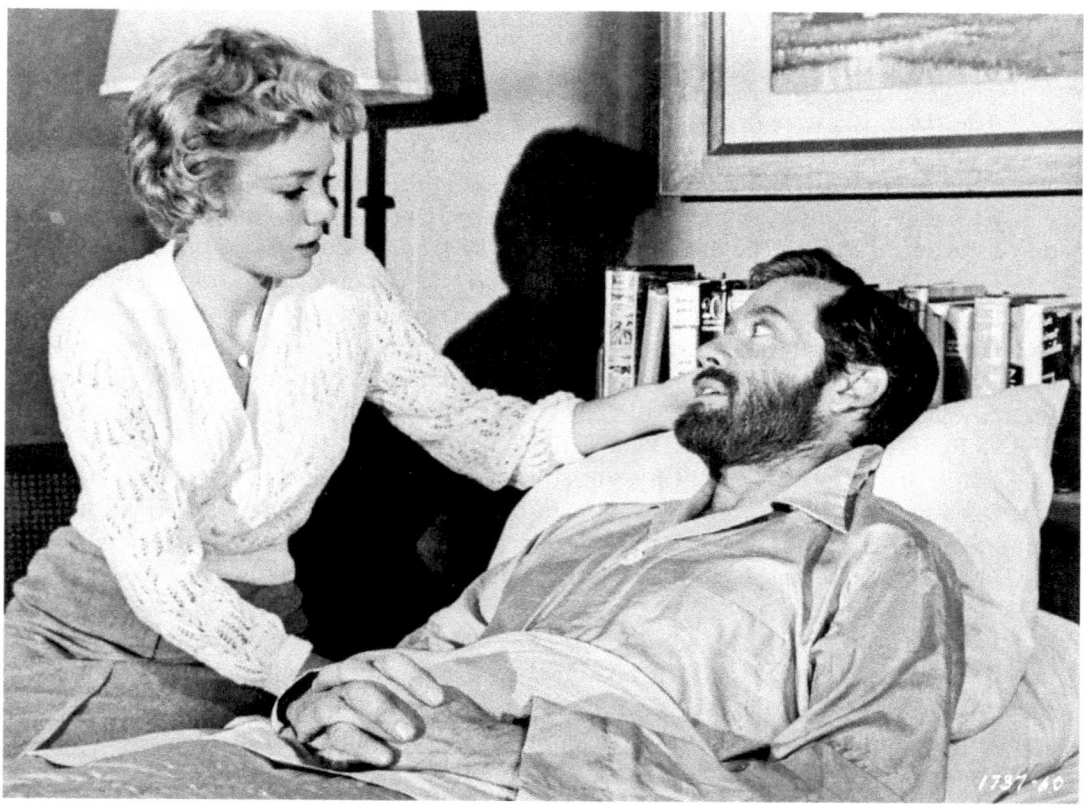

Sarah Crandall (Inger Stevens) nurses Benson Thacker (Mel Ferrer) back to health in *The World, the Flesh and the Devil* (MGM, 1959).

The World, the Flesh and the Devil is at its best during the first half. Ben's realization that the world has ended while he was trapped underground is unsettling, buttressed by striking visuals, such as the Brooklyn Bridge glutted with empty automobiles and New York City devoid of people. The radio broadcast Ralph replays is powerful, more disquieting than a visual broadcast would have been. Also, Harry Belafonte's bravura performance as Ralph makes us care about him—he is no "last man on earth" cipher.

As for a city of millions being completely vacant, it seems unlikely that everyone from New York could have or would have evacuated within the five days of the sodium isotope's potency. Some people would prefer to die in their hometown, and others might hang around for a looting spree. There should be some dead bodies in New York, but there aren't. Admittedly, the absence of human corpses is eerie, but just as in *On the Beach*, it's implausible.

The friendship between Ralph and Sarah is handled well enough; the movie starts to run into problems once Ben appears. Now we have a potential romantic triangle, plus the added element of the race issue. On the one hand, even suggesting that a black man and white woman could have a romance was shocking stuff for many 1959 Americans, especially those in the South. (Evidence: I grew up in Amarillo, Texas, during the 1960s, and the bigotry there was so thick that the African American portion of the city was commonly referred to with a derogatory racial slur that begins with "N" as in "N town.")

The movie has the courage to broach the race issue, but doesn't have the stamina to resolve it. When Sarah takes Ralph by one hand and Ben by the other hand at the finale, what is it supposed to mean? That they're all going to be good friends? That she will have a romantic relationship with neither Ralph nor Ben? That she will have a romantic relationship with *both* Ralph and Ben? The murky ending is apparently a bid to avoid offending anyone, but it is a gutless cop-out. It is cinematically unsatisfying.

The notion of poisoning the atmosphere with a sodium isotope that lasts only five days is novel, but is it plausible? Also, the movie doesn't deal with what led up to the atomic poisoning in the first place. Once the film becomes a romantic triangle, the initial desolate world situation becomes second-place. However, having Ralph stop at the U.N., while heavy-handed, is a nice touch, for it links the battle between Ben and Ralph as a microcosm of the hostilities that led to the atomic poisoning of the planet. By tossing his rifle aside and choosing to meet unarmed in the open with Ben, Ralph is announcing that the new world of which he is part will not be one in which conflicts are resolved by violence. In other words, Ralph won't be a party to World War IV. His gambit appears to pay off, even if the movie's dramatic ambitions don't.

The Last Woman on Earth
(71 minutes, Filmgroup, 1960)

Credits: Produced and Directed by Roger Corman; Screenplay by Robert Towne; Associate Producer: Charles Hanawalt; Music: Ronald Stein; Photography: Jacques Marquette; Editor: Anthony Carras; Production Manager-Assistant Director: Jack Bohrer; Sound: Beach Dickerson; Location Manager: Kinta Zertuche; Property Master: Stanley Watson.

Cast: Antony Carbone (Harold Gern); Betsy Jones-Moreland (Evelyn Gern); Edward Wain aka Robert Towne (Martin Joyce).

Color; Vistascope; 71 minutes; released in August 1960. Available on DVD.

The big question—was the "bigger and better bomb" Martin Joyce refers to a nuclear bomb or some other form of super-weapon? He also notes the apparent end of the world could be "an act of God. What difference does it make? The result's the same."

However, producer-director Roger Corman conceived the idea as a post-atomic movie when he asked Robert Towne to write the screenplay,[8] hence I am including this small apocalyptic drama filmed in only two weeks. The story concerns three characters: shady but wealthy businessman Harold (Antony Carbone), his acerbic lawyer Martin (Edward Wain aka Robert Towne) and Harold's dissatisfied wife Evelyn (Betsy Jones-Moreland). On vacation in Puerto Rico, they go scuba diving for several minutes, but once they surface, they realize something is wrong with the air. Their boat's porter is dead, looking as though he might have choked to death, and once they get to shore, they find other corpses.

Martin reasons that something happened to the air while they were underwater, but its effects were only temporary, yet long enough potentially to have killed everyone on Earth. Even given the lack of chatter on the radio, this is a huge leap for the movie to make—couldn't a new weapon have simply been tested nearby that affected only Puerto Rico, and perhaps played havoc with radio frequencies? And what about other people who would have been underwater, such as submarine crews, when the event happened?

The Last Woman on Earth is less interested in what killed everybody than in setting the stage for a romantic triangle. Harold, Evelyn and Martin take up housekeeping in a nice villa, where Harold immediately takes charge. He concocts a plan he fully expects Evelyn and Martin to obey. But even before the end of the world, Evelyn was tiring of Harold's domineering ways.

Martin is smart and sophisticated, and Evelyn begins an affair with the sardonic lawyer. Ultimately, she and Martin decide to make a break for it from Harold, but he catches up with them. While Evelyn goes into a church sanctuary, Harold and Martin fight outside. During the fracas, Martin is blinded and wanders into the church, followed by Harold. A concerned Evelyn assures Martin that she is there. But he dies, and Harold takes the blame for it. Harold and Evelyn walk away, hoping to find a new beginning.

The Last Woman on Earth is surprisingly well-written, but then again, it was scripted by the acclaimed Robert Towne, who went on to *The Tomb of Ligeia* (1964), *The Last Detail* (1973), *Chinatown* (1974), *Shampoo* (1975) and *Greystoke: The Legend of Tarzan, Lord of the Apes* (1984). (Readers of this book will probably also be interested to know that he wrote the episode "The Chameleon" for TV's *The Outer Limits*.) In *Last Woman on Earth*, Towne played Martin under the pseudonym of Edward Wain. He's not bad, but his snide lawyer character, a mocking nihilist, is obnoxious. His flippancy, annoying at first, eventually becomes insufferable. At one point, Evelyn asks him, "What do you believe in, Martin?"

"Nothing, Eve," he replies. "I'm too civilized."

Although the film holds one's interest, it proves ultimately unsatisfying. The end-of-the-world setup isn't convincing, the pacing lags midway, and this trio is not one you'd want to be trapped in a bomb shelter with. So does a movie *have* to have sympathetic characters to work? No. For example, if the writing, acting and direction are on the level of Billy Wilder's 1950 film *noir* classic *Sunset Blvd.*, the characters are so fascinating it doesn't matter that they are also less than admirable. But if the movie is simply technically okay, as in the case with *The Last Woman on Earth*, then one's attraction to said film is purely a matter of individual taste. For my money, *Castle of Frankenstein* #14 pegged it about right: "Rather weak drama shows aftermath of atomic war.... A few good moments, nevertheless."

According to Corman, this shoot was fun for all involved. "Most of us stayed in the beach house [in Puerto Rico]," he said. "It made the trip feel more like a vacation—except for Bob [Towne], who was closeted inside, racing the deadline so we could begin shooting."[9] Once *Last Woman* wrapped, Corman went on to prove that Speed Racer had nothing on him by filming *another* movie while they were still in Puerto Rico! (This was *Creature from the Haunted Sea,* and fortunately, this time it wasn't Robert Towne sweating bullets to get the script done in time, it was Charles Griffith, another one of Corman's regular writers.)[10]

One final thought concerning the mysterious doomsday device or bomb that decimates the planet: We know whatever it was, it sucked the oxygen out of the air. Hmm, does it seem as though you've heard of such a weapon before, used in the waters of Tokyo Bay? That's right, Dr. Serizawa's Oxygen Destroyer disintegrated both himself and Godzilla. Perhaps *The Last Woman on Earth*'s weapons builder and Dr. Serizawa were on the same wavelength.

Rocket Attack U.S.A. (Joseph Brenner Associates, 1960)

Credits: Written, Produced and Directed by Barry Mahon; Associate Producer: Al Baron (a.k.a. Barron), Steve Brody (a.k.a. Broidy), Rick Carrier; Photography: Mike Tabb; Editor: Alan Smiler; Sets: Al Baron (a.k.a. Barron); Wardrobe: Eaves; Assistant Camera Operator: Pat Tracy.

Cast: Monica Davis (Tanya); John McKay (John Manston); Phillip St. George (General Watkins); Jane Ross (Truck Driver's Wife); Arthur Metrano (Truck Driver); Sara Amman (Restaurant Dancer); Daniel Kern, Edward Czerniuk, Richard Downs, Herbert Flato, Ray Brewer, Janice Gilmain, Marco Behar, Frank Patrinostrow, Milton Fuchs, William Osborn, Ronnie Cooper, John Horner, Vladovia Lazareff, James Tura, Alan Smiler.

An Exploit Films production; black-and-white; 66 minutes; released "as early as 1960" (Bill Warren, *Keep Watching the Skies! The 21st Century Edition,* p. 706), March 1961 (AFI, TCM), 1958 (IMDb). Working title: *Guided Terror.* Alternate title: *Five Minutes to Zero.* Available as an Amazon Video Rental—but it's the *Mystery Science Theatre* version.

Regardless of one's politics, one would assume a movie about the nuclear destruction of New York City wouldn't be dull. Guess again, for *Rocket Attack U.S.A.* exhibits less life than the average resident at a county morgue.

American authorities are worried about the messages the Russian satellite Sputnik may be sending to its mother country. They fear the Soviets are ahead in their ICBM technology. Solution: U.S.A. spy John Manston (John McKay) sneaks into Moscow. Tanya (Monica Davis), his contact, tells him that the Russians now know enough to build a nuclear missile. How does she know? She is playing the role of the Soviet Defense Minister's mistress, that's how. "When the pig gets drunk," she says, "he talks."

America continues working on its own missile program while the Soviets argue about using their ICBM. In Tanya's apartment, a definitely happening place, the "pig"

This *Rocket Attack U.S.A.* poster brims with the same histrionics and cheapness found in the 1960 movie, appropriately released by Exploit Films.

falls asleep on the couch, and John and Tanya embrace and kiss. (Ah, young love.) Meanwhile, the U.S. launches a test missile, but it inadvertently explodes. British agent Steele (who sounds less British than Foghorn Leghorn) tells John to get to Leningrad because Tanya has major news. And boy, does she ever: She tells John that the Russians have decided to launch their ICBM at America that very night.

While Tanya and John rush to the missile site, a Russian shoots Tanya. John soldiers on. Thinking he has succeeded in sabotaging the missile, he races back to tell Tanya. "Hey, Tanya!" he yells as though the place isn't swarming with armed Soviets, "Tanya, we did it!" Needless to say, the Russians shoot him on the spot. And soon, the Soviets do indeed launch their ICBM. Target: New York City.

With John and Tanya dead, the movie switches viewpoints to several folks in New York, primarily spotlighting a radio reporter who tells his wife that despite the dire situation, he has to go on the air to help people during this emergency. Unconvincingly, he tells her that he will be fine.

Meanwhile, the Americans launch Nike missiles at the approaching ICBM, but they are too slow to catch it—we are told the Soviet missile is traveling at 18,000 miles an hour. A general moans, "If only we had an operational anti-missile device, we might give some hope to those people out there." But it's too late for hope, for soon the missile hits Manhattan Island: A split-second cartoon explosion segues into footage of an actual nuclear explosion. We hear that three million people have died. And the final credit warns us that this must not be "The End."

On the face of it, the histrionically shrill *Rocket Attack U.S.A.* appears to be a quasi-sincere attempt to sound a nuclear alarm bell. But it is so cheap, the script so idiotic at times, and the special effects so non-existent (the Soviet ICBM is portrayed by an obvious cartoon) that the only alarm audiences probably felt was the fact that they'd actually paid money to see this yawner. Its central premise makes little sense. Why would the Soviets launch one lone missile at the U.S.? For spite, or just pure Commie meanness? Even if you buy this premise, surely the Russians would realize there would be American retaliation. But the Soviets in this movie, like the Americans, are definitely not MENSA material.

Despite the movie's scant length, the filmmakers pad the film mercilessly to push it over the hour mark. For example, in a Russian nightclub, we see an exotic dancer writhe for what seems like a lifetime. And just when you think you're off the hook, a male Russian dancer immediately starts shuffling *his* Slavic feet!

Stock footage, the friend of many a cheap movie, likewise helps pad out the running time. In fact, we don't really see all that much of John and Tanya, the main characters. But we hear and see loads about missile construction. Toward the end, the abrupt viewpoint change to the radio announcer and his wife actually works better than the previous 45 minutes of would-be espionage. The movie might have been better off spotlighting them and other New York families. These are the only scenes that generate mild tension and even come close to giving the nuclear threat adequate treatment. Also, apparently to show us that nuclear war is no friend to the differently abled, a blind man asks for help to get to a bomb shelter, but in their fear and panic, everyone ignores him.

Even if the movie had dealt solely with New York characters, its total lack of pacing—the bane of many a low-budget movie—would still sink this listing ship. Not that the amateurish script is of much help either. And as for the actors, maybe it's best not to say anything.

Bill *Keep Watching the Skies!* Warren gives a fascinating overview of exploitation filmmaker Barry Mahon—I strongly suggest you read his entertaining entry on *Rocket Attack U.S.A.* Mahon sometimes dabbled in horror (1961's *The Dead One*) and trendy topics (1967's *The Pill*), but mostly gravitated towards sexploitation (1967's *Fanny Hill Meets Lady Chatterly*, for example). Considering the abundant lack of talent behind the camera of *Rocket Attack U.S.A.*, I was surprised to find out that this wasn't a one-off for Mahon, and that he actually had a hand in several films. But then again, so did Jerry Warren.

The Creation of the Humanoids
(Emerson Film Enterprises, 1962)

Credits: Directed by Wesley E. Barry; Story and Screenplay by Jay Simms; Produced by Wesley E. Barry, Edward J. Kay; Music: Edward J. Kay; Photography: Hal Mohr; Editor: Ace Herman; Art Director: Ted Rich; Set Decorator: Morris Hoffman; Makeup: Jack P. Pierce; Assistant Director: Melville Shyer; Sound Mixer: Ralph Butler, Charles Cooper; Special Eye Effects: Dr. Louis M. Zabner; Wardrobe: Oscar Rodriguez; Property Master: George Bahr; Lighting Engineer: Paul Butner; Set Continuity: Eleanor Donahoe; Production Assistant: Lynn Waring.
Cast: Don Megowan (Capt. Kenneth Cragis, "The Cragis"); Erica Elliot (Maxine Megan); Frances McCann (Esme Cragis Milos); Don Doolittle (Dr. Raven); David Cross (Pax); Richard Vath (Mark); Reid Hammond (Hart); Malcolm Smith (Court); George Milan (Acto); Dudley Manlove (Lagan); Pat Bradley (Dr. Moffitt); Gil Frye (Orus); William Hunter (Ward); Paul Sheriff (Police Officer); Alton Tabor (Kelly's Duplicate).
A Genie Production; color; 75 minutes; released on July 3, 1962. Available on DVD on a double-bill with the Italian-made *War of the Planets* (1966).

This may be the strangest movie in this book. Hailed as everything from a "classic turkey"[11] to an "underrated gem,"[12] this offbeat item depicts a post-atomic world very different from almost any other. It concerns itself with the essence of what it means to be human, pretty heady stuff for a low-budget science fiction film considered by some one of the worst movies ever made.

A narrator tells us that a nuclear war has killed 92 percent of the human race. Largely due to the scarcity of humans to perform various necessary tasks, the surviving men and women have created sophisticated humanoid robots. Although human society at large accepts the robots, which range from models R-21 (most primitive) to R-96 (top of the line), a reactionary organization known as the Order of Flesh and Blood strongly opposes them. Cragis, aka "The Cragis" (Don Megowan), a high-ranking Flesh and Blooder, discovers that a humanoid robot has killed Dr. Raven, a scientist involved in illegal operations. (Raven created the revolutionary R-96 robots to replace dead humans, and the R-96 automatons have all the memories of the original humans and in fact believe they *are* the original humans.)

Alarmed, Cragis rallies his fellow Flesh and Blooders at an emergency meeting. But then he discovers that his sister Esme (Frances McCann) is "in rapport" with an R-49 robot named Pax (David Cross). He insists she cease this relationship, but she defies him. During the argument, Esme's friend Maxine (Erica Elliot) arrives and finds herself

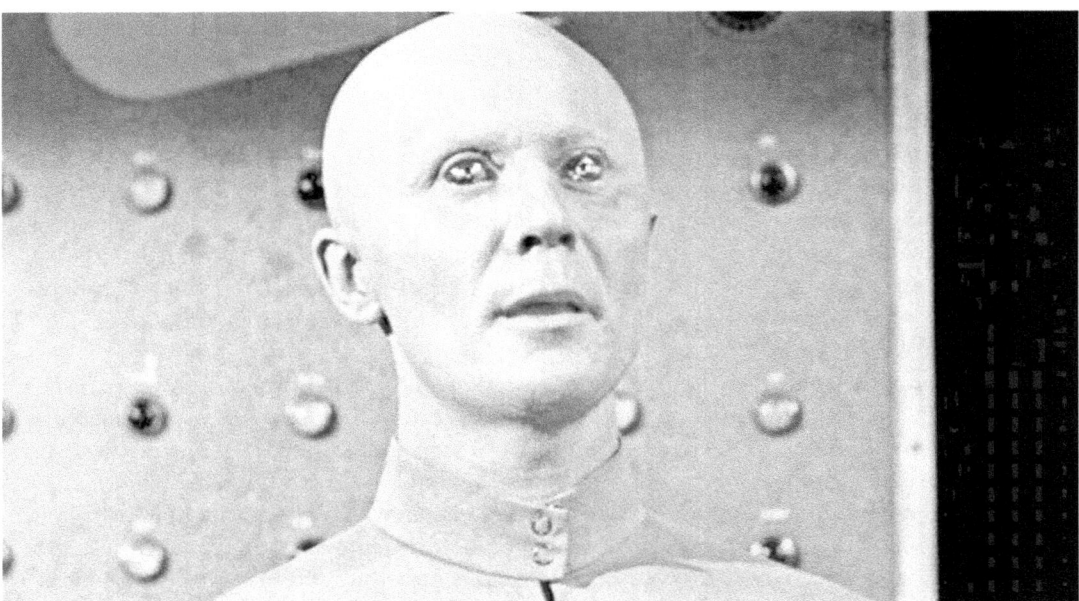

Acto (George Milan), a humanoid robot, seeks to help the human race avoid extinction in *The Creation of the Humanoids* (1962).

attracted to Cragis, who is likewise smitten with her. Departing, the couple find a private setting in which to talk over the possibility of being "in contract" (i.e., married). But unexpectedly, two humanoid robots arrive.

Fade to black.

When next we see Cragis and Maxine, they are in transparent glass tubes (a science fiction staple) inside "the Temple," the recreation and recharging center overseen by a master computer the robots call "Father/Mother." It turns out that both Cragis and Maxine are themselves robots, R-96 models that are human in almost every way. Dr. Raven, now reborn as an R-96 himself, decides Cragis should know the truth. Consequently, one of the humanoids tells the adamant Flesh and Blooder that he is actually an R-96. Cragis refuses to believe it, so one of the humanoids stabs him in the chest. Cragis feels no pain, and the resultant blood is green, the color of humanoid blood due to the copper tubing.

Dr. Raven reveals that Cragis actually died some time before, and that a thalamic transplant loaded all his memories and personality traits into the new, improved Cragis R-96. Gradually, Cragis and Maxine accept their lot as high-end automatons. Dr. Raven tells them that he can make them self-reproducing, thus being like humans in every way except that they are functionally immortal, which the film sees as a major improvement.

Detractors often criticize *The Creation of the Humanoids* as being stagy, slow and stilted. Those observations are accurate. The entire affair has a muted, dream-like quality accentuated by the minimalist sets and eccentric dialogue. The acting is competent, if unexceptional, the direction almost trance-like.

Also, the two robots shown close to the beginning of the film are inadvertently comical. One of them is the alien armor from 1956's *Earth vs. the Flying Saucers*, the other one from 1954's *The Bowery Boys Meet the Monsters*. This automaton looks cheap and ridiculous; Robby the Robot would be most embarrassed. At other points, the movie wavers between seriousness and satire. For example, when Maxine learns she is now an R-96, a humanoid tells her they made her new automaton form thinner than her human physique (a sexist touch?), for which she thanks them.

The film is also interesting, offbeat and imaginative. The themes offer a feast for idea-hungry SF fans. For example, the Flesh and Blooders derisively call the robots "Clickers," and lobby to limit their civil rights. Parallels to the Civil Rights Movement of the 1960s *vis-à-vis* African Americans are unmistakable, clear down to the Flesh and Blooders' abhorrence for "in rapport" relationships, the equivalent of interracial marriages. Also, the Order of Flesh and Blood clearly calls to mind the Klu Klux Klan. Even an "enlightened" non–Flesh and Blooder like Dr. Raven at one point says to a humanoid, "All Clickers look alike to me."

Equally thoughtful is the movie's exploration of what it means to be human. For example, Cragis is aghast that he could be a robot, certain that living as a literal machine makes him inhuman, no longer a man. But Dr. Raven asks if the loss of a man's legs and their subsequent replacement with artificial legs would diminish the man's soul. Cragis concedes it would not. Dr. Raven then goes on to explain that via a thalamic transplant, he has simply transferred Cragis' biochemical memories into an R-96 robot; the essence of what Cragis was, lives on. Raven says, "A man is only the subtotal of his experiences." And regarding the soul, the good doctor notes that what remains from the old Cragis is "the memory which includes a faith that there is a soul."

Also in this vein, it's interesting that the humanoids refer to their recharging center as "the Temple" and the computer that empowers them as "Father/Mother." Perhaps this implies that the closer a being is to becoming self-conscious, the more that being needs a spiritual frame of reference, including a personified Higher Power of some sort

Regarding the nuclear threat, the movie maintains that postwar radiation has drastically reduced the birth rate. Cragis tells Maxine, "Over 25 percent of the newborn are useless mutants." We never see any of these mutants, so it's unclear whether they quickly die, though at the least Cragis' words imply they suffer from serious birth defects.

Cragis also talks about how, as children, he and his sister played in one of the "old bombed cities." As Cragis tells it, they were "playing in ruins that were so hot with radiation that at night they shimmered in a blue light." This has left the adult Cragis sterile. (It's surprising it hasn't likewise left him dead.)

Dr. Raven notes the humanoid scheme to create "perfect humans" via R-96 automatons is intended to save humanity. Without this plan, "the human race would be extinct in a couple of hundred years." So the nuclear threat not only killed off most of the human race, but without the intervention of the sophisticated humanoids, the nuclear threat would have annihilated humankind. The implication: If the survivors of a nuclear war hadn't been able to create a technological society capable of producing sentient machines, then the human race would have indeed become as extinct as silent movies.

Panic in Year Zero! (AIP, 1962)

Credits: Directed by Ray Milland; Screenplay by Jay Simms, John Morton; Story by Jay Simms; Produced by Arnold Houghland and Lou Rusoff; Executive Producers: James H. Nicholson, Samuel Z. Arkoff; Photography: Gilbert Warrenton; Art Director: Daniel Haller; Editor: William Austin; Assistant Editors: Anthony Carras, Jerry Irvin;

Set Decorator: Harry Reif; Costumes: Marjorie Corso; Music: Les Baxter; Music Coordinator: Al Simms; Sound: Steve Bass; Sound Editor: Al Bird; Music Editor: Eve Newman; Special Effects: Pat Dinga, Larry Butler; Makeup: Ted Coodley; Hair Stylist: Betty Pedretti; Assistant Directors: Jim Engle, Les Gorall; Production Supervisor: Bartlett A. Carre; Still Photographer: Ed Jones; Script Supervisor: Billy Vernon; Unit Manager: Robert Agnew; Production Assistant: Jack Cash; Prop Master: Dick Rubin; Construction: Ross Hahn; Transportation: Allee B. Reed.

Cast: Ray Milland (Harry Baldwin); Jean Hagen (Ann Baldwin); Frankie Avalon (Rick Baldwin); Mary Mitchel (Karen Baldwin); Joan Freeman (Marilyn Hayes); Richard Bakalyan (Carl); Rex Holman (Mickey); Richard Garland (Ed Johnson); Willis Bouchey (Dr. Strong); Neil Nephew (Andy); O.Z. Whitehead (Hogan); Russ Bender (Harkness); Andrea Lane (Waitress); Scott Peters (Army Sergeant); Shary Marshall (Bobbie Johnson); Byron Morrow (Haenel—Evacuee from Newhall); Bud Slater (Complaining Diner); Ralph Clanton (Radio Announcer); Paul Gleason (Gas Station Owner); Hugh Sanders (Becker—Evacuee from Chatsworth).

An Alta Vista Production; 92 minutes; released on July 4, 1962. Re-release title: *The End of the World*. The *Castle of Frankenstein* #22 review claims that the film borrows from John Christopher's 1956 post-apocalyptic novel *No Blade of Grass* (a.k.a. *The Death of Grass*). Film is available on DVD and Blu-ray.

After World War III, when the going gets tough, the tough resort to theft, assault and manslaughter. Thus seems to be the major theme of the grim *Panic in Year Zero!* Too earnest to be dismissed as a cheapie, yet too inconsistent to fulfill its ambitions, the film's mood—and hero—shift through various multiple personalities.

Early one morning, the Baldwin family is journeying to the hinterlands outside of L.A. for a fishing trip. On a mountain road, lights flash from seemingly nowhere, and the radio goes dead. Before long, the Baldwin family sees a huge mushroom cloud looming in the direction over L.A. Teenage son Rick (Frankie Avalon) says, softly, "We've had it, Dad, haven't we?"

The Baldwin family—Karen (Mary Mitchel), Rick (Frankie Avalon), Harry (Ray Milland) and Ann (Jean Hagen)—watch a mushroom cloud rise over Los Angeles in *Panic in Year Zero!* (AIP, 1962). Milland also directed the film.

But Harry (Ray Milland) will brook no defeatism. On the road again, he announces to the family, "For the next few weeks, survival is going to have to be on an individual basis." At this point, he has clearly donned his survivalist persona.

After spending almost $200 buying canned food and other goods at a country store, Harry doesn't have enough money to buy guns at a hardware store, so he resorts to violence to take the weapons while Rick holds the hardware manager at gunpoint. Harry tries to make things right by assuring the hardware manager that he will pay him back when he can, but the man replies, "In my book, you're just a thug." Harry's wife June (Jean Hagen) is shocked at her husband's belligerent behavior, and teenage daughter Karen (Mary Mitchel) seems to withdraw into herself. Meanwhile, the radio announces that several major American cities, including L.A., have been hit, but "we have retaliated in kind."

To reach a desolate (i.e., safe) location, Harry knocks a greedy gas station manager cold, speeds through a roadblock and finds himself accosted by three roadside toughs. Rick shoots one of the three men in the shoulder, and the trio beat a hasty retreat. It turns out June purposely deflected Rick's aim, the reason Rick's shot didn't kill the man. Angry, Harry snaps at her, "Would you rather see one of us lying dead at your feet?" Nevertheless, he chastises Rick for enjoying the thought of maybe killing one of the men. Here he has (temporarily) donned his wise father persona.

Eventually, Harry discovers an out-of-the-way location, and the Baldwins set up housekeeping in a large cave. Harry and Rick run into the hardware manager, but Harry gives him the cold shoulder. Later, to pacify June, he and Rick go to ask the hardware man and his wife over for dinner, but they find the couple dead. The husband shot, the wife apparently raped before she was murdered.

Meanwhile, two of the hoodlums the Baldwins met on the road rape Karen; June shoots at them, but they escape unscathed. Harry and Rick track them down, and Harry kills them point blank. In the house's bedroom, they find Marilyn (Joan Freeman), a frightened young woman whom the hoodlums have victimized. Harry initially doesn't want to take Marilyn with them, but Rick convinces him to show some compassion, so they bring her back with them to their cave.

Later, as he talks with June, Harry appears to have had a change of heart, regretting his brutish, violent behavior of late. Now he has donned his repentance in sackcloth and ashes persona, and June consoles him. His confession: "I looked for the worst in others, and I found it in myself." As Jack Sheehan writes, "He comes by this philosophy rather belatedly."[13] Meanwhile, Carl, the third member of the hoodlum trio, sneaks up on Rick and Marilyn. Marilyn shoots Carl, but Carl shoots Rick in the leg. The serious injury requires a doctor's care.

They all drive to a nearby town and find a doctor who tends to Rick's wound. However, the doctor tells them Rick needs a transfusion of whole blood, so they take the road in the direction of nearby Wheaton. On the road, they meet what at first appears to be a threat, but then turns out to be two American soldiers patrolling the area. Upon realizing this, Harry utters, "You're the Army." To which June says, "Oh, Harry, thank God!"

The soldiers, emblems of American resilience in the wake of World War III, wave the Baldwins on, and one of them says, "Five more that are okay. They came from the hills. No radiation sickness."

"Yep," his companion replies, "five more good ones."

This ham-fisted and schizophrenic ending seems to belong to a different movie.

For 1962, this *Panic in Year Zero!* poster seems tailor-made for the adolescent drive-in crowd, the venue in which the film would probably have played best.

After all, we know via the film's radio reports that L.A. was badly hit, that plenty of U.S. cities are piles of deadly debris, that casualties must number in the millions. Even if this were a limited nuclear war, things would hardly ever be the same again, and civilization couldn't be immediately re-inflated as though it were a flat tire.

But after the film's first third, little is said of the fate of June's mother, who lives in L.A. and is most likely dead. The only member of the Baldwin family to touch on all they have lost is Karen. When the Baldwins hear on the radio that Operation Survival is underway by the U.S. government, June and Rick express relief, but Karen remains morose. "What's the matter, dear?" June asks her daughter.

Karen replies, "All our friends are probably dead. Our house, my school, everything's gone, everything's changed—including me!"

When Harry starts to go after her, June says, "Harry, she'll be all right, as soon as we get her home." Huh? As Karen has just noted, "home" has likely been wiped off the face of the map, and if not, at least riddled with radiation. And besides that, Karen was recently raped. How could that possibly be made "all right" by the Baldwins returning to civilization?

But could this be evidence of June living in denial in order to keep her sanity? Possibly. Maybe any World War III survivors who escape to the country would be in such shock that they would hold the long-term (and even the short-term) effects of the war at bay. But June's attitude is also an example of the movie's shifting tone.

The Baldwins are a safe distance from L.A. when they see the mushroom cloud. Yet early on, we hear one survivor talk about how shattered glass cut his wife to ribbons and another say he saw L.A. being ripped asunder. The Baldwins have no such immediately alarming memories to haunt them—for example, June holds the memory of her mother just as she was in the pre-aftermath world, not as one of the Bomb's badly burned victims. Still, by the finale, the movie seems to have switched to a far less troubled post-aftermath America than the first two-thirds imply.

The movie's mostly grim tone shows us an America irrevocably shattered by World War III. For example, the corpses of the hardware manager and his raped wife; the unspoken horror of what Marilyn's assailants did to her in her bedroom; the disheveled streets of Claxton with overturned cars and debris strewn about; the ominous radio message proclaiming, "Damages and casualties are extremely heavy."

Panic star Ray Milland also directed the film in a serious fashion. However, *Panic*'s meager budget hurts its ambitions. For example, at times, there are hardly any cars on the country roads, yet the roads should be clogged with bumper-to-bumper traffic. After all, the Baldwins wouldn't be the only ones striving to secure a safe haven. Another production problem is the terrible Les Baxter music score; its overstated jazziness doesn't fit with the movie's tone and more often than not becomes a distraction. Baxter turned in several agreeable scores for AIP, but this is not one of them.

As the intense and pressure-ridden Harry, Milland gives a good performance, and the apparent purpose of his character is to show how far one man might go to protect his family, without totally justifying or totally vilifying his actions. Harry kills the two men who raped his daughter in cold blood. But on the other hand, organized law and order appear to have vanished; there are no police to call to have the men arrested; the men have raped and killed more than once, and would probably have continued to do so if not for Harry's act of extreme prejudice.

That is not to say that such an act is "good"; I think that's why the script has Harry repent over the blood on his hands. It acknowledges that acting in a ruthless manner can start to eclipse one's soul—for example, due to his ever-hardening callousness, Harry has no interest in helping the victimized Marilyn. Here, Rick's compassion makes Harry realize that he has gone too far, that there is a level to which a man shouldn't stoop to keep himself and his family alive.

Some would argue that life after the Bomb could be analogous to fighting on the battlefield. In war, one sometimes has to do things one regrets. Even ordering surgical air strikes will inevitably result in some so-called "collateral damage," an antiseptic term for dead civilians. These strikes are hardly "good," even if they may be necessary for the greater good to be achieved, and this appears to be the stance of the majority of Americans. So Harry could be looked upon as not called to fight the good fight, but to fight the necessary one.

The film's most interesting character is seen very briefly, Dr. Strong. Slyly played by Willis Bouchey, Dr. Strong is no one's fool: He is cautious and compassionate and readily enough treats Rick's wound. But he exhibits a sardonic amusement about the post–World War III world in which he now finds himself. For example, speaking of the war, Harry tells Dr. Strong, "We won."

To which Dr. Strong replies, "Well, ding-ding for us."

This is the only moment in the film that acknowledges the lose-lose reality of a thermonuclear war between the era's two superpowers.

Critics have cut both ways on this doomsday drama. Bill Warren opined, "*Panic in Year Zero!* is earnest, but the earnestness emphasized the script's weaknesses.... It has a confused moral viewpoint."[14] On the other hand, in *Monsters from the Vault* #20 (2005 issue), Mark Clark wrote, "*Panic* proves remarkably effective. It has some nail-biting suspense sequences and boasts a fine cast."[15]

For its meager resources (director Milland reportedly rued the fact he didn't have time to film more footage),[16] *Panic in Year Zero!* is an interesting and well-made aftermath movie. However, its cop-out ending undercuts its attempt to warn viewers that a post-Bomb world would be Hell on Earth. Still, as a time capsule of the Cold War tensions of the early 1960s, it fascinates.

This Is Not a Test (Modern Films, 1962)

Credits: Directed by Fredric Gadette; Screenplay by Peter Abenheim, Betty Lasky, Fredric Gadette; Produced by Fredric Gadette, Murray De'Atley; Executive Producer: James Grandin, Arthur Schmoyer; Photography: Brick Marquard; Editor: Hal Dennis; Music: Greig McRitchie; Production Manager: Gordon Gadette.

Cast: Seamon Glass (Deputy Sheriff Dan Colter); Thayer Roberts (Jacob Elliot Saunders); Aubrey Martin (Juney); Mary Morlas (Cheryl Hudson); Mike Green (Joe Baragi; Alan Austin (Al Westeron); Carol Kent (Karen Barnes); Norman Winston (Frank Barnes); Ron Starr (Clint Delaney); Don Spruance (Peter); Norm Bishop, Ralph Manza, Jay Della, William Flaherty, Phil Donati, Boyle Cooper, James George, Jr. (Looters).

A GPA Production; black-and-white; 80 minutes. Available on DVD.

Growing up as a kid in Amarillo, Texas, during the 1960s, I recall when a test pattern would come on the Sears black-and-white portable TV and an authoritative voice would say, "This is a test of the Emergency Broadcast System. This is only a test." As I got older, it occurred to me how scary it would be for the same test pattern to pop up on the screen followed by the words, "This is *not* a test."

Something similar happens in *This Is Not a Test*, a well-made, albeit low-budget drama. (I first saw it on the same Sears black-and-white portable alluded to above.)

In the middle of the night, authorities order Deputy Sheriff Dan Colter (Seamon Glass) to set up a roadblock on a stretch of lonely mountain road. To do so, Colter parks his police car in the middle of the highway and orders drivers to pull over to the side of the road. In order of appearance, the drivers include Jake (Thayer Roberts) and his granddaughter June (Aubrey Martin); inebriated Cheryl Hudson (Mary Morlas) and her hipster boyfriend Joe (Mike Green); semi driver Al (Alan Austin) who is hauling a load for Discount World; and husband and wife Karen and Sam Barnes (Carol Kent, Norman Winston). Clint (Ron Starr), a hitchhiker who might or might not be a killer on the loose, hightails it into the hills.

Over Colter's police radio, everyone hears this message: "This is not a test. Condition Yellow. Air raid, air raid. Extreme emergency." Understandably upset, several rush to their cars to turn on their radios, but the mountain's high mineral content cuts off reception. However, everyone knows the message that squawked over the police radio has to mean nuclear war. Colter fires his rifle and confiscates everyone's car keys.

The police radio announces, "Condition Red. Evacuation. Evacuation scatter ... martial law emphasized."

After an altercation with Joe, Colter announces, with more bull-headedness than sincerity, "People survived Hiroshima. We can survive this." He orders everyone to dump the cargo out of the semi so they can use it as a bomb shelter. A final character arrives, Peter (Don Spruance), whom Colter likewise orders to help empty the truck.

While this is happening, everyone knows it won't be long before an enemy missile will hit a jet fuel factory only a few miles away, meaning all of them will be killed. The various characters handle this nail-biting situation in different ways. Karen dumps her husband Sam and has a fling with Al. Cheryl drinks. Her boyfriend Joe flirts with denial.

Deputy Sheriff Dan Colter (Seamon Glass) finds himself out of his depth as he enforces a roadblock due to incoming nuclear missiles in 1962's *This Is Not a Test*.

The next message on the police radio is dire: "Missiles! Missiles! Condition Red!" Cole orders Al to pull the semi about a quarter of a mile up the side of the road. Meanwhile, with her grandfather's blessing, June and Peter take his pickup in the hopes of reaching a mine shaft that will shield them from the upcoming blast. Sam, having lost his wife to Al, cracks under the stress and uses Colter's shotgun to kill himself.

Colter, Cheryl, Joe, Al and Karen lock themselves in the back of the semi. Nerves grate, and Colter helps nothing by strangling Karen's small dog Timmy to death so there will be more air for the rest of them. Al gets into a fight with Colter, and the door to the semi gets thrown open.

A group of looters from town greets Colter and the others. The looters mob Colter and steal his car keys, kidnapping Karen as they make a dash for it in Colter's squad car. Al, Joe, Cheryl and Clint jump into the back of the semi and lock it. Colter bangs on the semi's locked door, begging to be let in. But soon the screen goes negative, then white— we hear an explosion, and the title credit reads, "The End."

This Is Not a Test makes the prospect of nuclear war more immediate and frightening than many larger budgeted films. The characters are literally at Ground Zero waiting for the end of their world to arrive within the hour. As Bill Warren notes, some of this film's effectiveness derives from its limited budget, for we see the same characters in the same environment while the events transpire in real time.[17] This time limit ratchets up the film's tension.

The characters, though stock, are generally convincing. Deputy Sheriff Colter clearly knows he is out of his depth, but as the face of authority, he can't put his cards on the table. Colter, out of a sense of duty, a lack of imagination and a disposition of belligerence, can't think of any better solution than for all of them to take shelter in the back of the semi. But even in this dire situation, Jake convinces June and Peter to make a run for it to a nearby mine, where they might survive. Actually, the entire cast would have been better off trying this, but Colter probably wouldn't have allowed it.

Interestingly, no one in the film has any concern over how the war started or who started it. Instead, the characters' focus wavers between fatalism that they will soon all be dead and wishing that they will somehow survive. This is realistic for a number of reasons, not the least of which is that the immediacy of their situation would render blame irrelevant. Also, after an all-out thermonuclear war, not much would have been left of either superpower anyway.

Much of the film's strength comes from the frequent messages heard over Colter's radio. We move from "Condition Yellow" to "Evacuation scatter" to "Martial law emphasized" to "Missiles! Missiles! Condition Red!" The film bravely reaches its inevitable conclusion without pulling a punch.

I don't want to overstate *This Is Not a Test*'s power as a nuclear war cinematic timepiece, as it does suffer from its extremely low budget and variable acting. But it would have been far easier for an American of that time period to imagine himself or herself in a situation analogous to *This Is Not a Test* rather in one analogous to *On The Beach*.

Dr. Strangelove—or: How I Learned to Stop Worrying and Love the Bomb (Columbia, 1964)

Credits: Produced and Directed by Stanley Kubrick; Screenplay by Stanley Kubrick, Terry Southern, Peter George; Based on the book *Red Alert* by Peter George; Associate Producer: Victor Lyndon; Executive Producer: Leon Minoff; Music: Laurie Johnson; Photography: Gilbert Taylor; Editor: Anthony Harvey; Production Design: Ken Adam; Art Director: Peter Murton; Makeup: Stewart Freeborn; Hair Stylist: Barbara Ritchie; Production Manager: Clifton Brandon; Assistant Director: Eric Rattway;

Sound Supervisor: John Cox; Sound Editor: Leslie Hodgson; Special Effects: Wally Veevers; Wardrobe: Bridget Sellers; Assistant Editor: Ray Lovejoy; Dubbing Mixer: John Aldred; Sound Recordist: Richard Bird; Camera Assistant: Bernard Ford; Camera Operator: Kelvin Pike; Continuity: Pamela Carlton; Aviation Advisor: Capt. John Crewdson.

Songs: "We'll Meet Again": Words and music by Ross Parker and Hughie Charles; Sung by Vera Lynn.

Cast: Peter Sellers (Group Capt. Lionel Mandrake, President Merkin Muffley, Dr. Strangelove); George C. Scott (Gen. "Buck" Turgidson); Sterling Hayden (Brigadier General Jack D. Ripper); Kennan Wynn (Col. "Bat" Guano; Slim Pickens (Major "King" Kong); Peter Bull (Ambassador Alexi de Sadesky); James Earl Jones (Lt. Lothar Zogg); Tracy Reed (Miss Scott); Jack Creley (Mr. Staines); Frank Berry (Lt. Dietrich); Robert O'Neil (Adm. Randolph); Glen Beck (Lt. Kivel); Roy Stephens (Frank); Shane Rimmer (Capt. "Ace" Owens); Hal Galili, Laurence Herder, John McCarthy (Burpelson Air Force Base Defense Team Members); Paul Tamarin (Lt. Goldberg); Gordon Tanner (General Faceman); Victor Harrington (War Room Aide); Burnell Tucker (Mandrake's Aide).

A Hawk Films production; black-and-white; 95 minutes; released on January 29, 1964. Available on DVD and Blu-ray.

Satire doesn't get much more barbed than in *Dr. Strangelove*, producer-director Stanley Kubrick's valentine to the folly of nuclear war. A box office hit, the film was yet another feather in Kubrick's already impressive cap. He originally planned to shoot the movie as straight drama, but as it evolved, he brought humor writer Terry Southern on board and produced a classic Cold War comedy.

Slightly demented General Jack D. Ripper (Sterling Hayden) orders a bomber wing to fly into Russia and drop its hydrogen bombs. He meanwhile cuts off all communication ties to Burpelson Air Force Base. Ordering his men to fight off any invading troops, he warns them that the enemy might show up in American uniforms. Captain Lionel Mandrake (Peter Sellers), Ripper's British executive officer, tells him that since music is still on the radio, there can't be a Condition Red. However, after Ripper locks the doors, Mandrake slowly realizes that Ripper is a nut job dead-set on starting World War III.

President Merkin Muffley (Sellers again) confers with military and political leaders in the War Room, where General Buck Turgidson (George C. Scott) explains what Ripper has done and why his orders can't be countermanded. An unhappy President Muffley orders the Army to attack Burpelson Air Force Base and have General Ripper phone him immediately.

Hoping to prevent a counter-strike, Muffley calls Soviet Premier Dmitri Kissov to explain things, insisting that he is just as sorry about the situation as the premier. Shortly thereafter, Soviet Ambassador de Sadesky (Peter Bull) reveals that Russia has built a Doomsday Machine, a device that will turn itself on in the event of nuclear war; it will then proceed to shroud the Earth with a cloud of deadly radioactivity that will remain lethal for 93 years.

The president is astonished, but his science advisor Dr. Strangelove (Sellers one more time) takes the revelation in stride, calmly explaining that the logic of a Doomsday Machine is simply an extension of current nuclear deterrence strategy. Strangelove points out that unless such a device is made public, it is useless. Ambassador Sadesky admits that the premier, fond of surprises, was saving the announcement for the next party congress.

8. *Twilight's Last Gleaming: 1951–1964* (Dr. Strangelove) • 249

In *Dr. Strangelove* (Columbia, 1964), politicians and military men confer in the War Room as time is running out to stop an American bomber from penetrating Soviet airspace. This wonderful set was by Ken Adam, who also designed many of the sets for the original James Bond movies.

As this intrigue swirls in Washington and at Burpelson, one American bomber, commanded by Major T.J. "King" Kong (Slim Pickens), struggles to keep to its flight plan. A Russian missile damages the plane, meaning it can't hit its original target, but Kong decides they will drop the bombs at the next possible target, whatever it might be.

The Army secures Burpelson Air Force Base. General Ripper believes they will torture him to get the bomber codes, so he kills himself. Mandrake manages to persuade a dense Army colonel (Keenan Wynn) to shoot the lock off of a Coke machine for change to make a station-to-station call to the president.

Consequently, the Russians and the War Room's "Big Board" confirms that the American bombers either have been destroyed or have turned back—except for Major Kong's plane. Because of the missile damage, the bomb doors won't release, so Kong hurries to the bomb bay to fix the problem. He does. And when the bomber doors finally open, he rides one of the bombs as it plummets earthward, whooping like a rodeo star on a prize bull.

The bomb explodes.

Back in the War Room, Strangelove explains that despite the Doomsday Machine, a considerable number of Americans could survive at the bottoms of refurbished mine shafts. They could thrive underground for a hundred years, the time it would take for the surface world to become habitable again. Alas, the Doomsday Machine has already been triggered, and the movie treats us to a series of nuclear explosions set to Vera Lynn's World War II song "We'll Meet Again."

This film's players soar. Sellers is sheer genius in his multiple roles of President Muffley, Captain Mandrake and Dr. Strangelove. His phone call with Dmitri, the Soviet

In one of the most iconic movie scenes of the twentieth century, Slim Pickens "rides" an H-bomb as though it were a rodeo bull in *Dr. Strangelove* **(Columbia, 1964).**

premier, is hilarious. He also scores points as the long-suffering Mandrake and the wigged-out Strangelove. Peter Bull and George C. Scott likewise shine.

The script calls upon almost every level of comedy, from plays on words (Jack D. Ripper, Premier Kissov) to physical comedy (Turgidson tussling with Sadesky) to sophisticated spoofing (Dr. Strangelove's explanation of a Doomsday Machine). Brilliant lines abound. One of the best is the President saying, "Gentlemen, you can't fight in here—this is the War Room!" But not all the wit sparkles: Keenan Wynn's talk of "preverts" and "preversion" provokes eye-rolling rather than guffaws.

Nevertheless, Kubrick employs humor like a virtuoso to send up the philosophy of Mutual Assured Destruction (MAD), for 1964 audiences knew no one would be crazy enough to actually build a Doomsday Machine. Or would they?

Despite the laughs, Kubrick probably made 1964 audiences uneasy that maybe someone in the Soviet Union or the U.S.—or both—might attempt to construct such a device. However, MAD didn't go that far, which makes Stangelove's climax less scary; in the world of satire, it's fine to go too far, but when you do, the audience can be assured, consciously or unconsciously, that you stopped short of reality.

Critical reaction to *Dr. Strangelove* was mostly positive. Typical was David Kaufman's *Variety* review (January 21, 1964): "Nothing would seem to be farther apart than nuclear war and comedy, yet Kubrick's caper eloquently tackles a *Fail-Safe* subject with a light touch. While there are times when it hurts to laugh because somehow there is a feeling that the mad events in *Strangelove* could happen, it emerges as a most unusual combination of comedy and suspense." Reviewer Bosley Crowther (*The New York Times*, January 31) found the ending troublesome: "The ultimate touch of ghoulish humor is when we see the bomb actually going off, dropped on some point in Russia, and a jazzy soundtrack comes in with a cheerful melodic rendition of 'We'll Meet Again Some Sunny Day.' Somehow, to me, it isn't funny. It is malefic and sick."

However, comedy is in the eye of the beholder. Almost all comedy results from something unfortunate happening, from slipping on a banana peel to having one's pants fall down; it's simply a matter of degree. Crowther's objection assumes that some subjects and situations should never be treated humorously, and he apparently believes the annihilation of the human race to be one of them. If the movie had shown us scorched corpses and catastrophic carnage, I would agree. But as is, *Dr. Strangelove*'s ending is like a typical Monty Python punchline, outrageous but harmless. Almost.

Fail-Safe (Columbia, 1964)

Credits: Directed by Sidney Lumet; Screenplay by Walter Bernstein; From the novel by Eugene Burdick and Harvey Wheeler; Produced by Max E. Youngstein; Associate Producer: Charles H. Maguire; Photography: Gerald Hirschfeld; Editor: Ralph Rosenblum; Art Director: Albert Brenner; Set Decorator: J.C. DeLaney; Costume Design: Anna Hill Johnstone; Makeup: Harry Buchman; Sound: Jack Fitzstephens; Sound Mixer: William Swift; Continuity: Marguerite James; Assistant Director: Harry Falk, Jr.; Chief Electrician: Howard Fortune; Chief Grip: Edward Knott; Camera Operator: Al Taffet.

Cast: Dan O'Herlihy (General Black); Walter Matthau (Professor Groeteschele); Frank Overton (General Bogan); Edward Binns (Colonel Grady); Fritz Weaver (Colonel Cascio); Henry Fonda (The President); Larry Hagman (Buck); William Hansen (Secretary Swenson); Russell Hardie (General Stark); Russell Collins (Knapp); Sorrell Booke (Congressman Raskob); Nancy Berg (Ilsa Wolfe); John Connell (Thomas); Frank Simpson (Sullivan); Hildy Parks (Betty Black); Janet Ward (Mrs. Grady); Dom DeLuise (Sgt. Collins); Dana Elcar (Foster); Stewart Germain (Mr. Cascio); Louise Larabee (Mrs. Cascio); Frieda Altman (Jennie).

Black-and-white; 112 minutes; released on September 15, 1964. Available on DVD.

While General Bogan (Frank Overton) gives two Congressmen a tour of Strategic Air Command headquarters in Omaha, radar spots a UFO on the Eastern seaboard. This causes SAC's fail-safe protocols to spring into action: Groups of bombers fly to designated points on the Soviet Union's perimeter and wait there until the UFO is identified. The UFO turns out to be a passenger plane off-course, so SAC calls the bombers back. Due to apparent mechanical error, Group 6 does not receive these orders but believes a war is on and so flies toward its target: Moscow.

Group 6 can't be reached by radio, so the president (Henry Fonda) orders fighter jets to blast Group 6 out of the sky. The jets go to after-burner to overtake the bombers and shoot them down, but they fail in this task and, having run out of fuel, crash into the sea.

The president speaks with the Russian premier, who decides to use Soviet jets to shoot the U.S. bombers down. However, one American bomber gets through. The Soviets admit to having jammed the bomber's radio, thus preventing SAC from being able to communicate with the plane, but they now lift their radio jamming. The president directly orders the bomber to stand down. However, per his fail-safe orders, the pilot ignores voice commands at this point, since they could be an enemy ruse. When the pilot's wife pleads for him to return, he likewise refuses to listen.

At SAC, Colonel Cascio (Fritz Weaver) argues that the whole affair is a deliberate

Buck (Larry Hagman) translates for the president of the United States (Henry Fonda) as the latter and the Soviet premier seek a solution to a grave nuclear crisis in *Fail-Safe* (Columbia, 1964).

trick by the Soviet Union. He knocks General Bogan aside and attempts to take charge, but MPs arrest him, and Bogan again resumes command. At this point, the Americans and Soviets are divulging weapons secrets in order to prevent the U.S. bomber from reaching its destination.

The president makes the premier an offer: If the U.S. bomber gets through and does indeed drop two 20 megaton H-bombs on Moscow, the president will order two 20 megaton H-bombs dropped on New York City. The U.S. ambassador stationed in Moscow is on the line, and when the phone makes a high, shrill noise, they will know Moscow has been bombed. Unfortunately, this happens.

The president asks the premier if the gesture to have New York bombed is enough. It is not. So the president orders General Black (Dan O'Herlihy), an old college friend, to drop two H-bombs on New York. Black's wife and two young sons live in New York.

Fail-Safe is a taut, grim drama whose verisimilitude mesmerizes the viewer, even now in the 21st century and even knowing that some of the film's military technology was incorrect even at the time of its 1964 release. The direction is dynamic, the performances flawless. Walter Matthau plays Professor Groeteschele, a right-wing extremist, and he could have made the role flamboyant, but instead keeps it grounded in reality.

Director Sidney Lumet likewise doesn't show us nuclear explosions, though he could have. For example, we could have seen Moscow destroyed in a nuclear fireball, but Lumet uses a far more intimate method: Instead we hear the U.S. ambassador to Moscow say, "I can hear the sound of explosions from the northeast. The sky is very bright, all lit up." At this point, we hear a sharp whine over the phone, the sign that Moscow has just been vaporized. It is a chilling moment, far icier than a shot of a mushroom cloud billowing over the Soviet capital would have been.

The movie also captures the tensions of men under stress. For example, about midway through the film, American bombers have broached Soviet airspace, and Russian fighter jets are trying to shoot them down—this is with the SAC commander's full blessings, to prevent any of the bombers making it to Moscow. As the SAC commanders and staff watch the large view-screen showing two fighters closing in on an American bomber, the bomber fires a missile that destroys the two Russian jets. This elicits spirited whoops and cheers from the men, causing General Bogan to shout, "This is not some damn football game—remember that!" When another American bomber scores a victory over a Russian fighter jet, the chastened men remain silent.

Also of interest is that the film has no music score. This helps increase the documentary-like feel of the visuals, which basically take place in four areas: SAC headquarters, the Pentagon's War Room, an underground presidential bunker and the bomber's cockpit. The "common man" is divorced from the proceedings, as indeed he would have been in real life. In a subtle way, this could increase the average viewer's anxiety that he or she is helpless in the face of decisions made by the government and the military concerning the use of nuclear weapons.

This leads us to one of the film's most controversial points, i.e., the president's solution to obliterate New York City to atone for Moscow's accidental bombing. The film uses zoom-in freeze shots that spotlight typical episodes of human activity occurring in the Big Apple, at which point the screen goes white—the bombs have exploded. Chillingly, Groeteschele has earlier calculated that three million will die instantly, another million or two within five weeks of the blast, presumably from radiation poisoning, burns and other injuries.

The movie doesn't broach what might happen *after* two H-bombs have taken out New York, especially considering that it was the president who ordered the city's destruc-

Professor Groeteschele (Walter Matthau, left), who believes in a winnable nuclear war, confronts General Black (Dan O'Herlihy), who finds a winnable nuclear war an oxymoron, in *Fail-Safe* **(Columbia, 1964).**

tion. Would he be impeached? Would he declare martial law? Would he go into hiding for fear of his life? Would the military stage a coup *à la* 1964's *Seven Days in May*? Would the populace revolt? Would the president's political party be out of office en masse in the next elections?

And what of General Black? Having willingly H-bombed his wife and sons, along with millions of his compatriots, would he lose his mind? Spin into PTSD overdrive? Be locked in a padded cell for his own good? Blow his head off with a shotgun?

Given the inherent decency of the president as played by Henry Fonda, one assumes he would probably voluntarily step down and hand the presidency over to the vice-president, who is untainted by the affair since he was not involved in the decision. It's even possible the president might order himself arrested. Under the circumstances, many Americans would probably approve of such a move.

The solution to take out New York City is so drastic that it moves into the realm of the unthinkable, which is the way the movie regards the entire MAD (Mutual Assured Destruction) thesis. On one level, fittingly enough, MAD does indeed sound insane. Yet the film shows us that the military men and politicians caught up in this scheme are not insane. They're decent human beings trapped in a system that appears intractable. On a broader level, the same was true for every American and Soviet citizen.

For example, in the film, General Black speaks as the voice of reason when arguing that the entire MAD policy is out of hand. He questions the need for overkill. The right-wing Groeteschele argues just the opposite, strongly advocating that the U.S. should carry out a first strike against its "mortal enemy," the Soviet Union. Like real-life futurist Herman Kahn, he advocates a "winnable" nuclear war, even if "winning" means the near-total destruction of the United States. His character sees nuclear war as inevitable, and many political and military leaders of the day agreed with this thesis. Consequently, Groeteschele encourages the president to use this accidental situation to America's first strike advantage.

Groeteschele's political convictions aside, his disagreeable personality is the movie's major characterization weakness. While the characters speaking for the left and for the middle are good people, Groeteschele—the right's voice in the film—is despicable. Early in the movie, after a late-night party, he drives an attractive woman home who is taken with the idea of mass death. She clearly wants to have a sexual dalliance with him. But he slaps her and says, "I'm not your kind." His action is cruel and cowardly, and thematically unnecessary; his ideas should stand or fall on their own terms, not be front-loaded with ad hominem bias.

Concerning MAD's strategy, as I write this in 2016, we have an advantage over *Fail-Safe*'s 1964 audiences: We know there never was a thermonuclear war between the two twentieth century superpowers. The reasons for this are complex, and certainly beyond the purview of this book. But in a bizarre twist of history, could MAD have actually been our savior? As Jack Sheehan notes, *Fail-Safe*'s overriding theme is that the literal machinery of nuclear war had become so complex as to exceed the control of any one man or even group of men. As Sheehan writes, "The decisions regarding nuclear weapons are almost of a mystical nature, beyond capacity to comprehend or control."[18]

In the film, the president dismisses the Soviet premier's statement that no one is at fault. The President argues that the two of them, plus all the scientists, military officers and strategists, are jointly to blame for having created the system in the first place. As he says, "Today we had a taste of the future. Do we learn from it, or do we run the way we have?" This invites a fantasy scenario in which the United States and the Soviet Union put aside their differences and embark on a brand new day. Fat chance. For one thing, this argument assumes the differences between the two countries were not substantive. In addition, you again have to wonder how their respective nations are going to regard the president and the premier following this incident.

As I've already noted, probably the president would relinquish power. The Soviet premier would probably likewise step down, be forced to do so, or, in a worst case scenario, be removed from office by the military. What would happen if both countries experienced military coups? Would that make the probability of an all-out nuclear war more or less likely?

Let's take the Polyanna view: Suppose that following this incident, moderates in both countries rose to positions of political and military leadership. Suppose they jointly agreed to a "CoDominium," a concept developed by science fiction writers Jerry Pournelle and Larry Niven: All countries would be "frozen" where they were in terms of alliances with either the Soviet Union or the U.S. Neither the U.S. nor the U.S.S.R. would make a bid for expansion, and the bi-nation rule would quash any plans of nuclear exchanges by any secondary countries. Heaven on earth? Or just a logical solution of how to prevent any further fail-safe incidents? Or would the fail-safe incident portrayed in the movie inevitably lead to an all-out nuclear war?

The synopsis of *Fail-Safe* may sound strikingly similar to that of *Dr. Strangelove*, and here's why: Movie-wise, *Fail-Safe* was a victim of bad timing. It used the best-seller of the same name by Eugene Burdick and Harvey Wheeler as its source, but writer Peter George had written a 1958 novel called *Red Alert* that was very similar—indeed, George took Burdick and Wheeler to court for plagiarism. The case was settled out of court, but Stanley Kubrick had purchased the rights to film *Red Alert* (which eventually became *Dr. Strangelove*) and threatened a lawsuit of his own against Columbia since *Fail-Safe* was also on the studio's production docket. Consequently, Columbia agreed to release Kubrick's *Dr. Strangelove* before *Fail-Safe*. *Dr. Strangelove* was a box office hit, while *Fail-Safe* tanked. This, plus the fact that *Fail-Safe* treated the situation straight as opposed to *Strangelove*'s satirical approach, doomed the former's box office chances.

Critics gave *Fail-Safe* good notices. *Castle of Frankenstein* #9 (1966 issue) wrote, "Shattering suspense.... SF of high order, with disturbing message about mankind and machine-oriented society." *Variety*, noting the problem with *Strangelove*'s previous release, said, "*Fail-Safe* deserves to be seen." Critic Kenneth Tyman wrote that *Fail-Safe* "makes the logic of catastrophe seem much more intimate and irrefutable [than *Dr. Strangelove*]. Step by plausible step, we are drawn into an apocalyptic experience."

Strangelove is more entertaining than *Fail-Safe*, but due to its comedic nature, that was almost inevitable. *Strangelove* may have been dark satire, but it was still satire and generated laughs. On the other hand, *Fail-Safe* faces the issue of the nuclear threat stripped of all humor, and consequently, it is both more disturbing and more realistic.

In America, nuclear anxiety reached fever pitch in the early 1960s, so it's not surprising that the atomic age films of this period vigorously probed the possibilities of a nuclear exchange with the Soviet Union. After all, the Cuban Missile Crisis brought the U.S. and the U.S.S.R. closer to nuclear war than any other event during the decades-long Cold War.[19] On October 24, 1962, the United States went from DefCon 3 to DefCon 2, the only time in the nation's history this has happened.[20] SAC readied 2952 nuclear weapons exceeding over 7000 megatons of potential atomic devastation,[21] roughly the equivalent of 673,000 Hiroshima A-bombs. For its part, the Soviet Union was prepared to respond in kind. Millions of American adults, and people all over the globe, held their breath as the world teetered on the precipice of World War III.

If you were a young kid like me in October 1962, you didn't understand what was going on. But if you were a kid just two or three years older than I was, you knew all too well. One such friend—I'll call him Dale—lived in St. Petersburg, Florida, and was in the second grade during the Cuban Missile Crisis. He said his parents were careful not to talk about the unfolding events in front of him and his brothers. Unfortunately, the same can't be said for Dale's second grade teacher Mrs. Cleaver. One day during the crisis, Mrs. Cleaver burst into the classroom and ran up and down the aisles shouting, "We're all going to die, we're all going to die!" Dale told me he and his classmates were terrified. (By the way, Mrs. Cleaver did not lose her job over this.)

Another friend, a sixth grader, told me that flashes of lightning terrified him, for he was afraid he was seeing the burst of light that precedes a nuclear explosion. Then there were the "duck and cover" drills practiced in American public schools, including elementary schools.

The two best American nuclear threat movies of the 1960s—*Fail-Safe* and *Dr. Strangelove*—followed the Cuban Missile Crisis, so it's little wonder that both reflect the stuff of nightmares. However, Japan's two "purest" nuclear threat movies—1960's *The Final War* and 1961's *The Last War*—were released prior to October 1962, for in Japan, fear of nuclear war had been a constant public anxiety since 1945. The country's films had primarily used monsters and mutants to express the nation's atomic age fear. But by the early 1960s, the time had come for the Japanese to look cinematically at nuclear war without blinders, as we shall see in the next chapter.

9. Rising Sun Apocalypse

1956–1961

Godzilla was born in the hell of an H-bomb, but by the mid–1960s, his ties to the nuclear threat had become frayed. In fact, from 1961 on, Japanese giant monsters began to shed their atomic attachments, gradually at first, and then completely by the late '60s. For example, Toho released *Mothra* in 1961, but unlike Godzilla, Anguirus and Rodan, Mothra was not a metaphor for a destructive nuclear weapon. Mothra instead seemed to be a metaphor for justice and benevolence, two qualities rarely equated with the Cold War.

However, radiation mutated both *Dogora, the Space Monster*'s space amoeba and *Son of Godzilla*'s mantis-like Kamacuras, thus connecting them to Toho's string of nuclear threat monsters. Likewise, a nuclear explosion freed Daiei's super-turtle Gamera from the frozen Arctic à la *The Beast from 20,000 Fathoms*. (Tellingly, radiation does not weaken Gamera, and a nuclear explosion would apparently strengthen him.)

But by the mid–1960s, most Japanese giant monsters, Toho and otherwise, had been cut from the Bomb's radioactive umbilical cord. King Ghidorah (*Ghidorah, the Three-Headed Monster*), Baragon (*Frankenstein Conquers the World*), Gorosaurus (*King Kong Escapes!*), Gappa (*Gappa the Triphibian Monster*), Guilala (*The X from Outer Space*), Gyaos (*Gamera vs. Gyaos*) and other *daikaiju* orphans followed in the giant footsteps of Godzilla and company, only their footprints didn't send Geiger counters clicking.

However, during the 1960s, Japan had not dropped its nuclear anxieties. For example, 1964's *Godzilla vs. the Thing* featured a few fleeting moments of atomic age reflection. But America's 1959 epic *On the Beach* inspired two Japanese studios to leave monster metaphors behind and unveil the nuclear Gorgon for all to see in Toei's *The Final War* (1960) and Toho's *The Last War* (1961). In addition, two pre–1959 Japanese films, 1956's *Warning from Space* and 1957's *The Mysterians*, partially addressed nuclear threat concerns. We now examine all four worthy science fiction efforts.

The Mysterious Satellite (Japanese release: Daiei, 1956)

Warning from Space (America release: AIP-TV, 1965)

Credits: Directed by Koji Shima; Screenplay by Hideo Oguni, Based on the novel by Gentaro Nakajima; Produced by Masaichi Nagata; Photography: Kimio Watanabe;

Editor: Toyo Suzuki; Art Director: Shigeo Muno; Music: Seitaro Omori; Color Design: Taro Okamoto; Special Effects: Kenmei Yuasa.

Cast: Toyomi Karita (Hikari Aozora); Keizo Kawasaki (Toru Isobe); Shozo Nanbu (The Elder Dr. Isobe); Bontaro Miake (Dr. Komura); Mieko Nagai (Taeko Komura); Isao Yamagata (Dr. Matsuda); Kiyoko Hirai (Mrs. Matsuda); Kenji Kawahara (Dr. Takashima); Sachiko Meguro (Mrs. Tokuko Isobe); Toshiyuki Obara (News Reporter Hideno [Japan], Hoshino [USA]); Yuzo Hayakawa (Police Officer); Bin Yagasawa.

Japanese version: Color; DaieiScope; 87 minutes; released in 1956. Japanese title: *Uchujin Tokyo ni awawaru* (*Unknown Satellite Over Tokyo*). Alternate titles: *The Cosmic Man Appears in Tokyo, Space Men [Spacemen] Appear Over [in] Tokyo*.

American version: Possibly theatrically released (in Japanese-language theaters?) by Daiei International Films. Released to TV as *Warning from Space* in the early to mid–1960s by AIP-TV; color; pan and scan; 81 minutes. English dialogue by Jay A. Cipes and Edward Palmer. Available on DVD in various "bargain basement" collections, a typical example being *The Sci-Fi Invasion: 4 Movies on One DVD* (with *Cosmos War of the Planets, Assignment Outer Space* and *Voyage to the Prehistoric Planet*). Also available as a solo from Alpha Video.

Warning from Space is an odd duck. In the movie, a Japanese scientist has invented an explosive even more powerful than the H-bomb, and the world employs its arsenal of nuclear weapons towards the film's conclusion, but they use these weapons not to cause a catastrophe, but rather to avert one. In other words, *Warning from Space* is not an "aftermath movie"; instead, it might be considered a "pre-aftermath movie" warning us where our dabbling in ever more powerful theoretical weapons might take us.

Flying saucers are streaking over the skies of Japan, causing confusion. And human-sized, one-eyed starfish begin appearing across Japan, frightening fishermen, dock workers, party dancers and stage performers. For a time, the World Congress (a.k.a. the United Nations), determined to find the origin of the UFOs, forbids any country from launching rockets or satellites.

The cyclopean starfish aliens (obviously actors wearing cloth costumes) decide humans will be less startled if one of them takes human form, so No. 1 (Toyomi Karita) is "transmuted" into the form of popular Japanese entertainer Hikari Aozora. Found floating in a lake, the ersatz Aozora is rescued (though perhaps she was in no trouble in the first place) and soon finds herself in the company of scientists Dr. Matsuda (Isao Yamagata), Dr. Komura (Bentaro Miake), and Dr. Isobe (Shozo Nanbu). The pseudo–Aozora gives herself away almost immediately by making ten-foot jumps to return tennis lobs and passing through a glass door. When in the presence of Dr. Matsuda, she grabs his notes and begins tearing them up. Naturally, he demands to know why. She tells him that she knows his notes are for Urium 101, "the super-explosive so strong that even the H-bomb in comparison is a toy.... There's only evil in power used destructively." Dr. Matsuda counters with, "My formula was intended for peace, not destruction."

Then she literally disappears. The baffled physicist meets with his two other scientist friends to discuss this strange person. Before long, she appears before them and explains that she is from the planet Paira, which rotates parallel to Earth's orbit on the opposite side of the sun. She matter-of-factly tells them that Paira has been observing the Earth for thousands of years, and they have finally chosen to make contact to warn the earth of its imminent collision with a runaway planet. She adds that the world's collective nuclear arsenal might be able to change the planet's trajectory and thereby save humanity.

9. Rising Sun Apocalypse: 1956–1961 (Mysterious Satellite; Warning from Space) • 259

This Alpha Video DVD cover for *Warning from Space* (Daiei, 1956) depicts one of the "pillow case" starfish aliens. In the movie, the aliens are not gigantic but people-sized.

The Japanese scientists' appeal to the World Congress to use nuclear missiles to deflect Planet R (for Runaway?) is unsuccessful. The scientists decide that once telescopes can spot Planet R, the group of international politicians will change their tune. Dr. Matsuda notes that his formula for Urium 101 might work to change the planet's course, but he frets that no one has the technical prowess to manufacture it. Meanwhile, a black market weapons dealer tries to buy the formula from Dr. Matsuda, but he indignantly refuses.

Earth observatories spot Planet R and, just as the scientists predicted, the World Congress does an about face. A newscaster announces, "According to reports just received, the World Congress has convened an emergency session to reconsider Japan's proposal for the use of atomic weapons against Planet R."

Tokyo is evacuated, but some children stay in the observatory with the three scientists and a host of others. However, the black market weapons dealer kidnaps Dr. Matsuda, insisting that he surrender the formula for Urium 101. He refuses.

World Congress gives the green light for our Earth to pummel Planet R with nuclear weapons—but alas, it is too little, too late. As the runaway planet accelerates, our world heats up, and there are floods. When all seems lost, No. 1 (the ersatz Aozora) and some assistant Pairans free Dr. Matsuda and ask for his formula. After Dr. Matsuda is reunited with his wife and fellow scientists, the Pairans announce that they have used his notes to create a Urium 101 super-weapon, and it blows Planet R to bits. The children sing, nature relaxes, everyone smiles, and insightful viewers ask themselves, "In this movie, did Japanese scientists actually make a case for *using* nuclear weapons?"

This major plot thread certainly seems to have been woven into the movie by a schizophrenic seamstress. After all, Daiei produced this film in 1956, just 11 years after the atom bombings of Hiroshima and Nagasaki, two years after the *Lucky Dragon No. 5* incident. And yes, *Warning from Space* wants to have it both ways: make a point that a weapon more powerful than the H-bomb would be abhorrent, but likewise make the point that in some circumstances, such a world-destroying juggernaut might come in handy.

Of course, Planet R is not a person or even a collection of persons—we assume that the Pairans investigated the planet and verified that it was lifeless. Consequently, there is no moral obstacle in choosing to obliterate the runaway world. But the film nevertheless implies that because of the possibility of an imminent, world-threatening asteroid collision—a scenario that scientists agree could happen—we should not dismantle all our nuclear weapons.

But the movie clearly contradicts itself. For example, after ripping up Dr. Matsuda's Urium 101 notes, No. 1 says, "There's only evil in power used destructively." But the Pairans willingly and even ethically used Urium 101's power destructively to blow up Planet R, and the movie clearly doesn't believe this was an evil act. However, No. 1 was probably referring to Earthlings only, as she noted that Pairans are peaceful and in fact had destroyed the formula for Urium 101 long ago.

There are some interesting parallels between *Warning from Space*'s Dr. Matsuda and *Godzilla*'s Dr. Serizawa. Serizawa has done his best to hide his Oxygen Destroyer discovery from the world; Dr. Matsuda leaves his Urium 101 notes out in plain sight in his house, hence the reason that No. 1 spies them in the first place. Serizawa decides the Oxygen Destroyer can be used only once, and burns his notes. But Matsuda is indignant with No. 1's destruction of his scientific scribbles; likewise, he insists that he intends Urium 101 to be used only for peace. But Serizawa knows all too well that one nation or the other will use his Oxygen Destroyer to obliterate peace, hence the reason he commits suicide.

Also, Serizawa says to Ogata and Emiko that humans are weak, implying that he might give in to coercion—in the form of torture perhaps—and spill his guts about the Oxygen Destroyer. *Warning from Space* implies that the weapons broker had Dr. Matsuda roughed up off-screen, but still the scientist refused to fork over Urium 101's formula. However, what would Matsuda have done if the arms broker had threatened to torture his wife to death in front of him. Would he then still have remained silent?

It is quite interesting that in *Warning from Space*, it is a Japanese scientist who has discovered a weapon even worse than the H-bomb (recalling Serizawa of course). There is irony that a native of the only country to have suffered nuclear attack would devise a weapon stronger than any in the United States' atomic arsenal. However, unlike Robert Oppenheimer (or Serizawa), Matsuda doesn't seem particularly conscience-stricken about his discovery. And you do have to wonder what is going to happen later in the world of *Warning from Space*. Will one of the superpowers coerce the Urium 101 formula from him? Will the unscrupulous weapons dealer return and employ even more brutal tactics? Will the scientist have to go into hiding to protect himself and his secret? Or will he surrender the formula to Japan only, thus allowing the nation a potent defense against its nuclear-armed allies and enemies? The upbeat ending suggests such concerns may never materialize.

Earth Defense Force (Japanese release: Toho, 1957)

The Mysterians (American release by MGM, 1959)

Credits: Directed by Ishiro Honda; Screenplay by Takeshi Kimura; Story by Jojiro Okami; Adaptation by Shigeru Kayama; Produced by Tomoyuki Tanaka; Music: Akira Ifukube; Photography: Hajime Koizumi; Editor: Koichi (Hiroichi) Iwashita; Art Director: Teruaki Abe; Sound Recordist: Masanobu Miyazaki; Sound Effects: Ichiro Minawa; Lighting: Kuichiro Kishida; Production Manager: Yasuaki Sakamoto; Stunts: Haruo Nakajima; Assistant Director: Koji Kajita; Special Effects Director: Eiji Tsuburaya; Special Effects Photography: Sadamasa (Teisho) Arikawa; Optical Photography: Hidesaburo Araki; Special Effects Art Director: Akira Watanabe; Light Effects: Masao Shiroda.

Cast: Kenji Sahara (Joji Atsumi); Yumi Shirakawa (Etsuko Shiraishi); Momoko Kochi (Hiroko Iwamoto); Akihiko Hirata (Ryoichi Shiraishi); Takashi Shimura (Dr. Tanjiro Adachi); Susumu Fujita (General Morita); Hisaya Ito (Captain Teko); Yoshio Kosugi (Commander Sugimoto); Minosuke Yamada (General Hamamoto); Tetsu Nakamura (Dr. Tantobo Korda); Fuyuki Murakami (Dr. Nobu Kawanami); Yutaka Sada (Police Captain Miyamoto); Hideo Mahara (General Emoto); Ren Imaizumi (Adachi's Assistant); Takeo Oikawa (Head of Defense Meeting); Soji Ubutaka (Dr. Noda); Tadao Nakamura (Lt. Yamamoto); George Furness (Dr. Svenson); Harold Conway (Dr. DeGracia); Akio Kusama (Police Chief Togawa); Shoichi Hirose (Detective); Rinsaku Ogata (Policeman Ogata); Jiro Kumagai (Colonel Ito); Yoshio Tsuchiya (Mysterian Leader); Haruya Kato, Shin Otomo, Senkichi Omura (Doomed Villagers).

Japanese version: Color; TohoScope; 89 minutes; released on December 28, 1957. Japanese title: *Chikyu Boeigun* (*Earth Defense Force*).

American version: Originally to be released by RKO, but finally released by

MGM; color; CinemaScope; 85 minutes; released in May 1959. English-dubbed version supervised by Jay Bonafield; Dubbing script by Peter Riethof and Carlos Montalban. Available on DVD on Tokyo Shock in Japanese-language version with English subtitles and English-dubbed version (alas, not the dub of old, but a needless new one).

The Pairans in *Warning from Space* came in peace. The aliens in *The Mysterians* claim to come in peace, but at the same time they send forth a robot to demolish a Japanese town and kidnap Japanese women to use as "breeding stock." *The Mysterians* is unique in that the aliens are depicted as surrogate Japanese—what might happen to them, and us, if the world continues to stockpile nuclear weapons. Like *Warning from Space*, *The Mysterians* is a Japanese "pre-aftermath" movie, albeit one that ends on a more disquieting note.

In rapid succession, strange events occur in Japan: a forest fire in which the trees burn from the roots; an earthquake (the film calls it a landslide) that swallows a village whole; and a robot that attacks a town before the military dispatches it. People see flying saucers in the night skies. Eminent scientist Dr. Adachi (Takashi Shimura) believes we are experiencing, as a news headline screams, an "Invasion from the Moon!"

A large dome arises next to a Japanese lake, and its inhabitants, extraterrestrials called Mysterians, invite five scientists, including Dr. Adachi, to enter. The Mysterian leader explains that thousands of years ago, a major nuclear war destroyed their home world. "We had H-bombs when Earth was in the Neolithic Age," he declares. He also claims the Mysterians want only two things: a strip of land two miles in radius and "the right to marry your women. Due to the Strontium-90, 80 percent of our children are abnormal, so we dispose of them." Finally, he urges the scientists to have the military called off.

Later, from a television set, renegade scientist Ryoichi (Akihiko Hirata) speaks to his fellow scientist Joji (Kenji Sahara), his former betrothed Hiroko (Momoko Kochi) and his sister Etsuko (Yumi Sheriakawa), revealing that he is now allied with the Mysterians.

Despite the Mysterians' insistence that they are pacifists, the Earth authorities don't agree and attack the dome. The home team suffers serious losses. At the U.N., Dr. Adachi says, "America and the Soviet Union now face a common foe. Japan's trouble today will be theirs tomorrow." This appeal for international cooperation is typical of director Ishiro Honda's sincere desire for worldwide brotherhood and sisterhood.

Ryiochi appears on another TV screen to talk to a group of international scientists, Dr. Adachi among them. "One of the Mysterians' purposes on Earth," he reveals, "is to stop our atomic wars.... Otherwise, man will perish in 20 years." For this reason, he asserts, "Mankind should not rule the world.... No, only science can."

The Earth forces once again attack the dome, and the dome's ray destroys a rocket-like craft called Beta One. Apparently done with their "pacifist" ruse, the aliens announce that their territorial demands have now expanded to 75 miles. Plans are announced for the markalite, a weapon that deflects the dome's rays back on it and also has a potent ray of its own. A new electric gun will also be used against the aliens. Meanwhile, the Mysterians kidnap Etsuke and Hiroko.

During a major attack on the aliens' dome, during which two markalites blast away at the fortress, Joji steals into the Mysterians' underground base to free the kidnapped women. He is caught, but a repentant Ryoichi rescues him and the women. While Joji and the women flee to safety, Ryoichi uses a ray blaster to dismantle much of the Mysterians' interior equipment. At the last minute, the Earth's Beta Two mounted electric gun pummels away at the dome, heating it up (the aliens are susceptible to high temperatures) until the dome explodes. Although several Mysterian saucers escape to their orbiting space station. Dr. Adachi suggests the aliens are imprisoned in orbit.

As a science fiction movie, older (i.e., Baby Boomers) genre fans largely regard *The Mysterians* favorably. However, genre critics fault the film's story, but generally praise the visuals. Stuart Galbraith calls the movie "a generally silly but lively and colorful invasion epic."[1] Similarly, in *G-Fan #27*, Richard Pusateri writes, "[P]erhaps the biggest problem with *Earth Defense Force* is the story takes a backseat to the spfx exhibition. Without an underlying human drama to support the visual virtuosity the … battle scenes, however spectacular, fall into a mind-numbing series of pyrotechnic displays."[2] Peter H. Brothers opines, "Flamboyant if flawed, what *Earth Defense Force* lacks in cogent emotion it more than makes up for with unbridled enthusiasm."[3] Bill Warren perhaps sums up best the sentiments of most middle-aged fans when he writes, "As far as the film goes, it's entertaining enough."[4] Despite the movie's comic book atmosphere, Warren acknowledges that it has something important to say when it comes to the nuclear threat: "A slight attempt at something like maturity is made in the handling of the Mysterians, with the air of atomic tragedy that hangs over them."[5]

The movie repeatedly implies that what happened to the Mysterians could happen to us—and might be imminent. The most interesting motive the Mysterians have for taking over our planet is to prevent us humans from falling victim to a nuclear holocaust. The film makes the prediction that such an atomic war will inevitably happen within the next 20 years. (Fortunately, the filmmakers were wrong.)

The movie could have been far more mature if the Mysterians' dominant motive in taking over our planet had indeed been to save us from our own atomic annihilation. As depicted, the Mysterians are typical bad guy extraterrestrials who want to subjugate Earthlings. Been there, seen that. But what if instead, they had been conflicted aliens who had decided it was their ethical duty to save another sentient world from sharing their fate? Perhaps the Mysterians could be depicted with shadings—some against usurping humankind's free will, some seeing it as the only way to be truly compassionate. While such a film might have been a thoughtful endeavor, such a film would not have been *The Mysterians*, whose major power lies in its beautiful color photography, arresting miniatures and driving music score (the latter provided by the reliable Akira Ifukube).

Although practically drowned out by the movie's bombastic special effects and protracted battle scenes, Honda's theme of international cooperation is heard, albeit briefly. It is a wonderful fantasy, the notion that an invader or invaders would threaten our planet, thereby forcing us to come together for our own good. But such cooperation would not necessarily imply a moral equivalence between all nations. For example, if Orson Welles' 1938 *The War of the Worlds* Halloween broadcast had been true, and invaders from the Red Planet were indeed routing our world, this could cause the nations of our planet to unite against a common foe. But two of those nations would have been Germany and the United States, and one could hardly twist any moral parity between Hitler's nightmare regime and that of Franklin Delano Roosevelt's American presidency.

The Mysterians is an enjoyable excursion into 1950s Japanese science fiction, but the film's overwhelming action somewhat marginalizes its "pre-aftermath" message.

The Final War (Japanese release: Toei, 1960; American release by Sam Lake Enterprises, 1962)

Credits: Directed by Shigeaki Hidaka; Screenplay by Hisataka Kai; Photography by Tadashi Aramaki.

Cast: Tatsuo Umemiya (Shigero); Yoshiko [Yoshio] Mita (Tomoko), Yayoi Furusato, Noribumi Fujishima, Yukio Nikaido, Michiko Hoshi.

Japanese version: Black-and-white; ToeiScope; 76 minutes. Released on October 19, 1960. Japanese title: *Daisanji sekai taisen—yonju-ichi jikan no kyofu* (*Great Disaster of the World Waging War: 41 Hours of Fear*). Alternate title: *41 jikan no kyofu* (*41 Hours of Fear*).

American version: Black-and-white; Scope; 76 minutes; released on December 3, 1962. Released to American TV in 1965. The English-dubbed version includes footage from *Invasion of the Neptune Men* (a.k.a. *Space Greyhound*). The U.S. version cast: Jane Elliot, Carl Hansen, Frank Reynolds, Jack Wilson. Alternate title: *World War III Breaks Out*.

Unfortunately, as of this writing, the YouTube clip of this film has been taken down. But while it was up, I must have watched it 15 or 20 times. It showed several minutes from the film's climax. Unfortunately, the entire film is not officially available anywhere, neither on VHS, DVD or Blu-ray, either in Japan or North America. The movie did play on a Japanese TV network a few years ago, and a "gray market" copy circulated throughout fan circles. I have not seen the entire film, but I did get to watch the aforementioned YouTube clip, which from what I've read summarizes the film's overall tone.

The black-and-white movie depicts several strata of Japanese society: the middle-class family of teenager Shigeo; the upper-class Fujishimas; and the low-income Tonomuras. The prospect of nuclear war terrifies Shigeo to the point that along with a few friends, he tries to escape Japan in a yacht that belongs to a classmate's father. A typhoon overtakes the boat, but Masaki, a newspaper reporter, locates the boys and brings them back to Japan. For a time, Shigeo's fears of nuclear holocaust become front page news.

Meanwhile, Masaki begins dating Tomoko, a nurse, as geopolitical events around

During the climax of Toei's *The Final War* (1960), a nuclear blast obliterates Tokyo's Diet Building.

9. Rising Sun Apocalypse: 1956–1961 (The Final War) • 265

Toei's *The Final War* (1960) depicts the ruins of Tokyo after an atomic attack.

them start to spin out of control. An American plane blows up over Korea in a nuclear explosion. South Korea blames North Korea, and North Korea considers the event a prelude to war. NATO and Soviet forces mobilize in the region.

These Cold War tensions provoke panic in Japan, and thousands flee Tokyo, taking dubious cover in the subway system or in the woodlands outside the city. There are ugly incidents amidst the panic, including rape and assault. Some doctors flee the city as well, leaving their patients behind to fend for themselves. Nurse Tomoko compassionately refuses to leave the sick.

After thousands have fled Tokyo, a nuclear explosion consumes the city. At first, the refugees in the forests see a mushroom cloud rising over Tokyo in the distance, and perhaps some of them imagine themselves safe. But they are not. A bright light bursts over them just before they too are consumed in a nuclear blast.

Amidst shots of missiles taking flight, mushroom clouds blossom throughout Japan and the rest of the world. We see landmarks obliterated—San Francisco's Golden Gate Bridge; Moscow's Lomonosov Moscow State University; Tokyo's Diet Building.

The film returns to what's left of the woodlands surrounding Tokyo, thick forests having been reduced to acres of ash and tree stumps. The camera likewise pans over dozens of burned corpses—the remains of the Tokyo refugees. The scene switches to Tokyo, now a shambles. Reporter Masaki wanders through the ruins, calling out the name of his girlfriend Tomoko. Of course, she is dead. And Masaki himself winds up dying from the intense radiation.

The film clip once on YouTube showed the film from the time you see the Tokyo refugees huddled in the woods to the scene of Masaki searching the Tokyo ruins for Tomoko; this included the special effects shots, as well as the camera panning over the bodies of dead Tokyoites. These few minutes pack a wallop, evoking a bleak, despairing and fatalistic mood. According to people who have seen the film, this represents the movie as a whole.

The special effects shots, though not as plentiful as those found in Toho's 1961 *The Last War*, are quite effective. The miniatures of the Golden Gate Bridge and the Diet Building explode realistically, and several shots of the mushroom cloud over Tokyo appear ominous. On the other hand, at times, this mushroom cloud is an obvious static painting, such as a scene showing Tokyo refugees in the foreground while miles away the mushroom cloud remains unconvincingly frozen. However, the miniature missiles integrate well with stock footage of actual missiles.

The Final War's history in the States is an odd one. Film scholars such as Stuart Galbraith IV express uncertainty that the film had a theatrical release in the early '60s.[6] Bill Warren notes that the film apparently had a paucity of U.S. playdates.[7]

Proof that the movie at least showed in the New York City area is a license to exhibit it in New York State dated December 3, 1962 (this information came from the AFI website). Further proof that the movie at least showed in the New York City area is a brief mention in 1964's *Castle of Frankenstein* #4's "Frankenstein Movieguide": "Widescreen WW 3, destruction of world in atomic war. Japanese made." Later, *Castle of Frankenstein* #9 offered this brief review in its "Frankenstein TV Movieguide": "Japanese sf mainly of interest because familiar landmarks get the total destruction treatment."

Walter Manley Enterprises syndicated the film to U.S. TV in the mid–1960s (though this isn't absolutely certain, as one source attributes the TV version to Medallion). Kevin P., in an online article entitled "A Brief American History of *The Final War*" (exploder-button.com), notes a November 1965 listing for the film in *The Los Angeles Times*. He adds that the film probably stopped playing the U.S. television circuit around the mid–1970s, given an April 27, 1974, *Los Angeles Times* listing for a 3 p.m. TV airing. It seems as though few Baby Boomers got to see this film; however, for those who did, it left a lasting impression.

Responses to Kevin P's *Final War* series of articles came from folks who remember having seen the movie as youngsters. An example: "I saw this on TV in St. Louis when I was around ten years old in 1965 or so. It had a devastating effect on me and I've never forgotten it.... It seemed very stark and amazingly real.... Very powerful images." Another example: "All I know is this movie affected me as a young child. Saw the movie a handful of times. I was always thinking as a child, 'will I awake in the morning?'" And finally this one from a viewer who remembers a teacher showing the film to him and his young classmates: "I wonder how many impressionable minds [the teacher] permanently damaged as a result of [us] watching that picture? I remember being quite frightened at the time. It was NOT a fun picture."

This last comment may explain why the film has never had an official VHS, DVD or Blu-ray release. As Kevin P. notes, "*The Final War* pulled no punches.... It's undeniably well-made and effective to an extent that few of its ilk can match, but it's not very likable, and not the sort of thing that begs to be seen again and again."

Another interesting aspect of the American TV version of *The Final War* concerns the film's special effects. For years, fans assumed that impressive urban destruction scenes in 1961's *Invasion of the Neptune Men* (a.k.a. *Space Greyhound*) were actually taken from *The Final War*. But ironically, it appears that the American, English-dubbed TV edition of *The Final War* actually incorporated scenes from *Neptune Men*. The TV distributor

Seen in the English-dubbed TV version of *The Final War*, these two flying saucers (supposedly Soviet secret weapons) are actually footage from Toei's 1961 *Invasion of the Neptune Men* (a.k.a. *Space Greyhound*).

transplanted *Neptune Men* scenes of flying saucers destroying buildings into *Final War*'s climax. The explanation for the saucers: They were a Soviet secret weapon! In turn, Toei used at least the Tokyo Tower sequence from *Final War* for the Japanese theatrical version of *Neptune Men*.

From all accounts, *The Final War* paints an unappealing portrait of Cold War Japan, and indeed the entire Cold War world. The film apparently emphasizes Japan's helplessness at being caught between the nuclear superpowers, as well as what would be the probable result: the country's destruction. The film's ending is decidedly grim. While this is likewise true in Toho's *The Last War*, *Final War* apparently depicts panicked citizens at their worst, perhaps unintentionally suggesting that because of the debased nature of humankind, be it American, Soviet or Japanese, nuclear holocaust is inevitable.

The Last War (Japanese release: Toho, 1961; American TV release: Brenco, 1964)

Credits: Directed by Shue Matsubayashi; Screenplay by Takeshi Kimura and Toshio Yasumi; Produced by Tomoyuki Tanaka; Music: Ikuma Dan; Photography: Rokuro Nishigaki; Editor: Koichi Iwashita; Production Design: Teruaki Abe; Special

Effects Director: Eiji Tsuburaya; Assistant Director of Special Effects: Teruyoshi Nakano; Special Effects Photography: Teisho Arikawa, Motoyoshi Tomioka; Special Effects Lighting: Kuichiro Kishida; Art Director: Akira Watanabe; Optical Photography: Taka Yuki, Yukio Manoda.
Cast: Frankie Sakai (Mokichi Tamura); Nobuko Otowa (Oyoshi Tamura); Akira Takarada (Takano); Yuriko Hoshi (Saeko); Yumi Shirakawa (Teacher).
Japanese version: Color; TohoScope; 110 minutes; released on October 8, 1961. Japanese title: *Sekai daisenso* (*The Great World War*).
American version: Released to American TV (probably in 1964 or 1965) by Brenco Pictures Corp.; color; pan and scan; 79 minutes.
American credits: Executive produced by Edward L. Alperson; Produced by Stanley Meyer; Executive direction in charge of production by Sanezumi Fujimoto; Story (presumably dubbing script) by John Meredyth Lucas; Edited by Kenneth Wannberg; Sound by Ryder Sound Services; Dubbed voices by Paul Frees and others. Available on VHS, but unavailable on North American DVD or Blu-ray.

On the eve of nuclear war, an anguished father looks to the sky and asks, "Who has the right to take our lives, anyhow?"

This question sums up the theme of Toho's 1961 nuclear threat drama *The Last War*. A major departure from *Mothra* of the same year, *Last War* is as deadly serious as 1954's *Godzilla*, with a difference: *Godzilla* was a metaphor, but *Last War* was the real thing.

Although the Japanese version of *Last War* is substantially longer than the dubbed American version, the latter is more readily accessible to the majority of this book's readers since it is sometimes free online. For this reason, the plot summary will follow the American version, whose story is virtually the same as the Japanese version's.

The American version begins on a freighter following World War III. The captain asks the crew if they want to return to Tokyo even though the city has been destroyed and they will likely die from radiation. The men vote to go back, so the captain gives the order to do so.

We hear narration throughout most of the film from the ship's radio operator Takano (Akira Takarada). He flashes back to events before the war, most of which follow a Japanese family's ordinary lives set against a backdrop of the international crises leading up to World War III. Moichi (Frankie Sakai) drops his wife Oyoshi (Nobuko Otowa) and their two small children off at a shrine, then proceeds to work. On the way, he hears an unsettling radio news report about war games in the South Atlantic in which nuclear weapons are being used.

That night at supper, Moichi's young adult daughter Saeko (Yuriko Hoshi) gets into an argument with her father concerning the possibility of nuclear war. Moichi won't hear of it. "So," he says, "you're all set to having us blown to bits by a bomb. If we got blown up, it means that there's no God. No, I refuse to believe it."

Meanwhile, a plane is shot down over the Mediterranean, and concerned Japanese political leaders confer about the situation.

Takano returns from the sea and goes to visit the ship's chef Ebara, who is recovering from an ulcer operation; Ebara is helping his daughter with her daycare school. Next, Takano visits Saeko and the two of them plan to marry. They wonder how to break the news to Moichi, her dad, given his gruff nature.

Six nuclear missiles are unloaded to a Federation (a.k.a. the United States) missile site, activity spotted by an Alliance (a.k.a. the Soviet Union) spy plane.

Saeko and Takano discuss their upcoming marriage with Saeko's parents Moichi and Oyoshi. All have fun with the conversation except Moichi, but he gives the young couple his consent, somewhat abashed at hearing Takano call him "Father."

Japanese political leaders call for another East-West meeting to resolve the dangerous geopolitical situation. They also urge both sides not to use nuclear weapons.

Saeko and Takano go for a stroll. In the American version, they speak generally of war and human nature. In the Japanese version, their conversation is more pointed. Saeko asks Takano if it's true that only four hydrogen bombs can destroy Japan. Takano notes that the Japanese were the first to have gunpowder used against them, and now they are likewise the first to have experienced nuclear weapons. He worries that a miscalculation on the part of a missile operator could destroy the world.

An accident almost leads to World War III: On a Federation Mainland Missile Base, a short circuit nearly causes missiles to launch; the disaster is averted with only two seconds to spare. Meanwhile, hostilities break out on the 38th Parallel, and nuclear weapons are used. Japanese authorities fear the worst, but keep working for peace.

In a quiet interlude, Saeko buys four sweet potatoes from the local potato man, who tells her that ten percent of the money will go to the Hiroshima Bomb Fund. She silently reads a passage from his Bible, Psalm 140 verses 2 and 3, about the terror of war, as we see Tokyo, New York, London, Paris and Moscow. (In the Japanese version of the film, we hear her read James 4:1–3 on a similar theme.)

At a North Pole missile base, an accident occurs: An avalanche activates a nuclear warhead. The commander deactivates it in the nick of time.

At night, Saeko goes to the shore to stay with Takano until his freighter departs at 7 a.m. Moichi and Oyoshi discuss this situation, with a disgruntled Moichi expressing concern for his daughter, but a poised and pacifying Oyoshi assures him that everything will be fine.

Over the Arctic Circle, Federation and Alliance fighter planes clash and employ nuclear weapons. The U.N. issues a declaration calling for a ceasefire, or at least for neither superpower to use atomic armaments, asserting, "The use of nuclear weapons will mean the total destruction of mankind."

People in Tokyo panic, many fleeing the city. Moichi chooses to stay in Tokyo, and as the family sits down with him for an elaborate supper, the radio announces, "It is now certain that Japan will face a nuclear attack." Moichi, Oyoshi and Saeko know the score, but the two younger children don't comprehend the terror to come. Trying desperately to hold on to his certainty there won't be a nuclear war, Moichi says, "We won't perish!" He then hurries upstairs and rails at the skies, "Who has the right to take our lives, anyhow? Who? Why must I be so helpless now, why? If we only had some place to go."

But they don't, and that night, both the Federation and the Alliance launch their nuclear missiles. A lone ICBM obliterates Tokyo, and soon other ICBMs raze New York, Moscow, Paris, London…

The movie goes back to Takano's freighter and the men returning to Tokyo. Over these scenes, instead of dialogue, we hear the Disney song "It's a Small World." Next, we hear a portion of a speech by President John F. Kennedy in which he says, "Mankind must put an end to war, or war will put an end to mankind."

The Last War strives for excellence, for Toho apparently hoped the movie would gain a worldwide audience as evidenced by its international trailer. Dubbing rarely if ever helps any actor's performance, but even given the dubbing, the acting in *The Last*

War is of a high caliber. As Moichi, Frankie Sakai brings just the right combination of feigned crustiness and fatherly affection to his role as the besieged patriarch. Nobuko Otawa is likewise good as the sensible, long-suffering mother-wife, and both Yuriko Hoshi (as Saeko) and Akira Takarada (as Takano) bring energy and earnestness to their parts.

The movie features capable direction by Shue Matsubayashi, which generates a sense of unease during the closing minutes before Tokyo suffers nuclear death. In addition, Ikuma Dan's music score is haunting. Eiji Tsuburaya's special effects prove uneven—the lava flow in Tokyo is clearly a miniature—but considering the enormous task he and his special effects unit were given, few in the business could have done better. In fact, no American movie at the time attempted nuclear spectacle on the scale of that depicted in *The Last War*. Although 1960's well-regarded *The Time Machine* included the nuclear devastation of London, this sequence pales in comparison to the scope of Tsuburaya's *Last War* visuals.

The majority of his military miniatures, especially the jets, bombers and submarines, are first-rate, though his futuristic tanks do betray themselves as miniatures. In addition, the midair nuclear explosions between warring jets are ingenious, if not necessarily realistic. Tsuburaya's major accomplishment in *The Last War* is the nuclear obliteration of Tokyo, detailed and harrowing, and more often than not convincing. (Unfortunately, the American version leaves out footage of the huge atomic fireball dwarfing even Mount Fuji.) The angry red mushroom cloud towering over the landscape generates chills, and the viewer has no doubt that everyone in Tokyo has just been slaughtered.

When it comes to nuclear war, Moichi and his daughter Saeko represent different views; Moichi embodies denial, and Saeko fear. When Saeko brings up the subject of the potato man who sells his wares outside, and of the fact that he lost everything in Hiroshima and now gives money to anti-nuclear causes, her father pooh-poohs her. He insists that everything will go on as it has for years, and that you have to accept occasional international blips between the superpowers.

Saeko represents apprehension about the possibility of nuclear war. She is keenly aware of the subject, and it frightens her. Only her relationship with Takano diverts her from her atomic anxieties. Indeed, she continues to plan a future life with Takano, even though the movie's international events make this possibility seem increasingly remote.

Just as in *The Final War*, most people go on with their lives, regardless of worldwide tensions. For example, during the Cuban Missile Crisis in October 1962, American adults were no doubt on edge. But they still went to work, they still took the kids to school, and they still did the laundry. For the adults in *Last War*, World War III is likewise out of the average person's hands.

In this sense, the Japanese version of *The Last War* shows us a Federation missile base commanding officer (Harold S. Conway, who appeared as a "*gaijin*" actor in numerous Toho genre features) and his staff of soldiers discussing peaceful coexistence, and all of them say they think it's possible. But if given orders, we know they would still launch their missiles, thereby imperiling civilization. In fact, in the longer Japanese version of the missile base short-circuit sequence, just before the commanding officer presses the missile activation button, he says in an anguished voice, "God, please forgive me." It is a powerful moment, and it is unfortunate that the American distributor deleted it.

In depicting such a scene, the movie reveals its distinct Japanese outlook. When it came to nuclear tensions, Japan was in a unique position. Though officially allied with the U.S., the country did not have a "personal" stake in the disputes between the superpowers. However, while playing only a peripheral role when it came to the Cold War, Japan would sustain nuclear attack should the U.S. and the U.S.S.R. commence hostilities. *The Last War* depicts Japan's feeling of helplessness when it came to nuclear conflict, as if the nation was a pawn in a chess game being waged between the superpowers. In addition to international hostilities, *Last War* makes the case that an accident could trigger a nuclear war (the missile base short-circuit, the North Pole mishap).

In terms of credibility, *Last War* makes a near-fatal mistake in the depiction of its superpowers. For instead of being the real-life U.S. and U.S.S.R., the movie employs the non-existent Federation and Alliance. This shifts the movie more into the realm of science-fantasy, *à la* Rolisica as America's surrogate in 1961's *Mothra*. Perhaps the producers went this route to avoid offending America and Russia, and also perhaps because they hoped *The Last War* might receive theatrical distribution in both countries. But it was a mistake and weakens the film.

The Americanized version that Brenco supplied to American TV in the 1960s makes substantial changes from the Japanese-language version. For one thing, the American version runs only 79 minutes, dropping almost 20 minutes of the original. In addition, some scenes are jumbled out of order, and the structure changed into a flashback, whereas originally the film occurred in a single chronological sequence.

Also, the Americanization features music during some scenes that were originally left unscored. For example, in the Japanese version, there is total silence as a lone ICBM falls from the night sky over the Diet Building, an effective moment. In the Americanized version, music is playing and it blunts the scene's spooky impact. Also, the American producers cut some of the destruction footage, including the brightly lit freeze frames of world capitals before the nuclear blasts destroy them. Even a scene of the gigantic mushroom cloud looming next to Mount Fuji didn't make it into the American cut.

But the American producers' worst decision was to replay the opening few minutes of flashback at the end and dub the Disney song "It's a Small World" over the sequence; this is jarring enough to set one's teeth on edge. The Disney song is followed by a JFK speech about war, which features the key line, "Man must put an end to war, or war will put an end to mankind." This isn't a bad line, but it's out of place here because it distracts rather than enhances. Likewise, "It's a Small World" actually does have a connection to the nuclear threat; songwriters Robert B. and Richard B. Sherman, who composed the songs for 1964's *Mary Poppins*, wrote "It's a Small World" in the wake of the Cuban Missile Crisis. So the inclusion of this song and Kennedy's speech shows that the American producers' hearts were in the right place, but their heads were strictly MIA.

In the original version, pertinent dialogue, as well as silence, punctuates the final sequence aboard the Tokyo-bound freighter. While we see the faces of Takano and the ship's cook, we hear (instead of "It's a Small World") a poignant Japanese children's song. This segues into a view of what's left of Tokyo, lava-encrusted ruins around which radioactive mists swirl. We don't need to be shown what will happen to the ship's crew once they reach this new Tokyo, for it's a foregone conclusion they are dead men sailing.

Because *The Last War* received little or no U.S. theatrical distribution,[8] and only sporadically appeared on TV, English-language reviews of the film are scant. In *The Japanese Fantasy Film Journal* #13 (1981), editor Greg Shoemaker calls it "a personal film of incredible power ... awesome and frightening." Stuart Galbraith writes, "*The Last War* deviates sharply from similarly themed American films. [It] is a Japanese film told from a distinctly Japanese and—tragically—experienced point of view."⁹ According to an August 18, 2011, review on the online *Classic Sci-Fi Movies Blogspot*, *The Last War* "is interesting as a snapshot of Cold War mood. Told from the Japanese point of view (not one of the warring sides), it captures some of that helpless feeling most people had. The message is delivered with little subtlety, but even this conveys some of the sense of urgency people felt." An online *Toho Kingdom* review states, "Overall, this is a very epic piece of cinema in the traditional sense, not in the overused modern way."

As these reviews suggest, one of the movie's major purposes was to inspire activism on the part of early 1960s audiences; the ending of the Japanese version features an onscreen message urging viewers to work for peace. Toho obviously had no problem knocking down the "fourth wall" to make a plea for international understanding. Such an endeavor might seem naïve today and even overstated—certainly it's hard to imagine an American nuclear threat movie like *Fail-Safe* or *Dr. Strangelove* making such a plea (though arguably, *On the Beach* did with its camera focusing on the banner reading "There's still time ... brother"). But perhaps knowing first-hand the horrors of the A-bomb as well as H-bomb tests, Japan felt obligated to preach peace, even if only to the choir.

It is easy for a "lay person" to confuse *The Final War* and *The Last War*. After all, the titles are nearly identical, and so are the fates the films depict for Japan—utter nuclear devastation.

However, *Final War* is black-and-white, while *Last War* is in color. *Final War* also made do with a smaller budget than the more lavish *Last War*. Finally, Toho invested *Last War* with big Japanese stars (Frankie Sakai, Nobuko Otawa and Akira Takarada), whereas *Final War*'s players were not as celebrated. However, one fate both films suffered is poor distribution in North America. *Final War* had a minimal theatrical release, then enjoyed a sparse TV syndication for about a decade. *Last War* fared even worse, never getting a North American theatrical release, but going straight to TV.

To be fair, maybe American distributors were right; maybe neither film had much box office potential in the United States. Still, *Final War* and *Last War* might have made an interesting drive-in double feature: "Double your fear! Double your angst! See *The Final War* and *The Last War* while you still can before the bombs drop!" Surely this would have been a great theatrical program during 1962's Cuban Missile Crisis.

Seriously, it is a shame American distributors didn't accord Japanese nuke films much respect in the 1960s. In contrast, American nuke films generally received wide distribution, especially the big-budget ones like *On the Beach*, *Dr. Strangelove* and *Fail-Safe*. Even 1962's British-made *The Day the Earth Caught Fire* was treated better than *Final War* or *Last War*.

Nevertheless, *Final War* and *Last War* are more akin to their American counterparts than Japanese monster movies are to their American equivalents.

10. Aftermath vs. the End

In 1961's *The Last War*, an avalanche triggers a nuclear warhead at an Arctic missile base. An Alliance soldier falters, but his commanding officer says, "Ye gods, man, if a nuclear explosion occurs, our forces will think a surprise attack has been made. All-out retaliation will start. If that happens, it's the end of the world."

Twice more in *The Last War*, other characters—Takano and the prime minister—say that an all-out nuclear war will wipe out humankind. Toho's international trailer for *The Last War* states "The annihilation of all life!" No subtleties here, for Japanese nuclear threat cinema asserts that the nuclear genie will not stop until we, its victims, have perished.

Nevertheless, Daiei's *Warning from Space* ends with a cinematic smile: Urium 101 has destroyed the renegade planet that was hurtling towards Earth. Still, the movie warns that humankind might abuse Urium 101, just as it has abused the destructive power of the atom. The film displays unfettered optimism in its closing images of joyous children running from the observatory to greet their parents. But *Warning from Space* is the exception to the rule, for most Japanese nuclear threat movies offer not an open hand, but rather a clenched first.

For example, the aliens in *The Mysterians* represent what happens in the wake of a worldwide atomic war. A nuclear conflict literally blew their planet apart, and now the Strontium-90 in their systems results in genetic defects in 80 percent of their offspring. The Mysterians warn us that if we use H-bombs against them, they will respond in kind. Such a course of action "means Earth's ruin." Dr. Adachi echoes the sentiment that the Earth cannot employ H-bombs because of the grim global consequences, implying it would be better to be ruled by the Mysterians than to risk destroying all life on the planet by using H-bombs.

Further, the Mysterians have calculated that the Earth will experience a nuclear holocaust within the next 20 years; the Mysterians claim that they want to spare us from this fate. By the conclusion, the Earth forces have destroyed the aliens' dome, and the still living Mysterians flee to their orbital space station. Dr. Adachi says, "They're trapped in space forever. We must not repeat their error." The implication is that if the earth does wage nuclear war, as the Mysterians allege we will, we will meet the same fate.

Meanwhile, *The Final War* offers no hope at all for Japan, and little for the rest of the world. In the film, a nuclear conflict breaks out in Southeast Asia and ICBMs obliterate Japan, even though the country did not have a hand in the atomic conflict. *The Last War* likewise offers no hope, clearly foretelling worldwide doom as an aftermath of global nuclear war. For example, in the film, as the ship sails back to a demolished Tokyo, the vessel's cook wonders if any humans will be left alive.

One finds little hope in Japanese atomic age cinema of the '50s and '60s, and an abundance of hope in American nuclear threat movies of the same period. Two American films, *Day the World Ended* and *The World, the Flesh and the Devil*, have an end credit that reads "The Beginning." *Panic in Year Zero!* ends with a similar final credit: "There must be no end, only a new beginning." The narrator and final credits of *Rocket Attack U.S.A.* tell us "We cannot let this be—the end." Most exuberant of all, *Five* ends with the onscreen quotation of Revelation 21, which among other things proclaims, "And there shall be no more death.... No more tears.... Behold! I make all things new!"

While other serious American nuclear threat movies may not end with such a bold message, all of them examined in Chapter 8 offer hope except one, *On the Beach*. Even seemingly bleak films such as *The Last Woman on Earth* and *This Is Not a Test* offer a moonbeam of optimism. At the end of *Last Woman*, Harold and Evelyn plan to start a new life, and *Test* offers the possibility that June and Peter may make it to the abandoned mine shaft before the missiles hit. As June's grandfather tells them, "You two have got to believe there could be a new beginning."

Admittedly, *Fail-Safe* and *Dr. Strangelove* are "iffy" in terms of hope. But *Fail-Safe*, despite its grim ending, still leaves the bulk of the world in one piece; H-bombs have destroyed only Moscow and New York City. And the president's closing words with the Soviet premier suggest there might be hope somehow to dismantle the nuclear machinery that has entwined each nation.

On the other hand, *Dr. Strangelove* ends with the whole world buying it, right? After all, after the H-bomb falls in Russia, the Doomsday Machine automatically activates, resulting in the montage of mushroom clouds (presumably worldwide) with which the movie ends. However, there is evidence that not all homo sapiens died at the film's finale. On October 12, 2013, the online *The Verge* reported that Stanley Kubrick had the idea for a sequel called *Son of Strangelove* and asked *Dr. Strangelove* co-writer Terry Southern to write it; Kubrick had hoped that Terry Gilliam (*Time Bandits*, *Brazil*, *12 Monkeys*) would direct the film. The story would concern Strangelove and a harem of women surviving underground. This certainly implies that at the end of *Dr. Strangelove*, the Doomsday Machine did not kill everyone off, technically meaning there was still hope, even if it was a bit cockeyed.

In essence, American nuclear threat movies generally posited a survivable aftermath, whereas Japanese nuclear threat movies allowed for no aftermath at all, or at best, a limited one. There are American exceptions—for example, in the future Earth of *The Time Travelers*, the surface world has become uninhabitable. But those living underground have the hope of starting civilization anew on another planet courtesy of their starship. (Although the film's downbeat finale prevents this, the characters nevertheless escape via a time warp.) In the world of *Beyond the Time Barrier*, some survivors of the "nuclear plague" escaped to Mars and Venus to establish colonies, meaning there was still hope; and the finale in which the hero returns to the present day (1960), having inexplicably aged decades, should alert authorities to end atmospheric nuclear tests. (The Limited Test Ban Treaty of 1963 did ban atmospheric nuclear tests.)

However, as previously noted, like its Japanese counterparts, *On the Beach* allows for no aftermath, and therefore no hope: It is clear that the entire human race, or what is left of it, is marking time until radiation kills us all. It's interesting to compare *On the Beach*, probably the most "Hollywood" of American's nuclear threat movies, with *The Last War*, the most expensive of the Japanese atomic holocaust films. Certainly they overlap in theme, but also in many technical aspects.

Both *Beach* and *War* feature glamorous romantic leads: Gregory Peck and Ava Gardner in the former, Akira Takarada and Yuriko Hoshi in the latter. Both were big-budget films produced and released by major studios (United Artists and Toho), and their trailers emphasized each movie's importance and relevance. Yet despite these similarities, notable differences between the two reveal that *War* was a bit harsher, a general truism about Japanese nuclear threat movies in general.

For example, *Beach*, like many of its American ilk, concerns itself with the survivors of a nuclear war, whereas *Last War* and *Final War* feature protagonists who fear they will experience a nuclear war and, when it happens, perish. On the other hand, the American films *Five, The World, the Flesh and the Devil, The Last Woman on Earth, Day the World Ended* and *Panic in Year Zero!* all concern themselves with survivors of the nuclear war. But the Japanese saw the nuclear threat as more immediate, and also as something that would kill any survivors.

When it comes to graphic depictions of nuclear war casualties and property damage, the American films minimize the effects of the nuclear genie, hoping to rob the Pandora's Box specter of some of its power—in other words, to insert a smiley face (even if a bit tarnished) over the radiation warning sign. Granted, *Five* does show us a few clothed skeletons, and *The Last Woman on Earth* shows us some expired victims (not physically injured in any way). *Day the World Ended* goes further by displaying radiation marks on Radek's face, as well as a mostly mutated human who stumbles into the valley and quickly dies. But along with the film's three-eyed mutant, these are both stylized ogres, looking less like the result of a nuclear war than of a makeup chair. Indeed, the overwhelming majority of American films—*On the Beach, The World, the Flesh and the Devil, Rocket Attack U.S.A., This Is Not a Test, Dr. Strangelove* and others—depict no corpses of atomic conflict at all.

The genre's Japanese counterparts are not so squeamish. At the climax of *The Mysterians*, we see several aliens painfully expiring in their decaying dome, breathing heavily, with burns on their faces. In *The Last War*, following a nuclear weapons exchange in Korea, we see the ash silhouettes of soldiers as the wind blows their cinders across the battlefield. And *The Final War*, by 1960 movie standards of propriety, pulled out all the stops. Following a nuclear explosion in the woods near Tokyo, the landscape has been reduced to ashes and broken tree stumps, and the camera pans over dozens of burned corpses. The Japanese weren't afraid to "show it like it is."[1]

The Last War also wasn't afraid to show that children would suffer from nuclear attack. For example, the film's spotlighted family includes two young children. The father holds the sleeping daughter, the mother the slumbering son, as the family waits for nuclear obliteration, which arrives shortly. In addition, a single working mother is separated from her young daughter in a day care school, and the two are not reunited before the end comes. Likewise, several children lie asleep in the day care school while the teacher maintains a lonely vigil as she, like the rest of Tokyo, awaits nuclear doom. In the film's closing moments aboard the freighter on which Takano sails, we hear a poignant children's song (heard earlier at the day care school), a haunting moment signifying that memories are all that is left of Tokyo's children.

Given its relative optimism, American atomic cinema was even reticent about showing property destruction caused by nuclear weapons. The major exception here is *Invasion U.S.A.*, which does show New York City A-bombed. But most American nuclear threat movies, including the "A" pictures *On the Beach, The World, the Flesh and the Devil, Dr.*

Strangelove and *Fail-Safe*, abstain from depicting any physical carnage. Even though the radio announcer at the beginning of *On the Beach* says there has been an atomic war, when the submarine crew visits San Francisco and San Diego, each city is standing pristine, nary a brick dislodged. After a nuclear war, how is this possible? The producers couldn't have lacked money to depict two destroyed cities, given that the film enjoyed an ample budget; in other words, the decision to show these two major American metropolises untouched had to be deliberate.

On the other hand, in *The Final War*, we see Tokyo both before and after atomic attack; we likewise see the Golden Gate Bridge and Lomonosov Moscow State University blown to bits. *The Last War* depicts a more elaborate nuclear destruction of Tokyo, as well as ICBMs obliterating London, New York, Moscow and Paris. Perhaps considering the graphic nature of the devastation suffered by Hiroshima and Nagasaki in 1945, Japanese nuclear cinema had no qualms about showing that all the world's major cities could, in the blink of a gamma ray, become contemporary Hiroshimas and Nagasakis.

For Japan, the terms "atomic" and "fear" have been, since 1945, virtually synonymous. Akira Kurosawa's 1955 *Record of a Living Being* (a.k.a. *I Live in Fear*) depicts a middle-aged man so panicked by the notion of nuclear war that he plans to relocate to South America. The A-bombings of Hiroshima and Nagasaki cast a pall over Japan well into the 1950s and 1960s.

Not so for America. A 1945 Gallup poll showed that 85 percent of Americans approved of the A-bombings of Hiroshima and Nagasaki.[2] Why? Because for Americans, the nuclear obliteration of these two Asian cities looked like this:

On August 14, 1945, the news ticker in New York's Times Square proclaimed "TRUMAN ANNOUNCES JAPANESE SURRENDER." Thousands of Americans whooped, hollered and cheered until they were hoarse, the biggest crowd ever gathered in Times Square, with ticker tape piling up five inches high in the streets. The famous *Life Magazine* photo of a sailor kissing a woman in white best exemplified the country's mood. Across the nation, millions more joined the jubilation.

On a more intimate level, soldiers—Marines, sailors, pilots, paratroopers—came home. For a young wife who had anxiously waited a year as her husband served overseas, V-J Day meant a sight she feared she'd never see: Her husband walking through the door and embracing her as though their lives depended on it. Many a Dad came back as well, scooping up squealing sons and daughters, promising them he had come home for good. In addition, fathers and mothers of servicemen, many thanking God the war was over, could breathe a sigh of relief knowing their sons would soon return to American soil.

On the flipside, in American eyes, the atom bombings of Hiroshima and Nagasaki precluded Operation Downfall, the American invasion of mainland Japan, to have started on November 1, 1945, in which untold numbers of men would have died. As President Harry S. Truman wrote to his wife Bess on July 18, 1945, "Think of the [young soldiers] who won't get killed."[3] A diary entry of his stated, "Believe Japs will fold up before Russia comes in. I am sure they will when Manhattan appears over their homeland."[4] Lieutenant General Leslie Groves, who had overseen the Manhattan Project, issued a statement about this new weapon following its deployment: "It is an atomic bomb. It is a harnessing of the power of the universe."[5]

When the United States unleashed that power on Japan on August 6, 1945, the nuclear genie donned a more malevolent face for the Japanese than for the Americans.

A *pika-don*—a blinding flash burst over Hiroshima, punctuated by a teeth-rattling boom. Nuclear midnight eclipsed the morning sun.

The intense heat melted eyeballs, cooked flesh, boiled internal organs. The blast wave tore off clothes and skin and flattened buildings. Some survivors were burnt so badly that the front and back of their charred heads looked almost the same, the skin hanging limp off their hands and arms. One survivor said, "[W]e met some people from Hell. They were naked and their skin, burned and bloody, was like red rust and their bodies had bloated up like balloons."[6] A soldier said he touched his still-standing friends, and they crumbled into ash.[7]

Survivors—dazed, burned, bloodied—jammed into the only three hospitals still standing in Hiroshima. The doctors and nurses did their best, but medicine, food and water were scarce. Frantic parents searched for their offspring, injured children wailed for their mothers, and patients died by the hundreds. Survivors in serious condition wrote their name in blood on the wall by their hospital beds so relatives or friends could identify them.[8]

Soldiers removed the mounting toll of dead bodies, becoming numb to their grim task. One of the soldiers said, "There were objects that appeared to be lumps of flesh lying on the ground. Some of these squirmed from time to time, like exhibits in a freak show at a fairground."[9]

Because of the extensive damage to the city, non-hospitalized survivors found shelter wherever they could; one father huddled with his young son and daughter beneath a railway bridge. The boy, in the third grade, said, "There were almost no ordinary-looking people there. They had swollen faces and black lips." When the thirsty boy went to the now-polluted river, he had to shove corpses out of the way to find a place to get a drink.[10]

Many parents never did find their missing children. Because some children were at school when the A-bomb dropped, many had perished there. In one case, school authorities gave a mother and father two envelopes that allegedly contained the remains of their children. Inside each envelope were human vertebrae—of adults.[11]

Survivors who had escaped serious injury found themselves getting gravely ill days or weeks after the bombing. Temperatures rose, gums bled, hair fell out, stomachs heaved and life ended. Only later did the survivors learn that this mysterious "A-bomb plague" was due to radiation poisoning. The curse of radiation would return to haunt many survivors in the years to come via cancers of various kinds.

In Japanese eyes, had there been no atomic bombs dropped on Japan, this is how they saw the Allied Force's land invasion of the island nation:

Japan's *Ketsu-go*, or Decisive Operation, would have brutally engaged the invading Americans. Suicide planes would crash into Allied ships, human torpedoes would blast landing craft, Japanese civilians would assault Americans via guerrilla tactics, two divisions of Japanese troops would massacre Americans in the rugged terrain of Kyushu. Japan's leaders hoped that the massive Allied casualties would demoralize American civilians, who would then pressure Washington for a quick surrender. Japan's hoped-for result was not victory, but rather face-saving surrender terms, such as no American occupation, instead of the unconditional surrender America demanded.[12]

However, the United States did drop atomic bombs on Japan, and the country did unconditionally surrender, though the emperor was spared from being tried as a war criminal. For a people who revered honor as a veritable god, unconditional surrender to the Allies was humiliating in the extreme, the American occupation from 1945 to 1952 compounding the mortification. And throughout the '50s and '60s, the Japanese continued to pay the price for Hiroshima and Nagasaki.

I have painted these vivid pictures of what the World War II atomic bombings qualitatively looked like to America and Japan to illustrate the major reason that initially, the two countries regarded nuclear weapons so differently. To 1945 Americans, the atom bomb was a savior, but to the 1945 Japanese, it was a slayer. Following the two atomic bombings, the attitude in America grew more fearful regarding nuclear weapons, hence the reason for nuclear aftermath films in the '50s and '60s. But even then, many Americans saw nuclear weapons as perhaps preserving the nation from a hostile power or powers, reasoning that just as America won the war with Japan due to nuclear weapons, the nation could likewise win the Cold War with the Soviet Union due to nuclear weapons. *Invasion U.S.A.* and *Rocket Attack U.S.A.* blatantly tell us America needs to have its nuclear weapons ready at all times, because we don't know when the enemy might mount a sneak attack. *Panic in Year Zero!* tells us we won the war with the Soviet Union, presumably due to our superior nuclear arsenal.

In most American nuclear threat movies, atomic weapons and their metaphors—monsters and mutants—are dangerous, to be sure, yet still manageable; Americans always overcame the monsters and mutants because of the country's guarded optimism that we were in control of the nuclear genie, not the other way around, meaning our ingenuity, courage and brainpower would always force the cunning sprite back into its bottle. Still, over the 20 years following 1945, the American outlook on nuclear weapons mutated as surely as the giant ants in *Them!* By the early '60s, American nuclear paranoia had grown monstrous.

As for the Japanese, their initial 1945 attitude about nuclear weapons mutated as well, becoming increasingly fatalistic. Just as the Bomb destroyed Hiroshima and Nagasaki, they believed the Bomb could likewise destroy their country, and indeed the world. In addition to the A-bombings, the United States' 1954 Bravo H-bomb test (that pelted the *Lucky Dragon No. 5*'s crew with fallout) angered Japanese citizens, who circulated petitions to ban the H-bomb. By 1955, 32 million Japanese, a third of the nation's population, had signed such petitions.[13] A 1956 Japanese survey found that 60 percent of the Japanese saw even "peaceful" atomic energy (*à la* nuclear power plants) as more of a blight than a blessing.[14] Likewise, only a quarter of the Japanese people at the time believed the United States when it spoke of nuclear disarmament.[15]

The Japanese also did not see the atomic bombings of Hiroshima and Nagasaki as necessary to stop their nation's World War II aggression; rather, they saw themselves the innocent victims of aggressors, i.e., the United States. These attitudes are reflected in two 1952 Japanese movies that deal with the Hiroshima bombing—director Kaneto Shindo's *Children of Hiroshima* and Hideo Sekigawa's *Hiroshima*. The former relates the story of a teacher who has returned to Hiroshima to see what has happened to the children she once taught; she finds painful reminders of the city's atomic devastation. However, overall, the film is reflective and personal. The latter is in-your-face and political, an angry indictment of the United States for what it sees as a crime against humanity. It graphically depicts the immediate post–Bomb aftermath, accenting the suffering of children, and emphasizing that the civilians in Hiroshima were unarmed.

However, Westerners point out that American POWs endured brutal conditions in Japanese concentration camps, where thousands died from starvation and mistreatment.[16] In addition, thousands of Americans and Filipinos died in the Bataan Death March, in which Japanese troops beat and starved the participants, bayonetting those too weak to go on. Less known is Japan's World War II biological testing program Unit 731, in which thousands of Chinese were killed. One typical test consisted of infecting a man with plague and then vivisecting him without anesthetic.[17] The Japanese performed medical experiments on scores of American soldiers at Camp Mukden.[18]

While these brutal acts are reprehensible, Japanese civilians were not responsible. In addition, Japanese children were wholly innocent of these barbarisms, yet many children were killed, and many seriously injured, in the bombings of Hiroshima and Nagasaki.

A debate concerning the atomic obliteration of both Japanese cities has swirled in the West for the last several decades, some declaring the acts necessary to have prevented the aforementioned American invasion of Japan that would have killed millions as opposed to the thousands who perished due to the Bomb. Others hotly contest this assertion, insisting the two nuclear attacks were actually committed to show the Soviet Union the raw power the United States possessed. The pros and cons of this debate are beyond the scope of this book, but suffice to say, no one can deny that the atomic bombings were horrific, resulting not only in thousands of immediate deaths, but in subsequent deaths due to burns, injuries, radiation sickness and cancer. In addition, there is the traumatic psychological, emotional and spiritual toll.

For these reasons, Japanese nuclear threat movies, both those featuring monsters such as *Godzilla* and those treating the issue openly such as *The Last War*, depict the power of the atom as being almost exclusively harmful. As *Godzilla* director Ishiro Honda said upon witnessing the atomic ruins of Hiroshima shortly after the war, "There was a heavy atmosphere, a fear that the world was already coming to an end. Ever since I have felt that this 'atomic fear' would hang around our necks for eternity."[19] Historian Andrew J. Rotter notes, "Survivors of the bomb thought the whole world was dying."[20] A-bomb victims as diverse as a physicist, a writer and a Protestant minister saw the Japanese nuclear bombings as heralding humankind's apocalypse, the end of the age.[21]

Unlike America, Japan was not one of the warring superpowers whose military behavior could potentially engulf the world in a nuclear holocaust. Japan was a spectator of the U.S.S.R. and the U.S., and at times, if not often, a reluctant ally of the latter. However, as the only nation to have endured atomic attack, Japan believed it had more of a right than other countries to rally against the Bomb, and to be heard by both Russia and America. *The Last War*'s international trailer states, "We the Japanese are in a better position than people of any other nation to make a film such as this. We side with no one; we are inimical to no one. *The Last War* is presented as our appeal to the world." In the U.S., the film did not get a theatrical release, instead heading straight for TV, and this no doubt frustrated Toho. On a larger scale, Japan was continually discouraged that its pleas for nuclear disarmament seemingly went unheard.

The Japanese, to a major extent, saw a nationalistic parity between Russia and America. They liked Americans as individuals; the treatment of Occidentals in Honda's science-fantasies is always nothing less than cordial. For example, in *The Last War*, Federation (the film's ersatz United States) missile base military men discuss peaceful coexistence, and speak fondly of spending time with family. Honda favored the U.N., and clearly saw America as an essential part of this international body for peace.

However, though both America and Russia were members of the U.N., the two countries quickly became heated enemies, each competing fiercely against the other in the military and scientific arenas. Many in the U.S. military and government believed our nuclear arsenal was all that was keeping the Soviets from spreading totalitarianism across the globe. Once the Russians got the A-bomb in 1949, and the H-bomb in 1955, many Americans panicked. In 1958, given reports that Russia was assembling missiles hand over silo, Democrats criticized Republican President Dwight D. Eisenhower for allowing a "missile gap" between the U.S. and the U.S.S.R.[22] The administration rectified this disparity: By 1961 (under President Kennedy), the U.S. possessed 30,000 nuclear weapons, which equaled 1,360,000 Hiroshima A-bombs.[23]

President Kennedy championed Civil Defense, maintaining that survival after a nuclear war was possible (and that a nuclear war was, therefore, winnable); this implication echoed in several American nuclear threat movies, but in no Japanese films of this genre. Bomb shelter construction in America became a major preoccupation and controversy: Some said you would have to let strangers into your shelter or risk becoming a savage; others held that strangers could not be allowed into one's shelter due to the already limited resources. On September 29, 1961, the popular TV series *The Twilight Zone* aired an episode called "The Shelter": When authorities issue a civil defense warning, neighbors besiege a man and his family locked in their fallout shelter, the only such shelter on the block. Spencer Weart writes, "An aide warned Kennedy that the spirit of 'do it yourself' that had inspired the home shelter program was slipping into a mood of 'every man for himself.'"[24]

America's actions on the political, military and local fronts suggested one thing: There would be an aftermath following a nuclear war. For this reason, nuclear threat movies revered patriotism. With the possible exception of *On the Beach*, all American nuclear threat movies are at least implicitly patriotic, even if patriotism just means holding things together for the sake of civilization as in *Five* and *The World, the Flesh and the Devil*, or xenophobically depicting every last Soviet as scum as in *Invasion U.S.A.* and *Rocket Attack U.S.A. Fail-Safe* probably features the most realistic depiction of patriotism among the American military of the time, men of good will who want to do the right thing but find themselves caught up in the complexities of a nuclear defense apparatus threatening to blow a fuse.

Japan, despite being a formal ally of the U.S., saw itself as mostly neutral in terms of the nuclear policies of America and Russia. If Japan had been in charge of the nuclear arsenals of the U.S. and U.S.S.R. in this period, the nation would have no doubt called for the dismantling of nuclear weapons, given the country's basic ethos that nuclear weaponry was categorically evil.

While American nuclear threat films from 1959 through 1964 did not necessarily see nuclear weapons as evil, *On the Beach*, *Dr. Strangelove* and *Fail-Safe* did demonstrate a more pessimistic view of the nuclear threat than American science fiction films from 1951 to 1958. As already noted, *On the Beach* is thematically on the same page as *The Last War* in positing that, ultimately, after a short time there would be no survivors following a global nuclear war. And while *Fail-Safe* does not necessarily end with the fate of the world hanging in the balance, it does question the logic and morality of nuclear deterrence. Certainly the film implies that life after a nuclear war would be hard, to say the least. For example, when the American bomber is closing in on Moscow, and the airmen know the bomb blast will destroy the plane, one of them says, "There's nothing to go home to anyway."

Dr. Strangelove is even bleaker, though its satirical wit keeps it from seeming as grim. But it paints a near-future in which the Soviet Union has created a Doomsday

Machine that will render the world uninhabitable for 93 years. The device activates automatically, completely removing human decision-making from the world's nuclear fate. Like *Fail-Safe*, *Strangelove* argues that when it comes to the complexity of maintaining a national nuclear defense, accidents will happen, as they do in both films (though we see on-screen assurances that neither accident could actually have occurred given then-current SAC protocols).

Fail-Safe is disturbing in that it places the blame for the nuclear crisis on no single individual: The system, as personified by politicians and generals, is itself on trial. As the U.S. president says to the Soviet premier, "This disappearance of human responsibility is one of the most disturbing aspects about the whole thing." The premier later replies (through the translator), "It is true, Mr. President. Today, the whole world could have been burned without any man being given a chance to have a say in it." Notice that the premier's statement implies that a war between Russia and America could destroy the entire world and, by implication, humankind, a rare concept in American nuclear threat movies of the '50s and '60s.

Indeed, the nuclear genie is as free to run amok in these three American films as he is in their Japanese counterparts. Why? Perhaps a number of factors. For example, with few exceptions, the atomic age monster and mutant cycles had, by the early '60s, given up the radioactive ghost. In particular, Western giant monster films had petered out, the cycle having expired with Denmark's *Reptilicus* (1962). Meanwhile, traditional supernatural monsters such as werewolves, vampires and mummies, primarily courtesy of England's Hammer Films, had supplanted atomic ogres.

But nuclear fears did not evaporate from popular media. For example, during its five-year run from 1959 to 1964, *The Twilight Zone* featured six episodes related to nuclear war,[25] including the aforementioned "The Shelter," a direct response to the then-current Berlin Crisis of 1961.[26] In addition, Eugene Burdick and Harvey Wheeler's *Fail-Safe* was serialized in *The Saturday Evening Post* and released as a novel in October 1962, the same month as the Cuban Missile Crisis. The book sold an amazing two million copies and made the top-ten bestseller list for 1962, the only nuclear threat novel ever to have done so.[27] Evidently, the public hungered for serious nuclear threat cinema.

Although the Cuban Missile Crisis that brought the superpowers to the brink of nuclear war terrified Americans, that terror drove them to seek out a mirror image of nuclear reality in popular media. The movie *On the Beach* was ahead of its time as an example of thoroughly downbeat American nuclear cinema. The A-budgeted film had made money, and Hollywood sensed a potential trend. Columbia (who released both *Fail-Safe* and *Dr. Strangelove*) decided acquiring first-rate talent both behind the camera (directors Sidney Lumet and Stanley Kubrick) and in front of it (actors Henry Fonda, Dan O'Herlihy, Walter Matthau, Peter Sellers, George C. Scott) could result in brisk box office.

In an interesting twist, *The Last War*, despite having shown Tokyo and other world capitals destroyed, ends with the credits telling us that the film is only a fiction and that humankind can prevent this catastrophe. But there are no such assurances at the end of *Fail-Safe* or *Dr. Strangelove*. Their endings are ominous, with *Fail-Safe* freeze-framing on the moment of New York City's H-bomb annihilation, and *Dr. Strangelove* treating us to a montage of world-ending mushroom clouds. Perhaps the countenance of the nuclear genie in 1964 had grown as demonic for Americans as it already was for the Japanese. Perhaps, for both countries, it had corked its empty bottle—for good.

Epilogue

In both America and Japan, nuclear threat cinema changed radically from the early '50s through the mid–1960s. Japan moved from the "code" language of *Godzilla* and *The H-Man* to the overt fears of nuclear war via mushroom clouds over Japan in *The Final War* and *The Last War*. America's nuclear cinema likewise mutated, beginning with the escapist entertainment of Ray Harryhausen's Rhedosaurus in 1953 and ending with the realistic Cold War chills of *Fail-Safe* and *Dr. Strangelove* in 1964.

After 1964, the issue of nuclear war dropped almost entirely from the forefront of the news as well as from the front lines of cinema. On the one hand, the anti-nuke crowd had their own quasi-theme song with Barry McGuire's #1 1965 hit "Eve of Destruction." But on the other hand, just as that song explored more issues than just nuclear war, the much-ballyhooed "turbulent '60s" replaced protests against the Bomb with protests against the Vietnam War. In addition, the Civil Rights Movement was gaining ground and making major breakthroughs, its spirit epitomized in Dion's 1968 million-seller "Abraham, Martin and John."

Yes, the Bomb had become moribund. Scholar Spencer Weart states, "[T]he worldwide collapse of interest in nuclear war showed up in every indicator I have studied, including bibliographies of magazines, indexes of newspaper articles, catalogs of nonfiction books and novels, and lists of films."[1] He speculates that there were multiple causes for this nuclear apathy, including, but not limited to, a sense of helplessness in the face of such an overwhelming issue; a belief that a nuclear war would be so horrible that preparing for it would be useless; and the fact that after each new nuclear crisis, nothing had happened, which could lead people to convince themselves that nothing ever would.[2]

Ward Wilson contends that the key to understanding the rise and fall of nuclear anxiety is the extent to which the public believes the government is doing something substantive about the issue. For example, he theorizes that after the intense nuclear anxiety of the Cuban Missile Crisis, two events might have eased public fears: (1) the installation of the hotline between the U.S. and the U.S.S.R., which assured that leaders could speak to one another immediately rather than having to wait six to eight hours and (2) the Limited Nuclear Test Ban Treaty, which forbade aboveground nuclear testing.[3]

By the mid–1960s, nuclear cinema's icons had become well-established, and they continued to show up as blips from the late '60s through the '70s. The blip might be a low-budget independent (1967's *In the Year 2889*) or a big-budget blockbuster (1968's *Planet of the Apes*). The 1970s likewise featured a smattering of post-holocaust films such as 1973's made-for-TV *Genesis II* and 1977's theatrical *Damnation Alley*.

But thanks to sharp tensions between the Reagan Administration and the Soviet

Union, there was again a call for nuclear threat cinema in the 1980s, although this time, post-aftermath realism overshadowed Grade-B mutants. The nuclear freeze movement blossomed, and 1982 saw the single biggest anti-nuclear protest rally of all time, an estimated one million marchers in New York City.[4] Cinematically, the decade saw two major releases in 1983: *Testament*, a subdued PBS production in which Jane Alexander struggles to keep her family going after a nuclear war, and *The Day After*, an ABC-TV movie depicting the effects of a nuclear war on Middle America. The film was so controversial that a panel moderated by Ted Kopell followed the movie; the panelists included conservative pundit William F. Buckley and scientist Carl Sagan, well-known for his *Cosmos* TV series and his frequent appearances on Johnny Carson's *The Tonight Show*.

The following year, the BBC presented *Threads*, the grimmest post-aftermath movie ever made up to that time, depicting Sheffield, England, before, during and after World War III. Given all the nuclear war movies this author has seen, and I've seen almost all of them, *Threads* was by far the most disturbing (2012's *The Divide* is a definite close second). Other notable nuclear threat films from the 1980s include HBO's *Countdown to Looking Glass* (1984), the theatrical release *Miracle Mile* (1988) and *Godzilla* (1984), a Toho remake of the 1954 original known internationally as *The Return of Godzilla*. (New World, who released the movie to America as *Godzilla 1985*, re-edited it so that the Soviets appear to be the bad guys, whereas in the Japanese original, Russia and America are treated as moral equivalents.)

With the fall of the Soviet Union in 1991, nuclear tensions eased, and the nuclear movie boom went bust. Throughout the rest of the '90s, and now well into the 2010s, the public appears blasé about nuclear weapons. Despite the occasional post-aftermath film such as *The Divide*, Americans don't seem to be in the mood for mushroom clouds and fallout. Despite a fervent fan following, the CBS-TV series *Jericho* was short-lived.

But as plenty of experts have warned us, the odds of seeing one or more nuclear weapons used in our lifetimes have increased. On January 25, 1995, Russian President Boris Yeltsin held the nuclear-command suitcase in his hands, his nuclear keys activated. He had mere minutes to decide whether to launch a nuclear first strike on the U.S. From the northwest coast of Norway, scientists had fired a Black Brant XII four-stage rocket, its purpose to study the Northern Lights. Russian radar picked up the rocket as it soared to an altitude of 930 miles; the radar operators, believing it might be an American Trident nuclear missile, alerted the duty officer, who immediately notified his superiors. The military feared the missile might deliver an electromagnetic pulse that would take out Russia's early command and control system. Russian generals acted quickly, and President Yeltsin soon held the nuclear suitcase.

Fortunately, Russian radar indicated the rocket was moving away from Russia, not towards it. Presumably made aware that the rocket was not heralding a NATO nuclear assault, Yeltsin chose not to launch. No doubt more than one Russian general mopped his forehead in relief.

What had happened? A bureaucratic bungle. The Norwegian and American scientists had notified Russia in advance that they planned to launch the investigative rocket on January 25, 1995. However, this notification failed to go through the proper Russian channels, a blunder that almost resulted in a thermonuclear holocaust four years after the Cold War had ended.[5]

The relevance of this information: After the fall of the Soviet Union in 1991, Americans and much of the world had breathed a collective sigh of relief. Now everyone could stop worrying about a nuclear exchange between the superpowers; the threat of atomic war was over. At least, that's what most Americans chose to believe. This near-accident in 1995 showed that the reality of a possible nuclear holocaust was as relevant in the 1990s as during the height of the Cold War.

Other mishaps have occurred since then. In 2007, the U.S. Air Force "lost" six nuclear-tipped cruise missiles for almost two days. Similarly, in 2010, 50 Minutemen III missiles went offline for nearly an hour, and during this time, they were inaccessible to the missile crews.[6]

North Korean defectors have revealed that failures occur frequently within the country's nuclear program.[7] North Korea persists in making nuclear threats, including a short 2013 film called *Firestorms Will Rain on the Headquarters of War*, in which the White House is shown in crosshairs and the Capitol dome blown up. Russian President Vladimir Putin has rattled the nuclear saber more than once, bragging of his country's nuclear strike capability. Chillingly, Russia has announced that "it will launch a nuclear strike in response to large-scale aggression utilizing conventional weapons."[8] One has to wonder what Russia regards as "large-scale," for this certainly seems to be a warning against NATO and American interference in the country's apparent plans for forced expansion.

Perhaps the scariest idea of all is that America's online nuclear missile array could be hacked. Once in control, the hackers could fool the system into showing that Russia had launched missiles, which would require a counter-strike from the U.S. In another unsettling scenario, the hackers could cause unauthorized launch codes resembling the real thing to be issued to missile crews.[9] Needless to say, the results of either of these or similar cyber attacks could be catastrophic.

Perhaps today we need a rebirth of nuclear threat cinema. Or has the subject become too hackneyed to sustain public interest? Perhaps, like death and taxes, most Americans consider the threat of a possible nuclear war an inevitable part of the 21st century landscape, an international land mine we've thus far been lucky enough to sidestep. But one wrong move and … there goes the neighborhood!

It almost makes one long for the "good old days" of three-eyed mutants, bald giants and bugs the size of dump trucks. Now one can look back on those days—and I confess I do this myself—through a haze of nostalgia. Perhaps it should be unethical to enjoy "coded" Bomb stand-ins such as Godzilla and the Rhedosaurus, but perhaps it should also be unethical to enjoy any and all escapist entertainment.

But it isn't. At least, functionally.

And something tells me that the bottle-abandoned nuclear genie is having a good belly laugh over the whole thing.

Chapter Notes

Preface

1. Bill Warren. *Keep Watching the Skies! American Science Fiction Movies of the Fifties, The 21st Century Editon* (Jefferson, NC: McFarland, 2010), 9.
2. Ibid., 9.
3. Ibid., 9.
4. Peter H. Brothers. *Mushroom Clouds and Mushroom Men: The Fantastic Cinema of Ishiro Honda. Revised and Expanded Editon* (Seattle, WA: CreateSpace Books, 2013), 53.
5. Warren, 9.
6. Allen A. Debus, "Nuclear Dragon: Godzilla & the Cold War—1954," *G-FAN* #104 (March 2014), 22.
7. The mutant is actually monster designer Paul Blaisdell's titular ogre in 1956's *The She-Creature*.

Introduction

1. The late Ray Harryhausen was a pioneer in movie special effects, his works and career revered by the likes of Steven Spielberg and George Lucas. Indeed, at the 1992 Academy Awards ceremony in which Harryhausen received an honorary Oscar, Tom Hanks proclaimed his favorite movie to be Harryhausen's *Jason and the Argonauts*. Younger audiences may have trouble with Harryhausen's stop-motion model effects due to the strobing they produced, keeping the motions of his models from appearing realistically fluid. However, all art doesn't have to be photo-realistic, and as works of stylized art, Harryhausen's work still possess an undeniable charm. Likewise of importance to younger audiences should be that Harryhausen is one of a handful of fantasy movie artisans who set the stage for the lavish computer extravaganzas we take for granted today.
2. David Kalat. *A Critical History and Filmography of Toho's Godzilla Series*, 2nd ed. (Jefferson, NC: McFarland, 2010), 7.
3. Two non-genre Japanese movies, 1952's *Hiroshima* and 1952's *Children of Hiroshima*, had dealt with 1945's atomic bombings of Japan. These films do depict the aftermath of a nuclear attack, but as a past event, not a near-future one.

Chapter 1

1. Allen A. Debus. "Nuclear Dragon: Godzilla & The Cold War—1954," *G-FAN* 104 (March 2014), 29.
2. Bill Warren. *Keep Watching the Skies! The 21st Century Editon* (Jefferson, NC: McFarland, 2010), 10.
3. Ibid., 186.
4. Mark McGee. *Faster and Furiouser: The Revised and Fattened Fable of American International Pictures* (Jefferson, NC: McFarland, 1996), 49.
5. Alex McNeil. *Total Television*, 4th ed. (New York: Penguin Books, 1996), 516.
6. Michael Scheilbach. *Atomic Narratives and American Youth: Coming of Age with the Atom, 1945–1955* (Jefferson, NC: McFarland, 2003), 85.
7. Ibid., 90.
8. Martin Arlt. "The A.I.P. Monsters of Paul Blaisdell," *Mad Scientist* #6 (Fall 2007), 13–14.
9. Warren, 40.
10. Blaisdell's best monster design was for 1956's *The She-Creature*. This inspired humanoid beast sported interesting, cracked-rock skin (foreshadowing the Fantastic Four's The Thing), a belly flanked by what appeared to be three huge fangs on either side, and a suitably monstrous face bedecked with antennae and reptilian eyes. Blaisdell wore the outfit for the movie, and to make the She-Creature appear taller, he stood on Styrofoam blocks. For a photo, see Mark Clark's "Whither Saucer-Men?" in *Monsters from the Vault #21*, 2006 issue.
11. Paul Parla. "Remembering ... The Werewolf: Interview with Steven Ritch, the Werewolf of Big Bear Lake," *Scary Monsters Magazine* #20 (1996), 53.
12. Warren, 40.
13. Ironically, William Hudson would encounter Glenn Manning's colossal gender counterpart in the following year's *Attack of the 50-Foot Woman*.
14. Tom Triman. "The Amazing Colossal Worlds of Bert I. Gordon," *Scary Monsters Magazine* #59 (2006), 78.
15. "Operation Plumbbob—1957." *Atomic Heritage Foundation* (Washington, D.C.: American Heritage Foundation, 2015). Web.
16. Warren, 201.
17. Warren, 202.
18. Warren, 41.
19. Warren, 200.
20. Triman, 72.
21. Warren, 201. Indeed, Warren notes that Frees was paid the princely sum (by 1950's standards) of $5,000 for his vocal gymnastics—or should that be gymnasty-ics?)
22. Debus, 22–23.
23. In fact, Universal-International almost filmed a

sequel to *The Incredible Shrinking Man* entitled *The Fantastic Little Girl* in which Scott's wife Louise would also shrink, eventually meeting up with him in a microcosmos. However, the two would begin to grow again to their normal sizes.

24. Warren, 69.
25. Warren, 76.
26. Warren, 75.
27. This film inspired 1959's intentional comedy *The Thirty Foot Bride of Candy Rock* (Lou Costello's last film) and was remade as a heavy-handed HBO TV-movie in 1993 that starred Daryl Hannah.
28. It's also interesting that male mutants were rarely after women, but not vice-versa. For example, the colossal Colonel Glenn Manning seemed to want his fiancée Carol to keep away from him, whereas the giant Nancy Archer wanted Harry, as one of the characters says, "all to herself." Her motivation is vengeance against Harry for his philandering, but Manning's motivation is angst that causes him to shut Carol out.
29. *Karloff & Lugosi: Horror Classics (The Walking Dead / Frankenstein 1970 / You'll Find Out / Zombies On Broadway)* (Warner Home Video, October 6, 2009). DVD.
30. Warren, 315.
31. Triman, 86.
32. Two notable exceptions are *Mothra* (1961) and *Gorgo* (1961).
33. Jeff Rovin. *The Encyclopedia of Monsters* (New York: Facts On File, 1989), 4.
34. Debus, 28.
35. Debus, 24.
36. Warren, 364.
37. Rovin, 294.
38. "Like a Reverse Werewolf, Except Not … *The Hideous Sun Demon*," *The TellTale Mind* (4 March 2015). Web.
39. Tom Weaver. *Return of the B Science Fiction and Horror Heroes: The Mutant Melding of Two Volumes of Classic Interviews* (Jefferson, NC: McFarland, 1999), 86.
40. Warren, 365.

Chapter 2

1. Bill Warren. *Keep Watching the Skies! The 21st Century Editon* (Jefferson, NC: McFarland, 2010), 107.
2. Ibid., 108.
3. Ibid., 98.
4. Barry Atkinson, *Atomic Age Cinema: The Offbeat, the Classic, and the Obscure*. Baltimore, MD: Midnight Marquee Press, Inc., 2014, 90–91.
5. Warren, 98.
6. Eugene Archer. *The Horror of Party Beach*, *New York Times* (New York) April 30, 1964.
7. *The Horror of Party Beach / Curse of the Living Corpse* (Dark Sky Films, March 6, 2006). DVD.
8. Ibid.
9. Alex McNeil. *Total Television: The Comprehensive Guide to Programming from 1948 to the Present*, 4th ed. (New York: Penguin Books, 1996), 231.
10. Jim Arena. "There's Something About Larry," *Scary Monsters Magazine* 33 (1999), 41–42.

Chapter 3

1. Stuart Galbraith IV. *Japanese Science Fiction, Fantasy and Horror Films: A Critical Analysis of 103 Features Released in the United States, 1950–1992* (Jefferson, NC: McFarland, 1994), 356.
2. Bill Warren. *Keep Watching the Skies! The 21st Century Editon* (Jefferson, NC: McFarland, 2010), 121.
3. Ibid., 919.
4. Richard Pusateri. "*The H-Man*: A *G-FAN* Retrospective," *G-FAN* 34 (July/August 1998), 28–32.
5. Ibid., 31.
6. The first time I saw *The H-Man* was on cable TV circa 1981 courtesy of WTBS, and I found the cops and robbers plot tedious. However, I loved the special effects and the "monster" plot. I particularly liked the melting man visuals as well as the ghostly blue-green H-wraiths. Overall, I deemed this Americanization worth two and a half stars out of four stars movie, hampered by its dominating crime drama storyline, but still well worth the wait. Today, I view the film as a whole more favorably.
7. August Ragone. *Eiji Tsuburaya: Master of Monsters*. San Francisco: Chronicle Books, 2007), 54.
8. Warren, 353.
9. Galbraith IV, 38.
10. Allen A. Debus. "Nuclear Dragon: Godzilla & The Cold War—1954." *G-FAN* 105 (March 2014), 27.
11. Spencer R. Weart. *The Rise of Nuclear Fear*. Cambridge, MA.: Harvard University Press, 2012, 101–102.
12. Debus, 28.
13. Weart, 98.
14. Ed Godziszewski. *The Illustrated Encyclopedia of Godzilla*. Daikaiju Enterprises, 1996), 166.
15. Ragone, 94.
16. Richard Pusateri and J.D. Lees. "*Frankenstein Conquers the World*: A *G-FAN* Retrospective," *G-FAN* 30 (Nov/Dec 1997), 15.
17. Ragone, 94.
18. Peter H. Brothers. *Mushroom Clouds and Mushroom Men: The Fantastic Cinema of Ishiro Honda*. Seattle, WA: CreateSpace Books, 2013), 288.
19. Martin Arlt. "Frankenstein Conquers Japan," *Mad Scientist* 26 (Winter 2013), 25.
20. "2011 Japan Earthquake—Tsunami Fast Facts." *CNN Library*, Feb. 13, 2015): cnn.com. Web.

Chapter 4

1. Spencer R. Weart, *The Rise of Nuclear Fear* (Cambridge, MA: Harvard University Press, 2012), 97.
2. Kim Newman, *Apocalypse Movies: End of the World Cinema* (New York: St. Martin's Griffin, 2000), 85.
3. Weart, 115.
4. Robert Krulwich. "Five Men Agree to Stand Directly Under an Exploding Nuclear Bomb." *NPR Krulwich Wonders* (July 17, 2012). Web. This event occurred on July 9, 1957.
5. According to one source, the men all lived for several more decades and in fact three of them lived into their eighties. However, sources are inconsistent concerning the fates of two of the men.

Chapter 5

1. In addition, the trailer throws these three messages up on the screen: "Are we delving into mysteries we weren't meant to know?" "Is mankind challenging powers beyond the cosmic barriers?" "Will science unleash the fearsome forces of lost worlds?"

2. Harryhausen, Ray. Interview with Ray Harryhausen, "The Rhedosaurus and the Rollercoaster: Making the Beast." *Turner Classis Movies Great Films Classic Collection: Sci-Fi Adventures: Them!*, dir. Gordon Douglas; *The Beast from 20,000 Fathoms*, dir. Eugene Lourie; *World Without End*, dir. Edward Bernds; *Satellite in the Sky*, dir. Paul Dickson. Warner Home Video, 2010. DVD. Disc 1.
3. *Ibid.*
4. Mark Mawston, "Monster Musings: Letters from Monster Bashers." *Monster Bash Special* 1 (2013), 41.
5. Spencer R. Weart. *The Rise of Nuclear Fear*. Cambridge, Mass: Harvard University Press, 2012), 53.
6. Roger Corman with Jim Jerome. *How I Made a Hundred Movies in Hollywood and Never Lost a Dime* (New York: Random House, 1990), 20.
7. Carlos Clarens, *An Illustrated History of Horror and Science-Fiction Films: The Classic Era: 1895–1967* (New York: De Capo Press, 1997, copyright 1967 by Carlos Clarens), 132.
8. And just in case you're wondering what I consider the other five movies in that list of Top Ten Science Fiction Films of the 1950s, they are, in no particular order, 1951's *The Thing from Another World*, 1954's *Godzilla* (a.k.a. *Gojira*, Toho's 98 minute Japanese language version), 1957's *The Incredible Shrinking Man*, 1957's *Enemy from Space* (a.k.a. *Quatermass II*), and 1957's *Not of This Earth*.
9. Bill Warren. *Keep Watching the Skies! The 21st Century Editon* (Jefferson, NC: McFarland, 2010), 766.
10. *Ibid.*, 443.
11. "Giant Pacific Octopus (*Enteroctopus dofleini*)." *National Geographic* (National Geographic Society, 2015). Web.
12. Clyde Ropper and the Ocean Portal Team, "Giant Squid (*Architeuthis dux*)." *Ocean Portal* (Smithsonian Institution, 2013). Web.
13. John Baxter, *Science Fiction in the Cinema* (New York: Warner Paperback Library, 1970), 126.
14. Bryan Senn and Lynn Naron. "Battle of the Bugs: *Tarantula* vs. *The Deadly Mantis*." *Monsters from the Vault* 9 (Summer 1999), 44.
15. Roger Corman with Jim Jerome, 39.
16. Warren, 68.
17. Roger Corman Interview. *Roger Corman Triple Feature: Attack of the Crab Monsters; War of the Satellites; Not of This Earth* (Shout, 2004). DVD.
18. Kim Newman, *Apocalypse Movies: End of the World Cinema* (New York: St. Martin's Griffin, 2000), 85.
19. Of course, it might have been interesting if the two crabs had clashed. Perhaps one of them could have housed the minds of Hank, Dale, and Martha, and the other the intellects of the other characters. Maybe the Hank-Dale-Martha crab would try to defeat the more hostile Weigand-Deveroux-Carson crustacean.
20. Just how Ed got the bus-sized locust into the building's lab is unexplained, especially since the lab is several stories up. Gordon's *Earth vs. the Spider* poses a similar puzzle—how did the protagonists get the inert but super-sized arachnid into the local high school gymnasium?
21. Tom Triman. "The Amazing Colossal Worlds of Bert I. Gordon." *Scary Monsters Magazine* 59 (June 2006), 74.
22. *Ibid.*, 73.
23. Some AIP movies are an exception to this rule. For example, in *Attack of the Puppet People*, the hero and heroine watch *The Amazing Colossal Man* at a drive-in movie theatre. Tellingly, AIP never had its characters watching any sci-fi movies other than those released by its own studio.
24. Barry Atkinson. *Atomic Age Cinema: The Offbeat, the Classic, and the Obscure*. Parkville, MD: Midnight Marquee Press, 2014), 165. Though Atkinson uses the plural for the creatures, there was apparently only one actually built for the movie.
25. Warren, 588.
26. Paul Parla. "Remembering ... *Attack of the Giant Leeches*: The Leeches/Blood-Beast Interview." *Scary Monsters Magazine* 20 (September 1996), 135.
27. *Ibid.*, 139.
28. Lawrence McCallum. "The Slime People," *Scary Monsters Magazine* 17 (December 1995), 15.
29. Kim Newman, 85.
30. Warren, 221.

Chapter 6

1. J. Hoberman, "Poetry After the A-Bomb" booklet. *Godzilla* (The Criterion Collection, 2012). DVD.
2. Susan Sontag. "The Imagination of Disaster." *Science Fiction: The Future*, edited by Dick Allen (New York: Harcourt Brace Jovanovich, 1971), 314.
3. Galbraith IV, Stuart. *Japanese Science Fiction, Fantasy and Horror Films: A Critical Analysis of 103 Features Released in the United States, 1950–1992* (Jefferson, NC: McFarland, 1994), 9.
4. Tadao Sato, "New Interview with Japanese Film Critic Tadao Sato," Disc One, *Godzilla* (The Criterion Collection, 2012). DVD.
5. Bill Bussone, "Godzilla vs. the Bomb," *G-FAN* 63 (July/August 2003), 17.
6. Steve Ryfle. *Japan's Favorite Mon-Star: The Unauthorized Biography of "The Big G."* (Toronto: ECW Press, 1998), 33.
7. *Ibid.*, 33.
8. David Kalat. Commentary track for *Godzilla* (1954) (The Criterion Collection, 2012). DVD. Disc 1.
9. Peter H. Brothers. *Mushroom Clouds and Mushroom Men: The Fantastic Cinema of Ishiro Honda* (Seattle, WA: CreateSpace Books, 2013), 82.
10. *Ibid.*, 82.
11. Stuart Galbraith IV. *Monsters are Attacking Tokyo! The Incredible World of Japanese Fantasy Films* (Venice, CA: Feral House, 1998), 52.
12. Akiko Ono (translator), "Memories of Godzilla," *G-FAN* 12 (Nov./Dec. 1994), 48.
13. Kevin Chan and August Ragone (translators), "An Interview with Director Ishiro Honda," *G-FAN* 12 (Nov./Dec. 1994), 46.
14. Jon Inouye, "Godzilla and Postwar Japan." *The Japanese Fantasy Film Journal* #12 (1979), 36.
15. Ryfle, 57–58.
16. Burr was to reprise the role of Steve Martin almost thirty years later for *Godzilla 1985*, the New World Americanization of Toho's 1984 *Godzilla* remake. Just as before, Burr treated the role seriously.
17. Brothers, 87.
18. Galbraith IV, 18.
19. Ryfle, 63.
20. August Ragone. *Eiji Tsuburaya: Master of Monsters* (San Francisco: Chronicle Books, 2007), 47.
21. Steve Ryfle. Commentary track for *Godzilla Raids Again* (Classic Media, 2007). DVD.

22. Kalat, 37.
23. Melchior wrote or co-wrote several science fiction films, including *The Angry Red Planet* (1959, co-writer), *Reptilicus* (1962, co-writer), *Journey to the 7th Planet* (1962, writer, but with Sid Pink alterations), *Planet of the Vampires* (1965, co-writer), and two of my childhood favorites—*Robinson Crusoe on Mars* (1964, co-writer) and *The Time Travelers* (1964, screenplay writer, story by Melchior and David Hewitt; Melchior also directed this AIP release).
24. Brothers, 107.
25. Ibid., 109.
26. Ibid., 113.
27. Brothers, 178.
28. David Kalat. *A Critical History and Filmography of Toho's Godzilla Series*, 2nd ed. (Jefferson, NC: McFarland, 2010), 52.
29. Galbraith, 92.
30. J.D. Lees and Marc Cerasini. *The Official Godzilla Compendium* (New York: Random House, 1998), 29.
31. Ed Godziszewski. *The Illustrated Encyclopedia of Godzilla*. Daikaiju Enterprises, 1996), 18, 15.
32. Galbraith, 95.
33. Kalat, 69.
34. Raul Cruz. "*Gammera the Invincible*: A Re-evaluation." *G-FAN* 83 (Spring 2008): p.11
35. Kalat, 34.
36. J.D. Lees, "Mr. Yuasaka's G-FEST (Interview)," *G-FAN* 65 (Nov./Dec. 2003), 13.
37. Ibid., 13.
38. John LeMay. "Godzilla Takes a Holiday: *Godzilla vs. the Sea Monster* Retrospective," *G-FAN* 87 (Spring 2009), 24.
39. LeMay, 22.
40. Kalat, 87.
41. Galbraith, 150.
42. Ibid., 152.
43. Kalat, 102.
44. "Box Office Business for *King Kong vs. Godzilla* (1962) *Kingu Kongu tai Gojira* (original title). Gross $2,725,000 (USA)." IMDb.com.
45. Kalat, 57.
46. This is not a knock against Adams' acting—he invests his role with welcome spirit; however, not all American actors in Toho films did so. For example, in 1966's *War of the Gargantuas*, Russ Tamblyn not only phones in his performance, but was also apparently comatose at the time.
47. Ryfle, 37–38.

Chapter 7

1. Richard Rhodes. *Dark Sun: The Making of the Hydrogen Bomb* (New York: Simon & Schuster, 1995), 563.
2. Spencer R. Weart. *The Rise of Nuclear Fear* (Cambridge, MA.: Harvard University Press, 2012), 76.
3. Steve Ryfle. *Japan's Favorite Mon-Star: The Unauthorized Biography of "The Big G."* Toronto, Ontario: ECW Press, 1998), 43.
4. Bill Warren. *Keep Watching the Skies! The 21st Century Editon* (Jefferson, NC: McFarland, 2010), 600.
5. Kalat, 16.
6. Rhodes, 565–566.
7. Weart, 73.
8. Warren, 347.
9. Weart, 93.

Chapter 8

1. Arch Oboler experienced his primary fame and success via radio programs such as *Lights Out*. He also made a handful of films, and other than *Five*, his genre efforts included *Strange Holiday* (1946), *The Twonky* (1953), and *The Bubble* (1967), also known as *Fantastic Invasion of Planet Earth*.
2. Bill Warren. *Keep Watching the Skies! The 21st Century Editon* (Jefferson, NC: McFarland, 2010), 227.
3. Inspired by the success of the James Bond movies, *The Man from U.N.C.L.E.* ran on NBC-TV from September 22, 1964, to January 15, 1968. Vaughn played Napoleon Solo, a secret agent who, along with partner Illya Kurykin (a pre–*NCIS* David McCallum) primarily battled the forces of Thrush. Leo G. Carroll (Dr. Deemer in 1955's *Tarantula*) also starred as Alexander Waverly, who commanded U.N.C.L.E (the United Network Command for Law Enforcement). Many baby-boomers, including myself, look back on the series with fondness.
4. James Robert Parish and Michael R. Pitts. *The Great Science Fiction Pictures*. Metuchen, N.J.: Scarecrow Press, 1977), 310.
5. Warren, 745.
6. Roger Corman with Jim Jerome. *How I Made a Hundred Movies in Hollywood and Never Lost a Dime* (New York: Random House, 1990), 56.
7. Sheehan, 34.
8. Roger Corman with Jim Jerome, 71.
9. Ibid.
10. Ibid.
11. Warren, 171.
12. Scheib, Richard, *MORIA: Science Fiction, Horror and Fantasy Films Review*, 2015. Web.
13. Jack Sheehan. *Nuclear War Films*. Carbondale: Southern Illinois University Press, 1978), 48.
14. Warren, 652.
15. Clark, Mark. "Films from the Vault (Review of *Panic in Year Zero!*)." *Monsters from the Vault* 20 (2005), 51.
16. Parish and Pitts, 256.
17. Warren, 779.
18. Sheehan, 72.
19. The Cuban Missile Crisis began primarily due to the United States placing Jupiter ballistic missiles in both Italy and Turkey. Consequently, upon Soviet Premier Nikita Khruschev's orders, missile base construction began in Cuba. An American U-2 spy plane provided U.S. authorities with photographic proof that medium-range and intermediate-range missile installations existed in Cuba. President John F. Kennedy ordered a military blockade to prevent further nuclear missiles from entering Cuba, and he likewise insisted on the disassembly of nuclear missiles already in the Caribbean country. Kruschev and Kennedy negotiated a deal: Russia would take back the missiles and bombers already in Cuba and would deploy no more missiles to the country. In return, the U.S. publically agreed not to attack Cuba—and secretly, the U.S. also agreed to disassemble its Jupiter missiles in Italy and Turkey and deploy no more missiles to the region.
20. Richard Rhodes. *Dark Sun: The Making of the Hydrogen Bomb* (New York: Simon & Schuster, 1995), 572.
21. Ibid.

Chapter 9

1. Stuart Galbraith IV. *Japanese Science Fiction, Fantasy and Horror Films: A Critical Analysis of 103 Features*

Released in the United States, 1950–1992 (Jefferson, NC: McFarland, 1994), 28.
  2. Richard Pusateri. "*The Mysterians*: A *G-FAN* Retrospective," *G-FAN* 27 (May/June 1997), 31.
  3. Peter H. Brothers. *Mushroom Clouds and Mushroom Men: The Fantastic Cinema of Ishiro Honda*. Seattle, WA: Createspace Books, 2013), 130.
  4. Bill Warren. *Keep Watching the Skies! The 21st Century Editon* (Jefferson, NC: McFarland, 2010), 617.
  5. *Ibid.*
  6. Galbraith, 54.
  7. Warren, 266.
  8. Galbraith, 63, 362.
  9. *Ibid.*, 64.

Chapter 10

  1. However, graphic depictions of nuclear war victims abound in the British-made 1965 *The War Game*, an ersatz nuclear war documentary produced by the BBC, but which the network chose not to air because of its horrific content, instead allowing it theatrical distribution. But then, British science fiction films of the 1950s and 1960s always had a harder edge than American science fiction films of the same period, no doubt largely due to the fact that most British science fiction films of this period received an "X" certificate, meaning no one under sixteen would be admitted.
  2. Stokes, Bruce. "70 Years after Hiroshima, Opinions Have Shifted on Issue of Atomic Bomb." *Pew Research Center* (August 4, 2014): Pewresearchcenter.org. Web.
  3. Andrew J. Rotter, *Hiroshima: The World's Bomb* (New York: Oxford University Press, 2008), 187.
  4. *Ibid.*
  5. *Ibid.*, 193.
  6. *Ibid.*
  7. *Ibid.*
  8. *Ibid.*, 199.
  9. *Ibid.*, 203.
  10. *Ibid.*, 201.
  11. *Ibid.*, 200
  12. *Ibid.*, 185–186.
  13. Peter Kuznik "Japan's Nuclear History in Perspective: Eisenhower and Atoms for War and Peace." *The Bulletin of the Atomic Scientists* (April 13, 2011): the bulletin.org. Web.
  14. *Ibid.*
  15. *Ibid.*
  16. William Paul Skelton III, MD, FACP. *American Ex-Prisoners of War* (Veterans Health Administration, April 2002). publichealth.va.gov. Web. This source claims 12,935 American POW's died in Japanese camps; some sources peg the number higher.
  17. Nicholas Kristof. "Unmasking Horror—A Special Report; Japan Confronting Gruesome War Atrocity." *The New York Times* (Published March 17, 1995): nytimes.com (2016). Web.
  18. Daniel Barenblatt. *A Plague upon Humanity: The Hidden History of Japan's Biological Warfare Program* (New York: HarperPerennial, 2005, 178–183.
  19. Peter H. Brothers, *Mushroom Clouds and Mushroom Men: The Fantastic Cinema of Ishiro Honda* (Seattle, WA: CreateSpace Books, 2013) 45.
  20. Rotter, 204.
  21. *Ibid.*
  22. Spencer R. Weart. *The Rise of Nuclear Fear* (Cambridge, MA: Harvard University Press, 2012), 147.
  23. Kuznick, 8.
  24. Weart, 149.
  25. The six *Twilight Zone* episodes are "Time Enough at Last," "Third from the Sun," "Two," "The Shelter," "Old Man in a Cave," and "One More Pallbearer." Some might quarrel with the inclusion of "Two," since the war that has occurred isn't specifically said to be a nuclear war; however, Charles Bronson appears American, and Elizabeth Montgomery appears Russian, and one assumes any major war between the two countries would include nuclear weapons.
  26. This crisis between the superpowers revolved around East and West Berlin, and the Soviet Union gave East Germany permission in August 1961 to erect the Berlin Wall, thus stemming the flow of East Germans into West Berlin.
  27. Weart, 159.

Epilogue

  1. Spencer Weart. *The Rise of Nuclear Fear* (Cambridge, MA: Harvard University Press, 2012), 152.
  2. *Ibid.*, 156–157.
  3. Ward Wilson. "Why Are There No Big Nuke Protests?" *Bulletin of the Atomic Scientists*, vol. 71, no. 2 (2015), 56–59.
  4. Wilson, 57.
  5. Robert Johnston. "The World Was Never Closer to Nuclear War Than on Jan. 25, 1995." *Business Insider* (Aug. 7, 2012), businessinsider.com/2017. Web.
  6. Eric Schlosser. "Today's Nuclear Dilemma" *Bulletin of the Atomic Scientists* (volume 71, number 6, 2015), 13, bulletin.org/2015/November. Web.
  7. Schlosser, 12.
  8. *Ibid.*, 13–14.
  9. Franz-Stefan Gady. "Could Cyber Attacks Lead to Nuclear War?" *The Diplomat* (May 4, 2015), thediplomat.com/2015. Web.

Bibliography

Archer, Eugene. Review of *The Horror of Party Beach*, dir. Del Tenney. *New York Times* (April 30, 1964): NYTimes.com.

Arena, Jim. "There's Something About Larry." *Scary Monsters Magazine* 33 (Dec. 1999): 40–45.

Arlt, Martin. "The A.I.P. Monsters of Paul Blaisdell." *Mad Scientist* 16 (Fall 2007): 12–20.

Arlt, Martin. "Frankenstein Conquers Japan." *Mad Scientist* 26 (Winter 2013): 20–28.

Atkinson, Barry. *Atomic Age Cinema: The Offbeat, the Classic, and the Obscure*. Baltimore, MD: Midnight Marquee Press, Inc., 2014.

Ball, Howard. *Justice Downwind: America's Atomic Testing Program in the 1950s*. New York: Oxford University Press, 1986.

Barenblatt, Daniel. *A Plague upon Humanity: The Hidden History of Japan's Biological Warfare Program*. New York: HarperPerennial, 2005.

Baxter, John. *Science Fiction in the Cinema*. New York: Warner Paperback Library, 1970.

Brothers, Peter H. *Mushroom Clouds and Mushroom Men: The Fantastic Cinema of Ishiro Honda*. Seattle, WA: CreateSpace Books, 2013.

Burns, Bob, and Tom Weaver. Commentary track for *Frankenstein 1970*. *Karloff & Lugosi: Horror Classics* (*The Walking Dead*, dir. Michael Curtiz / *Frankenstein 1970*, dir. Howard W. Koch / *You'll Find Out*, dir. David Butler / *Zombies On Broadway*, dir. Gordon Douglas). Warner Home Video, October 6, 2009. DVD. Disc 1.

Bussone, Bill. "Godzilla vs. the Bomb: Cultural Differences as Reflected within the Giant Monster Genre." *G-FAN* 63 (July/August 2003): 12–18.

Chan, Kevin, and August Ragone (translators). "An Interview with Director Ishiro Honda." *G-FAN* 12 (Nov./Dec. 1994): 46–47.

Clarens, Carlos. *An Illustrated History of Horror and Science-Fiction Films: The Classic Era: 1895–1967*. New York: De Capo Press, 1997, copyright 1967.

Clark, Mark, "Films from the Vault (Review of *Panic in Year Zero!*)." *Monsters from the Vault* 20 (2005): 51.

Corman, Roger. Interview with producer-director Roger Corman. *Roger Corman Triple Feature: Attack of the Crab Monsters*, dir. Roger Corman; *War of the Satellites*, dir. Roger Corman; *Not of This Earth*, dir. Roger Corman. Shout, 2004. DVD. Disc 1.

Corman, Roger, with Jim Jerome, *How I Made a Hundred Movies in Hollywood and Never Lost a Dime*. New York: Random House, 1990.

Cruz, Raul. "*Gammera the Invincible*: A Re-evaluation." *G-FAN* 83 (Spring 2008): 8–11.

Debus, Allen A. "Nuclear Dragon: Godzilla & The Cold War—1954." *G-FAN* 105 (March 2014): 22–29.

Gady, Franz-Stefan. "Could Cyber Attacks Lead to Nuclear War?" *The Diplomat* (May 4, 2015): thediplomat.com/2015.

Galbraith, Stuart, IV. *Japanese Science Fiction, Fantasy and Horror Films: A Critical Analysis of 103 Features Released in the United States, 1950–1992*. Jefferson, NC: McFarland, 1994.

Galbraith, Stuart, IV. *Monsters Are Attacking Tokyo! The Incredible World of Japanese Fantasy Films*. Venice, CA: Feral House, 1998.

"Giant Pacific Octopus (*Enteroctopus dofleini*)." *National Geographic*. National Geographic Society, 2015. 10 Aug. 2015.

Godziszewski, ed. *The Illustrated Encyclopedia of Godzilla*. Daikaiju Enterprises, 1996.

Harryhausen, Ray. Interview with Ray Harryhausen, "The Rhedosaurus and the Rollercoaster: Making the Beast." *Turner Classis Movies Great Films Classic Collection: Sci-Fi Adventures: Them!*, dir. Gordon Douglas; *The Beast from 20,000 Fathoms*, dir. Eugene Lourie; *World Without End*, dir. Edward Bernds; *Satellite in the Sky*, dir. Paul Dickson. Warner Home Video, 2010. DVD. Disc 1.

Hoberman, J. "Poetry After the A-Bomb" booklet. *Godzilla*. The Criterion Collection, 2012. DVD.

Inouye, Jon. "Godzilla and Postwar Japan." *The Japanese Fantasy Film Journal* 12 (1979): 35–37.

Kalat, David. Commentary track for *Godzilla* (1954). The Criterion Collection, 2012. DVD. Disc 1.

Kalat, David. *A Critical History and Filmography of Toho's Godzilla Series*. 2nd ed. Jefferson, NC: McFarland, 2010.

Kristof, Nicholas. "Unmasking Horror—A Special Report; Japan Confronting Gruesome War Atrocity." *The New York Times* (Published March 17, 1995): nytimes.com. (2016).

Krulwich, Robert. "Five Men Agree to Stand Directly Under an Exploding Nuclear Bomb." *NPR Krulwich Wonders*. (July 17, 2012).

Kuznick, Peter." Japan's Nuclear History in Perspective: Eisenhower and Atoms for War and Peace." *The Bulletin of the Atomic Scientists*. (April 13, 2011): Thebulletin.org.

Lees, J.D. "Mr. Yuasaka's G-FEST (Interview with Noriaki Yuasa)." *G-FAN* 65 (Nov./Dec. 2003): 10–14.
Lees, J.D., and Marc Cerasini. *The Official Godzilla Compendium*. New York: Random House, 1998.
LeMay, John. "Godzilla Takes a Holiday: *Godzilla vs. the Sea Monster* Retrospective." *G-FAN* 87 (Spring 2009): 16–25.
"Like a Reverse Werewolf … Except Not—*The Hideous Sun Demon*." *The TellTale Mind* (March 4, 2015).
Mawston, Mark. "Monster Musings: Letters from Monster Bashers." *Monster Bash Special 1* (2013): 41.
McCallum, Lawrence. "The Slime People." *Scary Monsters Magazine* 17 (Dec. 1995): 14–17.
McGee, Mark. *Faster and Furiouser: The Revised and Fattened Fable of American International Pictures*. Jefferson, NC: McFarland, 1996.
McNeil, Alex. *Total Television*. 4th ed. New York: Penguin Books, 1996.
Newman, Kim. *Apocalypse Movies: End of the World Cinema*. New York: St. Martin's Griffin, 2000.
Ono, Arikiko (translator). "Memories of Godzilla," *G-FAN* 12 (Nov./Dec. 1994): 48. Print.
"Operation Plumbbob—1957." *Atomic Heritage Foundation*. Washington, D.C.: American Heritage Foundation (2015).
Parla, Paul. "Remembering *Attack of the Giant Leeches*: The Leeches/Blood-Beast Interview," *Scary Monsters Magazine* 20 (Sept. 1996): 133–144.
Parla, Paul. "Remembering *The Werewolf*: Interview with Steven Ritch, the Werewolf of Big Bear Lake." *Scary Monsters Magazine* 20 (Sept. 1996): 50–54.
Parish, James Robert, and Michael R. Pitts. *The Great Science Fiction Pictures*. Metuchen, N.J.: Scarecrow Press, 1977.
Pusateri, Richard. "*The H-Man*: A *G-FAN* Retrospective." *G-FAN* 34 (Jul./Aug. 1998): 28–32.
Pusateri, Richard. "The Myserians: A G-FAN Retrospective." G-FAN 27 (May/June 1997): 28–31.
Pusateri, Richard, and J.D. Lees. "*Frankenstein Conquers the World*: A *G-FAN* Retrospective." *G-FAN* 30 (Nov./Dec. 1997): 14–21.
Ragone, August. *Eiji Tsuburaya: Master of Monsters*. San Francisco: Chronicle Books, 2007.
Rhodes, Richard. *Dark Sun: The Making of the Hydrogen Bomb*. New York: Simon & Schuster, 1995.
Ropper, Clyde, and the Ocean Portal Team. "Giant Squid (Architeuthis dux)." *Ocean Portal*. Smithsonian Institution (2013).
Rotter, Andrew. *Hiroshima: The World's Bomb*. New York: Oxford University Press, 2008.
Rovin, Jeff. *The Encyclopedia of Monsters*. New York: Facts On File, 1989.
Ryfle, Steve. Commentary track for *Godzilla Raids Again*. Classic Media, 2007. DVD.
Ryfle, Steve. *Japan's Favorite Mon-Star: The Unauthorized Biography of "The Big G."* Toronto, Ontario, Canada: ECW Press, 1998.
Sato, Tadao. "New Interview with Japanese Film Critic Tadao Sato." *Godzilla*. The Criterion Collection, 2012. DVD. Disc 1.
Scheib, Richard, *MORIA: Science Fiction, Horror and Fantasy Film Reviews*. (2015).
Scheilbach, Michael. *Atomic Narratives and American Youth: Coming of Age with the Atom, 1945–1955*. Jefferson, NC: McFarland, 2003.
Schlosser, Eric. "Today's Nuclear Dilemma." *Bulletin of the Atomic Scientists*, vol. 71, no. 6 (2015): bulletin.org/2015/November.
Senn, Bryan, and Lynn Naron. "Battle of the Bugs: *Tarantula* vs. *The Deadly Mantis*." *Monsters from the Vault* 9 (Summer 1999): 40–46.
Shaheen, Jack G. *Nuclear War Films*. Carbondale: Southern Illinois University Press, 1978.
Skelton, William Paul III, MD, FACP. *American Ex-Prisoners of War* (Veterans Health Administration, April 2002). Publichealth.va.gov.
Sontag, Susan. "The Imagination of Disaster." *Science Fiction: The Future*. Ed. Dick Allen. New York: Harcourt Brace Javonovich, Inc., 1971: 313–324.
Stevens, Shannon. "The Rhetorical Significance of *Gojira*: Equipment for Living through Trauma." *The Atomic Bomb in Japanese Cinema: Critical Essays*. Ed. Matthew Edwards. Jefferson, NC: McFarland, 2015: 17–33.
Stokes, Bruce. "70 Years after Hiroshima, Opinions Have Shifted on Issue of Atomic Bomb." *Pew Research Center*. (August 4, 2014): Pewresearchcenter.org.
Tenney, Del. Interview with director Del Tenney. *The Horror of Party Beach / Curse of the Living Corpse*. Dark Sky Films, March 6, 2006. DVD.
Triman, Tom. "The Amazing Colossal Worlds of Bert I. Gordon." *Scary Monsters Magazine* 59 (June 2006): 66–99.
Tsutsui, William. *Godzilla on My Mind: Fifty Years of the King of the Monsters*. New York: St. Martin's Griffin, 2004.
"2011 Japan Earthquake—Tsunami Fast Facts." *CNN Library* (Feb. 13, 2015): cnn.com.
Warren, Bill. *Keep Watching the Skies! American Science Fiction Movies of the Fifties, The 21st Century Edition*. Jefferson, NC: McFarland, 2010.
Weart, Spencer R. *The Rise of Nuclear Fear*. Cambridge, MA: Harvard University Press, 2012.
Weaver, Tom. *Return of the B Science Fiction and Horror Heroes: The Mutant Melding of Two Volumes of Classic Interviews*. Jefferson, NC: McFarland, 1999.
Wilson, Ward. "Why Are There No Big Nuke Protests?" *Bulletin of the Atomic Scientists*, vol. 71, no. 2 (2015): 56–59.

Index

Numbers in ***bold italics*** indicate pages with photographs.

a-bomb 68, 86, 95, 96, 98, 99, 100, 101, 104, 106, 110, 113, 124, 148, 170, 203, 221, 222, 256, 275, 276, 277, 278, 279, 280, 289, 293; *see also* atom bomb; atom bombing; atomic bomb
Abe, Shime 190
Abe, Teruaki 175, 181
Abenheim, Peter 245
Ackerman, Forrest J 78
Adam, Ken 247, 249
Adams, Casey 150, ***151***
Adams, Harvey 225
Adams, Mike 18
Adams, Nick 97, ***98, 99***, 104, 202, 203
Adams, Stanley 16
Agar, John 135, ***136***, 138, 161
AIP 23, 24, 27, 33, 34, 36, 52, 53, 55, 56, 65, 66, 74, 78, 79, 80, 85, 97, 99, 100, 104, 108, 150, 156, 157, 183, 184, 185, 186, 223, 224, 225, 240, 241, 244, 257, 258, 289, 290
Akitsu, Hiroshi 181
Alaniz, Rico 55
Aldred, John 248
Aldridge, Daniel 74
Alexander, Van 16
Allan, Ted 18
Alland, William 134, 164
Alleborn, Al 126
Allen, Dede 52
Allen, Fred 16
Allied Artists 5, 30, 31, 37, 38, 40, 42, 45, 46, 48, 142, 143, 145, 146
The Alligator People 7, 58–61, ***59***, 110, ***111***
Althouse, Charles 150
Altman, Frieda 251
Amamoto, Hideyo (aka Eisei) 185, 196
The Amazing Colossal Man 7, 11, 27, 33–37, ***34, 3***, 39, 40, 44, 56, 64, 104, 107, 110, 178, 208, 214, 289
American International Pictures *see* AIP

American Releasing Corporation 23, 24, 107, 139; *see also* AIP
Amman, Sara 235
Anders, Merry 78
Anders, Rudolph 48
Anderson, Donna 225, 226
Anderson, James 217, 219
Anderson, Max W. 84
Andrews, Tod 40, 41
Angilas *see* Anguirus
Anguirus (character) 172, 174, 175, 176, 177, 178, 214, 257
Ankrum, Morris 69, 71, 147, 148, 165
Anthony, Ray 42
Araki, Hidesaburo 261
Archer, Eugene 77, 288
Arden, Arianne 65, ***66***
Arikawa, Sadamasa 97, 168, 181, 184, 186, 195, 198, 261
Arishima, Ichiro 202
Arkoff, Samuel Z. 23, 24, 33, 52, 55, 98, 185, 187, 223, 240
Arlt, Martin 287, 288
Armageddon 9, 205
Arness, James 127, ***128***, 130
Arnold, Jack 42, 44, 50, 52, 134, 138, 162
Astaire, Fred 225, 226, ***227***
Aten, L. (Larry) 67
Atkinson, Barry 153, 288, 289
atom bomb 8, 17, 200; *see also* a-bomb; atom bombing; atomic bomb
atom bombing 4, 90, 93, 101, 106, 109, 112, 168, 170, 214, 221, 260, 276, 278; *see also* a-bomb; atom bomb; atomic bombing
atomic bomb 12, 18, 26, 69, 96, 103, 1223, 128, 130, 171, 172, 203, 206, 212, 221, 223, 276, 277, 278, 279, 287, 291, 294; *see also* a-bomb; atom bomb; atom bombing
The Atomic Brain see *Monstrosity*
atomic breath 170, 176, 200, 209; *see also* Godzilla's ray
The Atomic Kid 16–18, ***17***, 109

atomic ray *see* Godzilla's ray
atomic tests *see* nuclear tests (inland); nuclear tests (Pacific Ocean region)
Attack of the Crab Monsters 25, 142–147, ***143, 145, 146***, 206, 289ch5n19, 293
Attack of the 50 Foot Woman 45–47, ***46***, 105, 208, 287n13
Attack of the Giant Leeches 4, 156–159, ***157***, 206, 289, 294
Attack of the Puppet People 55, 138, 289
August 6, 1945 4, 98, 102, 176
Austin, Alan 245, 246
Austin, Charlotte 48
Austin, William 240
Avalon, Frankie ***241***
Avery, Tol 132
Ayres, Ralph 126

Bahr, George 18
Bailey, Raymond 42, 135
Bakaleinikoff, Mischa 20, 27, 131
Bakalyan, Richard 241
Baker, Bob 125
Baker, Brydon 40, 139
Bamber, Judy 72, 73
Ban, Toshiya 198
Baragon 97, 98, 99, 100, 103, 114, 257
Baragrey, John 191
Barenblatt, Daniel 291, 293
Barison, Edward B. 168
Barnett, Ken 191
Baron (aka Barron), Al 235
Barrett, Jim 225
Barron, Baynes 40, 41
Barry, Donald 48
Barry, Wesley E. 238
Bass, Steve 241
Bataan Death March 278–279
Batson, Curly 142
Bau, Gordon 48, 126
Baxter, John 138, 289
Baxter, Les 241, 244
Bayz, Gus 217
The Beast from 20,000 Fathoms 15, 30, 88, 115–119, ***116, 118***, 120,

127, 130, 131, 134, 153, 173, 203, 204, 209, **210**, 212, 215, 257, 289, 293
The Beast of Yucca Flats 64, 65, 67–69, 73
Beauchamp, Clem 225
The Beauty and the Liquid People 88; see also *The H-Man*
Beck, Glen 248
Beck, John 202
Becwar, George 18, 55
Beginning of the End 7, 147–150, **149**, 206, **208**, 289ch5n20
Bekassy, Stephen 65
Belafonte, Harry 230, **231**
Bell, Rodney 139
Bellis, Richard 127
Bender, Russ 33, 55, 241
Benedict, Richard 147
Bennett, Bruce 58
Bennett, Jack 84
Bennett, Linda 20
Bercovitch, Reuben 97
Berg, Nancy 251
Berke, Irwin 48
Berkeley, Martin 134, 164
Bernds, Edward 30
Berne, Jack R. 33
Bernstein, Richard 40
Bernstein, Walter 251
Bernsten, G.W. 126
Berry, Frank 248
Bestar, Barbara 122, 123
Beyond the Time Barrier 65–67, **66**, 78, 80, 108, 111, 274
Bice, Robert 12, 220, 221
Bielema, Linda 67
Bijo To Ekatai-Ningen see *The H-Man*
Bikini Atoll see nuclear tests (Pacific Ocean region)
Binns, Ed (aka Edward) 251
Birch, Paul 23, 25, 83, 107
Bird, Richard 248
Biroc, Joe 33
Bissell, Whit 16, 50
The Black Scorpion 148, 162, 164, 212
Blaisdell, Paul 23, **24**, 27, 40, 107, 141, 287n10, 293
Blake, Larry J. 27, 147
Blake, Oliver 11
Blees, Robert 164
Block, Irving 12, 153
Blythe, Erik 220, 221
Bogeaus, Benedict 69
Bohem, Endre 153
Bohrer, Barbara 23
Bohrer, Jack 223
Booke, Sorrell 251
Bouchey, Willis 241, 245
Boutross, Thomas 61
Boyce, William 159, 160
Boyle, Edward 115
Bradbury, Ray 115
Bradford, Marshall 223
Bradley, Leslie 142, **143**, **145**, 223
Brainard, Karl 142

Brandon, Clifton 247
Bravo see nuclear tests (Pacific Ocean region)
Brennan, Kevin 225
Brenner, Albert 251
Bride of the Monster 7, 18–20, **19**, 64, 68
Britt, Leo 119
Brody (aka Broidy), Steve 116, 235
Brooks, Lola 225, 228
Brothers, Peter H. 172, 173, 179, 183, 200, 263, 287, 288, 289, 291
Broussard, Everett H. 42
Brown, Barbara 11, 12
Brown, C. Harding 226
Brummer, Andre 125
Bryant, William 132
Bua, Gene 191
Buchanan, Larry 84
Buchman, Harry 251
Bull, Peter 248
Buller-Murphy, Basil 225
Burdick, Eugene 251, 281
Burman, Ellis 223
Burns, Bob 49
Burr, Raymond 168, **169**, 173
Burton, Bernard W. 116
Burton, Robert 159, 160
Bushelman, John A. 48
Bussone, Bill 171, 289, 293
Butler, Artie 191
Butler, Larry (Lawrence) 165, 241
Buttolph, David 116
Byron, Jean 119

Cagle, John 67
Cahn, Edward L. 20
Calker, Darrell 40, 65
Camp Mukden 279
Campbell, Clay 27, 131
Campbell, R. Wright 223
Captive Women 5, 12–15, **13**, 84, 110, 111
Carbone, Antony 67, 68, 233, 234
Cardoza, Tony see Carbone, Antony
Carey, Leslie I. 11, 42, 50, 135
Carey, Philip 78
Carlson, Richard 119, 120
Carras, Anthony 233
Carrere, Fernando 225
Carrier, Rick 235
Carroll, Leo G. 135, 138, 290
Carter, Ellis W. 42
Caruso, Anthony 69
Carvahal, Carl 69
Carver, Tina 40, 41
Cassarino, Gianbattista (aka Richard Cassarino) 61; see also Cassarino, Richard
Cassarino, Richard 61, 63
Cassingham, J.L. 16
Casson, John 225
Castle, Peggie 147, 148, 220, 221
Castle of Frankenstein 21, 35, 39, 42, 63, 77, 80, 138, 148, 162, 180, 183, 219, 234, 241, 255, 256
Cerasini, Marc 187, 290, 294

Chan, Kevin 289
Chandler, Lane 20
Chaney, Lon see Chaney, Lon, Jr.
Chaney, Lon, Jr. 37, **38**, 58, 60, 63
Charles, Hughie 248
Charney, Kim 27
Chase, Frank 45
Chester, Hal 115
Chiaki, Minoru 175
Chikyu Boeigun see *Earth Defense Force*
Children of Hiroshima (film) 278, 287
Christian, Paul 116, 117
Christy, Ken 27
Cianelli, Eduardo 153
Civil Defense 25, 205, 280
Clarens, Carlos 127, 289
Clark, Ken 156, **157**
Clark, Mark 245, 287
Clarke, Marilyn 74, 77
Clarke, Robert 12, 61, 62, 65, 66, 111
Clatworthy, Robert 42
Clensos, Steven 12, 23
Clifford, Sidney 20
Cline, Rocky 12, 220
Cline, William T. 48
Close, John 147
Coates, Phyllis 220
CoF see *Castle of Frankenstein*
Coffin, Tristram 20
Cold War 2, 4, 142, 165, 194, 195, 245, 248, 255, 257, 265, 267, 271, 272, 278, 283, 284, 285, 287, 288, 293
Cole, Art 225
Coleman, Mary 58
Collins, Ray 11, 12
Collins, Russell 251
Collis, Jack T. 48
Colman, Booth 30
Colmar, Eric 12
Columbia 20, 21, 22, 27, 28, 69, 70, 87, 92, 105, 131, 132, 164, 181, 205, 217, 218, 220, 222, 247, 249, 250, 251, 252, 253, 255, 281
Conkling, Xandra 61
Connell, John 251
Connors, Mike see Connors, Touch (Mike)
Connors, Touch (Mike) 23, 25, 26
Conrad, Mikel 168
Conried, Hans 150 **151**
Consolidated Film Industries 37
Conway, Harold 181, 261
Coodley, Ted 241
Cook, Willis 116
Cooley, Stanley 153
Corday, Mara 135, 164, 165
Corman, Gene 156
Corman, Roger 23, 24, 65, 84, 125, 126, 142, 144, 156, 159, 162, 223, 225, 233, 234, 289, 290, 293
Correll, Robert Scott 127
Corso, Margo (aka Marjorie) 223
Cost, William 52
Costello, Ward 52

Courtney, Del 61
Cowan, Marie 225
Cox, John 248
Craig, James 37
Crandall, Robert H. 150
Crane, Kenneth G. 153
Crane, Richard 58, **59**
"Creation" 217
Creation of the Humanoids 238–240, **239**
Creature with the Atom Brain 20–23, *21*, *22*, 28, 47, 91, 122, 132
Creley, Jack 248
Crewdson, Capt. John 248
Cromwell, Rex 84
Cronkite, Walter 107
Crosby, Floyd 125, 142, 223
Crosby, Wade 220, 221
Cross, David 238
Cross, Jimmy 33
Cruz, Raul 191, 290
Cuban Missile Crisis, The 2, 8, 82, 216, 255, 256, 270, 271, 272, 281, 283, 290ch8n19
Curtis, Billy 42
Curtis, Donald 132
Cutting, Richard 142, 143
cyber attacks 285, 291, 293
The Cyclops 5, 7, 34, 37–40, **38**, *39*, 42, 56, 105, 113, 114

Dagora, the Space Monster see *Giant Space Monster Dogora*
Daiei (film company) 174, 190, 193, 194, 257, 258, 259, 260, 273
Daigo Fukuryu see *Lucky Dragon No. 5*
Daikaiju Gamera see *Gamera, the Giant Monster*
Daisanji sekai taisen—yonju-ichi jikan no kyofu see *The Final War*
Dalton, Audrey 150, 151, **152**
Dan, Ikuma 267, 270
Danch, William 125
Daniels, Glen 33
Darain, Diana 42
Dark, Christopher 30, *31*
Darrow, Barbara 150
Davis, Elaine 16, **17**
Davis, Jim 153, **154**
Davis, Monica 235
Davison, Jess 153
The Day After 284
The Day the Earth Caught Fire 5, 272
Day the World Ended 11, 23–27, **24**, 35, 83, 84, 85, 86, 106, **107**, 108, 110, 111, 112, 217, 225, 274, 275
The Deadly Mantis 47, 162, **163**, 164, 289, 294
De'Atley, Murray 245
Debus, Allen A. 1, 2, 4, 44, 93, 287, 288, 293
Dekker, Albert 191
De Kova, Frank 223, 224
The Del-Aires 74

DeLaney, J.C. 251
DeLuise, Dom 251
De Munde, Leonard 74
Denning, Richard 20, **21**, 22, 23, 25, 107, 110, 164
Dennis, Hal 78, 245
Dennis, John 48
DePatie, Dave 126
Descher, Sandy 127
DeWitt, Louis 153
Diamond, Jack 52
Dickerson, Beach 59, 142, 223, 224, 233
Dietz, Jack 115
Dillman, Bradford 72
Dillman, Dean, Jr. 72
Dinga, Pat 18, 241
Dixon, Richard 119
Dr. Strangelove—or: How I Learned to Stop Worrying and Love the Bomb 7, 9, 247–251, **249**, **250**, 255, 256, 272, 274, 275, 280, 281, 283
Doherty, Charla 84, **85**
Doleman, Guy 225
Domergue, Faith 132
Donahue, Troy 50
Donlevy, Brian 191
Donnelly, James H. 40
Donovan, King 119, 120
Doolittle, Don 238
Douglas, George 45
Douglas, Gordon 126
Douglas, Susan 217, **218**, 219
Downs, Bill 52
Downs, Cathy 33, 34, 58, 130, 140
Drake, Chris 127
Drake, Tom 37
Drumm, Steve 147
Dubov, Paul 23, 25, 26, 27
duck and cover drills 9, 30, 256
Duggan, Tom 48
Duke, Maurice 16
Duncan, Charles 159
Duncan, David 50, 150, 164, 178
Duncan, Pamela 142, 143
Dunham, Robert 181
Dunlap, Paul 48
Dunn, Harvey B. 18
Dwan, Allan 69
Dwiggins, Sue 72

Earth Defense Force 96, 261–263, 273, 275, 291
Eastwood, Clint 135
Eaton, Marjorie 72, 73
Ebirah, Horror of the Deep see *Godzilla, Ebirah, Mothra: Great Battle in the South Seas*
Eden, Keith 226
Edessa, Joe 74
Edwards, Blake 16
Eisenhower, Dwight D. 205, 280, 291, 293
Elcar, Dana 251
Ellerbe, Harry 119
Elliot, Erica 238

Elliott, Ross 50, 116, 135
Elliott, Walter 225
Emert, Oliver 11
Emmet, Michael 156, 157
Emmett, Robert 16
End of the World see *Panic in Year Zero!*
Endo, Seiichi 175
Engle, Jim 241
Englund, George 230
Eppich, George J. 147
Erickson, Jack 20, 131
Etcheverry, Fred 58
Eurist, Clarence 69
Evans, Charles 20
Evans, Douglas 12

Fail-Safe (book) 251, 281
Fail-Safe (film) 6, 8, 9, 65, 82, 250, 251–255, **252**, **253**, 256, 272, 274, 276, 280, 281, 283
Falk, Harry, Jr. 251
fallout 2, 3, 4, 11, 25, 29, 39, 40, 41, 44, 47, 66, 88, 90, 91, 93, 94, 95, 104, 107, 113, 115, 133, 134, 142, 144, 145, 170, 278, 280, 284
fallout shelter 280
Famous Monsters of Filmland 82, 98, 99
The Fantastic Little Girl 288
Fapp, Daniel L. 225
Farfan, Robert 18
Farrell, Wes 191
Faure, John D. 150
Feagin, Hugh 84, **85**
Fegté, Ernst 65, 153
Feindel, Jock 23
Feitshans, Fred R. 12
Fenton, John 16
Ferrer, Mel 230, **232**
Field, Margaret 12
Field, Rudi 40
Fielder, Pat 40
The Final War 6, 8, 9, 256, 257, 264–267, **265**, **267**, 270, 272, 273, 275, 276, 283
Finch, Stuart 226
Findlay, Diane 191
Fisco, Margie 72
Fitzstephens, Jack 251
Five 7, 8, 217–220, **218**, 221, 274, 275, 280, 290ch8n1
Fleischer, Stanley 126
Fletcher, Neil 84
Flick, W.D. 58
Florman, Arthur 52
Flournoy, Don 65
Fluellen, Joel 153
FM see *Famous Monsters of Filmland*
Fogetti, Howard J. 119
Follis, Stan 61
Fonda, Henry 251, **252**, 254, 281
Forbes, Louis 69
Foster, Preston 78
Foulger, Byron 119
Fowler, Frank 72
Fox, Michael 119

Francis, Alan 67, 68
Francis, Barbara 67
Francis, Coleman 67
Francis, Ronald 67
Franken, Steven 78
Frankenstein 1970 48–49, **49**, 288n29, 293
Frankenstein Conquers the World 8, 87, 97–104, **98**, **99**, **102**, **103**, 105, 106, 109, 110, 112, 113, 214, 257, 288, 294
Frankenstein vs. the Giant Devilfish see *Frankenstein Conquers the World*
Franz, Arthur 50, 51
Franz-Stefan, Gady 291, 293
Fraser, Sally 55, 56
Fredericks, Ellsworth 30
Freeborn, Stewart 247
Freedle, Sam 225
Freedman, Benedict 16
Freeman, Joan 241
Frees, Paul 37, 40, 88, 147, 175, 178, 268
Freiberger, Fred 115, 147
Fresco, Robert M. 134
Freulich, Henry 131
From Hell It Came 40–42
Fujii, Ryohei 97, 184
Fujika, Yu 186
Fujimoto, Sanezumi 186
Fujinawa, Shoichi 181
Fujishima, Noribumi 264
Fujita, Susumu 97, 185, 186, 261
Fujiyama, Yoko 185
Fukuda, Jun 178, 195, 197
Fukunaga, Takehiko 181
Fukushima power plant accident 104
Fuller, Dolores 18
Funakoshi, Eiji 190, 191, 193
Furankenshutain Tai Chitei Kaiju Baragon 98; see also *Frankenstein Conquers the World*
Furdeaux, Beatrice 52
Furness, George 261
Furuhata, Koji 97
Furusato, Yayoi 264

G-FAN Magazine 1, 2, 91, 187, 191, 196, 200, 263, 287, 288, 289, 290, 291, 293, 294
G-Fan Magazine see *G-FAN Magazine*
Gadette, Fredrick 245
Gadette, Gordon 245
Galbraith, Stuart IV 93, 170, 176, 187, 198, 263, 266, 271, 288, 289, 290
Gamera, the Giant Monster 8, 174, 190–194, **192**, **193**, **194**, 206, 209, 214, 257
Gammera the Invincible (Americanization of *Gamera, the Giant Monster*) 194–195
"Gammera Theme Song" 191
Gangelin, Paul 165
Gangelin, Victor A. 119

Gardner, Arthur 150
Gardner, Ava 225, 226, **229**
Garland, Beverly 58, **59**, 60
Garland, Richard 142, 143, **145**, 241
Garry, Robert 61
Garth, Michael 139
Gates, Nancy 30
Gausman, Russell A. 11, 42, 50
Gaye, Gregory 20, **22**
George, Peter 247
George, Roger 65
Germain, Stewart 251
Gershenson, Joseph 11, 42, 50, 135
Gerstad, Harold 58
Gerstle, Frank **72**, 73, 122
Gertz, Irving 58, 164
Ghidorah, the Three-Headed Monster 167, 183, 200, 201, 202, 209, 257
Ghidrah, the Three-Headed Monster see *Ghidorah, the Three-Headed Monster*
The Giant Behemoth 4, 45, 118
The Giant Claw 162, **164**, 165, 204, 206, 211, 212
The Giant Leeches see *Attack of the Giant Leeches*
"Giant Pacific Octopus (*Enteroctopus dofleini*)" 289, 293
Giant Space Monster Dogora 8, 91, 174, 184–186, 257
"Giant Squid (*Architeuthis dux*)" 289, 294
Gibson, Mimi 150, **152**
Gigantis, the Fire Monster 175, 177–178
Gillespie, A. Arnold 230
Gilmore, Stuart 12
Gladden, Owen C. 72
Glasgow, Bill 33
Glass, Everett 30
Glass, Jack 119
Glass, Seamon 245, **246**
Glasser, Albert 33, 37, 55, 147, 153, 156, 220, 223
Gleason, F. Keogh 230
Godzilla (1954) 167–172, **167**, **169**
Godzilla (character) 166, 174
Godzilla, Ebirah, Mothra: Great Battle in the South Seas 167, 195–197, 214
Godzilla, King of the Monsters! 172–173
Godzilla, Mothra and King Ghidorah: Giant Monsters All-Out Attack (aka GMK) 172
Godzilla Raids Again 175–177
Godzilla vs. Monster Zero see *Invasion of Astro-Monster*
Godzilla vs. the Sea Monster see *Godzilla, Ebirah, Mothra: Great Battle in the South Seas*
Godzilla vs. the Thing see *Mothra vs. Godzilla*
Godzilla's ray 170, 176, 188, 209; see also atomic breath

Godziszewski, Ed 187, 288, 290, 293
Gojira see *Godzilla* (1954)
Gojira, Ebira, Mosura: Nankai no dai ketto see *Godzilla, Ebirah, Mothra: Great Battle in the South Seas*
Gojira no gyakushu see *Godzilla Raids Again*
Gold, Ernest 225
Goldstein, Leonard 11
Golitzen, Alexander 42, 50
Goodwin, Bill 16
Goodwin, Ruby 58
Gorall, Les 241
Gordon, Alex 18, 23
Gordon, Bert I. 33, 34, 37, 55, 56, 147, 148, 149, 208, 287, 289, 294
Gordon, Flora M. 33, 37, 55, 147
Gordon, James B. 27
Gordon, Leo 69, 156
Gordon, Robert 131
Gordon, Roy 45, **46**
Gorgo (film) **174**
Gorn, Lester 147
Grace, Henry 230
Grady, Bill, Jr. 11
Granger, Michael 20, **22**
Graves, Peter 122, **123**, 147, 148
Green, Alfred E. 220
Green, Marshall 50
Green, Mike 245, 246
Greenwald, John 153
Griffin, Robert E. 153
Griffith, Charles B. 25, 142, 144
Griffiths, Chuck 132
Grimaldi, Hugo 175
Groesse, Paul 230
Gross, Charles 142
Gross, Jack J. 153
Grubbs, John K. 16
Gurney, Robert J., Jr 52
Guthrie, Carl E. 48
Gwenn, Edmund 127

H-bomb 4, 8, 25, 44, 61, 64, 90, 93, 94, 95, 96, 104, 109, 113, 113, 133, 134, 142, 166, 169, 170, 171, 173, 175, 176, 177, 179, 180, 186, 197, 201, 206, 211, 212, **250**, 252, 253, 254, 257, 258, 260, 261, 262, 272, 273, 274, 278, 280, 281; see also hydrogen bomb
The H-Man 8, 87–97, **89**, **94**, **95**, 101, 104, 105, 106, 107, 109, 110, 111, 112, 113, 114, 170, 185, 199, 283, 288ch3n6, 294
Haberman, Abe 150
Hagen, Jean **241**, 242
Hagman, Larry 251, **252**
Haller, Dan see Haller, Daniel (aka Dan)
Haller, Daniel (aka Dan) 156, 240
Hama, Mie 202
Hamamura, Jun 190
Hammer Films 65, 281
Hammeras, Ralph 165
Hammond, Reid 238

Hampton, Bill 61
Hampton, Orville H. 58
Hanawalt (aka Hannawalt), Charles 233
Hanawalt, Chuck 142
Hanna, Mark 25, 33, 45, 52
Hansen, William 251
Hardy [aka Hardie], Russell 251
Harris, Del 30
Harryhausen, Ray 4, 7, 116, 117, 118, 119, 131, 132, 134, 162, 204, 205, 207, 209, 211, 213, 215, 283, 287, 289, 293
Hart, Susan 159, 160
Hart, Teddy 11
Harvey, Anthony 247
Harvey, Don C. 147
Harvey, Phil 50
Haszillo, Louis 18, 153
Hathaway, Bob 52
Hatton, Raymond 23, 25, 26
Haworth, Ted 150
Hayden, Sterling 248
Hayes, Allison 45
Hayes, Chester 40
Hayes, Jack 126
Hayes, W. Donn 220
Hayne, Ben 125
Haze, Jonathan 23, 126, 223
Heermance, Richard 30
Henderson, Don (aka Donald) 159
Henley, Jack 11
Herman, Ace 238
Hernandez, Robert 55
Heron, Julia 50
Herrick, Fred 52
Hertz, Nathan *see* Juran, Nathan 45
Herzbrun, Bernard 11
Hewitt, David 78
hibakusha 93, 214
Hickox, Sid 126
Hidaka, Shigeaki 175
Hidari, Bokuzen 190
The Hideous Sun Demon 7, 61–64, **62**
Hiestand, John 42
Hilliard, Richard 74
Hiner, Phil 61
Hirai, Kiyoko 258
Hirata, Akihiko 88, 90, 168, 178, 179, 181, 195, 198, 199, 261, 262
Hirose, Shoichi 181
Hiroshima (film) 278, 287
Hiroshima bombing 4, 8, 15, 17, 18, 44, 93, 96, 97, 98, 99, 100, 101, **102**, 104, 106, 109, 113, 168, 170, 177, 186, 203, 212, 214, 246, 256, 260, 269, 270, 276, 278, 279, 280, 287, 291, 294; effects on victims 37, **95**, 277
Hirschfeld, Gerald 251
Hisataka Kai 264
Hoag, Doane R. 61
Hoberman, J. 166, 289, 293
Hodgson, Leslie 248
Hoffman, Bill 52

Hoffman, Harold 84
Hoffman, John 217
Hoffman, Maury 55
Hoffman, Morrie 40
Hoffman, Roswell A. 42
Hokanson, Mary Ann 127
Holcombe, Bill 74
Holcombe, Harry 202
Holden, Joyce 27, 52
Holland, Bill 11
Holland, Tom 159
Holland, William 42
Holman, Rex 241
Holsopple, Theobold 12
Holt, Tim 150, **151**
Honda, Ishiro 4, 87, 96, 97, 100, 166, 167, 170, 178, 179, 181, 184, 186, 189, 193, 197, 200, 201, 202, 203, 206, 209, 261, 262, 279, 287, 288, 289, 291, 293
Hones, Harry O. 37
Honthaner, Ron 61
Hopper, William 164
Horning, William A. 230
The Horror of Party Beach 64, 74–76, **75**, **76**, 77, 288ch2n7, 293, 294
Horsley, David S. 11, 135
Hoshi, Michiko 264
Hoshi, Yuriko 186, 187, 189, 268, 270
Hotaling, Frank 16
Hotta, Yoshie 181
Hough, Horace 116
Houghland, Arnold 240
Howard, Jane 135
Howard, Sandy 191
Howard A. Anderson Co. 65
Howlin, Olin 127
Hoyt, John 78
Hudson, William 33, **34**, 287n13
Hughes, Russell 126
Hughes, William 33
Hutchinson, Max 116
Hutton, Robert 159, 160, 161
hydrogen bomb 1, 29, 122, 167, 177, 182, 202, 248, 269, 290, 294; *see also* H-bomb
Hyke, Ray 116

I Was a Teenage Frankenstein 53, 225
I Was a Teenage Werewolf 24, 225
Ibuki, Toru 195
ICBM 3, 180, 235, 237, 269, 271, 273, 276
Icons of Horror Collection: Sam Katzman (The Giant Claw; Creature with the Atom Brain; Zombies of Mora Tau; The Werewolf) 21, 28
Ifukube, Akira 8, 92, 97, 100, 168, 172, 178, 184, 186, 202, 203, 261, 263
Iizuda, Sadao 184–185
Ike, Susumu 181
In the Year 2889 23, 84–86, **85**, 283

The Incredible Shrinking Man 11, 42–45, **43**, 50, 52, 64, 109, 110, 135, 139, 287n23 289ch5n8
Indestructible Man 30
Inescort, Frieda 58
Inoue, Akira 190
Inouye, Jon 172, 175, 289, 293
Invasion of Astro-Monster 98, 104, 125, 167, 183, 197, 200, 201, 202, 203
Invasion of the Body Snatchers (1956) 127, 147
Invasion USA 15, 217, 220–223, **222**, 278, 280
Iselin, Alan V. 74
Ishizaka, Mamoru 190
It Came from Beneath the Sea 7, 21, 23, 119, 131–134, **132**, 203, 204, **205**
Ito, Emi 181, 186
Ito, Hisaya 196, 261
Ito, Jerry 181, 182
Ito, Yumi 181, 186
Ivano, Paul 12
Iwanaga, Frank 168
Iwashita, Koichi 178, 261, 267
Iwashita, Koichi (Hiroichi) *see* Iwashita, Koichi

Jackman, Fred 20
Jackson, Thomas E. 45
James, Marguerite 251
Janiss, Vivi 139, 140
Japanese Fantasy Film Journal 271, 289, 293
Jennings, Al 230
Jens, Salome 52
Jergens, Adele 23, 25, 26
Jerome, Jim 289, 290, 293
Jessup, Robert C. 84
Jocelyn, June 55
Johnson, James Weldon 217
Johnson, Laurie 247
Johnson, Russell 142, **145**
Johnstone, Anna Hill 251
Jones, Gordon 150
Jones, James Earl 248
Jones, LaVerne 153
Jones, Robert 119
Jones-Moreland, Betsy 233, 234
Joseph, Al 42
Juran, Nathan 45, 47, 164
Justman, Joseph 220
Justman, Robert H. 230

Kagawa, Kyoko 181, 182
Kaiju shima no kessen: Gojira no musuko see Son of Godzilla
Kajita, Koji 97, 186, 261
Kalat, David 171, 178, 183, 198, 200, 287, 289, 290
Kanayama, Minoru 198
Kaper, Bronislau 126
Karita, Toyomi 258
Karloff, Boris 48, 288, 293
Kasama, Yukio 175
Kato, Haruya 181, 185

Katzman, Leonard 131
Katzman, Sam 20, 21, 27, 28, 131, 165
Kauer, Gene 67, 72
Kavigan, Joe 69
Kawahara, Kenji 258
Kawazu, Seizaburo 181, 185
Kay, Edward J. 238
Kay, Richard 168
Kayama, Shigeru 167, 175, 261
Keane, Ed 181
Kebroyd, Damon 74
Keith, Ian 132
Keith, Michael 202
Kellaway, Cecil 116, 117
Keller, Walter 55, 147
Kelley, Walter 156, *157*
Kennedy, Douglas 58
Kennedy, John F. 52, 269, 290*ch8n*19
Kennedy, Tom 220
Kenney, Jack 48
Kent, April 42
Kent, Carol 245, 246
Kent, Robert E. 27
Kevan, Jack 135
Kilbride, Percy 11, 12
Killers from Space 90, 122–125, *123*
Kimbell, Anne 125, 126
Kimura, Takeshi 87, 97, 175, 178, 261, 267
Kind, Loretta 18
King, Donna 61
King, Frank 178
King, Maurice 178
King Ghidorah (character) 125, 172, 197, 201, 202, 257
King Kong (1933) 4, 16, 35, 162, 176, 180, 216
King Kong vs. Godzilla 98, 166, 167, 171, 183, 184, 190, 200, 201, 202, 213, 290
Kiritachi, Harumi 190, 193
Kirkman, Robert C. 61
Kish, Joseph 30, 58
Kishida, Kuichiro 97
Kita, Takeo 87, 97, 168, 175, 181, 184, 186, 195, 198
Kita, Tatsuo 178
Kitahara, Yoshiro 190
Kloss, Marlene 37
Knight, Charles 72
Knight, Dale 18
Knoth, Fred 164
Knott, Edward 251
Knox, Ken 65
Knudtson, Frederic 225
Kobori, Akio 178
Koch, Howard W. 48
Kochi, Momoko 168, 169, 261, 262
Koike, Tadashi 185
Koizumi, Hajime 87, 97, 181, 184, 186, 261
Konna, Rika 97
Koseki, Yuji 181
Kosslyn, Jack 33

Kosuge, Yoshio 186; *see also* Kosugi, Yoshio
Kosugi, Yoshio 97, 181, 261
Kowalski, Bernard L. 156
Koyama, Hiroshi 97
Kramarsky, David 125
Kramer, Stanley 225
Krasne, Philip N. 153
Kress, Harold F. 230
Kristof, Nicholas 293
Kroeger, Barry 78
Krulwich, Robert 288, 293
Kubo, Akira 198
Kubrick, Stanley 4, 247, 248, 250, 255, 274, 281
Kuichiro, Kishida 88, 97, 168, 181, 184, 186, 195, 198, 261, 268
Kuno, Seishiro 198
Kuronuma, Ken 178
Kusama, Akio 181, 261
Kuznik, Peter 291

Lampkin, Charles 217, 219
Landau, Richard 48
Lane, Mike 48
Lang, Lisa 72, 73
Langan, Glenn 33, *34*, 35, 58
Langton, Paul 42
Lapenieks, Vilis, Jr. 61
Lapis, Joe 50
LaPorta, Fred 61
Larabee, Louise 251
LaSalle, Richard 78
Lasky, Betty 245
The Last War 6, 8, 9, 256, 257, 266, 267–272, 273, 274, 275, 276, 279, 280, 281, 283
The Last Woman on Earth 233–235, 274, 275
Laszlo, Alexander 156
Launer, S. John 20, *22*, 27, 28
Laurel, Allan 74, 75
Lauter, Harry 27, 132
Lava, William 164
Laven, Arnold 150
LaVigne, Emile 30
LeBlanc, Lee 230
Lee, Earl 217, 219
Leeds, Peter 11, 16
Lees, J.D. 1, 100, 187, 288, 290, 294
Leewood, Jack 58
Leicester, James 69
Leigh, Nelson 30, *31*
LeMay, Curtis 15, 205, 213, 225
LeMay, John 196, 197, 290
Levine, Joseph E. 168
Levitt, Ruby R. 42
Levy, Don 78
Levy, Jules V. 150
Lewis, Herman 223
Limited Test Ban Treaty (1963) 274
Linden, Eddie 27
Listz, Ralph 52
"Little Beauties" 181, 182, 186, 196
Lockwood, Alexander 50

Lockwood, Vice-Admiral Charles A., U.S.N. [ret.] 225
Locy, William Jenkins 217
Lodato, Carlo 37, 69, 156
Lohman, Augie 150
Long, Richard 11, 12
Loomis, Diana 37
Lourie, Eugene 115, 118, 119, 174, 215, 289, 293
Lovejoy, Ray 248
Lubow, Sid 217
Lucky Dragon No. 5 (Japanese ship) incident 44, 93, 95, 97, 109, 170, 171, 214, 260, 278
Ludwig, Edward 164
Lugosi, Bela 18, *19*, 20, 48, 288, 293
Lukather, Dorys 139
Luke, Keye 175
Lumet, Sidney 251, 252, 281
Lund, Jana 48, *49*
Lydecker, Howard 16
Lydecker, Theodore 16
Lyden, Pierce 139, 140
Lyndon, Victor 247
Lynn, George M. 27, 28
Lynn, Vera 248
Lyon, Alice 74, 75
Lyons, Lincoln 126

Ma and Pa Kettle Back on the Farm 5, 11–12, 109
Mabuchi, Kaoru 97, 100
MacDougall, Ranald 230
Machan, "Little Person" 198
Macready, George 58, 60
Madden, Robert L. 65
Maddox, Dean, Jr. 132
Maeda, Beverly 198
The Magnetic Monster 119–122, *121*
Maguire, Charles H. 251
Mahon, Barry 235, 238
Main, Marjorie 11, 12
Maki, Teruo 168
Mancini, Henry 135, 164
Manlove, Dudley 238
Mann, Edward 45
Manning, Knox 220
Manning, Patricia 61
Manoda, Yukio 97, 185, 186, 269
Mansbridge, John 58
March, Hal 16
Marco, Paul 18
Mark, Bob 16
Marlow, Hugh 30, *31*
Marquard, Brick 245
Marquette, Jack (aka Jacques) 233
Marquette, Jacques R. 45
Marshall, Darah 223
Marta, Jack 55, 147
Martin, Aubrey 245, 246
Martin, Bill 223
Martin, Strother 30
Martinson, Leslie H. 16
Maruyama, Kenichiro 198
Marzorati, Harold J. 230
Mascelli, Joseph 72

Masters, Jack 65
Matheson, Richard 42
Matsubayashi, Shue 267, 270
Matthau, Walter 251, 252, **253**, 281
Mawston, Mark 119, 289, 294
Mayor, Agustin 74
McCallum, Lawrence 161, 289, 290, 294
McCann, Frances 238
McCarthy, John, Jr. 16
McClory, Sean 127
McCormick, Joe 225
McCoy, Donald E. 18
McCoy, Tony 18
McCrea, Jody 150
McCurry, John 191
McGuire, Harp 225
McKay, John 235
McKinney, Austin 67
McNamara, John 40, 41, 55
McNeil, Alex 84, 287, 288, 294
McRitchie, Grieg 245
McVey, Tyler 156
McWhorter, Frank 12, 220
Meadows, Roy 125
medical experimentation on POWs 279
Megowan, Don 27, 28, 238
Meguro, Sachiko 258
Meikle, Richard 225
Meillon, John 225
Melchior, Ib 78, 80, 82, 178, 290
Mellor, Douglas 67
Mendelson, Herb 55, 58
Menken, Shep 122
Menville, Doug 61
Merrick, John 58, 122, **123**
Metrano, Arthur (aka Art) 235
Metty, Russell 50
MGM 174, 230, 231, 232, 261, 262
Miake, Bontaro 258
Mighty Joe Young (1949) 4, 117
Mikami, Choshichiro 87
Milan, George 238, **239**
Milland, Ray 240, **241**, 242, 244, 245
Miller, John 65
Miller, Peter 220
Miller, Tom 61
Milner, Dan 40, 139
Milner, Jack 40, 125, 139
Milo, George 16
Milt, Mike 30
Milton, David 30
Milton, Franklin 230
Minawa, Ichiro 168, 175, 261
Minoff, Leon 247
Mishima, Ko 181
Mita, Yoshiko (Yoshio) 264
Mitchel, Mary **241**, 242
Mitchell, Philip 45, 223
Mitchell, Steve 69
Miyazaki, Masanobu 87, 175, 178, 181, 261
Mizuno, Kumi 97, 98, 181, 198, 202, 258
Mizunoya, Kiyomi 178

Mohr, Gerald 220, 221
Mohr, Hal 238
Monster from Green Hell 7, 148, 153, 156, **154**, **155**, 206
Monster from the Ocean Floor 125–126
Monster Island's Decisive Battle: Son of Godzilla see *Son of Godzilla*
Monster on the Campus 42, 44, 50–52, **50**, **51**, 86, 110, 135
The Monster That Challenged the World 150–153, **151**, **152**, 206, 212
Monster Zero see *Invasion of Astro-Monster*
Monsters from the Vault 245, 287, 289, 290, 293, 294
Monstrose, Dave 27
Monstrosity 72–74, **72**
Montell, Lisa 30
Montgomery, Thomas 202
Moody, Doris 153
Moody, Titus 67
The Moons 191
Moore, Eulabelle 74, 77
Moore, Joanna 50
Mora (aka Morra), Irene 223
Moran, Paddy 225
Morgan, Boyd "Red" 65
Morgan, Ira 37
Morgan, William M. 135
Morheim, Lou 115
Mori, Iwao 168
Mori, Shigeru
Morin, Roland 67
Morlas, Mary 245, 246
Morley, Jay A., Jr. 42
Morrill, John 61
Morrow, Jeff 165
Morse, Terry O. 168
Morton, John 240
Morton, Judee 159, **160**
Moses, Charles A. 48
Moss, Joel 150
Most Dangerous Man Alive 69–71, **70**
Mosura see *Mothra*
Mosura tai Gojira see *Mothra vs. Godzilla*
Mothra (character) 96, 100, 167, 172, 174, 176, 186, 187, 188, 189, 190, 105, 196, 197, 199, 201, 204, 206, 209, 211, 212, 213, 214, 257
Mothra (film) 8, 88, 92, 132, 166, 181–184, 257, 268, 271, 288
Mothra vs. Godzilla 100, 167, 183, 186–190, 201
MST3K see *Mystery Science Theater 3000*
Mudie, Leonard 119, 120
Mueller, William 126
Mukoyama, Hiroshi 88, 168, 175, 178, 181, 185, 195, 269
Muller, Fred M. 122
Munekawa, Nobuo 190
Murakami, Fuyuki 168, 178, 261
Murata, Koji 87

Murata, Takeo 167, 175
Murton, Peter 247
Music, Shigeo 258
Mutual Assured Destruction (MAD) doctrine 250, 254
The Mysterians see *Earth Defense Force*
The Mysterious Satellite see *Warning from Space*
Mystery Science Theatre 3000 33, 115, 235

Nafshun, Irwin 67
Nagai, Mieko 258
Nagano, Takashi 198
Nagasaki bombing 4, 8, 15, 18, 37, 95, 97, 101, 106, 109, 168, 170, 173, 177, 186, 212, 214, 260, 276, 278, 279
Nagata, Hidemasa 190
Nagata, Masaichi 257
Nagel, Don 18
Nakadai, Fumio 168, 195
Nakajima, Gentaro 257
Nakajima, Haruo 97, 168, 175, 181, 186, 195, 198, 261
Nakamura, Nabuo 185
Nakamura, Shigeru 184
Nakamura, Shinichiro 181
Nakamura, Tadao 261
Nakamura, Tetsu 88, 181, 261
Nakamura, Yoshio 87
Nakano, Toshiko 88
Nakashizu, Tatsuji 190
Nakata, Yasuko 178
Nanbu, Shozo 258
Naron, Lynn 138, 289, 294
Nassour, Edward 175
Natsuki, Yosuke 185, 202
Naylor, Bill 119
Neill, Noel 220
Nelson, Ed 142
Nelson, Lori 23, **24**, 25, 83, **107**, 110
The New York Times 77, 183, 250, 288, 291, 293
Newman, Kim 108, 144, 162, 288, 289, 294
Newman, Samuel 164
Nicholson, Emrich 11
Nicholson, James H. 23
Nicholson, Meredith M. 65
Nickolaus, John M., Jr. 156
Nikaido, Yukio 264
Nimoy, Leonard 127
9/11 see September 11, 2001 terrorist attacks
Nishigaki, Rokuro 267
Nishikawa, Tsuruzo 87, 88
Nishimoto, Sadamasa 97
Nolte, William 18
Nonagase, Samaji 181
Norris-Smith, Royal Australian Navy Liaison Lt. Commander A.A. 225
nuclear tests (inland) 67, 115, 180, 213, 215, 274; Bikini Atoll 95, 170; fallout 107; Mike **167**;

nuclear tests (Pacific Ocean region) 4, 64, 95, 96, 126, 133, 134, 169, 171, 176, 186, 188, 189, 194, 211, 213, 272; Operation Bravo 94, 95, 96, 107, 170, 278; soldiers as guinea pigs 35, 108, 213; *see also* Limited Test Ban Treaty; Operation Plumbbob, 1957
nuclear waste 74, 77
nuclear weapons 9, 15, 88, 104, 118, 131, 147, 150, 162, 177, 184, 191, 192, 193, 196, 197, 199, 201, 202, 206, 213, 214, 215, 223, 253, 254, 255, 258, 260, 262, 268, 269, 275, 278, 280, 284, 291; *see also* a-bomb; atom bomb; atom bombing; atomic bomb; H-bomb; hydrogen bomb; nuclear tests (inland); nuclear tests (Pacific Ocean region)
Nye, Ben 58

Oboler, Arch 217, 218, 219, 220, 290*ch*8*n*1
O'Brien, Willis 164
Oda, Motoyoshi 175
Ogata, Rinsaku 178, 181
Ogawa, Toranosuke 168
Oguni, Hideo 257
O'Gorman, John 225
O'Hara, Quinn 84
O'Herlihy, Dan 220, 221, 251, 252, 253, 281
Oikawa, Takeo 261
Okami, Jojiro 184, 261
Oliphant, James 67
Olson, Don 65
Omori, Seitaro 258
On the Beach 5, 6, 225–230, **227**, **229**, 233, 247, 257, 272, 274, 275, 276, 280, 281
Onaka, Kiyoharu 178
Onaka, Seiji 198
Onda, Seijiro 175
O'Neal, Charles 58
O'Neil, Robert 248
O'Neill, Dick 191
Operation Bravo *see* nuclear tests (Pacific Ocean region)
"Operation Plumbbob—1957" 287, 294
Oppenheimer, Robert 61, 191, 261
Ordung, Wyatt 125
Osborn, Lyn 33
Otawa, Nobuko 268, 270, 272
Overton, Al 156
Overton, Frank 251
Owen, Tudor 69
Owens, Richard 48
Oxygen Destroyer 8, 141, 170, 171, 172, 173, 176, 192, 199, 206, 213, 215, 235, 260, 261
Ozawa, Eitaro 88

Pace, Roger 55
Paget, Debra 69
Pair Bambi 196

Paiva, Nestor 135, **136**
Palmentola, Paul 20, 27
Palmer, Gregg 40, 41, 69
Panic in the Year Zero! see *Panic in Year Zero!*
Panic in Year Zero! 6, 65, 71, 220, 240–245, **241**, **243**, 274, 275, 278, 290, 293
Paramount 88, 89
Parish, James Robert 225, 290, 294
Parker, Ed (aka Eddie) 50
Parker, Fess 127
Parker, Ross 248
Parkin, Dean 37, **39**, 55
Parks, Hildy 251
Parnell, Emory 11
Pate, Michael 69
Paterson, A.B. 225
Patrick, Dennis 78
Patterson, Hank 135
Paulmentola, Paul 131
Paxton, John 225
The Peanuts *see* "Little Beauties"; Shobijin
Peck, Gregory 225, 226, **227**, **229**
Pendleton, Steve 122, 123
Pennick, Jack 116
Perkins, Anthony 225, 226, **227**
Peters, Erika **72**, 73
Petersen, Paul 84, 86
Peterson, Nan 61, **62**
Peterson, Pete 84, 85, 86
Peterson, Richard W. 132
The Phantom from 10,000 Leagues 23, 24, 139–142, 171
Phillips, Leo, Jr. 78
Phipps, William 217, **218**, 219
Pickens, Slim 248, **250**, 281
Pierce, Arthur C. 65
Pierce, Jack P. 65, 238
Pine, Philip 139
Pinner, Dick 125, 126
Pitts, Michael R. 225, 290, 294
Pollexfen, Jack 12
Potter, Luce 42
Pratt, Judson 50
Prehistoric World see Teenage Cave Man
Prehoda, Frank 225
Pritchard, Robert 11, 42
The Purple Cloud 230
Pusateri, Richard 91, 100, 263, 288, 291, 294

Rabin, Jack 12, 149, 153, 220, 221
radiation made visible 209; *see also* atomic breath; Godzilla's ray
radioactive ray *see* Godzilla's ray
Radon see *Rodan*
Ragone, August 177, 288, 289, 293
Rand, Ed 135
Randall, Meg 11, 12
Randall, Stuart 12
Randell, Ron 12, 14, 69, **70**
Rattway, Eric 247
Ravick, Tom 65

Raymond, Paula 116, 117
Red Alert (book) 247, 255
Redd, Ferol 27
Redlin, William 78
Redmond, Harry, Jr. 119
Reed, Tracy 248
Reid, Cliff 135
Reif, Harry 23
Reilly, Thomas 126
Reitzen, Jack 220
Remington, Al 67
Remmington, B.F. 150
Reptilicus 80, 281, 290
Reyher, Ferdinand 230
"The Rhedosaurus and the Rollercoaster: Making the Beast" 289, 293
Rhodes, Richard 294
Rich, Ted 238
Ridgway, Suzanne 40, 41
Rimmer, Shane 248
Ritch, Steven 27, **28**, 287, 294
Roberts, Thayer 245, 246
Robertson, Blair 159
Robertson, Joseph F. 159
Robinson, George 134
Rock, Joseph 69
Rock, Phillip 69
Rocket Attack U.S.A. 235–238, **236**, 274, 275, 278, 280
Rodan (character) 1, 172, 174, 197, 201 202, 203, 206, 209, 213, 214, 257
Rodan (film) 8, 166, 178–181, 204, 215
Rodan the Flying Monster see *Rodan*
Roemheld, Heinz 150
Rogers, John W. 55
Rooney, Mickey 16, **17**, 18
Roope, Fay 16
Ropper, Clyde 289
Rosenblum, Ralph 251
Ross, Jane 235
Ross, Mike 45
Roth, Gene 156, 157
Rotter, Andrew J. 279, 291, 294
Rotunno, Giuseppe 225, 228
Rovin, Jeff 61, 63, 288
Rozsa, Miklos 230
Rubin, Richard 45
Ruggiero, Jack 65
Rusoff, Lou 23, 26, 139, 240
Russell, Henry 217
Russell, Jack 116
Russell, John L., Jr. 16, 220
Russell, Vy 72
Ruth, Roy Del 58
Rybnick, Harry 168
Ryder Sound Services 33, 37
Ryfle, Steve 171, 176, 177, 200, 206, 289, 290

SAC 225, 251, 253, 255, 281; *see also* Strategic Air Command
Sada, Yutaka 186
Saeta, Eddie 20
Sahara, Kenji 88, 89, 90, 97, 168,

178, 179, 181, 186, 187, 198, 202, 261, 262
Saijo, Yasuhiko 198
St. George, Phillip 235
Saito, Yonejiro 190
Sakai, Frankie 181, 182, 268, 270, 272
Sakai, Sachio 168
Sampson, Edwards, Jr. 125
Sanford, Blaine 119
Sano, Takeshi 195
Saperstein, Henry G. 97, 98
Sarino, Ben (aka Richard Cassarino) 61
Sato, Masaru 8, 87, 92, 175, 195, 197
Sato, Mitsuru 88
Sato, Tadao 171, 289, 294
Saunders, Gloria 12
Saunders, Russ 126
Sawamura, Ikio 186
Sawamura, Sonosuke 175
Sawtell, Paul 164
Scannell, Brank 42
Scary Monsters Magazine 1, 2, 29, 35, 86, 158, 161, 287, 288, 289, 293, 294
Schallert, William 12, 14, 42, 127, 220
Scheel, Hannah 78
Scheid, Francis J. 126
Schenck, Aubrey 48
Schiffer, Bob 33
Schiller, Norbert 48
Schlosser, Eric 291, 294
Schneer, Charles H. 131
Schoengarth, Russell 11
Schrage, Henry 37
Schreibman, Paul 175
Schwarzwald, Milton 11
Scott, George C. 248, 249, 281
Scott, John 74, 75
Scott, Mark 122
Scott, Walter M. 58
Searchinger, Gene 52
Sears, Fred F. 27, 164
Seay, James 33, 122, 123, 147
Sedgwick, Edward 11
Seeley, E.S., Jr. 61
Seely, John 61
Seiderman, Maurice 18
Sekai daisenso see *The Last War*
Sekita, Hiroshi 198
Sekizawa, Shinichi 100, 181, 184, 186, 190, 195, 197, 202, 203
Sellers, Bridget 248
Sellers, Peter 248, 249, 281
Senda, Koreya 88
Senn, Bryan 138, 289
September 11, 2001 terrorist attacks 222
Shapiro, Leonard J. 65
Shaw, Frank 135
Shayne, Robert 223
The She-Creature 23, 225, 287
Sheehan, Jack 228, 242, 254, 290

"The Shelter" (*Twilight Zone* episode) 280, 281, 291
Shelton, Don 127
Shepard, Jan 156
Sherdeman, Ted 126
Shiba, Kazue 197
Shiel, M.P. 230
Shigeaki Hidaka 264
Shima, Koji 257
Shimizu, Masao 175
Shimonaga, Hisashi 168, 195
Shimura, Takashi 97, 98, 168, 169, 175, 181, 202, 261, 262
Shin Godzilla 167
Shirakawa, Yumi 88, 89, 90, 178, 179, 261, 268
Shiroda, Masao 175
Shobijin 181, 182, 186, 188, 201
Showalter, Max 150
The Shrinking Man (novel) 42
Shute, Nevil 225
Shyer, Melville 238
Siegel, Sol C. 230
Similuk, Peter 61
Simms, Jay 238, 240
Simpson, David 74
Simpson, Frank 251
Sinclair, Ronald 23, 33, 55
Siodmak, Curt 20, 119, 120
Skarstedt, Vance 159
The Slime People 159–162, **160**, 289, 294
Smiler, Alan 235
Smith, Dick 58, 126
Smith, Hal 131
Smith, Malcolm 238
Smith, Robert 220
Smith, Shawn 30
Snegoff, Mark 78
Snyder, Earl 65
Sohl, Jerry 97
Sokoloff, Vladimir 65, 153
Solomon, Jack 33
Son of Godzilla 167, 197–200, 214, 257
Sonoda, Ayumi 88
Sontag, Susan 166, 289
Sora no daikaiju Radon see *Rodan*
Southern, Terry 247, 248, 274
Soviet Union 15, 20, 90, 95, 106, 125, 201, 205, 213, 216, 221, 222, 250, 251, 252, 254, 255, 256, 262, 268, 278, 279, 280, 284, 291; see also U.S.S.R.
Space Age Rentals 72
Speak, Jean 23
Spencer, Franz 220
Spiegel, Ed 217
Spruance, Don 245, 246
Stader, Paul 150
Stafford, Bing 67
Stahl, Francis E. 48
Stanton, Helene 139
Stapp, Marjorie 150
Starr, Ron 245, 246
"The Steel Monster" 69
Steensen, Clarence 12

Stein, Herman 134
Stein, Ronald 23, 45, 139, 140, 142, 233
Stell, Aaron 20, 147
Stephens, Roy 248
Sternad, Rudolph 225
Stevens, Angela 20
Stevens, Craig 164
Stevens, Eileen 45
Stevens, Inger 230, 231, **232**
Stevens, Leith 30
Stevens, Onslow 127
Stewart, Charles 55
Stewart, Douglas 37, 147
Stewart, Elaine 69, 70
Stine, Clifford 42, 134
Storey, Ray 78
Stoumen, Louis Clyde 217
Strategic Air Command 15, 205, 251; *see also* SAC
Stratton, John 52
Strauss, Robert 16, 17
Strock, Herbert L. 119
Stroheim, Josef von 33
strontium-90 204, 262, 273
Struss, Karl 58
Stuart, Randy 42, 44
Sugata, Michiko 190, 193
Sullivan, James W. 220
Sunazuka, Hideo 195
Sutton, Rod 159
Suzuki, Toyo 258
Swan, Robert 40, 41
Swerdloff, Arthur L 217
Swift, William 251

Tabb, Mike 235
Tadake, Kenzo 186
Tadashi, Aramaki 264
Taira, Echiji 87
Taira, Kazuji 175, 181
Taira, Yasnuobu 168
Tajima, Yoshibumi 88, 181, 186
Tajitsu, Yasuyoshi 184
Takahashi, Niisan 190
Takarada, Akira 168, 169, 171, 186, 187, 195, 196, 202, 203, 268, 270, 272, 275
Takashima, Tadao 97, 98, 181, 198, 202, 258
Takayama, Ryosaku 190
Takei, George 175
Talbott, Gloria 37
Talton, Alix 164
Tamai, Masao 168
Tanaka, Tomoyuki 8, 87, 97, 167, 172, 175, 178, 181, 184, 186, 195, 197, 201, 202, 203, 261, 267
Tanin, Eleanor 27
Tanner, Gordon 248
Tarantula 7, 33, 42, 44, 50, 134–139, **136**, **137**, 141, 148, 158, 162, 203, 204, 205, 206, 208, **211**, 212, 213, 215, 289, 290, 294
Tate, Dale 45
Tate, John 225, 228
Taylor, Alfred 72
Taylor, Carlie 37, 45

Taylor, Fred 52
Taylor, Gilbert 247
Taylor, Grant 225
Taylor, Kent 139, 140
Taylor, Ray, Jr. 37
Taylor, Rod 30, **31**
Tazaki, Jun 97, 185, 186, 196, 202, 203
Teague, George 165
Teenage Cave Man 6, 223–225, ***223, 224***
Teenage Caveman see *Teenage Cave Man*
Tenney, Del 74, 77, 293, 294
Terrell, Ken 45
Terror from the Year 5,000 52–55, ***52***, 108
Tezuka, Katsumi 168, 175
Them! 5, 7, 30, 33, 109, 116, 126–131, ***128, 129***, 133, 135, 147, 148, 149, 150, 153, 158, 165, 178, 179, 180, 191, 206, ***207***, 208, 209, 212, 213, 215, 278, 289, 293
The Thirty Foot Bride of Candy Rock 105, 288
This Is Not a Test 71, 245–247, ***246***, 274, 275
Thomas, Harry 40, 122, 125, 220
Thomas, Jerome 131
Thompson, Charles 223
Thompson, William C. 18
Thor, Larry 33, 34
Threads 284
Thurman, Bill 84
The Time Travelers 65, 66, 78–84, ***79, 81***, 108, 111, 274, 290n23
Tippit, Wayne 74
Tobey, Kenneth 116, 132
Tobolowsky, Edwin 84
Toei (film company) 8, 257, 264, 265, 267
Togin, Chotaro 195
Toho 8, 87, 88, 89, 91, 92, 96, 97, 98, 99, 100, 101, 109, 153, 166, 167, 169, 171, 172, 174, 175, 178, 181, 183, 184, 185, 186, 187, 188, 194, 195, 196, 197, 198, 199, 200, 202, 203, 257, 261, 266, 267, 268, 269, 270, 272, 273, 275, 279, 284, 287, 289, 290, 293
Tokumasa, Yoshiyuki 97, 185, 186
Tomioka, Mototaka 186, 195
Tomioka, Motoyoshi 97, 184, 268
Tomioka, Sokei 168
Tompkins, Darlene 65
Torpin, Don 30
Tors, Ivan 119
Toshimitsu, Teizo 168
Towne, Robert 233, 234, 235
Tracy, Pat 235
Tremayne, Les 159, 160
Triman, Tom 35, 39, 56, 150, 287, 289
Troiano, William 159
Truman, Harry S. 276
Tsuburaya, Eiji 88, 91, 97, 100, 168, 171, 175, 176, 178, 180, 181, 184, 186, 195, 198, 201, 202, 203, 261, 268, 270, 288, 289, 294
Tsuchiya, Yoshio 88, 97, 175, 187, 198, 261
Tsukiji, Yonesaburo 190
Turner, Barbara 153
Turner, Robert 126
Turner, Terry 168
Tuttle, William 230
The Twilight Zone 42, 80, 280, 281, 291ch10n25
"2011 Japan Earthquake—Tsunami Fast Facts" 288, 294
Tyler, Dick, Sr. 16
Tyler, Richard 147

Ubutaka, Soji 261
Uchida, Yoshiro 190, 191
Uchu daikaiju Dogora see *Giant Space Monster Dogora*
Uchujin Tokyo ni awawaru see *Warning from Space*
Uehara, Ken 181, 182
Ulmer, Edgar G. 65
Ulmer, Shirley 65
Umemiya, Tatsuo 264
Unagami (Kaijo?), Hideo 87
Unit 731 279
United Artists 119, 121, 150, 151, 152, 225, 227, 229, 275
Universal see Universal-International
Universal-International 5, 11, 12, 42, 43, 50, 51, 61, 67, 74, 134, 135, 136, 137, 162, 164, 202, 211, 221, 287
U.S.S.R. 125, 159, 192, 219, 221, 255, 271, 279, 280, 283; see also Soviet Union

Vaccarino, Maurice 142, 150
Vance, Jack 150
Van Cleef, Lee 116
Van Dreelen, John 65
Van Enger, Charles 11, 119
Van Marter, George 119
Vath, Richard 238
Vaughn, Robert 223, 224
Veevers, Wally 248
Verberkmoes, Robert 74
Vernon, Billy 241
Vernon, Lou 225
Ve Sota, Bruno 156
Vickers, Yvette 45, 156, 158, 159
Vieira, George 48
Vilardo, Henry 126
Vittes, Louis 153
Volkman, Ivan 225

Wade, Stuart 126
Wain, Edward (aka Robert Towne) 233, 234
Wakabayashi, Akiko 185
Wakamatsu, Akira 181
Wakayama, Setsuo 175
Wakeling, Gwen 69
Waldis, Otto 45, ***46***
Waller, Hal 115

Walters, Ken 12, 45
Walters, Nancy 50
"Waltzing Matilda" 225
The War Game 5, 291
War of the Colossal Beast 7, 34, 39, 55–58, ***56, 57***, 58, ***108***, 178, 214
War of the Gargantuas 110, 113, 203, 290
Ward, Al C. 168
Ward, Janet 251
Warde, Harlan 150, ***151***
Waring, Lynn 238
Warner Bros. 7, 49, 116, 118, 126, 128, 129, 130, 164, 175, 207, 209, 210
Warning from Space 257–261, ***259***, 262, 273
Warren, Bill 3, 4, 5, 27, 33, 39, 45, 49, 63, 64, 65, 67, 69, 92, 130, 144, 156, 162, 206, 219, 225, 235, 238, 245, 247, 263, 266, 287, 288, 289, 290, 291, 294
Warren, Eda 30
Warren, Gene 153
Warrenton, Gilbert 240
Watanabe, Akira 88, 97, 168, 175, 178, 181, 185, 186, 198, 261, 268
Watanabe, Kimio 257
Watanabe, Richi 190
Watanabe, Toru 196
Watari, Shin (Nobu?) 198
Watkin, Pierre 20
Watkins, Linda 40
Wayne, Ken 225
Weart, Spencer R. 215, 280, 283, 291
Weaver, Fritz 251
Weaver, Tom 49, 288, 293
Webster, Frank 40, 139
Weisbart, David 126
Welbourne, Charles S. (Scotty) 150
Welch, Jerry 48
Weldon, Joan 127, ***128***
"We'll Meet Again" 248
Welles, Mel 142, 143
Wells, Delores 78
The Werewolf 7, 21, 27–30, ***28***, 62, 110, 287, 294
Westcott, Helen 50
Westmore, Bud 11, 20, 42, 50, 131, 135
Westmoreland, Josh 20, 131
Wetzel, Hans 225
Whalen, Michael 139, 140
Wheeler, Harvey 251, 281
Wheeler, Loyd R. 58
White, Daniel 156
White, Harold 27
White, Les 150
Whitehead, O.Z. 241
Whitmore, James 127, 130
Whyte, Patrick 61, 63
Wilder, Myles 122
Wilder, W. Lee 122, 125
Wilkinson, Frank 135
Williams, Grant 42, ***43***, 44

Wilner, Ann 18
Wilson, Howard 16
Wilson, Ward 283, 291
Winkler, Benny 55
Winston, Norman 245, 246
Wisberg, Aubrey 12
Wittenberg, Paul 55
Wolfson, David 139
Wood, Edward, Jr. 7, 18
Woodbury, Joan 78
Woods, Donald 116
Woolman, Harry 159
Woolner, Bernard 45
The World, the Flesh, and the Devil 230-233, **231**, **232**
World War II 20, 24, 88, 90, 97, 101, 106, 166, 170, 171, 249, 278, 279
World Without End 30, 5, 11, 30-33, **31**, 35, 80, 82, 83, 84, 110, 111, 116, 127, 289
Worth, Frank 18
Wright, Gerry 16
Wyenn, Than 147
Wynn, Keenan 248, 250

X—The Unknown 88

Yagi, James 202
Yamada, Kazuo 195, 197-198
Yamada, Minosuke 88, 178, 261
Yamagata, Isao 258
Yamamoto, Ren 97, 168, 169, 175, 178, 181, 186
Yamashita, Junichiro 190
Yamauchi, Tadashi 190
Yanoguchi, Fumio 184
Yashiro, Miki 186
Yasumi, Toshio 267
Yates, George Worthing 48, 55, 126, 131
Yates, Lou 72
Year 2889 see *In the Year 2889*
Yeltsin, Boris 284
Yerke, Mary 48
Young, Jack H. 37, 55, 56
Youngstein, Max E. 251
Yuasa, Kenmei 258
Yuasa, Noriaka 190
Yuki, Taka 195, 269
Yuricich, Matthew 230
Yusuf, Osman 181

Zabner, Dr. Louis M. 238
Zarimba, John 119
Zavitz, Lee 225
Zimbalist, Al 153
Zsigmond, William 78
Zugsmith, Albert 12, 42, 220, 222